THE CINEMA OF THE REAL

SUNY SERIES, INSINUATIONS: PHILOSOPHY, PSYCHOANALYSIS, LITERATURE
CHARLES SHEPHERDSON, EDITOR

THE CINEMA OF THE REAL

HYON JOO YOO

Cover Credit: *The Tea-Tax-Tempest* (*The Oracle*), John Dixon, 1774.
Published by State University of New York Press, Albany
© 2024 State University of New York
All rights reserved
Printed in the United States of America

No part of this book may be used or reproduced in any manner whatsoever without written permission. No part of this book may be stored in a retrieval system or transmitted in any form or by any means including electronic, electrostatic, magnetic tape, mechanical, photocopying, recording, or otherwise without the prior permission in writing of the publisher.

Links to third-party websites are provided as a convenience and for informational purposes only. They do not constitute an endorsement or an approval of any of the products, services, or opinions of the organization, companies, or individuals. SUNY Press bears no responsibility for the accuracy, legality, or content of a URL, the external website, or for that of subsequent websites.

For information, contact State University of New York Press, Albany, NY
www.sunypress.edu

Library of Congress Cataloging-in-Publication Data

Names: Yoo, Hyon Joo, author.
Title: The cinema of the real / Hyon Joo Yoo.
Description: Albany : State University of New York Press 2024. | Series:
  SUNY series, insinuations: philosophy, psychoanalysis, literature |
  Includes bibliographical references and index.
Identifiers: LCCN 2024011297 | ISBN 9798855800159 (hardcover) | ISBN
  9798855800166 (ebook)
Subjects: LCSH: Reality in motion pictures. | Motion pictures--Philosophy.
  | Psychoanalysis and motion pictures.
Classification: LCC PN1995.9.R325 Y66 2024 | DDC
  791.43/6612--dc23/eng/20240418
LC record available at https://lccn.loc.gov/2024011297

10 9 8 7 6 5 4 3 2 1

CONTENTS

Acknowledgments — vii

Introduction: Real Life, Real Cinema — 1

Chapter One: The Cinema of the Real — 35

Chapter Two: The Cartography of the Real Body — 71

Chapter Three: The Chronotope of the Drive in the Cinema of the Real — 113

Chapter Four: The Feminine Cinema and Feminine Universality — 163

Notes — 209

Bibliography — 227

Index — 237

ACKNOWLEDGMENTS

I am grateful to my primordial family Mark Stein, Chang Seok Yoo, and Young Joo Yoon for opening the path to consider emancipation as a matter of practice. I am deeply indebted to my friends and fellow travelers Hilary Neroni and Todd McGowan for allowing me to wrestle with the theory of emancipation. I stand on the shoulders of thinkers who have pursued both the theory and practice of emancipation.

A version of chapter two appeared in "The Cartography of the Abject Nation in *Thirst* and *Still Life*," *Studies in the Humanities* 44, nos. 1–2, and 45, nos. 1–2 (March 2019), 113–131. A version of chapter three appeared in "The Chronotope of Trauma in National Cinema," *Journal of Japanese and Korean Cinema* 7, no. 1 (May 2015), 73–92.

Introduction

REAL LIFE, REAL CINEMA

The Real Cinema, The Real Drive

Psychoanalysis defines the human as *the subject of suffering*. As speaking subjects, we suffer from what psychoanalytic theory terms an ineradicable *lack*. Language, our only means to relate to our experience of being, signifies the world for us but operates through a chain of metonymies. This leaves a gap between the speaking subject and its perceived objects, which the speaking subject seeks to grasp as meaningful. This gap creates the sense that we have lost some essential piece of ourselves. We experience this condition as the lack, which propels our desire for some phantasmatic object, one that we believe can fill the gap and deliver us from a state of being where we lack the ability to form a meaningful connection between ourselves and our experience. Our suffering comes from encountering this lack in the Other, who cannot deliver us from it. Psychoanalysis, therefore, creates a new subject who is free to act, to break out of the established trajectory of the drive, in which we forever seek out the object of desire. Psychoanalyst Tracy McNulty emphasizes that, in this context, we can free ourselves from the condition of lack by traversing the fantasy space, wherein we are tethered to the death drive—the name for our tendency to repeatedly follow the same painful trajectory in our lives.[1] Perhaps we are reminded of friends who repeatedly involve themselves in romantic relationships that end disastrously.

The death drive means that we remain on the trajectory wherein we repeatedly experience the lack of the object that, we fantasize, will fulfill our desire for what the Other does not have. That object, however, does not exist, since our belief in such an object is merely the effect of our existence as a linguistic subject. The death drive keeps us on the track of not having "it," that elusive object. But the trajectory of the death drive, wherein we repeatedly fail to obtain the satisfying object, arrives where the way of desiring through what Jacques Lacan calls the Symbolic order loses its hold on us. The Symbolic order is the foundation of the linguistic order that organizes how we make meaning in a given society, which is to say, it structures the way we as social subjects experience our reality and the world that encompasses it. According to this prescription, our desire has a well-defined goal: to finally obtain the object that allows us to have a meaningful place in the world that the Symbolic order organizes. For example, a capitalist subject of desire approaches this goal through the accumulation of commodities. Here, the Amazon warehouse is our place of belonging: we are obliged to see our place in society through what we desire and how we obtain our object of desire, and Amazon defines how we fulfill these obligations.

Within the trajectory of the death drive, we exist in a state of desiring whatever we nominate as capable of eradicating the lack, and we experience the eternal suffering that desire creates as we forever fail to have the object that is to eradicate the lack. After we traverse the fantasy space where our desire is enacted, the trajectory of our desire brings us to its limit, and we devise a new trajectory for our desire. I call this new trajectory the *emancipatory drive*, where we transform our relationship to the Other and the perceived traumatic lack that the Other brings into our relationships.

The emancipatory drive articulates the psychical structure in which we emerge as the political subject. It is a way of moving beyond the recognition that we exist along the trajectory of the death drive. As foundational to this book, the emancipatory drive is a concept I articulate throughout this chapter and in the chapters that follow. For now, I will relate the following personal experience to gesture toward this "beyond." Coming of age in South Korea during the military dictatorship, I participated in protests in many public spaces, from the plazas of university libraries to the steps of the city halls around the country. I witnessed others opening themselves to the ideals of the people's revolutionary movement to fight dictatorship and embrace democracy. I watched, and was subjected to, the violent oppression of such movements on the street. I was bloodied and blinded by tear gas. I witnessed friends and strangers being beaten and arrested, and I sat in courtrooms to observe their trials in a court mandated by the National Security Act that undergirded the fascistic regime.

These experiences left me with the question that has driven my intellectual inquiry: How did South Koreans crash through the militaristic and, more importantly, psychical barriers to open up that space of protest and political revolution that has persisted for nearly the entire modern era, until as recently as the candlelight revolution of 2016–2017? The law that persecuted those who fought for democratization, the National Security Act, still delimits political freedom. How do South Koreans continue to confront the Symbolic of the nation-state that this act showcases? How do they continue to reveal what is in them that is more than who they are on the street, in the public sphere? How do we, as subjects of the Symbolic, connect the transformation of our desire's trajectory to the revolutionary act of political emancipation in the plazas of the world? Through terms such as *the emancipatory drive, the life drive,* and *the Other's drive,* which I discuss throughout this book, I offer answers to these questions in order to articulate a universal psychical structure, of which revolutionary South Koreans represent but one of many examples.

What I call *the cinema of the Real* offers a theoretical framework for illuminating the ways in which cinema visualizes the look and feel of existence within the emancipatory drive. It explains how some films create a space of exploration that activates the radical potential of being a viewer. Within this framework, the viewing subject's eyes are a conduit for opening up what Lacan calls "the Real." The Symbolic order is founded on this psychoanalytic Real and yet cannot incorporate it, because the Real reveals the revolutionary possibility of undoing the Symbolic order itself. In this book, I describe how, as viewers, we move from viewing and encountering the Real in cinema to exporting that cinematic experience into our own lives, thus transforming ourselves into subjects who have the potential to exist in the emancipatory drive. It is this extension of the philosophical, and ultimately political, implications of Lacanian thought through transtextual analysis of the transnational cinema of the Real that constitutes this book's novel intervention. I chart a path that initially emerges within Lacan's *philosophical* terrain and leads to unexpectedly new *political* terrain. Transnational cinema is pivotal to this intervention.

My point of departure is the recognition that Lacanian psychoanalytic theory includes the possibility that one form of *jouissance*—psychoanalytic "enjoyment"—can be replaced by another and thus may transform subjectivity itself. Lacan's notion of "traversing the fantasy" creates, from this, the emancipatory possibility. Consider as one good example of this the finale of Michael Haneke's *The Piano Teacher* (2001), in which the central character stabs herself and walks away from the concert hall, leaving her lover behind. In reference to the same scene in Elfriede Jelinek's novel of the same title, on which Haneke's film is based, Slavoj Žižek asks: "What if this self-inflicted wound is to be conceived as 'traversing the fantasy'? What if, through striking at herself, she got rid of the hold of the masochistic fantasy over herself? . . . What if the ending is 'optimistic': after being raped by her lover, after she got her fantasy back at her in reality, this traumatic experience enables her to leave it behind?"[2] In this scene, we witness a human subject transcend jouissance as pleasurable suffering in a masochistic fantasy. This transcendence of the experience of trauma dislocates her from the drive that has sustained her previous mode of being. This trauma, which is "the structural first cause of subjectivity,"[3] alters the trajectory of her drive. She enters the emancipatory drive, which produces a different kind of jouissance, and subsequently establishes and sustains a new way of being. Through this transformation of jouissance, the subject shifts from the death drive to the life drive and continues on her path of emancipation. Her abandonment of the love object signifies this newly articulated jouissance.

In the following chapters, I expand the conceptual boundary of the psychoanalytic drives by introducing the emancipatory drive and the life drive, the latter of which involves a new articulation of desire. Following the life drive entails moving from the singular trajectory of desiring to this new articulation, transforming in the process the death drive into the emancipatory drive and the subject from the subject of the death drive to the subject of the life drive, a transformation that is itself an emancipation. All drives, in Lacanian thought, are death drives, because our drives are chained to language, which is always ultimately lacking in its capacity to fulfill.[4] According to the death drive, the subject is forever chained to ideology, which is articulated and materialized through the dead language. The life drive, on the other hand, is the drive toward emancipation in a social and political sense; hence, we experience the life drive as emancipatory, even from ideology. The cinema of the Real offers a picture of how it feels and looks to be on a trajectory in which the subject and her world changes.

Byung-Chul Han begins his contemplation of how such changes may occur in the world by citing Giorgio Agamben: "A rabbi, a real cabalist, once said that in order to establish the Kingdom of Peace it is not enough to destroy everything nor to begin a completely new world. It is sufficient to displace this cup or this bush or this stone just a little, and thus everything. But this small displacement is so difficult to achieve and its measure is so difficult to find that, with regard to the world, humans are incapable of it and it is necessary that the Messiah come."[5] Han notes that in this scene "the holy is not transparent,"[6] which I interpret to mean that the most radical change in the world (the "holy" that the Messiah is to bring, disrupting the law of the world with an incomprehensible new divine law) is unable to be harnessed by our existing language, whose efficacy depends on its transparency; ideology is a prime example of transparent language because, for ideology to operate, it must be comprehensible to everyone. Agamben's scene could also be interpreted as indicating how humans might accept an unknown Otherness, which would change the entire scene. In this case, it is not the Messiah but a revolutionary new trajectory that emerges through a series of slight displacements that incorporate unknown Otherness into our way of being. This incorporation of Otherness suggests how the life drive works toward emancipation. Han continues: "Not just the space of the holy but also that of desire offers no transparency. . . . The Lady (*frouwe*)—the object of desire in courtly love—provides a 'black hole' around which desire thickens."[7] Regarding an object of desire, around which our desire congeals, Han posits that its "its impenetrability and hiddenness, prohibits its image to be fashioned. It defies representation."[8] The point at which we encounter the Real of our object of desire—the void that this object leaves in the absence of satisfactory representation—propels us into the life drive. It is here that we transform our relationship to the object and, along with it, to the Other who coincides with or appears alongside the object of our desire. Han's "lady," no longer a sublime object but a black hole, does not guarantee the fulfillment of our desire. Rather, she thwarts desire and propels us into a new drive where the way we desire must change. It is this change that holds the emancipatory potential. Joan Copjec writes that the drive "so wills what occurs that the object it finds is indistinguishable from the one it chooses,"[9] which allows us to imagine the object as unmoored from our desire for a particular ideological object. Where desire is defined by a specific object, the drive, as Copjec sees it, can emancipate us from the object of desire and thus release desire itself from its reified position that determines our trajectories.

At this juncture, it is useful to survey notable thinkers' positions on the theory of the drive, in order to clarify my critical intervention in the concept. While the drive emerges from language, all drive is understood to have a bodily dimension, the body being a location within the chain of signifiers. Mari Ruti, for example, conceptually conflates the drive with the bodily drive, which is "amorphous, hard to pin down," and thus unruly, and differentiates it from desire, which, she writes, is "still more orderly—more coherent and consistent—than the drives."[10] One of this book's interventions is to reformulate the drive that sustains bodily jouissance such that it contains emancipatory political possibilities.

Todd McGowan's approach to the drive aligns with my position. McGowan posits that we actually enjoy, in psychoanalytic terms, dissatisfaction, that is, the state of not having the object that fulfills our desire. Citing Freud, McGowan states, "The subject finds satisfaction in repeating loss. . . . The subject's satisfaction is inextricable from failure."[11] The paradise lost of the mother's breast or of the Lady whose attention one can never have are examples of objects that stand in for this permanent, fundamental loss—a state of being that describes the death drive, which stems from the loss and lack of the object whose meaning is meant to be sustained by language. We can see the death drive's emancipatory potential if we observe that the *satisfaction* of our drive is fueled by our desire for an object (the Lady, for example, or the breast) that we can never hope to have. As such, our drive enters a new path, and we create a new relationship to our objects of desire. Critically, this new path of the drive must entail a new relationship to the Other, especially the Other's drive, a concept to which I will return shortly. Lack and the loss of the object that fuels our desire are, in this new context, life affirming. Through this new relationship to lack and loss, we leave off from continually circling the object that we imagine will make us whole. We can also emancipate ourselves from the dead language of the paternal order as the originator and guarantor of meaning and enter the life drive, which leads away from the path set by the pregiven order of things and ideologies, and anchored in the pregiven meaning of the object. McGowan's notable intervention in Lacan's concept of the drive—that we find satisfaction not in an object itself but in the *path* we take to obtain the object—emphasizes that "the subject finds ways to miss [the object] and to ensure that it [the object] remains lost."[12] This drive to miss the object of desire and ensure that it stays lost is what allows us to combat the pull of the desire for "the sublime object of ideology."

My theoretical framework also figures this missing and loss as a means through which we jump to a new trajectory of the life drive. Crucially, the life drive frees us from the tyranny of the Lacanian big Other as an entity that authorizes and guarantees meaning within the Symbolic order, which is sustained by our investment in the existence of some sublime object, and allows the subjective Other's life drive to appear in the field of our own trajectory. In this sense, I am free when I recognize the Other's drive in the sphere of my drive as the stain that muddles the waters of my desire, which I imagine to be unspoiled by the Other's desire, and that undermines the meaning of sublime objects of my desire.

To provide a conceptual foundation for the Other's drive, which appears in the sphere of one's own drive and changes its trajectory, I offer a succinct example from a 1998 episode of the television series *The X Files* that is aptly named "Drive."[13] Crump, a roofer from Nevada, leads the police in a high-speed car chase as his wife inexplicably writhes in agony in the backseat. He is captured but then escapes the ambulance that is transporting him for treatment of what seems to be a brain ailment. He hijacks Fox Mulder's car, which had been following the ambulance, and orders Agent Mulder, at gunpoint, to drive west at increasingly higher speed. Mulder comes to understand that low frequency sound waves, emitted from a secret naval military research facility adjacent to Crump's property, has affected his inner ear and set up a ticking bomb of rising pressure that could explode and kill him. This was the fate that Crump's wife had met; his high-speed getaway had been in desperate pursuit of the direction and speed that would alleviate the pressure building inside her skull.

When Mulder recognizes the Real of the situation, he decides to save Crump's life by continuing a mad dash past the police lines set to capture him. No longer a hostage, Mulder embarks on the life drive that emancipates both Crump and himself from the grids of power they drive through—all the way to the point where the land meets the Pacific Ocean. Crump's head explodes before they can reach the point where an emergency measure to relieve the pressure could be carried out. Mulder's trajectory reflects a subject's (Mulder's) decision to allow the Other's drive to enter his own drive's path and change its trajectory. Together, they follow the trajectory of manifest destiny only to demonstrate its impossibility: the end of that trajectory inevitably coincides with the death of the white male subject.

This episode deviates from the series' usual trope, in that what drives the narrative is not the excavation of absent causes of the phenomena that reveal the Real of reality but the formal characteristics of the chase genre, so much so that the investigation of the absent cause is largely neglected. In a moment of meta-awareness, Mulder mutters as Crump orders him to drive faster and faster, "I've seen this movie before." This formal choice makes room in the episode for philosophical rumination about Mulder's actions. It allows us to see that accepting the Other's drive is a political act that confronts the Symbolic order, which undergirds manifest destiny as the national myth that continues to insert itself in global capitalism. Mulder, as the subject of the death drive that keeps pursuing elusive, absent causes, acknowledges the Other's subjectivity and its existential condition as the origin of the ethical demand one must heed. In doing so, he articulates his own trajectory of the life drive. The Other, in all its monstrosity (both criminal and lethal), is personified by Crump. The government agent has embarked on the life drive, which defies the space predetermined by societal power relationships. He violates the police lines and deviates from the trajectory the police enforce on the landscape. The subject's ability to change the trajectory of his drive and create a new path, as exemplified by Mulder's actions, emancipates him from the path of the death drive on which he has been traveling. An action that creates the new path for his life drive constitutes his freedom.

When the subject of the death drive cannot change its trajectory upon encountering the death drive of the monstrous Other, a deranged comedy might well ensue, as in the compilation film *Wild Tales*.[14] In one segment, we ride along as two drivers get into an altercation. One is a suave upper-class man in a luxury car, the other a rough-hewn working-class man in a tattered truck loaded with indistinguishable junk. The conflict initially plays like a predictable road rage scenario. Set in the breathtaking Argentine countryside, the action offers multiple opportunities for one of these men to quit the trajectory of his own drive and allow the Other reasonable space to keep driving. After many acts of visceral, mutual destruction, which include defecating on the luxury car, shoving the truck over a cliff, and brutalizing each other's faces and bodies, they end up together trapped in a car that they manage to set ablaze following a cartoonish fusillade of slapstick blows in attempts to wrestle their way out of the vehicle. After the resulting explosion, the detective who examines the corpses, which are fused in a death parody of a lovers' embrace, offers his reading of the situation: "A crime of passion?"

Here we can reconceptualize the heretofore monstrous Otherness of the neighbor as the only condition of our freedom to say "no" to the sublime object. The subject of the life drive is propelled by this freedom to emerge from their existence as a linguistic subject, in which they are imprisoned by the death drive. In my pursuit of this freedom, my neighbor's life drive disrupts the cohesiveness of the meaning that I confront. Žižek summarizes the subject's relationship to her neighbor according to Emmanuel Levinas: "The existence of the subject [is] grounded in its openness to an irreducible-unfathomable-transcendent Otherness—there is a subject only insofar as it is not absolute and self-grounded but remains in a tension with an impenetrable Other; there is freedom only through the reference to a gap which makes the Other unfathomable."[15] Notably, the Other's life drive does not originate from Levinas's "irreducible-unfathomable-transcendent Otherness." The Otherness that propels the Other's drive exists within the context into which the Other is thrown; it is not only knowable by us but also part of our condition of existence. That is, the Other's context cannot be separated from my own context, which has a global dimension (the Real of capitalism, notably) and is thus structurally intertwined with my own: the subject and its Other are together historical subjects in a universal condition of existence. The transnational cinema of the Real that this book takes up casts the Other's drive in this light: as a recognizable and knowable phenomenon that I traverse via my own drive. Herein, we recognize the life drive as an ethical trajectory; we enter the ethical subject position just as the Other does in their own situation. This freedom to make ethical choices transcends the boundaries that create differences between the subject and its Other. Žižek posits, "My very status as a subject depends on its link to the substantial Other: not only the regulative-symbolic Other of the tradition in which I am embedded, but also the bodily-desiring substance of the Other, the fact that, in the core of my being, I am irreducibly vulnerable, exposed to the Other(s)."[16] The life drive describes how I relate to the Other through "finitude and vulnerability"[17] in my move toward emancipation from an intricate matrix of suffering. This book follows the life drive as the universal term of human subjectivity, as articulated by the cinema of the Real across national boundaries.

Lacan differentiates *automation*, which is repetition within and the preservation of the Symbolic order, such as signifiers and law, from *tyche*, which is a gap in the chain of the automation.[18] On this point, Alenka Zupančič cites Mladen Dolar: "In the tiny gap between one occurrence and the next one, a bit of real is produced. In every repetition, there is already, in a minimal way, the emergence of that which escapes symbolization, the haphazard contingent object appears which spoils the mere repeating of the same, so the same which returns is never the same although we couldn't tell it apart from its previous occurrence by any of the positive features or distinguishing marks."[19] This "bit of real" changes the material and ideological trajectory of the Symbolic order. The repetition that produces the Real constitutes the subject's drive. The life drive emerges at a point where one set of repetitions changes into a new set that involves an unexpected jouissance that comes from existing in the field of the Real. This existence in the Real and experience of the Real jouissance is what the cinema of the Real visualizes. As in Dolar's statement above, I posit that the life drive transforms the form and context of our existence and, thus, renders the piece of the Real, that which escapes symbolization, visible. The life drive changes the scene where the subject exists, and this change is marked by negativity, by the disintegration of the cohesiveness and integrity of the Symbolic subject; hence the subject of the Real emerges in our field of vision.

Zupančič argues in *The Odd One In* that it is via a "crack" between repetitions that the subject emerges. I add to this the idea that at the scene of the subject's emergence there is found the Other's life drive, which is foreign to the subject. All life drive entails a mode of jouissance that is different from what we have known from our experience of the death drive. Our historically specific trauma is the origin of our life drive, which leads to our emancipation. The Other's life drive originates from a context of trauma that is different from our own. An unfamiliar context of trauma creates a new trajectory for the subject's life drive. Transnational cinemas address this complexity and allow us to encounter the Other's life drive. We in turn can allow it to inflect our own life drive's trajectory, or we can also erase it from our reality. In one recent effort to erase the Other's life drive, a group of former Stanford students created an app that turns all accents—which materialize how speech is haunted by specific contexts of trauma—into a standardized, "neutral" (Midwestern) accent, thereby attacking the universality of our being. Universality resides in the fact that our subjectivity originates from the traumatic Real, which in turn originates from the linguistic "cut" that formulates our social existence.[20] Accents indicate how linguistic subjects' enunciations differently carry the sign of the traumatic yet universal cut, depending on their historical and social contexts.

As Žižek points out, our relationship to the Other is possible only through the Symbolic order, through some kind of common language and law, which Žižek calls a "mediator": "In order to render our coexistence with the [neighbor] Thing minimally bearable, the symbolic order qua Third, the pacifying mediator has to intervene: the 'gentrification' of the Other-Thing into a 'normal human fellow' cannot occur through our direct interaction, but presupposes the third agency to which we both submit ourselves—there is no intersubjectivity (no symmetrical, shared, relation between humans) without the impersonal symbolic order."[21] I suggest that the mediator must have capacity to allow us to change our own life drive as we engage that of the Other. We cannot treat our and the Other's life drive as a matrix for particular differences throughout humanity. Nor can we homogenize the universal trauma we all share as social subjects who emerge through the cut from nature. This trauma is a fulcrum of universal subjectivity, founded on the universal lack of an object of desire that sustains our fantasy—be it ethnic, racial, sexual, and so on—in support of another level of our fantasy, the wholeness, or potential for wholeness of our being. We all share access to a universal mode of being through our life drive. What matters is not the particular content of our drive but the trajectory toward universally meaningful emancipation. Through the life drive, we continue to encounter and confront the Real that has the potential to transform our way of being. The life drive includes the jouissance that opens a gap in the established way in which we desire. The force of this jouissance affirms that I would rather be a revolutionary than a lawyer; the unexpected jouissance in the drive toward revolution changes me and unravels the Symbolic order. It also unravels my location within it by propelling me out of the death drive, as formulated within the Symbolic order, and into the Real of my existence, keeping my desire going along the trajectory of the emancipatory desire.

The Real Cinema and Feminine Jouissance

The cinema of the Real dramatizes the transformation of the drive as I have delineated thus far, creating a visual field wherein the Real emerges through cinematic elements. The Real ruptures the reality that the Symbolic order strives to secure, even at the cost of a subjects' survival and progress, and this rupture is not a simple fraying of the Symbolic order's fabric. The cinema of the Real shows how point of view—be it that of the spectator, the diegetic character, or the gaze that emanates from outside the clearly defined cinematic frame, which reflects ideological boundaries—functions as a conduit through which the visual field of the Real opens up. The viewing subject, whose eyes are a conduit into the Real, comes to exist within the space of the Real and thereby to experience what it feels like to encounter the Real. Through this experience, the viewing subject can enter the situation where the Real, in a particular historical and political context, transforms the subject's relation to the world and the Other. Jean-Luc Godard says, "Without cinema, I wouldn't have known I have a history of my own."[22]

This statement is, however, not simply about making "a memory of this history."[23] Film is a way to engage with history as the Real condition of our being. As I will show in the following chapters, many South Korean films represent the subject entering the emancipatory drive through an encounter with the Real of history that strikes down historiography as written in the dead language of the Father.

The transformation of subjectivity necessitates a corresponding transformation of jouissance. For Lacan, jouissance stems from the path toward an object along which the subject moves, not from the acquisition of that object. There is something profoundly comedic about being on this path, which the subject enjoys traversing, heedless of consequences and indifferent to actually getting the object. This is why we cannot fully explain a truly comic character's way of being through any rational character arc. Their jouissance is tied to the path of the death drive, not to its supposed object. Eluned Summers-Bremner posits that the death drive's path dissolves "the parameters of the known,"[24] which correlate to the boundaries of the Symbolic subject and the pregiven order of things within which that subject exists. As such, the death drive is the origin of the human subject, who emerges through trauma as "the structural first cause of subjectivity and history."[25] Summers-Bremner goes on to theorize that humanity is "exiled from the world of instinctual satisfaction that marks the animal domain" and that the signifier passes across the body, "severing us from simple need and rendering each impulse . . . alive with unmasterable meanings."[26] Such is the trauma of becoming a linguistic subject, whose act of meaning-making is possible only through language, which is defined as the dead letter of the Father in Lacanian theory. This traumatic entrance into the language is "written on and by the body whose singular fragility allows the fiction of a common language."[27] The subject is then forever beholden to the dead letter, stuck "in the form of jouissance . . . to its ends in death forms."[28]

But the subject can also transform the means of obtaining jouissance and, subsequently, the drive as the path to obtain it. As the following chapters on the transnational cinema of the Real will show, these transformations occur in history- and locality-specific situations, setting the death drive, inscribed in historical and geopolitical contexts, on a new path, toward a new kind of jouissance that ultimately leads to political emancipation and a new path of history.

The concept of the life drive, as I theorize it, is rooted in psychoanalytic theory. Žižek, for example, asks, "What if the very structure of a drive (as opposed to instinct) provides a solution? [Animals' instincts focus on achieving their goal, which is satisfaction, unlike humans' drive for the path itself, remaining indifferent to arriving at the goal.] We are stuck on a knot around which drive circulates, yet it is this very stuckness that pushes us again and again forward to invent ever new forms to approach it."[29] Žižek hints that, through the death drive, we approach the Real of the historical and political existence that forms our knot, something unresolvable in the Symbolic order of society that renders the social totality unstable.

Elements of psychoanalytic theory also support my thesis that the Other's drive is the crucial element that pushes us "forward to invent ever new forms to approach" the Real. Theorizing that our being holds a kernel of the trauma of becoming a linguistic subject, Ruti posits that this kernel defines us as individual human beings, as it "expresses something about the idiosyncratic intonation of our desire."[30] Ruti goes on to say that "the conditions we are thrown into shape our life-world, giving us a specific set of obstacles and opportunities. . . . Much depends on how we meet the world . . . how we bring together the particulars of our constitutions and the particulars of our environment."[31] In our encounter with the world, we inevitably encounter the Other's drive, which is formed in the same way. It would be an ethical failure not to recognize, in these encounters, the universality of every subject's life drive toward emancipation from all manner of oppression.

As a way to ponder the Other's drive, consider an elderly Jewish man named Dov Eschel, a Holocaust survivor.[32] His last name is the name of a tree, specifically, the tree that the Old Testament figure Abraham planted when he settled in the land to which god had led him after commanding that he leave the land of his fathers, taking nothing with him. Abraham planted the tree after making a treaty with Abimelech, king of the Philistines, in whose land Abraham had set up his new home according to god's instructions (see Genesis 21:22-34). The tree is the symbol of agreement, of treaty, and of faith in the god whose might and power were the reason Abimelech, an invincible warlord, decided to work with Abraham rather than destroy him. But Dov's original family name, back in Poland/Austria/Germany, was Altschuler, which means "member of the old synagogue."[33] So his name went from attachment to a culture and history that the Nazis tried to obliterate to the symbol of uneasy truce with the prevailing local monarch, backed by god's threat. Abimelech even stole Abraham's wife Sarah until god came to the ruler in a dream and told him that if he didn't give Sarah back to Abraham, he was a dead man. Don't mess with this god. Such a treaty, volatile and uneasy it is, must be continually renewed. It is so that "Eschel"'s life drive could continue to transcend that of "Altschuler." His life drive can transform even the death drive of "Abimelech" into Abimelech's own life drive. When we acknowledge and accept the multiple trajectories along which we pursue our desire, we transition to the life drive. Different historical and social contexts and the particularities of people's means of experimenting with the paths their life drives take create divergent trajectories, which is the Real of the universal human existence.

The cinema of the Real depicts how the subject enters the Real as an ontological condition and, critically, is transformed into the subject of the Real, often through the violent breakdown of subjectivity. This cinema creates for the spectator the subjective experience of the Real via visual and aural descriptions of subjects moving beyond the economy of desire prescribed by the Symbolic order. The spectator enters the Real through the eye, which generates the poetic shock that accompanies the faltering of subjectivity. The subject of the Real appears in what I term *the Real body*, which ruptures both spatial organization, defined as the proper social space where social identities are made visible, and temporal organization, defined as the biographies and historiographies that move toward telos, that is, meaning comprised of the ultimate object of desire. It is in these organizations that the Symbolic order finds its material manifestations, which are then undone via the encounter with the Real body.

A notable example of the Real body is the assigned embodiment, in any human body, of feminine subjectivity as a universally ethical subject. Feminine subjectivity reveals the Real condition of all human subjects, who can never possess the object that is represented as (in psychoanalytic terms) phallic, and promises the fulfillment of all desires. The jouissance of feminine subjectivity comes specifically from *not* having it. Phallic jouissance, in contrast, draws enjoyment from the fantasy of finally obtaining the phallic object, the phantasmatic source of everlasting satisfaction. I note that feminine subjectivity and its jouissance is universal because it provides a universal subject position that anyone can take up, regardless of the specific contexts of their own traumatic cuts, through which they have become social subjects.

The phallic and the feminine, of course, are not founded upon biological, or even morphological, differences, nor can they be defined as purely cultural constructions of identity. Rather, they are two different ways of responding to the impossibility of unified subjectivity within the Symbolic order. As Jennifer Friedlander states, "Sexual identity arises not from biological difference but rather occurs as a result of the symbolic's *in*difference to the subject's need for a solid identity, and identity that may be implemented in either of two ways: the 'male' or the 'female.'"[34] In other words, our sexual identity emerges because the Symbolic order cannot sustain a unified and concrete mode of identity and thus sexual differences are presented to us as a fulcrum of the Symbolic subject. The way we make sense of ourselves within the Symbolic order, in other words, is through sexual difference organized around the perceived presence or absence of the phallus. But we have established that such lack is central to *all* subjects. The phallus is the signifier of the lack that represents the imagined object par excellence, which does not actually exist. As such, the phallus is "a structuring absence that sets the subject on a lifelong course of unfulfillable desire."[35]

Gender identity, then, is a fantasy through which the linguistic subject copes with the impossibility of fulfilling the desire for the object that can eradicate the lack. The feminine and the masculine are two different responses to that lack, two means (or poles, as Friedlander puts it) of coping with that lack. No gender identity can guarantee a unified subject position. In psychoanalytic thinking, the Real destabilizes the Symbolic order's gender scenario, in which the fantasy of ultimate fulfillment of desire is tied to gender identity. It is in this light that we understand Lacan's notion of the not-all (*pas-tout*) of woman. This not-all (*pas-tout*) of woman does not refer to what is constituted as women's biological truth, authenticating the natural state that lacks the phallus. It means that there exists a position that transcends even the seemingly all-important sexual difference between men and women. In this position, the subject—no matter how it matches up with the accepted lines of sexual differentiation—can free itself from the phantasmatic phallic object that is believed capable of successfully defining the order of gender and sexuality. This position foregrounds the fact that the lack creates a split subject, which no amount of language can unify and deliver to the Symbolic order as a secure social subject that abides by that order's ideologies, including those that determine gender and sexuality. The Lacanian subject is a split subject, an empty place in the linguistic and Symbolic order. The Lacanian subject's relationship to some object that subjects might otherwise fantasize will anchor the certainty of their being is mediated by the chain of the signifiers and never by the thing itself. Thus, language only confirms the absence of that phantasmatic object, forever undermining subjectivity itself via the lack of an epistemological and material power to construct a subject as whole and complete. As such, it is impossible to occupy a stable subjectivity, and from this split emerges feminine jouissance.

We become (and continue to exist as) social subjects through the meaning we assign to the phallus, which represents an object that promises to deliver us from the lack. Feminine jouissance exposes the emptiness behind the linguistic veil, the signifier that shields the phallic object. Consider the Calvin Klein underwear commercial featuring sports hero David Beckham: Behind a visual barrier—the pristine white underwear—is believed to be the phallus. But there is, in reality, nothing more than a pound (more or less) of flesh. The subject of feminine jouissance contains the possibility of emancipation from the existing social order that upholds the meaning and promise of the phallic object, which we fantasize will fulfill all our desires. Having moved beyond the fantasy of ultimate fulfillment, the feminine subject defines subjectivity via the impossibility of ever obtaining what Lacan calls "little object 'a,'" (*objet petit a*) wherein "a" is an object that elicits our desire by promising its ultimate satisfaction. The phallic object signifies this "a," which stands in for something that has no actual, material existence. As linguistic subjects, we only have access to the objects of desire that we misrecognize as "a," rather than the Thing-in-itself, which does not, in reality, exist. The subject of phallic jouissance ignores (or is ignorant of) the Real, namely, that the little object "a" does not exist and that we are thus fated to be the subjects of the lack.

Michelangelo Antonioni's *Blow-Up*[36] visualizes what is at stake in the cinema of the Real with regard to feminine jouissance. The film follows a day in the life of Thomas, a London fashion photographer whose engagement with the world involves aiming, shooting, and capturing the Other in still images. He occupies a powerful position of looking, whether the object he frames in a tight spatial and temporal organization is a group of homeless men or provocatively dressed fashion models. This framing places the Other within the comfortable order of class and gender. The world is his garden, framed through the visual apparatus of eye and camera; he exercises mastery over the representation of objects in it. The film follows him, a subject with a comfortable place in the world of meaning-making, as he moves at exhilarating speed, shooting scenes, cavorting around town, at ease even when he procures an absurd, apparently meaningless object on a whim, even when he engages in reckless behaviors.

When he inadvertently captures what appears to be a corpse, he manipulates the images such that they build a logical narrative that suggests a murder. When these images are stolen from the studio, he loses the means to master their meaning, and the reality he has confidently navigated falters. The empty wall where photographs hung is now a gaping wound where the fabric of reality has been torn away, and the Real emerges from the gap in meaning. The enjoyment to be had through possessing and giving meaning to objects is phallic in nature, founded upon the meaning of the phallus, a symbolic object of unlimited potency, as the guarantor of all meaning in the Symbolic order. Phallic jouissance promises final ownership of the object of desire. In Thomas's case, this object is the image that guarantees his subject position as the rightful and effective giver of meaning. His capacity as the maker of meaning is crystallized in his accidentally captured image of a corpse. Appearing as a stain in the field of vision, this image does not immediately yield signification. When blown up, a series of contiguous images turns it into evidence of the existence of a meaningful object, which Thomas can build into a cohesive narrative.

Thomas's position as the giver of meaning shatters when he cannot locate the concrete object, the body that certifies the meaning he has conjured. When he returns to the scene, the object/body is nowhere to be seen. The lack of the object, the loss of an unambiguous signifier, forces Thomas to enter the field of the Real. The stable relationship between signifier and meaning breaks down, and all objects that have been anchored by that relationship, rendered safe and meaningful for the phallic subject of knowing, are cast into an anarchic state. In the closing scene, Thomas follows the volley of an imaginary tennis ball, hit by a troupe of miming clowns playing in the early morning on an empty court. The film's final shot seems to swallow and erase Thomas, as we withdraw to a bird's-eye view, until the protagonist becomes a speck in the vast open field. The trauma of the Real is shown as the empty field where a reality populated by meaningful objects has vanished. It is the field of the Real where the subject of phallic desire—desire that anchors itself to the object that the desiring subject fantasizes will eradicate the lack of meaning—faces the impossibility of ultimate fulfillment. Facing the Real, the subject of desire, formerly bound to phallic objects, can become a new subject of feminine jouissance, for whom there is no phallic object that fulfills desire. This new subject accepts the lack as an existential condition and embarks on the emancipatory drive. All subjects of the emancipatory drive, therefore, are feminine, regardless of the biological, morphological, or cultural prescriptions written on their bodies.

In McNulty's formulation, a new way of desiring creates a new object, and this new object can "create a space for the subject that was not there before."[37] The freedom to act consists of a freedom to accept objects as incidental and partial, which indicates that the meaning of objects is never complete and is really only ideologically constructed. This contingency replaces the previously necessary phallic object perceived to possess definite meaning and thus to be complete and full. As we let go of the impossible phallic object, we no longer turn to the Other as the subject who possesses, and therefore withholds, this object par excellence. We lose the drive to eviscerate the Other's body to extract and possess the object. We become a new subject by allowing the Other to coexist along the path of our emancipatory drive, in which the law of desire, organized around the phallic object, doesn't determine our actions. I describe this new subject of the emancipatory drive as the *universal feminine subject*.

The Real Cinema and the Other's Drive

In the emancipatory drive, the universal feminine subject resists the preexisting temporal order, which the law of desire prescribes as motion toward teleological fulfillment, and likewise rejects the prescribed social organization of space, in which identities are meant to be formulated and affirmed. For an example of the temporal and spatial organization in which teleology (i.e., history's progression) and identities (i.e., how subjects exist in the space where teleology occurs) converge, let us consider the film genre of the Western, wherein the temporal order sets up the movement of the body in space toward a goal. In the space of the Western, we watch "wilderness" turn into "garden," an imperial object of desire, and human subjects are imbued with gender, sexual, and racial identities. These subjects populate the scenes of conflicts between the desire for teleological progress (coded as masculine) and various impediments (coded as feminine); Westerns are full of feminine bodies standing in the way of cowboys' movement in space toward the horizon. These types of subject also appear in conflicts between imperial citizens who build the garden and savages who belong to wilderness.

Through resisting the pregiven order of temporal and spatial organization, the universal feminine subject confronts the drive within the law of desire that unfolds within the Symbolic order. In the cinema of the Real, we see the subject move from a mode of desire emanating from various ideological formations of nations and societies to the emancipatory drive. One point of departure for this shift toward the emancipatory drive is the capitalist nation's scopic desire to contain the subject and the body, which signify intolerable Otherness, within its ideological boundary, using visual images as the metaphoric and material means of containment. This intolerable Otherness comes most notably in the form of feminine jouissance that disrupts the subject of phallic jouissance, which is held together by a chain of meaningful signifiers. The emancipatory drive supports a break from the desire of the nation-state and capitalism, according to which we are to pursue the object that ideology constructs as essential to our being. In the emancipatory drive, there is no phallic object. All objects are partial, which is to say, objects lack an inherently unified and complete meaning. Accepting the lack of the phallic object makes it possible for the subject to subvert the law of desire. The emancipatory drive allows us to recognize, within its sphere, that which exceeds the signifiers that support the Symbolic order. This is the radical possibility contained within the Other's life drive that continually confronts the desiring subject. The Other's life drive disrupts phallic jouissance and, therefore, the normative cohesion of the phallic subject whose position is consolidated though believing in the completeness of the phallic object. In this way, the Other's life drive creates the possibility for the emergence of the new subjectivity of feminine universality. It forces the subject of the death drive to transform its drive.

Throughout history, we see this process unfold, whereby the subject encounters the Other, and both speak and experience the encounter as inherently traumatic. The traumatic dimension explains what Dominick LaCapra has described as the contradiction of historiography: on the one hand, we have the form of history-writing that excludes or downplays "a dialogic relation to the other recognized as having a voice or perspective that may question the observer [the historiographer] or even place him or her in question by generating problems about his or her assumptions, affective investments, and values"[38]; on the other hand, we have "a radical constructivism" that argues that "there is an identity or essential similarity between historiography and fiction, literature, or the aesthetic on structural levels" and emphasizes "the fictionality of structures in all these areas."[39] The perspective missing from both positions is that historiography is the writing of the traumatic relationship between the subject and its Other. Our relationship to the Other necessarily involves a traumatic dimension because, as Lacan posits, subjectivity is not located where subjects believe it to be. The subject that speaks from a perceived stable social location is threatened and haunted by something problematic inherent to any act of speech: the persistence of some kernel of trauma that the system of signification cannot encompass.

Signification comprises chains of metonymy and metaphor. The Thing-in-itself, with which we have no direct relationship, exceeds the linguistic boundary. Its proxy is Lacan's little object "a," which we mistake for something we have lost, something that has been taken, something that can be recovered. This causes us to suffer from the lack that cannot be mended. Linguistic descriptions cannot pinpoint precisely what this "a" might be, so subjects are haunted by their own continual enunciation of impossible desire. For this reason, when subjects verbalize their desire, what they actually describe is the cut in our undifferentiated drive and the ensuing lack. The Other to whom I speak cannot respond to the desire that drives me to speak to the Other in the first place. My relationship to the Other is, thus, defined by my trauma over my lack of the unattainable object of desire. Since speech is necessarily haunted by this enunciation of incurable lack, it cannot guarantee a secure subject position in relation to the Other. What the Other brings to the interaction is, thus, a gesture that reveals the traumatic kernel of desire, an elusive something that defies signification. Instead of comforting by providing what is desired and demanded, it baffles. The Other, in turn, confronts me with her own enunciation that I likewise cannot comprehend.

The Other's enunciation has a historical dimension of its own, since the Other's own subjectivity emerges through its specific context of trauma. That is, the Other has its own context for the emancipatory drive. Every society has its own way of cutting the subject off from the linguistically undifferentiated Thing-in-itself, instituting the subject who speaks a specific language. The encounter with the Other that speaks, thus, places the subject in double jeopardy. First, there is the universal nature of language that fractures subjectivity into a series of enunciations that subjects perceive as the articulation of their own desire for that little object "a." But these enunciations serve only to destabilize the secure position of the speaking subject, because, as Lacan points out, the subjects of speech are not where they believe themselves to be located. That is to say, my speech always involves that traumatic kernel, that elusive thing, which cannot be signified and therefore fractures my speech, leaving a gap in my meaning that cannot be filled. Since my speech cannot attest to a unified subjectivity, not only the meaning of my speech but also my position as a speaking subject is derailed whenever I speak. Second, there is the indigestible kernel of the Other's subjectivity, the result of her own trauma in becoming a speaking subject, which escapes the encountering subject's epistemology.

A friend once complained to me about the strange behavior of his lover, a polished, graceful, young woman with an active social and professional life. It seems she would never flush the toilet when she stayed over at his place. In his own bathroom, he thus continually confronted what was inside her, but was more than her, constituting an excess. Her gesture, like the kernel that found its metonym in his toilet, reveals what exceeds the boundary of her subjectivity, which is perceived as the location of the functioning ego, as a subject without lack. The presence of the kernel of the Other that he saw in the toilet metaphorized her own little piece of the Real that eludes what the Other's statement signifies: the woman as a unified subject position. In the face of the Other, all subjects encounter the impossibility of desire. In this case, the fact that it is impossible to read the Other's desire prompts the question, "What does a woman/an Other want?"

Just how scary is the encounter with the Other's drive? Let us start with what Žižek calls "the encounter of the 'enigmatic signifier,' of the desire of the Other in all its impenetrability."[40] According to Žižek, this encounter can involve an experience of utter alienation as one becomes obsessed with the Other's inaccessible desire. It involves a separation that stems from "insight into how 'the secrets of the Egyptians were also secret for the Egyptians themselves,' i.e. into how our alienation generates what Lacan calls separation as the overlapping of the two lacks."[41] I posit that to encounter this overlapping of two lacks can be transformative, world-remaking, and foundational to a universal condition of being. This is why encountering the Other's drive can be emancipatory, pushing us away from the death drive of colonization and the annihilation of the impenetrable Other. Emancipation, then, is the third option available to us in our encounter with the Other's drive, beyond scary alienation and separation.

Through the encounter with the Other, we confront the limit that the Other imposes on our way of desiring and our subsequent drive to fulfill that desire. As a result, we must recreate our way of being, emancipating ourselves from the law of desire within the existing Symbolic order. I meet the gaze of the Other in my field of vision and confront my own scopic drive, which is part of the death drive and through which I pursue my desire to know and possess sublime objects through seeing them. In that confrontation, I, the subject, face the Real of the scopic drive: the impossibility of knowing through seeing. In this way, the Other's drive derails the trajectory of the drive that supports my coherent subject position. The Symbolic subject, assembled by properties of identity, can be made to unravel via the gaze. This is especially true of the phallic subject, who fantasizes possessing the sublime object through the scopic drive: the phallic subject believes that the scopic drive allows him to command the meaning of the object. Freedom, in this context, is the ability to create a new trajectory for the drive, wherein the Other's jouissance informs my own jouissance, that of *not* having the phallic object of scopic desire. Žižek associates the Lacanian notion of the visual drive with the notion that "our fundamental striving is not to observe, but *to be part of a staged scene*, to expose oneself to the gaze—not a determinate gaze of a person in reality, but of the nonexistent pure gaze of the big Other."[42] The visual drive, in other words, solidifies the Symbolic subject's attachment to the big Other, and, hence, this drive secures the subject's location within the big Other's sphere of the Symbolic order. The Other's gaze, emanating from its own life drive, ejects the scopic subject from that sphere.

The Other's drive compels subjects to vacate their symbolic position. Consider the case of Alan Heyman. I first came across a man called "Hae Euiman" in a South Korean TV program that presents, as objects of curiosity, people who do not quite fit into the perceived boundary of norm in South Korean society. Hae Euiman was a phenotypically white man, ancient-looking, with a bent back. He appears wrapped in a well-worn Korean traditional garb, with an unruly mop of white hair. The camera follows him with barely veiled pornographic pleasure as he ambles through the street. This humble elderly figure, a fixture in a largely working-class neighborhood, was well known for his fluent Korean. Noting that he has taken shelter in lower-class quarters while his Korean wife resides in their modest middle-class apartment nearby, the reporter follows him to his refuge. His living space is filled with a random array of household goods and a surprising trove of traditional Korean musical instruments. We learn that he is a naturalized Korean citizen, originally from the United States. No mention is made that he is also Jewish, a fact I uncovered later from documents archived in the National *Gugak* Center, the South Korean center for traditional music.[43] Hae (his last name) Euiman is a Korean phonetic translation of his given name, Heyman. The viewers learn that he is also a noted and respected musician and scholar of traditional Korean music. Many consider him to be the master of the *taepyungso*, a double reed woodwind instrument.

The trajectory along which Alan Heyman, a Jewish student of classical music from New York City, became Hae Euiman has the potential to be the banal tale of a white man going native, with a tragic conclusion: mere fodder for voyeuristic entertainment. It could also be the story of a "possessive investment" in Otherness. Hollywood certainly has no shortage of horror stories about westerners who go native and then go bad. Consider the 1942 MGM film *White Cargo*, set in the 1910s on an African rubber plantation. The film features Austrian Jewish actress Hedy Lamarr, in blackface, playing a half-Egyptian woman named Tondelayo. We can speculate that knowing there is a phenotypically white face underneath the black surface keeps the audience at a safe distance from the traumatic Real that an intimate encounter with the Black body opens up: there is no safeguarding whiteness from the monstrosity of Otherness. At the same time, an intertextual understanding of Lamarr's Jewishness likely makes it feel more acceptable that she has exchanged a white facade for Blackness, signifying unruly jouissance. In the film, Tondelayo has been banished from the white magistrate's district for her sexual transgressions, but a white plantation manager, Langford, marries her and then is poisoned by her. Subsequently, the dark feminine menace is, within the film's structure, properly punished. Langford, however, remains unconscious. His limp body, carried on a ship to civilization for medical treatment, is the eponymous white cargo. It signifies a human subject that has lost its humanity after intimate contact with the "native," and it is rendered as nothing more than an object, packaged for transport.

Heyman, in contrast, through his encounter with the Other, shifts from one subject position to another, rather than becoming an object fit only as cargo. According to biographical accounts available in South Korea, Heyman as a young man was deployed to the front line of the Korean War. Lying in the trenches at night, surrounded by the North Korean army, invisible in the dark, he and the other soldiers were forced to listen to the enemy's nightly performance of traditional battle march songs, accompanied by percussion and woodwinds, a classic warfare tactic to intimidate the enemy to the south. As he lay listening to sounds he had never before encountered, Heyman was gripped by what he later learned was the *taepyungso*. He was moved not by fear of the invisible enemy that the music signified but by something he sensed exceeded the linguistic structure of music as he knew it. This encounter likely shattered his understanding of sound as a signifier. After the war, he returned to South Korea to learn the instrument and later gained renown within traditional music scholarship and performance circles.

Beyond a postmodern rendition of a deterritorialized subject, Heyman's is the story of an encounter with the Other's drive that finds its linguistic response in a subject that changes his location in the world in order to accept the Other's drive, in this case carried out through music. Reading his own account closely, we understand that it was not simply a novel experience of beauty that moved him. The sound exceeded the boundary of the language of Western music to which he was accustomed and compelled him to vacate the subject position that defined his way of desiring a beautiful object. The *sound* appeared to him as the *gaze*. Issuing from the space of the Other's drive, its undulations metaphorizing how the Other's drive unfolded, the sound allowed him to forget about the violent death that could arrive at any moment. Heyman responded to the Other's drive by creating a new subjective trajectory, for which he needed to abandon the communal identity that had anchored his subjectivity up to that point.

The subject does not, of course, always respond to the Other's drive this way. The film *Even the Rain*,[44] set in 2000 in Bolivia during what is known as the Cochabamba Water War, a popular uprising against the privatization of water resources, involves a film crew, led by a Spanish producer, Costa, and a Mexican director, Sebastian, that arrives to shoot a movie about Christopher Columbus. The European investors backing the production intend to promote a politically conscientious portrayal of Columbus's conquest. They choose their location because, in the producer's words, "the poor natives will work their tail off for two dollars a day." During the production, we see the Other's drive disrupting the metropolitan subject's desire, represented by Costa and Sebastian, through the actions of Daniel, an indigenous actor who plays the role of Atuey, leader of the indigenous rebellion against the church and Columbus's army. He is also an organizer of the largely indigenous popular resistance in the Water War. The Water War throws the filmmaking into turmoil, especially after Daniel's arrest. Daniel, as Atuey, appears in the scenes of the indigenous resistance against the church, and as an activist he appears in news footage of fierce demonstrations against the state violence that has allowed comprador global capitalists to usurp, through the water monopoly, the people's right to life. The film production team watches grainy TV news footage of violent attacks on indigenous bodies carried out by military police. This scene is soon followed by a location shoot of the key moment where Columbus's priests and army burn the resisting indigenous fighters, including Atuey, at the stake. The Columbus film's producer has bribed the police to have Daniel temporarily released to shoot the scene. The wounded, indigenous body we previously saw in the news footage haunts the scene of filmmaking, which recapitulates the colonial violence. Daniel's face, as we have seen in the news, appears again at the scene of massacre and immolation.

Daniel embodies the Other whose political act forces entry past the safe boundary of the metropolitan imagination. Likewise, Atuey crosses the colonial boundary by inserting himself into the empire's death drive as the kernel of Otherness. The viewer is invited to imagine the close-up of Daniel's face in the news footage overlapping Atuey's face as he shouts from the stake, "I despise you, I despise your god, I despise your greed." As he burns to death, this speech becomes a collective chanting of all those burning alongside him. The diegetic villagers, surrounding the site of execution, join in. The face and the speech constitute the kernel of trauma that cannot be removed from the imperial desire: they are the gaze of the Other that it must confront.

The film, however, is not sanguine about the possibility of the Other's drive propelling the subject of desire into the emancipatory drive. The narrative makes it clear that Atuey's and the villagers' chanting is successfully staged and framed for cinematic effect, endowing the film within the film with an aura of resistance to the imperialist narrative. The filmmaker had been striving to achieve this emotional impact as a signifier of successful filmmaking all along, so much so that he singles out Daniel from the sea of extras; he sees Daniel as the authentic personification of what the indigenous should represent to the metropolitan spectator. In the closing scene, the Spanish producer, Costa, rides a taxi to the airport to leave Bolivia. Moved by the plight of Daniel's family, he has ignored the protection of his investors' capital as the highest priority to search for Daniel's daughter, who had gone missing during the protest. In the beginning of the closing scene, he intently scans the people and the streets passing outside the taxi window. Holding up a vial of water that Daniel has given him as a gift, he speaks aloud the word *yaku*, which in Daniel's language means "water." Then the speed of the film framing Costa's view intensifies, at first seeming to mimic the speed of the car and soon accelerating to blur the scene outside, rendering it as jumbled abstract brushstrokes whose shape we cannot discern, until the scene fades to white. This conclusion visually demonstrates how that which appears as the knot at the center of the metropolitan subject's drive—a thing that exceeds epistemological and material understanding of the Other and disrupts the subject's given way of existence—might fade into a perceptual dead end without any lasting effect. In this instance, the Other's drive does not meaningfully change the trajectory of the desiring subject's drive toward that of the emancipatory drive.

In the following chapters, I investigate how such a transformation might happen. For now, I posit that to move toward the emancipatory drive, we must abandon our pregiven subject position, especially when the Other appears and articulates her cut. In doing so, we emancipate ourselves from the demands of the big Other and the insistence of our own desire, which is based on the illusion that we can fulfill those demands. This cycle tethers us to the death drive, in which we pursue our object of desire even unto the destruction of ourselves and the subjective Other. As I will show throughout the book, in the emancipatory drive subjects live with the jouissance of the wounded Other, a mode of jouissance that calls for us to change the way we narrate and live out our desire.

The Real Life

Psychoanalysis proposes the creation of a new subjectivity; the cinema of the Real shows what it is to exist in the life drive of this new emancipated subject. How, then, do we apply this understanding to life? How does the viewer translate the emancipation represented in cinema into a way of being? Is the gap between art and life too significant to cross?

The cinematic space where we, as subjects, construct meaning is, in theory, a conduit to the life space where that meaning is realized. I draw my conceptual connection between the Real of life and the Real of cinema from earlier works that see the political potential in the relationship between cinema and viewer; Hilary Neroni's reading of Jane Campion's work as feminist cinema is one example. Neroni recognizes that in Campion's films, the spectator is made "to look from what Campion posits as the perspective of the drive."[45] Such a position of looking shows that Campion envisages "political change as the result of learning to look differently rather than as the result of seeing new things."[46] In the cinema of the Real, the cinematic field serves as the ontological field where we face the ruin of the Symbolic order that had previously prescribed our subject position. By aligning ourselves as spectators with the cinematic vision, we might occupy the space of the Real. In the cinema of the Real, the viewing subject is herself a formal element, as her eyes are the visual apparatus that unfolds the Real. Eyes register the poetic shock of an image that dislocates the viewing subject's position of knowing. The narrative, technique, and technology of cinematic production often work to obscure the fact that while real life is framed according to a particular set of ideas, the poetic shock of the cinema of the Real can disrupt the narrative space that circumscribes normal life, placing the viewer in touch with the traumatic Real. These films may explicitly spectacularize the traumatic encounter with the Real, or they may allow the traumatic Real to peek through the cinematic images and spaces with subtlety.

In the recent French film *Cuties*,[47] Amy, an eleven-year-old Senegalese girl, struggles to find her place in a French *banlieue*. She faces the ideological force of the regional practice of Islam that dictates femininity through rituals and customs, overseen by a community matriarch. As Amy's mother makes preparations to bring her husband's second wife from Africa to France, Amy begins to resist the confinement imposed on her by the local religious-patriarchal apparatuses. Amy's story reflects the reality of many feminine subjects who struggle against the collaboration of family and religion to sustain the Symbolic order.

Amy attempts to escape her confinement, confronting family and religion while seeking to secure her subject position and negotiating the enforced norms of gender and sexuality in a larger social context outside the *banlieue*. In this process, she is driven to a dead end of performative femininity, a commodity in capitalist patriarchal societies that violently reenforce confinement within the signifiers of femininity. Amy adopts the lurid sexuality found in commercial exhibitions of commodified adolescent sexuality. She engages with the linguistic norms of the proper feminine subject, which tie her to the Symbolic order that prescribes that norm. Through this engagement, however, we encounter the gaze of the Real in two scenes of magical realism, which serve as aesthetic devices for indicating a mode of violence that the film cannot properly represent. These scenes of magical realism disrupt the filmic reality to reveal the Real of the feminine condition. Through this encounter with the Real, the feminine subject can shatter the reality of femininity to create a new subjectivity, independent of her external conditions.

These scenes feature an object that metaphorizes Amy's confinement: an intricately embroidered, flowing dress that she is to wear at her father's wedding. Amy watches the dress, tucked among other clothing in a wardrobe, slowly swing back and forth, its elaborate lace sleeves rustling as if blown by the wind, although there is no diegetic indication that an actual, physical wind is blowing through the room; the other pieces of clothing remain motionless. It is as if the dress is animated by the force of familial and religious ideologies, compelling her to put it on, an externalized femininity sewn together in accordance with the Law of the Father. This scene comprises a subtle revelation of the unspeakable violence upon which it is founded. In another scene, the dress bleeds. The dripping blood forms a dark red puddle that spills onto the floor, indicating an encounter with the Real of femininity as the bloody cut in the Symbolic order. Amy will ultimately refuse to wear this dress and to attend the wedding, a sign that she will transform her way of being through refusal to invest in the femininity to which she has been relegated.

The poetic shock of these scenes has a visceral effect through which we encounter the complex layers of existence outside the boundary of our sense of reality and what we perceive to be our subjecthood within it. Therein lies the possibility of feminine jouissance that resists the signifiers of the feminine that the Law of the Father, which authorizes family and religion, inscribes. In the film, the expression of feminine jouissance is conveyed mostly through the gestures of Amy and her friends, all of whom come from the same impoverished neighborhood and live with similar restrictions on how to embody the feminine. But these gestures, despite their emancipatory dimension, are confined to the normative language of the feminine, as when they choreograph and perform sexually explicit numbers in a dance competition.

Feminine jouissance, in this instance, seems to be mainly about the transgression of familial and religious ideologies and less about the creation of a new subjectivity. This limited scope may be the film's way of acknowledging that the creation of a new feminine subjectivity involves wresting meaning out of what is forced upon feminine subjects, as there is no pristine emancipatory language available to us. We may wrestle with god, the master signifier, but the expression of feminine jouissance nevertheless alters our perception of reality as we wrestle. The gesturing body that conveys feminine jouissance gazes at us as it embodies the Real of gender and sexuality; it alters what is assumed to be permanent reality with all its physical and ideological trappings.

Feminine jouissance originates where the phallus—the master signifier that promises the smooth operation of the chain of signifiers by denoting identities such as gender and sexuality—does not exist. This recognition, mediated by film, comes as a shock. In *Tomboy*,[48] we meet Laure, a fourth-grader who decides to be a boy named Mickaël. To participate in a swim meet with other boys, she constructs a penis from clay to put in the swim trunks she has fashioned by cutting down her bathing suit. After successfully embodying a boy swimming in the lake, Laure stores the detachable penis in the small box where she has kept her baby teeth. The sight of a clay penis lying among discarded teeth shocks us by revealing the Real of the phallus, upon which we found masculine subjectivity: it is an empty signifier that refers to a pound of fabricated flesh, an accidental object.

The poetic shock induced by the disruptive kernel of the Real unravels our sense of reality. This is how cinema opens the abyss of our being. We stand at the precipice, the edge of what we believed to be our material and symbolic reality and our imagined location within it. We come to comprehend the Real world through this experience of poetic shock, to see the flaws in the fabric of what we had accepted as reality. The Real gazes at us through those imperfections, and we recognize that reality itself is an arbitrary ideological framework. The gaze that emanates from the cinematic screen can, in this way, follow us into the bright daylight outside the theater.

My experience teaching South Korean cinema in a predominantly white North American university has provided ample opportunity to observe the cinematic gaze follow spectators, my students, out of the "theater," a stadium-seating on-campus screening hall. In one class, we screened and discussed the South Korean film *A Taxi Driver*.[49] Set in 1980 during the Gwangju Uprising, an armed civilian resistance against the military dictatorship, the film follows real-life German journalist Jürgen Hinzpeter, who first reported the uprising and the military's massacre of civilians. The taxi driver, also based on a real-life figure, accompanies the reporter on the perilous journey through the city, which has been shut down by martial law. The real-life taxi driver died shortly after the journey to Gwangju, but his identity was not discovered until the release of the film. *A Taxi Driver* represents a historical event about which American audiences are largely ignorant, a civil uprising in a tiny country that is still mostly outside the understanding and consciousness of many Americans, veiled as it is behind the glossy spectacles of BTS and other K-pop sensations. The uprising reveals that the intricate structure of global capitalism necessitated military rule in South Korea within the Cold War world order, wherein the divided Korean peninsula stands in as a mainstay, and led to a bloody struggle for democracy. Facing the Real of modern history through local details, the viewer experiences its visceral effect, rendered through the film's hybridization of the historical melodrama and action genres. This hybridization taps into viewers' usual ways of consuming the cinematic spectacle even as it jolts them out of their comfort zone by introducing cinematic elements that exceed generic expectations. Trauma leaves its trace in the film's textuality: it is written on the cinematic body and also on the linguistic (both visual and narrative) composition of *A Taxi Driver*. The most profound effect on my students seemed to come from the face of the taxi driver himself. Close-ups of his face, like those of Dreyer's Joan of Arc, suggest something that doesn't quite fit within the diegetic time-space of the cinema. These unusual close-ups exceed the expected economy of identification with the character that provides a shortcut to what we assume is the character's psychological truth. Both the taxi driver and Joan of Arc appear to be looking at something outside the order and ideologies that enfold them. Gilles Deleuze, in a similar vein, posits that a close-up removes the face "from its spatio-temporal coordinates."[50] The close-ups of the taxi driver's face indicate a universal emancipation of the historical subject that transcends the temporal and spatial confinement that global capitalism imposes. These close-ups place us, as viewers, in a time-space that doesn't belong to what we see or believe to be our stable reality as historical subjects and viewers of film.

The close-ups also indicate what the historical subject undergoes in facing the Real of history. They first convey the driver's disbelief and horror as he witnesses the scenes of massacre and then mark the point at which he changes from passive witness to political actor. When my students encounter the close-up of the taxi driver's face, they experience an "a-ha moment," in which they recognize the Real of history unfolding. They often describe finding it impossible to look away from the face. It pulls them into the event that disrupted the reality of the global capitalist political economy that sustained the Cold War. Through viewing the face that conveys the impact of historical trauma, which gazes at them from the midst of the bloody Real of history that language is inadequate to describe, they encounter the trauma of the Other that demands they see and hear its wounding. The gaze that appears at the site of that wound pulls them from a comfortable position of seeing and knowing and gets lodged in their eyes like a kernel. Through the act of seeing, they enter the Real. When they change their understanding of the world because of the gaze, they access the potential to live in the Real, to forever alter the way they live. In this way, the cinematic space can intersect with the life space.

In considering madness, we see another way of linking cinema to life. Madness is a mode of being that follows the blueprint of our own persistent death drive. In ferocious repetitions, the subject gone mad stages a death-driven encounter with the big Other. The big Other's demand has shattered the subject of madness, unlike those who occupy a stable position in the Symbolic order and are able to successfully assimilate themselves within the linguistic order through the encounter and construct a functioning ego. The subject gone mad repeatedly stages her own death, believes that she has lost something precious in the encounter with the big Other, and has suffered a virtual death. By restaging that deathly encounter, the subject experiences a fleeting reunion with that lost object, a temporary resurrection, rather than a much more frightening encounter with the Real of human existence, namely, the lack. The cinematic experience may likewise stage the experience of such repetition. The repetitious viewing of favorite films, the popularity of genre films, and the satisfaction of repeatedly experiencing the visual and aural renditions of a specific position in auteur films may be a method of avoiding confrontation with the Real through the more palatable repetitions that the cinema stages. The death drive allows us to keep going without having to move to the life drive, where we turn living with the lack into the emancipatory drive.

In the cinema of the Real, our encounter with the Real also occurs through repetition, but each repetition pushes the subject a little further off the path, away from the trajectory of desire and its object, so that the subject walks the untrodden toward creating a new path of the life drive.

Let us look at this relationship between cinema and reality from a slightly different perspective. Deleuze argues that "the cinema is the machine for going back into the past" to change the past, which is to say, to open up the past to a range of potential reinterpretations.[51] When such reinterpretations of the past become available, we are no longer bound by our subjectivity or tethered to fixed interpretations of history that we had formerly accepted as immutable. The unconscious, meanwhile, no longer delineated by the fixed past, opens up revised temporalities that can change our ideas about, and practice of, who we are. Cinema, enfolding multiple temporalities of the unconscious, can do the same work. Deleuze asserts that the cinematographic mechanism produces material images rather than representations or illusion.[52] The images we encounter in the cinema have a material dimension, in that they generate an effect that can alter our mode of existence. Through the conduit of the eye, we experience the reverberating effect of those images. This is why spectacle has political potential. I posit that, through the eyes, the spectator experiences becoming the subject of the Real who is emancipated from the pregiven term of subjectivity and that this creates the political potential of cinema.

An important concept that allows us to explore the relationship between cinema and life is the Law of the Father, upon which the Symbolic order is founded. The Law of the Father is a psychoanalytic term that refers to the ideological and material structure of society. The Law prescribes and maintains the order of things and the terms of our existence by nominating proper ways of desiring and the appropriate objects we are meant to desire. Cinema can show how we might encounter the Law in life. I posit that this encounter comprises two distinct modes: the masculine, which upholds and identifies with the phallic jouissance that the Law of the Father promises, and the universal feminine, which confronts the Law with feminine jouissance.

As an example of the masculine mode, I offer an obscure 1941 Ernst Lubitsch comedy called *That Uncertain Feeling*.[53] Throughout the film, Mrs. Baker's outfits allow her to visually blend in with the bourgeois norm. In a doctor's office, she wears a dress with geometric details, as if mirroring her role as a properly scientized object of medicine. In the bedroom, she dresses up like a doll. Mr. Baker, an insurance executive, lacks the visual details that could render him as an object to behold. These visual details affirm the bourgeois norm of gender identity. However, in the end, such a norm cannot hide the crack in the law that it upholds, allowing the Real of the law, its obscene underpinning, to peak through.

In one scene, a bourgeois couple in New York City, Mr. and Mrs. Baker, meet in a lawyer's office for divorce proceedings. The lawyer informs the couple that they must establish a plausible cause for divorce and that in New York State this requires that one of them have an extramarital affair and identify the partner thereof. The husband volunteers to take on the role of the unfaithful spouse in an elaborate ploy to win back his wife by impressing her with his high-mindedness.

In the end, they cannot agree on whom this fictitious paramour should be. This leads to a conflict, and the husband's ploy to win his wife back fails. They decide to divorce in Pennsylvania, where the law requires one of them to take up residence in the state and further mandates that one partner be physically cruel to the other.

Comedy ensues when they try to stage the scene of cruelty in front of a witness. After the husband pours insults on the wife about her family, the wife is supposed to call the husband a "cheap second-rate insurance peddler," the line that is meant to be his cue to slap her. The lawyer's secretary is present to serve as the legally required witness to the act of cruelty, though she has no clue that she has been made into a chess piece in an absurd game of performative conformity to the letter of the law. Mr. Baker recognizes that the law demands that he be a lawful subject, one who follows the letter of the law, which demands that he slap his wife, but he is unable to follow through. He tries several times and finally drinks himself silly to be able to perform the required act. This absurd scene captures how we stage our best performances for the big Other. We present the best possible justification of our actions in the eye of the law, especially when it involves our most personal and intimate matters. The couple and their lawyer go beyond turning the law into a banal theater where they perform petty justifications for their actions. The law demands justification, and subjects of the law work as hard as necessary to meet that demand. Ernst Lubitsch, a Jewish filmmaker who fled his native Germany when the Nazis came to power, smuggles into this formulaic, genre-based work an absurd picture of the American bourgeoisie answering to the law, even if their obedience is based on performing the most obscenely banal act.

In contrast to the lawful subject represented in *That Uncertain Feeling*, the ethical subject must confront the law in life. In *Eichmann in Jerusalem*, Hannah Arendt discusses the ethical subject as theorized by Immanuel Kant. According to Arendt, "Kant's moral philosophy is . . . closely bound up with man's faculty of judgment, which rules out blind obedience."[54] Kant's categorical imperative is that "the principle of my will must always be such that it can become the principle of general law."[55] Any action must, in Kant's formulation, have a universal resonance, applicability, and meaning. Arendt states that "from the moment Eichmann [who said that he read Kant] was charged with carrying out the final solution he had ceased to live according to Kantian principles. . . . He had consoled himself with the thought that he no longer 'was master of his own deeds,' that he was unable to change anything."[56] Thus, simply carrying out crimes legalized by the state becomes the way of being.[57] To do so is to act as if the principle of action were the same as that of the state's law, where its sanctioned criminal act, the final solution to the Jewish question, is a simple matter of legislation and administration.

Certainly, the choices available to individual subjects regarding moral judgement and action were there all along: to choose the universal law of life in freedom (regardless of the consequences) or to choose the Nazi's state law as the personal moral imperative. Arendt relates the story of two German peasant boys who were drafted into the SS, refused to sign, and were then sentenced to death.[58] In the last letter they wrote to their family, they said: "We too would rather die than burden our conscience with such terrible things. We know what the S.S. must carry out."[59] We can say their moral judgments and actions constitute an example of the Kantian ethical subject, whose choices and actions have universal meaning and application. By refusing to participate in genocide and instead choosing death, they upheld life in freedom for all. Their ethical act allows them to become the universal feminine subject. The boys are satisfied with knowing that satisfaction will, for them at least, never arrive.

The ethics of universal feminine subjectivity involve confronting the Law of the Father that the nation upholds, the chain of signifiers that sustains the lawful subject's Symbolic existence. Accepting the Other's trauma, the universal feminine subject emerges through the traumatic encounter with the Real of history to which the Other's trauma points. Through this process, some Germans living under the Nazi regime emerged as feminine subjects of universal ethics. In Rainer Werner Fassbinder's 1972 film *The Bitter Tears of Petra von Kant*,[60] Petra von Kant arrives at the precipice of her Symbolic existence, facing the traumatic loss of that which supports her subjectivity. A fashion designer, Petra loses her lesbian lover, Karin, a working-class woman who refuses to be marooned in the space that Petra constructs as the limiting sphere of desire: all of their interactions are staged in her bedroom. Crucially, she also loses her factotum Marlene, who has provided capitalist value for her like an indentured servant, through both domestic and professional labor, without speaking a word throughout the film. She serves tea and creates the detailed fashion illustrations that Petra claims as her own. In the end, Marlene, initially tethered to Petra in what appears to be an eroticized sadomasochistic relationship, packs her suitcase and leaves. The loss of the Other who sustains one's desire, whether fascist or bourgeois, must happen before a subject can move on to the emancipatory drive.

In turning the Holocaust into a simple matter of legislation and administration, the law reveals its obscene jouissance. The law's very appeal is in how it justifies ardent participation in obscene jouissance. Robert O. Paxton argues that fascist movements rely not on terror but on "mobilizing passions." The emotions and sensations that I posit accompany jouissance allow fascists to be moved by "the beauty of violence and the efficacy of will."[61] We, through emotions and sensations, likewise occupy an imaginary subject position in which we identify with the ideologies that support the Symbolic order, which then inform our political behavior.

We escape the Imaginary and Symbolic sphere of being that has been prescribed to us by claiming the universal feminine position, but the only way to emerge as the universal feminine subject, which is to say, the ethical subject, is through an encounter with the Real. According to Bruce Fink, "The I is not already in the unconscious. It may be everywhere presupposed there, but it has to be made to appear."[62] Although Fink's statement is made in a clinical context, I believe this process can likewise be applied to the creation of a new subjectivity, the universal feminine subject that comes to exist in the emancipatory drive by encountering the Real of our being. Fink continues, "I must come to be where foreign forces—the Other as language and the Other as desire—once dominated. I must subjectify that otherness."[63] This we may apply to the process of becoming the ethical subject in relationship to the big Other. This process happens through language. To become a new subject, overcoming what is fated to us by parents, nation, culture, community, society, religion, and so on, we must transform the dead language of death drive and, with it, the sense that we are an object in the sphere of the big Other's desire. In learning to wrestle with the paternal language, we move from one linguistic sphere, where we are locked into the objectification of the big Other's desire, to another sphere that holds a space of emancipation, where our relationship to the Other is not mediated by being the Other's object or by demanding that the Other fulfill our own desire for the pound of flesh we believe we have lost.

Lacan's emphasis on the imperative of speech attests to the possibility of our emerging as an ethical subject through confronting the language that is given to us in the Symbolic order, which defines our relationship to the Other through the object of desire. Lacan states, "Psychoanalytic experience has rediscovered in man the imperative of the Word as the law that has shaped him in its image. It exploits the poetic function of language to give his desire its symbolic mediation. May this experience finally enable you to understand that the whole reality of its effects lies in the gift of speech."[64] The emerging new subject speaks the language of feminine jouissance as a means of revealing the *lack* as the Real of desire. Perhaps returning the gift to the giver, this subject enjoys freedom from the law of desire, which is organized around the signifier of its object. Alessandra Raengo posits that the body "organizes the textual system" of film[65] and that film is a formal challenge that presents new aesthetic possibilities.[66] I extend this postulation with the idea that the body that belongs to the subject of the Real, the Real body, can challenge the linguistic system of both film and life and present new linguistic possibilities. As I will demonstrate throughout this book, the Real body of the universal feminine challenges the cinematic textual system. In showing us the Real body, the cinema of the Real explores and expands the linguistic and political potential of the cinema.

Throughout the following chapters, I undertake transnational and transtextual approaches, staging a dialogue between global theory and local trauma and outlining elements of universality in local contexts. Chapter 1 theorizes how the cinema of the Real *Real-izes* the subject through form. This chapter also outlines how my conception of the cinema of the Real expands upon the existing theory of the Real in film and in psychoanalytic thinking, a point that subsequent chapters will clarify. Chapter 2 focuses on the Real body that figures as the traumatic kernel in the Symbolic order. This chapter also looks closely at feminine jouissance as the emancipatory subject position. The key concept in chapter 3 is the emancipatory drive. This chapter looks at how we can conceptualize the drive as politically meaningful and emancipatory through the traumatic encounter with the Other. Chapter 4 theorizes feminine universality. It looks at feminine cinema that focuses on space as the cartographical metaphor of trauma, as well as historical scenes where feminine universality emerges, connecting cinema and life and advancing the position that it is possible to transform the world through feminine jouissance.

CHAPTER ONE

The Cinema of the Real

What's in a Name? The Real in the Cinema

As articulated in the introduction, the cinema of the Real transforms the viewing spectator into the subject of the Real by transforming the visual field itself into the field of the Real, thereby disrupting the concrete certainty of the body and its subject position. As something that cannot be mapped within the temporal and spatial order of a given definition of reality, the Real exceeds the usual chain of visual signifiers, appearing as an indigestible kernel that fractures the smooth surface of the image onscreen. This fracturing inevitably pressures the film form itself, which must devise a new visual language to reflect this disruption. What, then, is the aesthetic and thematic organization of the cinema of the Real? What does the Real look or feel like? How does the Real figure as an ontological condition, a state of being? Furthermore, how does the cinema of the Real make the revelation of the visual and ontological field of the Real possible?

To begin to answer these questions, I turn to the South Korean film *The Front Line*,[1] which is set during the Korean War and includes a scene of South Korean soldiers waiting for a battle against the Chinese army to commence. Both sides will incur enormous casualties in their determination to claim a hill that signifies progress on the chessboard of war. The silence in anticipation of the uproar of the battle is shattered when illumination flares reveal a sea of Chinese soldiers sweeping down upon the South Koreans. This scene reflects how China figures in the South Korean experience of history. In the contemporary context, China's long-standing sponsorship of North Korea has been a defining factor in the North-South relationship, which includes sustained, often sharp tensions in the peninsula as China uses the North as a buffer against the United States. North Korean communists fought alongside the Red Army for the establishment of the People's Republic of China, before repositioning themselves in North Korea. In this scene from *The Front Line*, the hill functions as a threshold, across which is staged the traumatic encounter with the Other. Through this encounter, the subject faces the Real of national history: the nation-state cannot shield the national subject from a traumatic encounter with the Other. From the vanishing point that the mountain occupies, which serves as the limit of seeing, the Other emerges to annihilate the subject.

In a Lacanian context, the Real is that which reveals how the assumed, pregiven order of things *really* works, a constitutive element of the Symbolic order that underpins the established order. The Symbolic order refers to the collection of ideas, beliefs, and assumptions that we construe as the principles around which law, ideology, and other systems of belief and action organize our society and social subjectivity. The Symbolic order cannot successfully accommodate or incorporate the Real because the Real ruptures the presumed reality that the Symbolic order strives to guarantee, and it does so by exposing the points where the Symbolic order falters. The pregiven order of things, including ideology, society, and subjectivity, collapses in that rupture.

The Front Line exemplifies what I call the cinema of the Real. As such, the film shows the cinematic structures and elements that frame the emergence of the Real for the audience. This film launches our exploration of how the cinema of the Real transubstantiates the visual image into the Real, transforming the visual field itself into the field of the Real. The cinema of the Real likewise transforms the spectator into the subject of the Real, who emerges through the violent shattering of subjectivity and encounters the Real as produced by the visual form. My analytical emphasis is on the visual, rather than narrative or thematic, elements and moves beyond identifying the enigmatic visual elements through which the fabric of the Symbolic order may be seen as torn apart. I focus on how, in some films, a point of view, particularly one inscribed as that of the spectator, works as a conduit through which the visual field of the Real emerges. Beyond seeing and encountering an object that signifies or marks the eruption of the Real, the spectator enters, and exists for a time, within the sphere of the Real.

It is worth noting that I do not aim to create a binary opposition between the narrative form and the visual form. We must consider how narrative and formal elements together achieve an effect that the viewer viscerally experiences. If a film destabilizes "reality" through the visual form, the narrative form materializes this destabilized reality. In an essay on King Hu's classical *wuxia* films, particularly *A Touch of Zen* (1971) and *Raining in the Mountain* (1979), Héctor Rodríguez points out that a formal quality (what he calls the "de-realized" visual tone that King Hu uses in his construction of the cinematic space) permeates the entire narrative of these films. Rodríguez also notes that when the narrative lacks a stable diegetic space—which characterizes King Hu's construction of diegesis, for which he uses fragmentary human movement through estranging cinematic space—the viewer experiences reality as "fluid, fleeting and unstable," and this experience undermines the viewer's "sense of ontological security."[2] Here, we see how the narrative form is formulated through the suffusion of formal qualities. King Hu's narrative form is organized around, and propelled by, a seemingly endless meandering of characters through space that is rendered through "fragmentary pro-filmic gestures."[3] For King Hu, the need to show the impossibility of the subject's "sensory-motor control over objective space" is what drives the narrative's organization and movement.[4] His narrative form builds the world through precarious diegesis, and this narrative drive informs the filmmaker's formal choices regarding the construction of space. Human subjects wander, seemingly after an object of desire, but in the end, it is the wandering that is the focus. The repetitious and circular sense of time is rendered tangible in that space. In this context, Rodríguez describes King Hu's method as follows: "Drawing on a vividly haptic metaphor, the director has himself described the narrative space of his films as an experience of groping in the dark, 'not seeing one's five fingers while holding up one's hand.'"[5]

We can observe how the narrative form, thematic form, and visual form together materialize existential subjectivity in the South Korean Netflix TV drama, *My Liberation Notes*. The drama's narrative drive follows characters' movements toward an ethical position regarding the Other, and we watch that process unfolding through diegesis centered on characters walking and musing on existential questions. The paths characters take are often surreal. A moonlit and windswept field of reeds that looks like a no-man's-land is juxtaposed with a hyperreal rendition of the cityscape and the mundane scenery of the countryside. Characters move from the mundane to the surreal on their walks, as if their quest leads them to the sphere outside the norms of morality in a neo-Confucian capitalist society. As one watches these characters walking side by side, elucidating their existential condition without resorting to emotional exchange, one wonders if the image of walking itself precedes the narrative drive toward the theme of existentialism.

In my articulation of the aesthetic and thematic organization of the cinema of the Real, I locate the cinema of the Real in a transnational framework, traversing various configurations of global filmmaking, often represented by auteur films.[6] In Werner Herzog's *Aguirre: The Wrath of God* (1972), the Amazon River, a significant body of water surrounded by a curtain of forest, marks the limit of seeing, functioning as the opaque, impenetrable perspectival point. On this waterway, which extends the space of looking endlessly while simultaneously prohibiting true visual penetration, Aguirre's expedition team, which had come to seek El Dorado and declare a new empire, is decimated by arrows flying from above the line of vision, the forests, and the river. At the point where visual penetration fails, the subject encounters the Real of imperial history. The waterway is the field of the Real.

To comprehensively structure how the Real emerges in the cinema of the Real, I now turn to Joan Copjec's *Imagine There's No Woman*. In this book, Copjec argues that the linear perspective of Renaissance paintings, a departure from medieval representations of space, organizes the visual field of the cinematic screen and brings about the possibility of disrupting the Symbolic order.[7] The transcendental point built into the perspectival horizon not only indicates the space beyond the frame of the image but also reveals what exceeds the visible phenomena. On the surface, the perspectival horizon suggests an ever-expanding vision, the purview of the imperial spectator that encompasses the visible world. This purview is key to understanding the social subject of enlightenment and, therefore, conveys and mimics the privileged position of the subject of knowing. This perspective is located within the Symbolic order, where seeing is thoroughly bounded and defined by the "rules of the game" that overdetermine our modes of being and action, as in the order of imperialism or patriarchy. The originality of Copjec's argument is this: What seems to support the Symbolic order—by delineating the position of the subject of knowing through seeing in relation to the objective world—in fact disrupts the Symbolic order. The vanishing point on the horizon interrupts the omniscient spectator's looking, which is meant to harness the world to his point of view. What appears in the visual field is empirically impossible to comprehend for a subject who exists in the Symbolic order.

In this context, the perspectival arrangement of images indicates the Real. The Real reveals constitutional elements of the Symbolic order, but it ruptures the Symbolic order by also revealing potential points of fracture in those elements. The omniscient position of looking that the use of linear perspective seems to establish is ontologically and phenomenologically impossible. The Symbolic order that seeks to offer such a position as a possible place of emergence for the subject of seeing and knowing falters at the vanishing point on the horizon. It is on this ground that I, with Copjec, argue against the widely accepted notion in cultural studies that perspective is primarily the expression of imperial vision, in which the world is circumscribed as a garden where the wilderness of the savage landscape is tamed and redesigned according to the Symbolic order of the imperial nations. Rather, Copjec asserts, perspective reveals the unknown and allows us to visualize what is ineffable within the Symbolic order: that is, the Real. Perspective transforms the horizon in the field of the image not into a point from which extends a boundless imperial vision but into a potential disruption of that field and its corresponding vision. The horizon does not represent a metonym of a telos, an object of history, through which the arc of our looking tames the wilderness and the strangeness of the world it encounters. The horizon is where the Real appears as the breaking point in the Symbolic order.

In the aforementioned filmic scenes, the boundary of visual perspective represents the breaking point where the encounter with the traumatic Real occurs, threatening the Symbolic order. The images hold a point from which the Real erupts, and our encounter with the Real creates a traumatic rupture of subjectivity. In these films, this rupture threatens the Symbolic order in which subjects occupy their assigned social, cultural, and historical positions—that is, subjectivity. This rupture thus pertains to national and imperial subjectivity.

The analyses of these scenes are further informed and clarified by psychoanalytic theses regarding human subjectivity, such as the notion that, though we anchor our sense of reality to seemingly tangible and concrete objects, human reality is "the world of make-belief [le monde du semblant]."[8] The Symbolic comprises the way society arranges and gives meaning to our relationships to objects. In patriarchy, the phallus functions as a pure signifier that gives meaning to all the other objects. The phallic signifier gives value and meaning to the body in this order by "[clothing it] with a gender identity."[9] As such, the body appears to us as a concrete object equipped with meaning and is arranged in relation to other bodies by following these enforced gender identities. In the Iranian film *Offside*,[10] the bathroom serves as the social space where conflict over this arrangement of bodies takes place. A group of young Iranian women sneak into the soccer stadium dressed as men, because the law prohibits women from attending sports events. They are eventually captured and held by the soldiers who guard the stadium. A conflict ensues when a soldier is charged with taking a woman in drag to the male-only public bathroom because the stadium lacks facilities for women. Her entrance creates chaos by disrupting the strict gender boundary, which the soldier desperately tries to maintain, holding men at an imaginary line that separates them from the newly queered sphere the woman presently occupies. The men flow across the imaginary boundary, and so does the woman, escaping into the stadium.

Jacques Lacan's notion of "little object 'a'" (*objet petit a*) disrupts the concrete certainty of the body as an object, as with the gendered body that representatives of the ruling regime seek to sustain in *Offside*. A missing object that cannot be materially located, this "a" represents a radical lack of the phallus, which neither society nor biology can guarantee as the foundation of sexual and gender difference. Ideology seeks to buttress sexual and gender difference as the fulcrum of the Symbolic order. There is, in this context, no object that guarantees the meaning of the body. The body that the Symbolic order organizes, assembles limb by limb so that it coheres along the lines of sexual and gender difference, is a "defensive elaboration of what's lacking,"[11] namely, the phallus as the foundation of all meaning. If we treat the body as the representation of sexual and gender difference, then we continue to make believe that the phallus exists, and thus the substantial foundation of the Symbolic order remains intact. It is, however, possible that the body reveals the Real: the lack of the phallus. A transgender body can indicate this lack; it can be a site at which we perceive "a," the something that is missing. The transgender body is often in transit, on the way to form the final piece that will make for a perfect exemplar of gender identity. Thus, the transgender body can obscure the uncomfortable notion that we all lack something, an object that will complete us as a phallic subject. This lack is inherent in the speaking subject, because speech can never coincide with the *thing itself*, which language, being a chain of signification, displaces into a signifier.[12] Besides occupying the impossible body, we are also the image of that body, and this image is the essence of our pleasure.[13] Our pleasure in identifying with the image of the Real can lead us to the unexpected pleasure of a traumatic encounter with the Real in cinematic form. I return to this point by looking at how cinematic sight and sound convey this traumatic pleasure through the spectacle of feminine jouissance, which we see in, for example, Lars von Trier's films.

Now, we begin to explore how film can organize the field of vision such that it transforms the visual field of the cinema into the field of the Real, wherein we might experience the pleasure that exceeds what is prescribed by the Symbolic order as proper enjoyment. I focus on how, in some films, a point of view particularly inscribed as that of the spectator works as a conduit through which the visual field of the Real appears. In my theorization of the cinema of the Real, the spectator encounters the Real by occupying a subjective place of looking that traverses the cinematic space, which constitutes the ontological field of the Real. Anywhere the spectator looks, they find the scene of the Symbolic order's ruin. As the spectator traverses the screen that materializes the Real, the spectator goes beyond simply encountering an object that signifies the eruption of the Real and instead grapples with the cinematic image in order to exist in the Real itself. In this way, the cinematic vision—beyond staging an antagonistic and destructive encounter among the subjects on screen with whom the spectators identify—produces a subject position situated in the space of the Real.

In Lacanian film theory, represented by the work of Slavoj Žižek, the Real appears through an object that creates an uncanny flaw in the visual field. In that theorization, discussions regarding the disruption of narrative cinema—moments when the Symbolic order falters and the Real erupts—often focus on Hitchcockian blots.[14] These discussions focus on images within a film that exceed the narrative's diegesis and cause the meaning of objects to falter. The crop duster that is dusting crops where there are no crops in *North by Northwest* (Alfred Hitchcock, 1959) or the windmill that rotates against the direction of the wind in *Foreign Correspondent* (Alfred Hitchcock, 1940) are examples. In this light, one starting point of theorizing the Real in cinema might be to ask what the object that opens up the Real looks like. As I have noted elsewhere,[15] Todd McGowan, in his own theorization of the Real in the cinema in *The Real Gaze: Film Theory after Lacan*, first discusses films that build a narrative around desire. Specifically, these films show that it is impossible for the subject to obtain its object of desire. Through textual analysis, McGowan demonstrates how the cinematic subject encounters the Real of desire, which is the impossibility of attaining the object of desire.[16] Desire cannot be satisfied, because the subject can never obtain the desired object. This object stands in as a missing phallic object that is supposed to deliver final satisfaction: "If only I have it/her/him, my life will be perfect." This reveals the dimension of our existence that compels our pursuit of the impossible object as a source of painful enjoyment deriving from not having it. This revelation is directly connected to the experience of the Real.

In McGowan's analyses, the Real emerges as a point that reveals the impossibility of fulfilling desire, but through what manner of visual aesthetics does the Real appear? With this question in mind, I seek to expand the theoretical scope of the cinema of the Real to explore how certain films achieve, through their formal rendering, the Real itself as an ontological position. These films visually depict the jouissance inherent in the Lacanian drive, an ontological state where the subject no longer seeks to satisfy their desire but rather enjoys the ongoing and inevitable failure of such satisfaction. It is from this perspective that I examine how films, often through the spectacle of jouissance, show the aesthetic impulse to depict the Real as a condition of being. I will demonstrate that there are films that *Real-ize* the subject through form, that is, the visual field of the film, which contains all the formal elements that are visually apprehended. In these films, the visual field itself becomes the field of the Real. Thus my emphasis is on the visual field itself, not on the appearance of an object disrupting that field. This cinematic form has the capacity to work as "a form [that indicates] the repressed traumatic content."[17] This traumatic content is what I describe below as the kernel, the Real of our being.

The kernel is that which neither a film's form nor its content can digest. The kernel is that which "survives every confronting test with the pure signifier," the phallus.[18] In Lacanian analysis, the phallus is an ultimate missing piece that we believe we have lost when we enter the Symbolic order. It appears as an elusive object "a," and our desire drives us onward as we pursue it. Because the phallus is a signifier, and not a thing itself, every time we encounter what seems to reify the phallus, we are disappointed by the emptiness of the encounter. Willy Wonka's Everlasting Gobstopper expresses the fantasy of obtaining the ultimate object that fulfills desire ad infinitum, which is the meaning of the phallus. The Wonka factory, however, continues to produce objects that only approximate the Everlasting Gobstopper, items for consumption that promise only the possibility of something that can finally and permanently fulfill desire but do not themselves effect this fulfillment. The kernel of our being consists of surviving this traumatic encounter with the lack of the phallus. This represents the Real of our situation with respect to our desire: the phallus that we desire to obtain does not, cannot, exist.

In the visual field of the Real, both the human subject and the image reveal the kernel that we cannot map or conceptualize within any temporal and spatial order of a given definition of reality. As such, it implies the existence of a contingency that escapes the law of logical causality, haunting our temporally and spatially defined reality. It may appear as a stain-like, strange object, constituting a gap in the organization of meaningful subject-object relationships. The subject in the cinema of the Real exposes this haunting presence of the kernel, and the body figures prominently in this haunting. In referencing Lacan's designation of the signifier as a material cause, something that has real-life consequences, Samo Tomsic in *The Capitalist Unconscious* reiterates Lacan's assertion that the body is the site of the production of subjectivity and of jouissance.[19] Because the signifier does not coincide meaningfully with the signified, the signifier appears with the haunting excess: "a," an elusive, trauma-inducing fantasy object that we cannot locate in our own sphere of reality.

The body-as-signifier functions in a similar way. The body appears as an "a" that exceeds the scope of the signified (that which makes sense in the Symbolic order), undermining the reality that the Symbolic order seeks to establish through language, particularly through the system of signification. The image of the body haunts the linguistic and imagistic structure of what the Symbolic order constructs. The image of the body exceeds, and thus disrupts, the formation of a stable cinematic language, and it figures as the traumatic kernel in both the cinematic form and the subjectivity that the cinematic form anchors in the Symbolic order. For Lacan, the signifier appears as "an apparatus of jouissance,"[20] and the body as an image/signifier is likewise an apparatus of jouissance. Here, jouissance is the kernel that escapes the mode of enjoyment that the Symbolic order prescribes: that we all learn how to enjoy ourselves properly.

The Real in the Transnational Cinema

The cinema of the Real and its depiction of the kernel as I have described thus far can work as a paradigm across various global, social, and cultural formations. In Lars von Trier's *Breaking the Waves*,[21] the feminine body represents such a kernel of jouissance. The image-value of the feminine body diminishes as the signifier of protagonist Bess's embodiment shifts from the body to the wound (she suffers fatal sexual violence) to the sound of a bell (at the end of the film, we see church bells toll in the stratosphere as if to signify the remnant of her material existence). This transformation of the feminine body reaches a point at which it is no longer a discrete human subject but the kernel, that which has survived the encounter with the phallic signifier and its injunction imposed by hypermasculine entities such as the law of the church and obscene male enjoyment. Bess's death not only means that annihilation through biological demise has occurred but signifies what Lacan calls the "second death"[22] as she, like Antigone, walks into the "tomb." This walking involves a jouissance that confronts the Symbolic order with its excessiveness. She climbs into a vessel where she encounters the violent phallic desire that destroys her body, and through this destruction she continues her life into the Real. In this kind of event, the subject becomes the kernel.[23]

Another such example is the Israeli film *Or*,[24] which follows Ruthie and her teenage daughter, Or, who are Mizrahi Jewish women living in Tel Aviv. Ruthie is a prostitute and as such embodies an ethnic feminine identity that figures as the Other within the Israeli nation proper.[25] Her otherness is expressed through a wounded body: her vagina bleeds from sexual violence. Even when she seeks a different way of living, as a housekeeper for a middle-class Ashkenazi Jewish family, she is connected to filth. Her daughter, Or, who is introduced collecting empty bottles on the city streets, also connecting to cleaning discarded objects, eventually becomes an escort. These women are confined within a society that fantasizes itself as homogeneously Western. As Mizrahim, they serve as the ethnic feminine Other who embodies the object of the phallic desire and, as such, supports the hypermasculine national fantasy. The film conveys the sense of their confinement to a socially ascribed position through stationary, long-take shots. There is no editing within these scenes; women walk in and out of the fixed shot, their heads or bodies often cut off by the tightness of the frame. These women's visually mutilated bodies seem to gaze unflinchingly at the audience. The subversive outcome of this visualization of confinement is that the film formally denies the audience a visual space within which the phallic fantasy can unfold through a position of looking that conveys mastery over the feminine body and the cinematic landscape within which that body is situated. The film form militates against the ideological inscription of the feminine subject in support of the hypermasculine national fantasy. In this way, the film undermines the classical norm of narrative cinema, in which the masculine position of looking expresses mastery over the landscape in which the feminine Other is situated.

Through the gaze of the feminine body, constructed limb by limb, the film frames the space where the Real emerges, revealing violence that feeds the Symbolic imagination that connects the feminine Other to a signified object within the sphere of phallic enjoyment. In this way, these women embody the kernel. Here, the cinematic space no longer functions as the fantasy frame, because it forces the viewing subject to face the limit of a previously secure ontological position. The fixed camera simultaneously presents the bloodied, aging body and the young, fetishized body of women as the point of the gaze, thus removing the safe distance that would allow the viewer to imagine control over the image. The suspension of the cinematic aesthetics of established, shot-reverse-shot editing deprives the audience of a safe place of knowing and forces it to experience the traumatic destabilization of subjectivity. It might seem that well-established cinematic codes can create a similar effect. Consider, for example, a scene from George Romero's *Night of the Living Dead* (1968) in which a child zombie murders her mother with a spade. The horror genre's specific editing of a gruesome scene of matricide generates the visceral effect of horror, but the film preserves space for the viewer's knowledge, and thus comfortable mastery of the horror image, through its generic semantics and syntax.

The viewer in *Or*, on the other hand, exemplifies the subject who is seized by what the Real reveals: that the violent Real of the gender order disallows a safe subject position, which forces the viewer to encounter the kernel of the social being. The normative subject can no longer suspend its anxiety about the Othered subject through aesthetic distance from that Othered body. Without the comfort of knowing that distanciation provides, the film places the audience in a direct encounter with the Real of the nation's desire. This encounter exposes the "anxious sign" of the Othered body and places us in the space of "'non-knowledge' and non-understating"[26] within the national boundary, prompting the viewer to abandon the pregiven way of looking as an ontological support. It also reveals that our desire for proper subjectivity can be rendered through the cinematic form. The aesthetics that constitute the cinema of the Real thus have a political dimension. The disorganization of those structures upon which the norm of subjectivity is founded entails the transformation of subjectivity into the kernel; the subject of trauma as it experiences the disintegration of the regime of looking thus occupies the place of the kernel in the Symbolic order.

In Park Chan-wook's *Oldboy*,[27] the cinematic aesthetics that lead to the revision of subjectivity find expression in spatial organization, especially in a scene where two antagonists come together for a final confrontation. The main character, Dae-su, is imprisoned in a private jail cell for fifteen years by Woo-jin as part of an elaborate revenge plot against Dae-su. Woo-jin holds Dae-su responsible for the death of his (Woo-jin's) sister, with whom he was having an incestuous relationship. In the scene, Dae-su discovers that Woo-jin has successfully manufactured a situation to hoodwink Dae-su into a sexual relationship with his own daughter. In a larger context of the film, this revelation of the Real of masculine desire has a simultaneous, devastating impact on the Law of the Father and that of the patriarchal nation. Immediately preceding this revelation is a scene in which the filmmaker reveals a technical quilting point in the filmic image: we see three reflections of two men in a mirror. The quilting point is a Lacanian term that refers to an instance which reveals that the relationship between the signifier (such as an image) and that which is signified (meaning of the image) are not natural; they are, in fact, sewn together. There is the knot of tension in this sewn-together unit of meaning (the image with comprehensible meaning attached to it) because the sign that signifies always exceeds the signified, a cohesive meaning secured in the Symbolic order. Opting for the strenuous construction of a shot that frames two men such that three different images appear in one frame, the filmmaker reveals the artifice of image construction on a green screen. The grainy image noticeably differentiates the shot from the rest of the technically smooth film. This artifact jarringly exposes the technique of visuality. This scene displays the fracture in the unified boundaries of both masculine subjectivity and cinematic space in a film that has otherwise been edited to hide the underlying artifice of filmmaking. This scene, through its visualization of the eruption of the Real of masculine subjectivity through the quilting point, anticipates the emergence of the visual field of the Real in which the gendered subject undergoes the revision of subjectivity: the loss of logos, metaphorized by the loss of the tongue that Dae-su self-amputates, deprives the subject of phallic jouissance.[28]

The visualization of the Real in South Korean cinema has the potential to extend the political impact of the Real. As a formerly colonized nation-state, South Korea functions as a linchpin of global capitalism in East Asia. The line of division in the peninsula spatially delineates the antinomy that constitutes the global capitalist world order in which geopolitical contestations among neo-imperial forces, from the United States (Japan also participates in the Western sphere that the United States represents) to China and Russia, prescribe the movement of humans, resources, and ideas. The traumatic condition of South Korean modernity lies in an encounter with the Real of these historical situations, and this encounter, in turn, constitutes a social and cultural condition of

South Korean subjectivity. Here, we note that Japan has, since the colonial era, figured as part of the Western hegemony by employing what Max Horkheimer calls "instrumental reason,"[29] which pursues modernity as a justification for its colonial and neocolonial endeavors. Contemporary geopolitics are, in part, an extension of the Korean historical trauma that originated from colonization. The Korean War solidified the Cold War order in the region by extending the neocolonial condition in which South Korea serves as an object of neo-imperial epistemological scrutiny and political and economic containment. The application of postcolonial teleology (colonization, decolonization, the birth of a postcolonial nation) becomes problematic in this context because South Korea continues to experience modernity as colonial modernity. With the South Korean modern nation-state as the fulcrum of geopolitical alliances and hostilities in the region, Asia's Cold War configuration continues to inform South Korea's modern subjectivity. As noted, the divided Korean peninsula continues to function as a linchpin in the divisive order of global capitalism, in which a new imperial configuration has emerged notably involving the antagonism among the United States, China, and Russia. This neo-imperial configuration extends colonial modernity, which first placed the Korean peninsula in the sphere of Japanese colonialism.

In the past decade, South Korean cinema has produced an increasing number of films that seek to rework the notion of colonial modernity, in which Japanese colonialism figures as a backdrop for various subject formations. Some of these films focus on the indigenous enjoyment involved in that process. In Choi Dong-hoon's *Woochi* (2009), a final showdown between good and evil happens on a soundstage arranged to depict a modern urban space during the height of Japanese colonialism. In this film, colonial history appears as a pastiche of the spectacle-driven Korean blockbuster formula that pursues the enjoyment of an action genre film. But in Park Chan-wook's *The Handmaiden* (2016), a film that deals with the horror of feminine jouissance, such jouissance destroys phallic jouissance as the foundation of masculine authority rooted in colonial modernity. The scene of this destruction constitutes the cinema of the Real.

Before we delve into feminine jouissance, recall that phallic jouissance involves belief in a phallic signifier, an object that is misrecognized as the thing that can deliver final satisfaction. The subject of phallic jouissance fantasizes that it can obtain this singular object, for which the most salient metaphor is the phallus, and achieve final satisfaction of all desires. Like Willie Wonka's Everlasting Gobstopper, this fantasy object provides satisfaction that never diminishes no matter how long you enjoy it. Feminine jouissance begins with the recognition that all objects, no matter how strongly desired, will fail to provide relief from the lack. The subject of feminine jouissance accepts that, as the Rolling Stones would have it, you "can't get no satisfaction." The subject of feminine jouissance, therefore, organizes itself around *not* having, via the lack. The subject obtains jouissance through disavowing and resisting phallic jouissance organized around desirable objects. The feminine subject of jouissance reveals the Real condition of all human subjects, shattering ideological phantasy: we do not have the phallus that guarantees the satisfaction of all our desires; we cathect only to the phallic signifier, the Everlasting Gobstopper, through which we maintain the fantasy of having the phallus of everlasting satisfaction.

The Handmaiden, set in the era of Japanese colonialism, allegorizes the colonial and paternal authority's obscene jouissance through the pornographic novels that the patriarch of the household collects and treasures in order to prescribe the mode and means of exclusively phallic enjoyment. The patriarch in the film, a native Korean, masquerades as Japanese, thereby enlisting the colonizer's authority as the foundation of his own phallic authority, but it turns out that phallic jouissance cannot enclose feminine jouissance, which denounces the phallus as the primary source of enjoyment. While the patriarch masquerades as a phallic subject through Japanese costume and customs that he uses like prosthetics, a subjectivity founded on feminine jouissance emerges through the female characters: the eponymous handmaiden and her mistress, who is to be wedded to the patriarch, her uncle. This incestuous union supports the obscene jouissance that sustains patriarchy rather than weakening it. The emergence of feminine jouissance is marked by the destruction of objects, the signifiers of phallic jouissance, such as the snake head that stands as sentinel in the library of pornography, the pornographic paintings and books, and the library itself. It seems, then, as if indigenous life, represented by the feminine subject, carves out its own subversive place of being in the cinematic space and engages in what Homi K. Bhabha calls "colonial mimicry," that is, using the master's tools, the cinematic language, for its own sly negotiation to destabilize the colonizer's modernity.[30]

Some see as fetishistic the disavowal of phallic jouissance that the subject of feminine jouissance makes, specifically in the sense that this subject achieves pleasure without having to obtain an object of desire. Although he does not directly make a connection between feminine jouissance and fetishistic disavowal, Henry Krips argues that fetishism "through a 'perverse' structure of disavowal, openly displays the splitting of the subject," as demonstrated by the subject's assertion of fetishistic disavowal, "I know very well, but just the same I . . . ."[31] This subject denies that the missing object is actually missing, having misrecognized it in the form of some other, present, incidental little object "a." In Krips's example of this form of disavowal, mother's missing penis is replaced by an object that instigates desire, such as a knee or a piece of fur.[32] In this context, the subject can disavow the phallic jouissance that depends on actually obtaining the missing sublime object (mother's penis, for example) and opts to explore a new form of jouissance, feminine jouissance, that accepts that there is no sublime object at all, instead drawing its jouissance from present, partial, imperfect objects. In this sense, fetishistic disavowal holds the subversive and political possibilities within its structure.

Fetishistic disavowal also functions as the fulcrum of ideology. Paul Eisenstein and Todd McGowan state that fetish "enables the subject to believe with deniability, to believe while clinging to the posture of the nonbeliever. . . . Even more than in Marx's time, the ruling fetish is now the commodity (and the free market that facilitates its exchange). Like God, the commodity and the free market provide an ultimate ground of explanation for all phenomena and offer the promise of a final and lasting satisfaction."[33] Here, fetishistic disavowal leads to, not away from, the belief in that ultimate satisfaction. Fetishistic disavowal, with its potential to pervert the structural order of things, does not necessarily enable the emancipation of the subject tethered to phallic jouissance.

The same can be said of *méconnaissance*. In "The Mirror Stage as Formative of the *I* Function as Revealed in Psychoanalytic Experience," Lacan describes *méconnaissance* in the mirror stage that places the linguistic subject on the path of "alienating destination." In the mirror stage, the subject obtains the agency of the ego (the I function) but also undergoes the process in which misrecognition of the self as that-which-it-is-not occurs. In this process, "I" emerges through the image of the ideal ego as a point of the imaginary identification, which is imposed on subjects by the social and linguistic contexts within which they develop. This imaginary identification is the misrecognition of myself as another, as the image of the ideal ego that is not biological or an essential constitution of the self. Thus, the process of becoming a human subject is the process through which we are sutured to, or attached in the flesh to, an identifiable, albeit unattainable, location within the Symbolic order. This "seeing the self" is Lacan's *méconnaissance*: the misrecognition of the self as a Symbolic (thus, attainably ideal) entity. Within *méconnaissance*, independent and objective subjectivity is impossible. The phallic subject is the response to this impossibility.

Méconnaissance also "sutures the gap between the natural or biological support of the body and the social determination of the subject,"[34] thus constructing the phantasmatic unity of the subject. Furthermore, *méconnaissance* sustains ideology, or what Žižek calls "ideological phantasy." Žižek states, "What [individuals] overlook, what they misrecognize, is not the reality but the illusion which is structuring their reality [of capitalism], their real social activity [such as using money]. They know very well how things are [that money has no magical quality to satisfy our desire], but still they are doing it as if they did not know. The illusion is therefore double: it consists in overlooking the illusion which is structuring our real, effective relationship to reality. And this overlooked, unconscious illusion is what may be called *ideological phantasy*."[35]

The subject of feminine jouissance shatters ideological fantasy. The emancipatory possibility of the feminine subject of jouissance merits exploration beyond what it makes possible through its structural configuration, such as fetishistic disavowal. Its political possibilities need to be examined as practical in application, including through political action. Cinema's mode of visualization of this social, political subject can shed light on the material contours of feminine jouissance.

South Korean modernity is embedded in a matrix of national trauma related to colonization and the subsequent developmental capitalism. As I have noted elsewhere,[36] this leads some mainstream South Korean genre-driven films set in colonial modernity—including such actions films as Choi Dong-hoon's *Assassination* (2015) and Kim Jee-woon's *The Age of Shadows* (2016)—to focus more on the presentation of the wounded body than on a history-specific interrogation of colonialism. In these films, pastiche seems to displace history, rendering them a reservoir of fungible postmodern artifacts, but it is important to see how genre-driven films can unexpectedly change the visual language, using the genre form as the "Master's Tool" to dismantle the master's house: the theater where epistemological and ontological truths may only be invented by the right (Japanese/Western) cinematic discourse. *The Age of Shadows* goes beyond the displacement of history with pastiche by presenting a subject of historical trauma whom the modern nation fails to enclose with its promise of sublime objects of desire and the possibility of becoming proper national subjects, once we accept as truth the idea that the nation-state can provide us with all the sublime objects we desire. The film does so by unmooring the generic form from the narrative drive organized around an object of desire, the lost nation. The film foregrounds the spectacle of destruction without redemptive possibility (i.e., the formal drive) over the resolution of conflicts (i.e., the narrative drive) toward a recuperation of the masculine position of mastery. Thus, the subject of trauma in this film undoes the national project that binds subjects to its ideology and historiography, which delineate the imaginary and symbolic contours of national subjects. This undoing is an intervening challenge to modernity through genre filmmaking.

Here Is the Real Looking at Us

We become social subjects through accepting the meaning of the phallus, and we exist as social subjects in relation to that meaning. This is why, in Lacanian thinking, the feminine holds the possibility of resistance and emancipation, not just by resisting the patriarchal norm of gender and sexuality but, more importantly, through undermining the Symbolic order that the meaning of the phallus supports. Recall that the feminine is a subject position, not a biologically grounded denotation of sexual difference: the feminine position aligns with political emancipation from the pregiven order of things. The subject of the Real who can disrupt the Symbolic must be located in Lacan's *feminine pas-tout*, "not-all."[37] This feminine "not-all" goes beyond the binary opposition to the masculine "all": it designates a position beyond the bounds of the antinomies of not-all and all. The masculine "all" is a fiction that depends on its also fictional binary opposite, the feminine "not-all." Hence the opposition of having and not-having the phallus. No subject, however, has the phallus constitutive of sexual difference. It exists only as a principle that must be present to impose a categorical imperative and thereby keep the world as we define it from unraveling. In the feminine not-all, the lack of sexual difference that designates men and women persists, though the phallus avoids this lack by insisting on that difference in order to conceptualize "all." The masculine subject—not the feminine, as Mary Ann Doane argues in her notion of the feminine masquerade[38]—dissembles to hide the absence of the phallus. Jennifer Friedlander points out that phallic subjects are those who masquerade as if they had it.[39] In this sense, we can argue that we are all feminine subjects. We can all be the subjects of the Real, whose being reveals that there is no phallus that sustains a subject's ethical, social, and symbolic validity, whether that subject identifies with the masculine or the feminine.

Cinematic form expresses the subject position of the Real. As noted, Todd McGowan theorizes the impossible desire that leads the subject to face the Real.[40] He develops the notion of desire as the original point of lack, which leads the subject to the Real. In this way, McGowan helps clarify what critics like Teresa de Lauretis could not quite articulate. Positing that feminine desire inscribes itself on and disrupts narrative driven by masculine desire in *Alice Doesn't: Feminism, Semiotics, Cinema*, de Lauretis does not account for the condition that implicates the subject in the impossibility of desire.[41] The theorization of the Real in cinema that McGowan's work (notably, *The Real Gaze*) represents moves the discussion of human subjectivity beyond the feminine subject's disruption of the masculine narrative. This theorization expands the political possibility of the cinema beyond a focus on the parasitic opening in the hegemonic narrative that the feminine subject manages to create, a theorization that falls short of introducing something akin to the Real, the destructive effect of which leaves untenable not only the ideological order that the narrative holds together but also any human subjectivity consolidated through desire.

Thus far, we have expanded our theoretical endeavor beyond an encounter with the Real on the narrative level, which focuses on a plot through which the subjects encounter the Real via an incidental or incongruous object or via a contingency for which the narrative cannot neatly account; this theorizes an approach to the Real primarily through the investigation of form that allows the Real to emerge. Thereby, we have extended a reading of film beyond the desire-driven narrative structure in which gendered desires clash and inevitably take the binary form of a masculine narrative and its feminine fracture. This also moves us beyond the two most widely accepted notions of the cinematic Real as articulated through contingent objects: that they appear as blots that reveal fractures in the Symbolic order (e.g., Hitchcock's windmill and crop duster) and that they reveal the way desire creates torsion of the visual field (e.g., the gush of blood from a pristine toilet in Coppola's *Conversation*). We must, then, clarify exactly how form works to accomplish the emergence of the Real, and we do so by looking at notable works in transnational cinema.

In his study of Japanese cinema, Eric Cazdyn posits that films of history "work through *on their formal level* (not necessarily in their narrative content) the most crucial events of their own historical moment before there is a common language to speak about these events,"[42] which is to say, films mark a specific historical context and work as the expression of critical historical junctures—in Cazdyn's case, historical moments in which Japanese national capitalism is registered on the filmed body—generating their meaning primarily through form, which, as Cazdyn puts it, is the crucible of meaning. Cazdyn describes aesthetics as "a symptom of something unrepresentable . . . something that cannot be directly represented by everyday discourse."[43] Nor, I would add, can it be directly represented by narrative. It is in this light that Cazdyn considers pornography. The pornography industry has exploded in Japan since the 1960s, an era that paralleled Japanese capitalism's equally prodigious growth. Cazdyn argues that a formal relationship between pornography and nonpornography emerged in that era. From this formal relation, the truth of the social body in the modern Japanese imagination may be seen in the pornographic body that not only complements the national body proper as its binary opposite but also reveals what the imaginary national body cannot represent. I suggest Cazdyn is here delineating the process that generates what I define as the dimension of the Real of the national body in a specific local context.

In films like Oshima Nagisa's *In the Realm of the Senses* (1976) and the significant production of mainstream films that straddle porn and nonporn categories, we see that the pornographic form of the body reveals what cannot be revealed in the Japanese national body. Cazdyn explains this phenomenon by describing pornographic aesthetics as functioning primarily to formulate commodity fetishism. The body is the commodity at the center of composition in pornography, as well as all sorts of nonpornography fetishistic advertisements. Cazdyn implies that what is unrepresentable is the process of commodity production that involves the systematic exploitation of the body and all the ways that bodies generate exchange value. Pornography is less about content than how the body is represented in the frame, particularly "the way films and images relate to libidinal and psychic desire . . . the way spectacular content fetishizes social relations of power."[44] Consider the "money shot," which implies that the telos of the narrative of sexuality has been reached. It is in this context that the pornographic emerges in various media, such as live or recorded scenes of war and disaster around which the nation-state galvanizes the national subject position.

We can apply Cazdyn's notion of the pornographic to the cinematic spectacle. It is, perhaps, significant that the first apparatus of cinematic scopophilia was Thomas Edison's "peeping hole," which allowed viewers to fetishize the image and thus to enjoy the sense that they possessed a spectacular object. This operation is built on investment in the image that generates the fantasy of possessing the object of desire, which is the economy of the pornographic image and could also be a means of hiding what is truly unrepresentable: the impossibility of fulfilling desire through objects. In this context, I consider film *form* to be a way to express the Real, a topography of our being where we experience the Real as the kernel of our subjectivity. Hence, I describe the subject position of looking as a means through which we become subjects of the Real. Arguably, Hollywood enlists spectacle and effects to produce regressive fantasies of resolution in the face of social contradictions.[45] Spectacle in the cinema of the Real, however, goes beyond the expression of scopic desire as a constitutive element of spectatorial pleasure that upholds ideology through the phantasmatic resolution of contradictions (the resolution is the elimination of the barrier to the object of desire, the process of which is staged in cinematic spectacle). Through its capacity to open up the field of the Real, spectacle has political potential; because the spectacle's effect is not independent of the unconscious but rather is its symptom, we gain through that effect access to the repressed kernel, the Real, of our consciousness. Spectacle with visceral effects appears in South Korean cinema, for example, as a way to introduce the Real in the process of grappling with social contradictions that lack resolution.

A film can formulate the feminine position of looking as a path to the Real, but the mere fact of the feminine position as the origin and center of looking does not guarantee the appearance of the Real. *Rosetta* (1999), a Dardenne brothers film that deals with the feminine subject's difficult social position in European bourgeois society, follows the point of view of the eponymous female protagonist. Although the film's narrative does reveal the Real of desire and its impossibility, the film does not open up the field of the Real. Even though Rosetta's pursuit of an end, to exist at the margin of bourgeois society as a propertyless young woman, moves the narrative forward to the point of failure, the film's mise-en-scène and cinematography, centered on handheld shots, keep the Real from erupting. The film refuses a position of looking that is extraneous to the narrative space, a position that would emanate from the Real, specifically, that of feminine jouissance. Tightly controlled realism leaves few gaps in the spectator's identification with a stable position of looking in the diegesis. There is no appearance of the image of the Real, as the visual field is filled with objects and incidents that economically and structurally sustain the continuity of the viewer's subjective position. The viewer can maintain a safe position of looking at the trials of Rosetta's life and thus never loses mastery over the image. In *Rosetta*, formal technique strengthens the realism and invites the viewer to observe the rhythm of the feminine subject's psychical undulations and physical movements. The viewer occupies a position of the secure observer, that is, the position of knowing. Realism as a form in this film arguably prevents the emergence of the Real and further prevents the visual field from turning into the field of the Real.

One example of formal elements that do open up the Real in the filmic diegesis occurs in Hong Sang-soo's *Nobody's Daughter Haewon* (2013). In this South Korean film, a main character uses a tape recorder during emotional moments in scenes that otherwise contain no diegetic sound. The tape recorder functions as a device that makes sound, as a filmic formal element, strange and presents a surprising nonbelonging to the contemporary film experience, both as a result of its antiquated technological form and of the distressed quality of analog sound it produces. Sound is usually used to promote verisimilitude, but in this film it punches a hole in the fabric of verisimilitude, estranging the formal element itself. This sound surely functions as the gaze that grabs our attention, as something that does not belong, destabilizing our imaginary position relative to it. In addition to this function, this formal element brings to the scene a temporality that is extraneous to the narrative, signified by the static analog sound that stands out in the film's overall soundscape. When a viewer experiences the opening up of another temporality, the viewer has entered the field of the Real where the teleology that supports the Symbolic order falters. For a native viewer, it is possible to say that the character is facing the Real of his temporal being, of modernity that expresses itself through a sense of remoteness and nonbelonging, which produces an effect of surprise, estranging him from his own sense of time as he encounters multiple temporalities.

The spectator may experience, through the spectacle-driven image, the opening of the Real. In the films of Lars von Trier, spectatorship means experiencing the rending of subjectivity, achieved through the spectacularization of feminine jouissance. In *Medea* (1988), feminine jouissance turns the world awry, defying the physical laws of time and space. This disruption is visualized in the sequence in which Medea's spell creates a new chronotope that imprisons Jason, making it impossible for him to move forward. Jason circles the same field until his horse collapses. This new chronotope, which destroys the progress of teleological time, is that of feminine jouissance. In *Antichrist* (2009), feminine jouissance constitutes radical evil that strikes down patriarchy. The central character of this film is simply noted as "she." She has been disfiguring her toddler son's feet in an act that symbolizes the blemishing of patriarchal lineage, and she allows her son to fall to his death. She then enters what the intertitle names "Eden," a primordial forest where a different temporal and spatial order seems to prevail. When we first see "she" entering this territory, the tempo of her movement changes, signaling a different temporal order. While the film's speed reflects this new temporality, the film's change in tonality conveys the vision of the world devoid of lively colors, expressing the transformation of the space that feminine jouissance creates. As such, Eden is the land of feminine jouissance where a new chronotope prevails. In Eden, "she" castrates the Father: she mutilates her psychiatrist husband's genitalia, then screws a gigantic grindstone to his leg, rendering him impotent and immobile.

The visual elements in *Breaking the Waves* and *Dancer in the Dark* (2000) express the ontological status attached to feminine jouissance by showing the mode of looking and existing that is particular to the subject of feminine jouissance. These films offer no place to which we can divert our eye from the way of being in and looking at what is cinematically rendered to be the Real, thereby traumatically rendering a stable symbolic subjectivity impossible. Everywhere, we see the chronotope of feminine jouissance that dismantles the subjective position of looking and being as we know it. In *Dancer in the Dark*, the feminine subject's way of seeing and being organizes the sensuous experience of the cinematic image and sound embedded in the time and space she imagines. In the film, high-saturation colors and song and dance numbers express the main character Selma's interiority, which is distinctively different from the part of the film where actions unfold that advance the narrative and its color palate. For example, a drab factory floor where Selma toils turns into a sumptuous musical space as she breaks into song and dance. She changes factory time to play time, redefining the space of value production as the field of the Real of her jouissance, which escapes the temporal and spatial boundaries of the accepted social order. In *Breaking the Waves*, we are imprisoned in the feminine subject's jouissance, brought forth by the painful destruction of her body. In the uncanny space of feminine jouissance, her embodied femininity disappears, but the bells toll in the firmament, their sound enwrapping the world below like the gaze that emanates from the indestructible kernel of the subject of feminine jouissance. For Lacan, "woman" does not exist,[46] which is to say, "woman" functions as a way to indicate the quilting point of the fiction of sexuality. The Real of this fiction is that the phallus is not the nodal point of sexuality but a partial object made to convey phallic jouissance, the only kind of jouissance possible within the Symbolic order. The phallus is an impossible object in that it has no inherent or necessary meaning as an organ of pleasure. In this sense, it is an ideological object. The kind of jouissance that comes from tearing up the world through experiencing the Real exposes the terrain where "woman" and "phallus" do not exist. We can envision the delight of the Real that comes from the spectatorial sensation of jouissance at the dismantling of subjectivity.

In cinema, the satisfaction of desire, expressed through the organization of images, is frequently accomplished via continuity editing. Through this technique, narrative cinema seeks to embed the spectator in the film's ideological system. The opening of the visual field of the Real entails a failure of the classical, generic expectations that typically function to advance the ideological aims of the film. This failure produces the transgressive poetic shock. As articulated in the introduction, poetic shock accompanies our encounter with the Real and the subsequent faltering of subjectivity. Because this term allows us to explore the impact that the cinema of the Real has on the viewer, I mobilize it here as I look at examples of form that express the Real. We experience poetic shock when an image appears that exceeds and frustrates not simply the expectation of narrative resolution but also the anticipated effect of the image itself. Here, form works as a transgressive drive that challenges not only the authority and cohesion of the narrative but also the desire underpinning that narrative.

Poetic shock comes not from a simple lack of, or twist in, the process of narrative resolution but invokes the film's own deliberate arrangement of formal elements such that narrative conflicts fail to arrive at a stable ideological conclusion. Slavoj Žižek points out, in *The Plague of Fantasies,* that art fails to concretize ideas. This means that art could fail to arrive at an ideologically coherent point.[47] In the cinema of the Real, form visualizes that ideological failure and in doing so generates the subjective experience of the Real for the spectator. This experience pushes the spectator outside the economy of desire as the fulcrum of subjectivity in the Symbolic order. Importantly, the corresponding shock marks the moment when subjectivity falters and enters the field of the Real.

The Poetic Shock of the Real

Moments of poetic shock can appear as cinematic spectacle. They mark the return of the body—not the Foucaultian body, as the site of biopolitics or of pleasures different from those allowed by the social norm,[48] but the impossible Lacanian body, assembled limb by limb. Lacan sees in the hysteric's perception of the body a prototype that appears in the form of disjointed limbs or fantasy objects, what he calls "exoscopic partial objects," such as organs with wings.[49] Such a body signifies the disintegration of individuality: if the body is the site of the subject's symptomatic expression, then the disjointed body symptomatizes fragmented subjectivity. The body as the material site of the subject is assembled in the ideological realm, where limbs and organs are understood to create the fantasy of a unified subjectivity. The ideological realm is a phantasmatic realm; its substance is fantasy. The object of desire that the national body politics seeks is, for example, the nationalist fantasy, the phantasmatic body of the unified nation. We become a national subject through our desire for phantasmatic objects that the nation necessitates by speaking of what we perceive as the lack, such as a cohesive racial identity in Nazi Germany. This process implies a teleological trajectory toward the objects that we fantasize will fill the lack. The rise of an ethnically pure nation as an imperial fantasy is one example. The unified national body is itself a phantasmatic object.

To further explore the phantasmatic dimension of the body, consider a case, described to me by a psychiatrist, of a Hindu woman whose psychosis involves obsessively fantasizing a mechanical device that she imagines Muslim men planted in her vagina and that constantly generates orgasms. The horror of this fantasy is her mortal fear that she cannot and must not live with persistent orgasm, which, it is possible to conjecture, she sees as a foreign desire she must not enjoy. This fantasy likely originates from anxiety that the Muslim Other is too close and has taken complete hold of her body, disturbing the social and cultural bodily identity that both binds a subject and separates a subject from the Other. This condition makes her identity untenable. The invasive orgasm involves the organ that functions as a central piece of her cultural, gender, and political identity as a Hindu woman. It is an expression of the aggressiveness that she, as a subject, fears that the ethnic and racial Other harbors, and it is also an expression of her own desire for the Other. The jouissance of the Other, which the subject fantasizes in a particular form, may also represent a lethal assault on the subject. At the same time, the Other represents jouissance from which the subject is excluded, an unknowable enjoyment in which the subject also wants to participate (or steal if participation is barred or limited by the Other), but which the subject must also disavow, as it is perceived to be too foreign and obscene to be included in the Law of the Father. In this subject's case, the Other, by generating uncontrollable orgasms through which the kernel of her desire appears (something the patriarchal Symbolic order cannot contain), makes it impossible for her to progress with her social identity. Phantasmatic viscerality, rather than providing her with a solid ground as an embodied subject, throws her into the impossible place in the Real, shattering her subjectivity.

The cinema of the Real creates moments in which an organ, notably the eye and the viscera, take the place of the subject. The great early example of this can be found in a scene in *Un chien andalou* (Luis Buñuel, 1929), where the slitting of an eyeball represents the assault on the subject of looking. The subject remains fragmented as its body figures as disjointed partial objects and organs: eyes that see and guts that feel. The subject is elided by a material effect of the disjointed corporeal form that is made to appear through the viscerality of organs. Subjectivity then is a surplus, something added that is more than the constellation of body parts. Similarly, in capitalism, surplus economic value exceeds the totality of the material elements of the commodities that are used in production of consumer goods. Experiencing subjecthood in this way as something impossible and illusory is what the cinema of the Real makes possible.

The body, put together limb by limb, organ by organ, is, rather than an a priori reality, an effect of ideation that renders exoscopic objects scientifically comprehensible and symbolically meaningful. Ideation is not limited to abstract thought; it has material effects. Linguistic, that is, symbolic, subjects suffer from a fundamental lack, because subjects can exist only in a chain of metonyms, a continual displacement of the thing itself by signifiers. The desire derived from this condition drives us to seek a particular form of the body. Transgender desire, for example, shows this desire-driven body as much as the heteronormative body does. In both cases, (re)formulation of the body, in pursuit of the means to fill the lack, to obtain what we believe we are missing in order to be the subject who inhabits sexual difference, reflects the relationship of desire to the body. While Foucault's is a desiring body that is always awaiting inscription of erotogenic zones (here, desire and erotogenic zones coincide), the Lacanian body emerges through the impossibility of the body and the desire coinciding. For the Lacanian body, erotogenic zones do not bind and sustain desire, because what we desire cannot be localized. When erotogenic zones do bind the body, the body becomes the phantasmatic location of ideology. It is the impossibility of binding desire through erotogenic zones that necessitates the ideological invention of the body. The cinema of the Real reveals this ideological process through a spectacularization of feminine jouissance that tears apart that invention of not just the body but the subjectivity that the body houses.

While Foucault's body emerges as the surface on which desire is written, the Lacanian body is an effect of desire that can never be satisfied. For Lacan, the body is assembled from parts, and we instrumentalize these parts to sustain the fantasy that our desire will be satisfied. Here, limbs and body parts represent partial objects of desire that lack inherently necessary meaning. This is the radical, and perhaps irreconcilable, difference between Lacan's psychoanalytic body and Foucault's biopolitical body. For Foucault the body, as the constellation of erotogenic zones, always already exists, although biopolitics will continue to organize and reorganize its aim and function. The biopolitical body is a way of arranging those zones and of solidifying their boundaries. For this reason, imagining a body beyond the biopolitical body, for Foucault, necessitates reconfiguring the erotogenics of the body and assembling a particular kind of body with organs; this reconfiguration is opposed to the Deleuzean body without organs, the body without the structural organizing principle that the Law of the Father dictates, and likewise is opposed to Žižek's organ without a body, a kernel that the Symbolic boundary of the body cannot contain. This distinction is meaningful because the kind of spectatorial experience I theorize for the cinema of the Real involves experiencing the shattering of the fantasy of the unified body, leaving the kernel upon which the Symbolic order cannot anchor itself, the disarticulated organs and limbs of the Lacanian body. The body is experienced as the kernel around which meaning fails; it is the Real body as the kernel. This is the affective outcome that the cinema of the Real produces. The body is, through the affect registered on its surface, to be placed in the inescapable spectacle of the Real.

In this light, my conceptualization of the camera eye is different from that of the eye as an organ without a body. Žižek focuses on the camera eye as an organ independent of human subject positions within the film, gesturing toward the realm beyond the frame of the image and beyond the ideas in and of the Symbolic order. Žižek takes the camera eye as the location of the gaze[50]: in *Psycho* (Alfred Hitchcock, 1960), the camera eye impersonates the gaze of the phallic mother, through which the Real peeks. In the cinema of the Real as I theorize it, the eye that looks at the spectacle on screen, belonging to both the viewer and the on-screen character whose looking the viewer follows, is the conduit through which the subject experiences the pain of having its self shattered.

The visceral affect attaches the eye to the screen. This means that looking, or rather, eyes are the opening onto the Real. Through the eye, "I" occupy a position where subjectivity is impossible, because I now consist of disarticulated organs: the eye and perhaps a throbbing heart. My looking transforms the field of vision into the field of the Real, a no-man's-land, to which I am sutured, from which I cannot move my eye. This is not simply an alternative kind of suturing to an image. This position of looking makes the classical sense of the viewing subject's suture to the image field impossible, as it makes impossible not only any suture of a subject onto the Imaginary—the spectacle of the Real overwhelms and destroys the viable imaginary position—but also the pregiven notion of subjecthood itself. By occupying the place of this nonsubject of looking, the viewer experiences the shock of her own opening into the visual field of the Real. The visual field itself looks awry, borrowing Žižek's description of the spectacularity of the Real. It is not simply that objects appear in disjointed and fragmented form, as in Hieronymus Bosch's painting *The Garden of Earthly Delights*, which Lacan takes as an example of partial objects that elucidate impossible phallic objects. The objects of the Real defy perception or any complete conception of their contours and organization. The whole visual field becomes a disjointed and fragmented world that cannot be grasped and mastered through looking.

The development of the visual technique that produces this emergence of the Real involves identifying what is refused and silenced in social and historical discourse. Eric Cazdyn observes in the formal aesthetic transformations in Japanese cinema the marking of the trauma of modernity that is not allowed a place of enunciation in public discourse. To extend Cazdyn's observation in my conceptualization of the Real, I posit that Japanese auteur Imamura Shohei's *The Pornographers* (1966) experiments with the opening of the Real in the modern Japanese nation, that is, the untenability of national subjectivity, by framing the gendered body and its social milieu through the eye of the on-screen pornographer. However, the film stages the erotic in such a way that it is devoid of the jouissance that one might expect in the violent undoing of the Symbolic order of the nation through illegitimate carnality. Through the subject of the lack for whom even the binding of jouissance is impossible, the film signals the end of phallic jouissance as the constitutional element of national subjectivity.

The experience of the Real conveys the end of phallic jouissance. This traumatic ending has a historical dimension. In *The Element of Crime* (Lars von Trier, 1984), Europe is visualized as the field of the Real representing the ruin of phallic jouissance. The protagonist, a detective now living as an émigré in Egypt, can virtually return to Europe only when hypnotized by an Egyptian analyst. Referred to simply as "Europe," without national designations, this postapocalyptic landscape is shot with low-saturation red tints, rendering it surreal. Bereft of temporal markers, it is possible to read the state of the landscape as the universal condition of a Europe that serves as a chronotope of the Real. We traverse the ruins of cities and dwellings drenched in perpetual rain and deluge. What little dry surface of the earth and buildings that exists is covered with layers of useless refuse: rusted keys, empty soda bottles, crumpled lottery tickets, and such. In the flooded archive, the detective tries to assemble evidence of a serial murder of girls. In waist-high standing water, torn pages float by. This space signifies the impossibility of historiography, which the film allegorizes through the crime narrative that the detective seeks to construct. Both historiography and narrative involve temporally coherent chains of motive, cause, and effect. The narrative and historiography both fail to reach a telos, because those chains are a phantasmatic structure that the master discourse produces. They fail to harness a coherent historical and narrative time and space because to do so is fundamentally impossible.

In *The Element of Crime*, no action results in the progressive movement of plot that we are accustomed to follow in narrative cinema. Though the detective is compelled to try to understand and solve the serial murder of young girls, he can only circle around the elusive traces of the killer, traversing the devastated European wasteland. In the process of investigating murders in what seems to be the landscape of the unconscious, he encounters the Real of Europe, that is, a Europe that makes no sense in the narration of the Symbolic order. This is also the process by which the male subject reaches the end of phallic jouissance, the enjoyment that comes from investing in and obtaining the phantasmatic object of desire. That end signifies the end of the economy in which the phallus is endowed with capacity to eradicate the lack and thus of the values of objects that are measured in terms of the phantasmatic fulfillment of desire. What the protagonist finds at the end of his pursuit is the hanged body of his mentor, who supposedly knew the identity of the murderer. It turns out that the mentor has followed, analyzed, and ultimately begun to impersonate the killer, Harry, after the killer's own unexplained death. The detective then also begins to impersonate Harry, following his mentor's example. To narrativize the serial murder, that is, to organize an event in an epistemological order, he reasons, you must insert yourself into the logic of the trajectory that the killer has established, following his movements and mimicking his gestures. This means mimicking the enjoyment of the Other. In the end, it is impossible for the masculine subject to sustain his desire; he cannot obtain the object that would bind him as a subject of desire. He possesses nothing, not even coherent spatial and temporal coordinates, let alone the phantasmatic object, whether that turns out to be the body of the killer or a victim's life saved, which would make the logic of desire possible for a consolidated subject of desire. All this reveals the loss of phallic jouissance. The protagonist's screams as he suffers agonizing physical pain, induced by an aphrodisiac given him by an Asian prostitute, Harry's former lover, allegorize his inability to know/enjoy the Other's jouissance, as well as the pain of the loss of phallic jouissance that he experiences. The detective screams "I love pain" while floating through an underground sewer, the exact course of which is unclear, except that it crosses the territory of the killer's movements, which the detective himself traverses. The physical pain he experiences is symptomatic of the loss of the subjectivity, allegorizing the annihilation of the European subject.

Commenting on the quintessential modern European experience, Paul Virilio describes blitzkrieg as the culminating moment of the fear of modernity and speed as a response to that fear.[51] Lars von Trier's *Europa* (1991) depicts the ruin created by the modern regime of fear created through speed and technology. The film is set in 1945 Allies-occupied Germany, though throughout the film the narrator uses the word *Europa* to designate the place we navigate along with Leopold Kessler, a German-descendant American sleeping car conductor. We feel trapped in the train with Kessler, with the mise-en-scène of the train emphasizing this feeling, creating the space that deprives us of the sense of being a subject capable of action and movement. On this train, we encounter a car that holds Jewish prisoners in a dreamscape restaging of wartime images of a concentration camp. The train car becomes the concentration camp where we meet the gaze of the Jewish prisoners as if we are dreaming it. This staged apparition, by invoking the truth that the industrialized transportation system, as a hallmark of scientific rationality of the modern state, is implicated in unspeakable violence, takes away from the viewer the sense of recognizable temporality, despite the narrative persistence of diegetic temporality denoting the post–World War II Europe. The past exists in the present like a haunting.

Fear and speed lead to the pursuit of phallic jouissance, which is the foundation of the Law as it defines the proper ways of desiring proper objects, such that the properly juridical subject may participate in that jouissance in modern Europe. But Lars von Trier's vision of Europe shows us that, although fear is dispersed across a Europe of garbage-strewn urban spaces and destroyed landscapes, the body politic, dwelling in those places aimlessly and subjected to blind violence, cannot systematically administer a regime of speedy forward movement away from that fear. The train, the primary apparatus of movement in the film, never arrives at its destination: Kessler detonates a bomb that Nazi saboteurs have installed as a means to escape the train and, by extension, Europa. As the train is submerged underwater, the omniscient voiceover of narrator Max von Sydow (a quintessential European who doubles as the hypnotist) invites the spectator to stare at the slow death by drowning of the main character, Kessler, but it is his drowning body that gazes at us.

Where the speedy occupation by arms, technology, and constructivist images once prevailed, we see the image of ruin through a camera eye that has no clear subjective position beyond that of the narrator who invites us to the spectacle of that ruin and to face the "real gaze." The field of vision is the Real called "Europe." The eye marks the place that the spectator is forced to occupy as she enters the visual field in which the cinematic subject loses subjective standing, while the subject's sense of distinctive time and space is destroyed. Further obfuscation of the sense of time comes from meticulously staged scenes of Kafkaesque bureaucracy, meant to construct the temporal management of the whole conveyance unfolding in the midst of the explosive situations throughout the train cars. Confusion with regard to space also comes from Lars von Trier's use of color. The screen often splits into two domains, one in black-and-white and one in color. Characters, some in black-and-white and some in color, appear in the same visual space. They move in and out of two chromatically distinct spheres, rendered in color in the monochromic world and in monochrome in the full-color world. This movement constitutes the field of the Real. The state of bewilderment, signifying the end of phallic jouissance, is the affect that the film generates. In this state, subjecthood itself, which functions as an agency with which to pursue a phallic jouissance, is no longer possible.

As if visualizing the impossible subject, *Europa* ends with the drowning of Kessler after the train's explosion. While the narrator counts to ten, we watch the long, slow process of drowning, spared none of the pain and agony on the drowning man's face. We are fixed by the gaze that emanates from the image of death. The final shot of *The Element of Crime* is of a captured animal, trapped in a hole in the ground. The close-up of the animal's dilated pupils, blind, black, and shiny, characteristic of subterranean life, expresses the viewing subject's condition of entrapment in the Real. Both Lars von Trier films visualize the destruction of phallic jouissance, but we need to push this destruction even further to allow feminine jouissance to emerge and show us what the world looks like through the eye of its subject. The cinema of the Real helps us to see this world.

The World according to Feminine Jouissance

Feminine jouissance defies the gender binary. In *Hunger*,[52] a film that dramatizes the hunger strike of prisoner Bobby Sands, a member of the Irish Republican Army (IRA), the masculine body itself acquires a strange look, as if feminine jouissance is inscribed upon it. In the film, fragmented objects allegorize the disarticulation of the masculine body of phallic jouissance: the wounded knuckles of a prison guard who tortures IRA prisoners with his fists, streams of urine released by political prisoners under their cell doors that flood the prison corridors, excrement and filth that stand in for a subject, most notably the feces used to paint a whirlpool on the cell's wall, signifying the vortex of the drive as it circles around a "nothing," a bull's-eye made of human waste. The circles visualize the drive that renders the object cause of desire (the Irish nation, properly idealized masculinity) as excrement, as nothing with inherent symbolic value. Although it is possible to read this film by following its ostensible narrative trajectory in a way that conceptualizes Bobby Sands as a subject of desire who seeks an independent nation-state, as a national hero, and as an ideological subject, the film's visual construction indicates otherwise. *Hunger*'s pornographic spectacularization of Sands's emaciated body generates a poetic shock through visualizing the disintegration of the masculine subject's body into a body part, into wounded flesh. Although his hunger strike and subsequent death did, at least partially, achieve his goal—namely, the treatment of the hunger-striking prisoners as political subjects—a political reading of this film should focus on feminine jouissance, not on the recovery of lost objects such as the nation that would enable phallic jouissance. Regarding image creation in the film, the filmmaker states, "I want this movie to be like a smell"[53] to confront the viewer. Judging by many reviewers' comments, the filmmaker indeed created an image that "smells like shit." The film's fecal image doesn't just confront viewers; it forces the spectator to enter the field of the Real where jouissance itself "smells."

In *Hunger*, the prison is, rather than a field of political struggle with identifiable and obtainable objects of desire, the visual field of the Real. Bobby Sands's dying body, shot through sweeping, unstable close-ups, is reduced to stains on a white sheet. In the final sequence, shots of Sands's moribund body and face are intercut with shots of Sands as a boy running through the forest. The scene then cuts to an image of a bird fluttering into the room where he lies dying, then finally to a shot of a bird feather floating midair. These shots signify Sands's transformation from body to stain to feather, until he is no longer a wholesome and discrete human subject but a residual thing-ness, matter that cannot be sublimated or tamed into a particular symbolic meaning. Like the smell and image of shit, the images transport the viewer into the world of the Real where the

Symbolic subject as we know it no longer exists. Beyond the subject's annihilation through biological death, we see the suggestions of the second death, like that of Antigone as she walks into the tomb only to continue her life beyond Symbolic and legitimate mourning into the Real. Feminine jouissance strikes down the Law of the Father, drives Antigone into the tomb and Bobby Sands into the form of a feather. Sands's body, as the focus of our looking, invites us to occupy the subject position attached to feminine jouissance. Horror in this film is in the form of the destructive effect of feminine jouissance.

While *Hunger*, which can be read as a political film, exemplifies filmic representations of the horror of feminine jouissance, the horror genre is crowded with women whose jouissance destroys phallic jouissance. Monstrous women refuse to settle for the normative objects of desire. They embark on a quest to destroy the object that they once coveted, such as a lover, a child, or a family. When we follow the looking of the feminine subject in those films, objects no longer support phallic jouissance, and we witness feminine jouissance rendering such objects impotent. In the South Korean film *The Wailing* (Na Hong-jin, 2016), we see the feminine embodiment of the Real in the form of a ghost that lurks at the edge of a village. As the only subject who knows the Real of history responsible for the horror, here Japanese colonialism, enveloping the village, the female ghost confronts the proper subjects of family, religion, and the state. Patriarchal law, personified by a father who is also a police officer, fails to protect and preserve law and order from monstrous enjoyment, which finds its expression in a young girl who becomes possessed by foreign desire—embodied by a devil who appears as an elderly Japanese man, himself a representation of the imperial Other as the origin of lethal desire.

In the Realm of the Senses is among the films where we encounter feminine jouissance and that do not conform to generic categorization, despite its aesthetic alignment with the pornographic form particular to Japanese modern cinema, as Cazdyn delineates it. The film turns the expressive space of the pornographic form into a political space that showcases the looking that emanates from feminine jouissance. In this film, the woman's looking keeps the male body not simply as an object of desire but as the impossible object that does not deliver the *objet a*. The male body becomes an object that signifies the lack, especially the penis, which is an abject object that symptomatizes the lack of the phallus. The materiality of the penis as visually rendered in the film only affirms that it is an empty signifier, having no capacity to bring the satisfaction of desire that the phallus, a phantasmatic object that the penis stands in for, promises to fulfill. This lack unleashes feminine jouissance; the phallic object is an ordinary object that cannot satisfy her desire. Hence, for her, it is a useless and impotent object that testifies to the impossibility of ever possessing the *objet a*, and thus it cannot be sublimated in the Symbolic order. After the man dies from asphyxia during sex, she cuts off his penis and carries it around in her purse, as if it is a mundane object one might find in such an ordinary location. My reading of this film differs in this way from the reading Teresa de Lauretis undertakes. In de Lauretis's reading, the feminine desire moves the film's narrative forward, and the film is counterpolitical because the feminine desire counters the masculine desire that narrative cinema privileges.[54] I argue, however, that it is the failure of the woman's desire, that is, her failure to turn into a subject of phallic jouissance, that makes the film counterpolitical. This trajectory of failure inhibits and halts the narrative.

In the Realm of the Senses is organized around points where the feminine subject's phallic desire—which initially keeps her in the realm of phallic jouissance, where desire targets the jouissance that the phallic object is supposed to deliver—is increasingly heightened and yet fails to lead to satisfaction in the form of obtaining of *objet a* that the phallic object is fantasized to be. Rather, the phallic object (penis) itself becomes increasingly disappointing. The sadomasochism that ensues dramatizes the demand for the object in order to elicit and prolong the fantasy of finally having the *objet a*. These points stall, rather than advance, the narrative. We cannot simply say that the feminine subject usurps the narrative and that therefore feminine desire pushes the narrative forward. It would be more accurate to say that the drive of the feminine jouissance halts the narrative. Such stasis, which privileges the spectacle of sex, causes the film to veer away from the narrative cinema form, despite its utilization of pornographic structures evident in cinematography that provide the backbone of narrative cinema, moving toward a telos, or the money shot.

The pornographic sex scenes in the film are often staged in expressionistic settings, creating a sense of surreality in jarring contrast to the realism of genital exposure and copulation. High-saturation colors, bordering on gaudiness, emphasize the theatricality of these scenes, which is further augmented by the presence of onlookers, some open about their scopophilia, even situating themselves in the scene, and others peeping, implied as extradiegetic spectators. Their presence suggests that looking, in marking the place of the Other, is always involved in the scene of desire. But the looking of the spectator, and of the onlookers who stand in for the spectator, is not simply voyeuristic; it points toward a place outside the narrative. These scenes disrupt the narrative with the kind of enjoyment that cannot be subsumed by the narrative's ideological presuppositions regarding sexuality and gender. Even when the looking is part of the film's diegesis, it appears as a hole in the film's field of the image. The presence of those who look is part of the diegetic space, yet it punctures the filmic image, rendering it difficult to read. This hole is a formal supplement for the fissure that the feminine drive generates, a break in narrative film introduced through the visual metaphor of those onlookers. If Laura Mulvey's voyeurism explains how the ideology of narrative cinema works,[55] this theatrical look shows where that ideology falters.

The Vision of the Real and the Cinema of Failure

To further theorize this novel form of cinema using a psychoanalytic framework, I return to the unconscious as the core of the cinema of the Real. The unconscious is not individual and does not exclusively express itself in an individual sphere. Rather, we can say that a mobile unconsciousness traverses the cultural and social spheres. Let us consider this traversal through the Warner Brothers cartoon *One Froggy Evening* (1955) and its sequel, *Another Froggy Evening* (1995), where the box that contains a singing frog exemplifies the unconscious. The sequel expands on the original's premise: a man accidentally comes to possess a mysterious box that contains a spectacular singing and dancing frog, but he fails to harness the elusive object, the frog, as the phallic object that will fulfill his desire for fame and fortune. The frog box mysteriously appears in different historical locations, from ancient Rome to modern New York City, though the frog never seems to age or die. Those who happen to gain possession of the box and discover the singing and dancing frog within all attempt to make a fortune, but the troublesome amphibian won't perform in accordance with the wishes of its owner. Onstage, the frog that was moments earlier singing and dancing for its new owner sits and croaks like an ordinary frog. Eventually disappointed, each owner abandons the box, and the frog along with it, though it is only a matter of time before a new owner stumbles upon it and has the same disappointing result. The box that traverses different historical settings figures as the mobile unconscious of society. The precious object it carries, a singing frog, always turns out to be useless for those who desire it. The coveted object never delivers what those who covet it seek to obtain from it. The movement of the box follows the trajectory of a drive that circles around a useless object without ever obtaining satisfaction. The frog is the stuff that the Lacanian Real is made of, a kernel that cannot be harnessed or grasped through the Symbolic order and imaginary identification and that alludes to something beyond the visual and ideational frame of what we perceive as reality. The cinema of the Real reveals this area beyond the ideological frame of cinema.

Here, I return to the question of how the Real appears in cinema. In *The Element of Crime*, we are alerted to our own act of looking from the very beginning through a sweeping shot of unrecognizable insects buzzing through crates. The shot is disorienting; it offers no position of looking that might anchor the viewer securely in the time and space of the film's diegesis. The film *Irreversible* (Gaspar Noé, 2002) uses similarly sweeping and disorienting opening shots to extend a sense of destruction to a cohesive cinematic chronotope; such shots have the effect of opening up the moment in which the Real appears via our looking. *The Element of Crime* also features shots that cause the viewer to lose a proper topological sense, such as a man's image reflected upside down on the wet floor. The film's circularity also defies the viewer's sense of chronology, beginning and ending with the voice-over of a protagonist whose temporal location is unclear, except that it is situated in a time where a historiographical grasp of events is not possible. We are made to wonder about the temporal location of what we see, such as the ritually suicidal acts of skinheads and the killing of young girls. In this uncertain temporality, we encounter objects that do more than announce the presence of the Real as the point where the utilitarian and fantastic dimension of objects falters. We also see the inauguration of the drive, following circular paths around objects that are impossible to harness in spatial and temporal meaning-making and leading the viewing subject as well as the diegetic subject into the field of the Real.

Point of view is itself a gap or hole through which the Real emerges. In *The Element of Crime*, the undefinable land of the Real, an impossible chronotope, exists as the only landscape that the viewing subject beholds. Our eye itself becomes the breach, materialized in the dark pupils of the trapped animal, through which the landscape of the Real appears. Everywhere, we see only the ruin that the Real has created in the Symbolic order, and the image leaves no place to which we can avert our vision. At one point in this film, we are placed in the subjective position of a dead girl's looking, forced to take up her corpse's perspective, that is, the view from the Real. The Real appears not simply as an object or its image but as a structure of our looking.

The cinema of the Real may have a depthless, infinite surface, and our visceral/visual pleasure in seeing it comes from encountering the visual materialization of the Real as a depthless surface. There is no hermeneutic depth underneath, no hidden underside to its surface. The visceral pleasure that we experience looking at that surface comes from the appearance of what is impossible in the system of signification. In *The Element of Crime*, one example of the Real appearing as the surface is the hole in a dead donkey through which water and blood gush as if direct conduits into some unspeakable realm. The watery ground shines like a red blur that lacks any substantial properties in its ever-shifting shape, as if all things solid might melt away. These constitute the scenery of the Real. Here appears the shocking strangeness of the image, a sign without a thing signified. The image of the hole is meaningless, except as a point of visceral shock that generates the painful pleasure (and pleasurable pain) of seeing a wound open on the cinematic surface.

In the cinema of the Real, the visual subject, as long as it sees, cannot escape the Real. The act of looking traverses the field of the Real. In terms of the cinematic effect, the line or angle of looking delineates the shape of the Real. The look itself always evokes, wakes up, and creates the Real. For the subject of vision, there is no other place of existence but the Real.

The cinema of the Real reveals the Real through sensation, through the viscerality of the shock that the viewing subject experiences in no-man's-land. In *Europa* and *The Element of Crime*, that experience comes from the encounter with Europe, entering or existing within Europe as the field of the Real. In *The Element of Crime*, characters assert "we are Europeans," although a discernable, cohesive Europe has ceased to exist. In both films, Europe signifies an impossible place where European-ness exists, not simply as an object of desire and an identitarian designation but as a "European-Thing," something spectral yet persistently registering the failure of all desires to be the core of subjectivity. The traumatic Real is what everyone trapped in that impossible chronotopical location of the European-Thing must face. History exists only as a perpetual registration of trauma, where the European-Thing is the kernel that the subject of phallic jouissance cannot digest. It marks the absence and impossibility of an identification that secures subjectivity.

Europe, as such, does not exist, and Europeans in these films suffer from an irrecoverable lack. There is no European nation and no transnation of Europe. Egypt figures as the screen upon which the sign of the European-Thing and its fundamental lack of chronotopical certainty is conjured. On this screen is projected the unconscious of a male European subject. In his memory, the image of Europe is that of the ruin of civilization: the violence of blitzkrieg has destroyed any possibility of building the national and social body. Carnality is concentrated in the bodies of murdered children and an Asian prostitute, over whom the masculine subject does not hold a position of mastery. For the masculine subject who should occupy the position of knowing through looking as a means of mastery, to be in the Europe of this film is to be in a hell of the Real of blinding pain and to suffer the loss of oneself.

As in von Trier's films, McQueen's *Hunger* focuses on the cinematic frame as the field of the Real where strange, partial objects tear the fabric of the Symbolic order, such as the painting of fecal swirls on the wall, looking like the concentric lines that form the eye, or the prisoners' urine streaming from underneath cell doors along the corridor. There is a shot of a prison guard mopping up the flood of urine, the extent of that flow exaggerated by a wide-angle lens. The image of these objects immerses the spectator in a realm beyond humanity, that of the inhuman kernel. The unwashed, starving, and naked bodies of the prisoners, the intricate movements those bodies make as they are beaten and tortured, also figure as partial objects. They stand in as pure matter upon which meaning cannot be ascribed. Kafka's hunger artist disappears, leaving nothing behind except the pile of hay upon which his diminishing body lay, signaling the complete negation of the subject, whereas in *Hunger*, the body leaves the residue of thingness, of pure matter. It remains a kernel, the undead that the codes of national and imperial law cannot erase. The material persistence of the body, a thing that exceeds the symbolic inscription of order and meaning, is evinced by the spectacle of filth that the body generates. The spectacle of the kernel finds its ultimate expression in Bobby Sands's dying body. The camera presents the spectacle of the body in ruination, lacerations on the skin, bloody traces on the sheet, the remainder (or thing itself) that escapes the ideological cohesiveness that we desire of the body. As such, the film stages the dimension of the Real of subjectivity, reminding us of the impossibility or precariousness of corporeal subjectivity.

The cinema of the Real, which transubstantiates the image into the Real and transforms the spectator into a subject of the Real, is the cinema of failure. It visualizes the failure of the subject to bind its desire within the Symbolic order. But it also visualizes the subject of the Real that enjoys the image itself, viscerally experiencing its effect. In a Lacanian sense, the category of the "all" that defines proper subjectivity obscures the lack that produces the drive to circle around the lack, as a means to contain the constitutive lack that makes us who we are, a fluctuating surface upon which is reflected the shape of the kernel.

In the visual field of the cinema of the Real, we experience the pain of losing ourselves, as much pain as is involved in the drive, for the drive is not an "effortless" and banal action that repeatedly passes through a form or structure.[56] As a subject of the drive, we cannot sustain our cathexis to the *objet a*;[57] we opt for its painful and perpetual lack, and therein exists the emancipatory possibility of the drive. The spectacle of the Real involves registering the visceral pain of that loss of an object as the affectation that the subject suffers. We have seen that Lars von Trier's films focus on visualizing the visceral pain that accompanies the annihilation of the subject to a literal degree, as in the genital mutilations in *Antichrist*. Enjoyment of the visual image in von Trier's films is equivalent to enjoying the pain of the Real. We are bound to the Real through our eyes. The spectacle pains us, but it also inaugurates for us the subject of the Real.

The cinema of failure affirms that *objet a* does not exist, but beyond that it is also able to involve the spectator in the experience of that object's absence. The spectacle, as it constitutes the visual drive, allows us to experience that lack and loss. Through that experience, the subject of the Real emerges. However, the subject of the Real does not engage in self-pulverization or mere destitution of subjectivity. Rather, it opens up the space where it becomes possible to imagine the new subject. The cinema of the Real shows the violent shattering that is necessary for the emergence of the new subject. The following chapters will look at that emergence in national cinemas.

CHAPTER TWO

The Cartography of the Real Body

What Is the Real Body?

The cinema of the Real places the viewing subject in an encounter with the Real via poetic shock, accompanied by the violent shattering of subjectivity, as I have delineated in chapter 1. If this shattering is a precondition for the emergence of a new subject, how does the cinema of the Real visualize this subject? I argue that the new subject appears as what I call the *Real body*, whose movement ruptures the spatial arrangement that binds social organization, notably that of the sovereign nation-state in the Symbolic order of capitalism. The Real body is, in this sense, the embodiment of feminine subjectivity as this new ethical subject's position.

As we have established, subject formation occurs in the wounding that results from our entrance into the Symbolic order as a speaking subject. Subsequently, while the Symbolic order constructs our daily "reality," the Real remains invisible. Investigating it can, however, reveal significant underlying truths.[1] I am reminded of how a student once described, during a class discussion, his own encounter with the Real of capitalism. Unboxing his brand-new iPhone, he opened the battery/SIM card cover to find a smudged fingerprint, most likely belonging to a Chinese factory worker. This hidden sign of the labor utilized in creating the phone was, for him, evidence of the Real of capitalism: the accumulation of surplus value through the exploitation of labor. The Real erupts onto the shiny, unblemished surface of the commodity and disrupts the smooth functioning of capitalism by uncovering the inherent contradiction in capitalist accumulation. For the student, the exploitation of a heretofore invisible subject, a member of an undercompensated, disposable labor force, disrupted the myth of infinite gratification through unchecked acquisition. The cinema of the Real relies on the smudge, one that stains the shiny surface of filmic reality.

Before we explore the concept of the Real body as a crucial element in the cinema of the Real, let us revisit the question of subjectivity from which we tease out the subject of the Real that the Real body houses. As we visualize how the Real body appears in cinema, we move conceptually from the linguistic subject to the subject of feminine jouissance as the subject of the Real and finally to the Real body. As linguistic subjects, we lose access to the Real because language, a chain of metonymy and metaphor, forever displaces and obscures the thing that it represents. The Real exceeds the language that unifies the Symbolic order's material organization. Appearing as a structural, formal disruption of the Symbolic order's material organization, the Real marks the place of the little object "a" (*objet a* in Lacanian terms) we can never grasp because it does not exist as a material reality. As a phantasmatic object that we think we have lost, it becomes the object that causes our desire. Our only possible relationship to the Real is through its displacement through language. We experience this loss of access to the Real as a wounding, one that cuts "a pound of flesh" from our being. This lost part of us is what we retroactively construe as the piece of "I" that we believe had been in direct and intimate contact with the Real. This loss constitutes us as the subject of the lack, and through our experience of lack we establish our relationship to some object, *objet a*, which comes to signify the lost object, the inaccessible thing itself. This "a" also allows us to defer an encounter with the horror of the impossible thing itself that is beyond signification. Horror films are full of moments of encountering the Thing (consider John Carpenter). This interaction extends to our relationship to all objects.

This is not to say that we once had, or can possibly regain, contact with the Real; we never had contact with the Real in the first place. We enunciate our being through language that conveys the cut in our undifferentiated drive, like sexuation, which opens up the psychic and social position for us to occupy as the linguistic subject. The Real is the symptom of the cut and the ensuing lack, and language provides us with a formal structure through which we relate to the Real. But the Real always bursts the seams of that structure.

As shown in previous chapters, two subjectivities emerge around the lack: the feminine and the phallic. Each entails its own mode of jouissance and implies subsequent positions regarding objects. Phallic jouissance is formed around belief in an object that is connected to the phallic signifier, an object that promises to deliver us from lack. The subject of phallic jouissance fantasizes that it can obtain *objet a*, the singular object, for which the most salient metaphor is the phallus, that can satisfy desire that comes from the wounding loss of the pound of flesh.² This is the phallic subject position, which is coded masculine. Feminine jouissance, on the other hand, begins with the recognition that all objects, no matter how desirable they seem, will fail to provide relief from the lack.³ The feminine subject, in response, pursues feminine jouissance, the subject position of the lack.

We have established that these two different kinds of jouissance do not align with gender, sexual, or morphological differences. Rather, they are two poles that subjects occupy to respond to the lack as the existential condition. But they do differentiate bodies. One, the linguistic and Symbolic body of phallic jouissance, is founded on belief and trust in the phallic signifier and, thus, belief and trust in language itself and the Symbolic order. The other is the Real body of feminine jouissance. To understand the Real body, we need to return to the Lacanian notion of the body as distinct from the biological living organism. As Colette Soler summarizes, Lacan understood the body as a linguistic body that receives the mark of the signifier.⁴ Here, the difference between "man" and "woman" depends on "the way in which an individual inscribes him/herself in the phallic function."⁵ Thus, the difference between "man" and "woman" depends on which side of phallic jouissance one stands. "Woman" codifies the feminine side that denounces phallic jouissance, while "man" codifies the phallic, which culturally is represented by the masculine subject that invests in the goal of obtaining the phallic object. The "sexual destiny" of the body, configured along the lines of "man" and "woman," is determined by the discourse⁶ of society and culture that draws a line between these two different kinds of jouissance. Soler further asserts that in Lacanian thought, there is antagonism between signifier and jouissance.⁷ Paul Verhaeghe states that the patriarchal monotheistic system, a conflation of the authority of the father with the monotheistic God as the sole locus of truth, is the basis of the Law of the Father. In this role, it designates objects of pleasure, ranging from food to sexuality.⁸ In this system, sexual and gender difference, of which "man" and "woman" are signifiers, are determined by "the One Man," whether he is the primal father or God the Father.⁹

In my theorization, the sovereign nation-state also appears as that One Man. Feminine jouissance, as we will see in this chapter, disrupts this arrangement of signifiers, an antagonism between signifier and jouissance that is particular to feminine jouissance. Here, we end up with two bodies: the body of the signifier, or phallic jouissance, and the body of feminine jouissance, which I call the Real body. This Real body, which is the effect of the wounding lack, relates to *objet a* as the Real object. Soler explains the Real object as follows: ". . . of the body and its jouissance, the only thing that can be approached by psychoanalysis . . . is this object, which we can describe as real. Real, not because it has the materiality of a body, or spatial extension—it has neither of those things—but it is real precisely, in Lacan's definition, in so far as it is impossible to apprehend by means of the signifier; that is to say, the signifier circles around it."[10]

The patriarchal system of the sovereign nation-state—likewise, the monotheistic system, in the sense that it centers around a figure of One Man, another name for the big Other, who consolidates sovereign authority—summons the linguistic body to signify the possession of *objet a* by representing it through phantasmatic phallic objects. The Real body, in contrast, reveals *objet a* as something exceeding the body, something that escapes the organic and linguistic boundary of the body, something that we cannot grasp through any signifier within the Symbolic order. The resulting monstrous Otherness of feminine jouissance is a thing from which "man," invested in phallic jouissance, flees. The patriarchal state must render the Real body abject, because the Real body transgresses all of the patriarchal state's borders, unsettling its cartography that designates the location of the body. We see these transgressive lines of movement of the Real body in the cartography of the sovereign nation-state in the South Korean films *Thirst*[11] and *Poetry*[12] and in the Chinese film *Still Life*.[13]

Before we engage in analyses of these films, let us establish how the Real body appears in the cinema of the Real. As noted, in the cinema of the Real, the visual field is the field of the Real. That is, the cinema of the Real transforms the visual field into the field of the Real through the viewer's encounter with the imagery of the Real: hence my focus on formal elements that render that field on the cinematic screen. In this chapter, I focus on the image of the Real body that destabilizes cinematic language's formal elements, figuring as the traumatic kernel in both the cinematic form and in subjectivity itself. The kernel confronts the phallic signifier and its injunction as articulated in the patriarchal system, and it survives that confrontation. Different films stage that confrontation using different formative tendencies. The spectacle-driven films examined in this chapter allow visceral experience of the Real (*Thirst*). Films anchored in realism (*Poetry, Oasis, Still Life*), while not viscerally disturbing, likewise place the spectator in the subject position of the Real. Both types of film map the Real body in the cinematic visual field and, in doing so, display the transgressive force of the Real body that upsets the spatial arrangement of the sovereign nation-state. The image of the Real body unsettles both the expectation of resolution through action in narrative and the anticipated effect of the image itself. In this sense, poetic shock, which I conceptualize in chapter 1, permeates the appearance of the Real body. It reveals the kernel of being that survives an encounter with the signifier[14] and continues to cleave to feminine jouissance. In these films, that body appears as a vampire, as migrant workers, as violent women, or as ailing women.

As in previous chapters, I use a transnational approach in my analyses. This is a comparative method that moves across geopolitical boundaries to locate universal structural threads that manifest differently in particular local contexts. In interrogating transnationally universal structures as well as the eruption of the Real in local contexts of those configurations—notably the way the Symbolic order works in various configurations of patriarchal-monotheistic systems in nation-states, societies, and regions—the comparative approach calls for placing various theoretical methodologies in dialogue. The aim is to see the relationship between a global theory of subjectivity and local conditions of subjectivity, as we reconfigure the established terrain of the theorization of subjectivity itself. As I have pointed out elsewhere, citing Naoki Sakai,[15] "the West" in that terrain sees itself in binary opposition with "the Rest." The West, in this binary, designates itself as *Humanitas*, representing transcendental and universal humanity and likewise designates the Rest as *Anthropos*, an empirical object of inquiry.[16] This binary implicitly supports the claim that only the West is capable of producing theory and is by extension solely responsible for generating a universal mode of knowledge that defines the order of things. This Humanitas/Anthropos binary structures a relation of looking and knowing that supports the modern power dynamic that continues to define our epoch.

However, we must note that the Humanitas/Anthropos binary is not limited to this "West and the Rest" binary written across Orientalist geopolitics. We can, for example, recognize a binary that the neo-imperial impetus imposes upon the racial and ethnic Other in China's neo-imperial posture in East Asia. For example, China has invested its ideological apparatuses in a revisionary history in what is called the Northeast Project of the Chinese Academy of Social Sciences. Therein, China bolsters its territorial claim to what is construed as the "Northeast," an area that includes Manchuria, by rewriting histories of ethnic groups outside of the majority Han Chinese as part of the long duration of Chinese national history, which is imagined as cohesive and unified. Here the Chinese nation-state imagines itself as the only national entity in possession of the power and knowledge to narrate history in the Northeast as opposed its own Rest/Anthropos, the Chinese nation-state's ethnic and racial Other.[17]

A transnational approach encompasses different frameworks for theorizing the human, such as around *the abject* and *homo sacer*, which are important in this chapter's theorization of the Real body. A transnational comparative approach asserts that Anthropos (the theorized) can theorize Humanitas (the theorizer) and expand the scope of universal theory by allowing Anthropos to appear as the subject in theorizing the human, in direct opposition to the established order of theory formation. In building a universal framework in which we can reconfigure the relation of looking as well as the power relations involved in universal theory, we can draw from Susan Buck-Morss's method of working "through the historical specificities of particular experiences." Buck-Morss suggests "approaching the universal not by subsuming facts within overarching systems or homogenizing premises, but by attending to the edges of systems, the limits of premises, the boundaries of our historical imagination in order to trespass, trouble, and tear these boundaries down."[18] The universal should imply a historical and critical paradigm that encompasses material and ideological conditions of subjectivity across geopolitical borders, locating the margins and limits of epistemology within the mapping of human existence. For Buck-Morss, the Haitian revolution exemplifies universality: it is a historical struggle at the margins that enables us, both Humanitas and Anthropos, to create a universal paradigm of history as a history of emancipatory struggles.

The transnationality I employ undermines prevalent approaches of area and regional studies and of national studies of separate nations. This method calls "into question the notion of space encircled by clear boundaries for national and civilizational discourses"[19] that allow for ethnic nationalism. The universal Real body transgresses the boundaries that those discourses draw in the theoretical and material movement of subjectivities. More importantly, transnationality counters the cosmopolitanism informed by the humanistic notion that Kwame Anthony Appiah exemplifies: to be a cosmopolitan means to be responsive to "what Adam Smith called 'reason, principle, conscience, the inhabitant of the breast.'" Appiah sees that cosmopolitan engagement as "moral conversation between people *across* societies" in which we expect disagreements about questions of values.[20] Appiah suggests that once this moral prerequisite is accepted, we will be able to eradicate extreme poverty in twenty years with about 150 billion dollars a year, assuming the people of the richest nation would be willing to raise the money "at about 45 cents a day."[21] In contrast, transnationality as a framework gives us ways to counter global capitalism by looking at how the new universal might emerge to counteract the capitalist universal and does so by articulating a new human subjectivity that participates in a history of emancipatory struggle. The revolting Haitian slaves must insist upon their visibility in the new expression of the human, facing off against the benevolent citizens of the richest nations.

Transnational analyses must involve a framework through which we interrogate global theory and aesthetic form that are intricately involved in local articulations of the human. South Korean cinema, for example, hybridizes cinematic forms and conventions to draw from global formal aesthetics. Genre films especially imbue a hybridized cinematic form with South Korea's own local expression of trauma, leading critics such as Jinsoo An to state that "what is novel and dominant in South Korean cinema can be summed up in two words: *trauma* and *globalization*."[22] In the modern nation, subject formation occurs through the individual apprehension of national trauma. Here, globalization is an occasion in which national trauma finds a globally recognizable visual form. National cinemas contribute to the formal and thematic transformation of global cinema by using local contexts of trauma and allowing the appearance of the traumatic kernel in the shape of the metaphorical stain on the cinema's visual surface. The viewer encounters what Lacan calls "the gaze" at the point where the stain appears. This is the point through which the Real erupts and the unreadable "local" desire exceeds the "global" generic norm. Although South Korean cinema often shows an uneasy coevality of modern trauma and global postmodernity, where history can be turned into a reservoir of fungible cultural commodities, these films include a formal excess that marks the point where they heighten the empathic and intellectual impact of local contexts, thereby disrupting the global language of genre cinema. Here, the margin shapes the universal discourse of modernity and its aesthetic representations. The cinema of the Real that undertakes a global expression of local trauma articulates the universal by, in the words of Buck-Morss, "attending to the edges of systems, the limits of premises, the boundaries of our historical imagination."[23] The cinema of the Real attends to local trauma that is invisible from the perspective of Humanitas. It does so "in order to trespass, trouble, and tear these boundaries down."[24] It moves us away from film theory and form founded on the binary of Humanitas and Anthropos and toward the universal.

What, then, is the relationship between the traumatic cut of language and empirical, historical trauma? I posit that historical trauma gives structure to the psychic experience of the cut of language. In this way, historical trauma frames our relationship to *objet a*, that phantasmatic, impossible object that is supposed to have been cut off from us by language. The public dimension of trauma resides here. Through historical trauma "the borders between the psychical and the social, the private and the public," open up.[25] Trauma puts us in an impossible subject position, where the pregiven temporal and spatial coordinates, which hold a subject position together, fall apart. This undoing threatens our phantasmatic grip on *objet a*. Freud recounts a dream in which a father is reproached by his deceased child. In the father's dream, his dead child appears to him and says, "Father, can't you see I am burning?" The father has fallen asleep while a knocked-over candle starts a fire in the child's room. I posit that this provides us with an example of what it looks like to be a subject, about to be awakened to traumatic loss. In this scenario, the father wakes up to an irreversible loss that constitutes the lack. This is reality for the linguistic subject: we wake up every day to the lack of an *objet a*. In this sense, trauma is structurally similar to the linguistic cut, in that both figure as the structure in which the subject experiences the lack. Historical trauma leads the subject to experience the lack as that of the nation, community, social subject, or any other ideological object that stands in as the *objet a*. Trauma knocks the subject off the temporal and spatial foundation upon which the historical subject is ideologically and materially anchored. Therein lies the emancipatory possibility for a new subject of the Real to emerge.[26]

Historical trauma also reveals how our subjectivity is anchored by *objet a*. This condition makes it difficult to resist the hold that the Symbolic order has over the national subject, by persuading her to believe in the existence of *objet a*, which neither she, nor anyone, possesses. Colonization unleashes a proliferation of such lost objects: mourning over the loss of *objet a*, which appears as national sovereignty, territory, traditional social organization, and ideological principles, obscures the linguistic cut that founds all social subjects. It is in this context that decolonized nation-states reclaim ownership of the heritage objects stolen from them. The spectacle of modernization in South Korean cinema consists of bodies breaking apart, limb from limb, to signify the vacuum in subjectivization that colonial modernity introduces; Korea's experience of modernity is intricately enmeshed in that of colonization. Exposing the unraveling of the premodern way of being finds expressions in the body of the national subject and invokes the belief that this broken body can be reassembled into an object "a," an embodiment of a national subject. We see this in the rehabilitation of the Father in films, such as the aptly named blockbuster *Ode to My Father* (Yoon Je-kyoon, 2014). In this film set during the Korean War, which violently propelled the nation-state into a modern capitalist order, the wounded nation is metaphorized by indignities and sacrifices that a father suffers during the war. In the course of the nation's postwar rehabilitation, the father's authority must be recovered and upheld, especially by women who suffer indignities and sacrifices in a patriarchal family. The spectacle of the breakdown of the subject and its body could also consist of scenes of destruction of urban and rural space, superimposing pathways for new and shiny objects of modernity: highways, bridges, skyscrapers, and the like.

To resist the rehabilitation of *objet a*, the cut must be included in national memory-making so that new national narratives do not gloss over the wound of the traumatic Real. I once attended a lecture given by a female Muslim academic who researches the Shoah. In that talk, simultaneously fetishizing herself as the Muslim feminine body inserted in the imaginary of the Holocaust and claiming authority to speak in both the Muslim and Jewish spheres, she glossed over systematic Muslim anti-Semitism with anecdotal memories of good will on the part of Arab people and nations during the Nazi occupation. Her approach leaves little room to interrogate the psychical investment made in the Jewish body undergirded by the obscene jouissance coming from enjoying the destruction of the Other, which can be a scene of enjoyment. The theoretical antinomy emerges around the Other as exemplified in this particular case of a Muslim woman's claiming of the narrative of the Holocaust: the Lacanian cut as opposed to a Foucauldian will to power/knowledge, which cannot properly explain the obscene enjoyment that desire for "a" elicits. The cut needs to remain visible as the foundation of our desire for *objet a*, which is ferocious enough to find its signifier even in the Holocaust.

This book's transnational comparative film analysis creates a dialogue between global theory and local trauma to locate the subject of the Real and the Real body that the Lacanian cut creates. Applying the notion of the Lacanian body to analysis of transnational horror films, for example, allows us to see the abject body in these films as representations of the universal Real body of jouissance that tears down the normative, linguistic body. When we attend to local trauma, we observe that jouissance has a public dimension. Through it, the Real body confronts the law of the sovereign power and its violent governmentality, which have a local historical context. In the following section, I use South Korea as a context within which we may interrogate the sovereign state's structure, which Giorgio Agamben describes as "the camp." In Agamben's "camp,"[27] the abject body of *homo sacer* appears as the limit figure between the law (prescribing life with civic rights) and the state of exception (describing the sphere where life exists without rights and thus can be killed with impunity). *Homo sacer* simultaneously belongs to the law and to the lawless sphere that functions to define the boundary of the law.

The bare life that *homo sacer* represents is forfeit to the law through governmentality's brutal exercise of power, which takes life and then bans it from the juridical sphere. *Homo sacer* is a lawless form of life in that it can be abandoned and killed with impunity. And yet, it is also taken by law, not only in the literal sense of being killed but also in being rendered precarious and disposable. For bare life, subjection to law is indistinguishable from dispossession of life.[28] Subjection to the law, for *homo sacer*, implies losing rights to civic and also natural life, as experienced by Jewish people under the Nazi regime. Despite this loss of civic rights, *homo sacer* remains integral to the law, since the politically meaningful life of the citizen, which the juridical system protects, can be defined only in relation to the lawlessness of bare life. Lawlessness itself is a positive, that is, constitutive, element of law. There is no way that this situation "leads us back to a space without law—and therefore without abandon and bare life—back to the *homo non sacer*."[29] With this statement, Anton Schütz argues that, as Kafka illustrates in "Before the Law," "the gate of the law is wide open."[30] Because our way of being is juridically defined and determined, and *homo sacer* is life designated as the integral part of law and governmentality underwritten by law, we are all *homines sacri*.[31] To the extent that a sovereign power exists that administers the body of *homo sacer*, all lives are subject to that administration. I will return to this point later in this chapter in relation to the Real body of abjection in the cinema of the Real.

Agamben, in his critique of modern sovereignty (in his book *Homo Sacer*), advocates for a politics that is liberated from law created and preserved by violence and for political action that "severs the nexus between violence and law."[32] In theorizing a new political subject in the form of a "whatever singularity," which defies pregiven identarian categories, Agamben says that "the coming politics [will be] a struggle between the State and the non-State (humanity), an insurmountable disjunction between *whatever singularity* and the State organization."[33]

Agamben's *whatever singularity* leaves space for particular articulations of human subjectivity. The Real body is one such articulation. In the sovereign nation-state, an Agambenian camp wherein all life exists as *homo sacer*, the *whatever singularity* figures as the subject of the Real that emerges within that camp, confronting law and its violent inscription of the state of exception, the lawlessness that undergirds law. I locate the possibility of emancipatory politics and the formation of the new subject, one that the law and norm of subject formation cannot contain, in the kernel that occupies the core of the subject of the Real that the Real body houses. The kernel, though within us, is more than ourselves, more than our linguistic and imaginary capacity. This kernel survives the encounter with the signifier or system of signification. It allows the subject to remain unsubsumed. The kernel is the Real of subjectivity that confronts the Symbolic order and allows the subject of the Real to escape subjection to the regime of signification, the method by which law determines and inscribes on our body, through governmentality, meaning itself. The cinema of the Real depicts the subject of the Real and its Real body.

The Real Body Rewriting the Sovereign Cartography

As a way to examine how the Real body exists in the space of the sovereign nation-state and how we may map its patterns of movement, I take a close look at South Korean auteur Lee Chang-dong's films *Poetry* and *Oasis*[34] and the way the Real body takes shape in these films. In the landscape of the Real where the Real body emerges, the viewers experience the shattering of their subjectivity. In these films, compromised bodies (in *Oasis*, Jong-du, a cognitively disabled man, and Gong-ju, a woman with cerebral palsy, who become lovers; and in *Poetry*, Mija, a woman who is facing looming dementia) figure as the primary registers of physical, emotional, and sexual ethoses and, more importantly, the sites of the political articulation of subjectivity. These bodies represent the Real body that reveals the kernel of being that enables the formulation of a new ethical subjectivity. Through this body, the ethics of feminine jouissance confronts the Symbolic order, which permeates the relationship between the subject and its Other. It is in this context that these films elucidate the universality of the Real body located in a local context.

Ethics must have a universal dimension.[35] The ethical subject position is unthinkable without allowing a place for the Other in ontological, social, and spatial organizations of existence. The Other appears from beyond the horizon of the Symbolic order, exceeding the pregiven way of looking, and transforms the subject's own mapping of all these organizations. Specifically, universality emerges "from a place of exclusion ... from the very place of deprivation and dispossession,"[36] which is the place of the marginal Other. According to Žižek and Badiou, as Mari Ruti references, "What is exiled from ... the symbolic order, the big Other, or the situation ... gives rise to the universal in its authentic sense."[37] Ruti continues by citing Žižek: "Universalist ethics would take as its starting point those who are 'part of no-part [of the Symbolic order, the big Other]' ... who are out of place in the social totality [that the Symbolic order and the big Other dictate and impose]."[38]

Oasis and *Poetry* show us this marginal Other, embodied by our lover and our neighbor, in their monstrosity. It is monstrous either because its feminine jouissance is too disturbing (*Oasis*) or because it demands us to exhume what lies buried and unheard in a deprived and dispossessed state at the margin (*Poetry*). In both films, the Real body appears as bare life. In *Oasis*, it is the disabled body that the patriarchal order seeks to subsume under law yet leaves susceptible to punishment and destruction. In *Poetry*, it is life that remains nondead even after it is destroyed.

To understand the local context of these films, it is useful to note that in a sovereign nation-state, shaped through the history of class- and gender-related trauma generated by the geopolitics of global capitalism, from imperialism to neoliberalism, oppressive social relationships emerge. For the nation-state to function within global capitalism, society requires a means of discipline by which social subjects are forced to conform to norms. Hence, the patriarchal gender order and neoliberal class order prevail in individual lives. In films that successfully reveal how history, which is to say, historical trauma, permeates the personal, the result is often formal cinematic innovation. These films move between the aesthetic regime of realism and cinematic elements that subvert that regime.

In *Oasis*, the lovers' hardship reveals the encrustation of historical trauma surrounding class and gender that is written on individual bodies. A woman with severe cerebral palsy is confined by her family in a gloomy apartment while they occupy the special subsidized housing meant for her. Her location allegorizes the entrapment of the feminine body in the sphere of ideology concerning gender and sexuality. The man who becomes her lover is a "lumpen-proletarian" whose cognitive disability puts him outside the boundary of a normative masculine position. His body is subjugated to the patriarchal sovereign state's violence: the system demands that his body represent *homo sacer* imprisoned in the camp of the nation-state, allegorized by incarceration for crimes of which he is innocent. The Otherness of their bodies represents something monstrous that exceeds the normative (i.e., linguistic) body. Their disability reveals the kernel of Otherness that the normative, linguistic body obscures from view. But the horror that these bodies elicit derives from more than their difference or monstrosity in relation to the bodies of normative civic subjects. They reveal that all the linguistic subjects that linguistic bodies represent, all of whom are at all times subject to the sovereign, are *homines sacri*, subject to the law and its violent exercise of a linguistic order that determines the rights and death of all life.

The sex act between two disabled social subjects depicted in *Oasis* is seen as monstrous by the relatives and neighbors who behold it. They react with shock and outrage and characterize it as the rape of a helpless paraplegic by an idiot; they call the police to the scene of copulation so that the lovers are brought to the law to reckon with the criminality of their desire. In this scene, society faces the jouissance of the Real body and, by criminalizing it, seeks to reinstate the law of phallic jouissance as a means of enforcing the proper way of desiring and the appropriate object of desire within the Symbolic order. The social apparatuses that the sovereign state defends seek to confine Jong-du and Gong-ju's bodies in a cartography of the body politic that upholds the middle-class myth of proper social subjectivity.

Gong-ju, the woman with cerebral palsy (played by an actress who does not have that condition), has a middle-class-aspiring brother. He abandons Gong-Ju after he and his pregnant wife use her disability to obtain tenancy in a well-appointed special housing unit for the disabled. She exists as the invisible monstrous body in exile. When Jong-du takes her out of the apartment, ushering her body into public space, she imagines a different way of being, with a capacity for action and voice. In a scene captured with handheld camera cinematography, we see her rise up from her seat on the subway to playfully hit Jong-du's head with an empty plastic water bottle, seemingly liberated from her condition. This is an act that expresses her feminine jouissance and defies the existential delimitations in which she exists only as the disabled body that cannot act or speak. The scene then returns to her paraplegic body writhing in the seat. This transition from the body that expresses her jouissance to her disabled body that comes to signify her gender-based unfreedom in this film occurs through the economy of editing we see in films of realism. Later in the film, we see her moving fluidly and singing a love song to Jong-du in a subway station, devoid of the usual flow of people, as if opening up an impossible space for her jouissance. In these eruptive scenes, there is no accompanying musical score—even the banal background noise is silenced—and they are rendered again in handheld cinematography and in one continuous take. Jong-du responds and listens to Gong-ju's singing, as if he hears the sound of feminine jouissance in this scene that superimposes its own law of jouissance on reality. In this mixing of the elements of realism and surrealism, the verisimilitude of realism is interrupted by the scene of feminine jouissance.

Jong-du has served a prison term for a vehicular manslaughter committed by his own older brother, a small business owner. Upon release, his brother houses him in a cramped room in the back of the garage, sequestered from his extended family. Both he and Gong-ju are the subalterns who cannot speak, subjects who do not have representation in a proper Symbolic order of gender and class. This status is mapped in the Agambenian camp that entails the invisible, lawless margin for the subaltern. The film renders their interior life in a sphere of magical realism that clashes with the film's overall realistic aesthetics, which more commonly depict gritty urban reality. It is as if the Real bodies of these characters crash through the formal boundary to reveal their monstrous desire, expressed through sexuality and their shared experience of trauma. Through the formal combination of realism and magical realism, the film allegorizes how national trauma that the patriarchal system cannot sublimate erupts through the Real body. In this case, the disabled body symptomatizes a communal trauma: the history of violent political regimes, including military dictatorship and the unsparing implementation of capitalism, which render all life that of *homines sacri*. The disabled body, in turn, threatens the national fantasy of the healthy body politic.

The Real body in the film, appearing through both realism and magical realism, rewrites the sovereign nation's cartography, where space opens up in which the disabled body is no longer confined by the spatial constriction that sovereign cartography imposes upon it: In a dilapidated slum apartment, Gong-ju breaks a mirror and butterflies burst forth from the shards. In the middle of highway traffic jam, Jong-du gets out of a car, carrying Gong-ju, then dances with Gong-ju in his arm to a Rolling Stones tune playing on a car stereo, flooding the space with their own jouissance. As in the aforementioned subway scene, the materiality of space itself changes as Gong-ju and Jong-du's jouissance overwhelms it. In Gong-ju's cramped bedroom, a surreal scene is staged wherein an elephant marches through and an Asian Indian woman and her children dance around Jong-du and Gong-ju; their appearance brings about changes in lighting and mise-en-scène, as if an unknowable jouissance of the neighbor is merging with their own subjectivity.

Finally, Jong-du escapes from jail after having been arrested for a fabricated charge of raping Gong-ju, only so that he can climb a tree outside her window and saw off the branches that cast shadows on her bedroom wall that Jong-du knows she finds frightening. This scene maintains a delicate balance between realism and magical realism. The scene opens with Gong-ju lying in the dark at night facing the foreground. Then the viewer sees the large shadows of the branches behind her shaking as the limbs are sawed off, accompanied by the sound of the handsaw cutting them. The shadows of the branches loom over Gong-ju and shake rhythmically, resembling a shadow play projected on the dingy wall of a cramped apartment in an abstract and surreal manner. The scenes that follow include Gong-ju turning up the radio volume high with great effort so the sound of a pop song playing on it resonates in the entire alleyway of her cramped and dilapidated working-class neighborhood, and Jong-du, standing on a tree limb with the police squad surrounding him below, dancing to the tune. In this mixing of the realism and surrealism that pervades this film, we watch Jong-du and Gong-ju reconfiguring the landscape and grids that confine them. It is worth noting that the film does not place these characters in the sweeping open space to laud the reconfiguration of the landscape through jouissance. At no point in the film are characters shot in a frame that depicts openness of space, even in Seoul, one of the largest metropolises in the world. The film chooses to show the cartographic transformation while these characters are materially situated in the underbelly of an advanced capitalist society. This way, the film emphasizes that an ethical act that Jong-du undertakes, transforming the cartography of Gong-ju's existence, emerges under the crushing weight of the oppressive human condition in which both the subject and its Other are tethered. This act exemplifies the way the subject of the Real responds to the call of the Other to change the linguistic shaping of social space in the sovereign state. *Homo sacer* confronts the camp's boundary, the law, and by transgressing that boundary disengages the violent inscription of the law from social space it normally occupies. Likewise, through the movement of the Real body, we create the space of the Real that the Symbolic order cannot contain in its spatial arrangement.

In *Poetry*, Mija is an elderly home caregiver and housekeeper whose charge is an elderly man with debilitating paralysis. Mija is herself in the early stages of dementia. While gradually losing her grip on language, she struggles to write poetry for the first time in her life. Mija knows that as her condition worsens, she will continue to lose not only words but also the most familiar and socially acceptable modes of propriety and the confidence of purposeful gestures and actions. In this setting, she discovers that her teenage grandson, whom she is raising alone, participated in the gang rape of a young girl. The girl's drowned body is discovered in the opening scene, in the river into which she has thrown herself. Mija is obliged to pay a portion of the compensation money to the dead girl's mother. The parents of other boys who participated in the assault, the school principal, and even a local reporter see this as the only rational choice to protect the boys from any further repercussions for their actions. Mija meets the obligation by blackmailing the man in her care, threatening to file a complaint for a sexual advance he had previously made. But she also mourns the dead girl; the film takes some time to show us the depth and desperation of her mourning. The film implies, through ellipses, that she ultimately leads a policeman to arrest her grandson. The poem that she leaves behind, with the implication that she has thrown herself into the same river, is a conversation between herself and the dead girl, Agnes.

In the final sequence, we hear Mija's disembodied recitation of her poem, in which Agnes is given voice to describe her suffering: the voice that narrates the poem segues from Mija's to the girl's and then to that of Agnes alone, opening up the space of existence for the girl, which is unthinkable in the patriarchal society depicted in the film. Finally, we see Agnes, standing on the bridge where she threw herself into the river below, turn to look directly at us, a faint smile on her lips. In this closing scene, the voices of two dead women are the point of emergence of the Real, something that we can not see and yet founds these women's new subjectivity: the extraordinary form of life that crosses from death to life, into the Real. Agnes's face supplements the voices as evidence of that transformation. Through their voices, Mija survives the loss of logos, and Agnes survives the material destruction of sexual violence. More importantly, together they enter the field of the Real of feminine subjectivity, jouissance of the undead.

The film opens and ends with the same river. In the opening, we see a child silently watching a floating object like a stain in the bucolic rural landscape. We then cut to a shot that affords a closer look at what is revealed to be the corpse of a young girl in her middle-school uniform. In the closing scene, following the shot of Agnes's gaze, we watch the torrents of river water, their overwhelming force rendered by the rising crescendo of their sound. The image of the water then fades to black; the sound continues through the ending title. Ultimately, the river no longer affords the same cartographical point of patriarchal violence. Mija has rewritten the meaning of the river, has changed the river from a site of biological death to a scene of the emerging ethical subject from the margin, both in the form of Mija, who answers the call of the traumatic Real, and of the girl. This girl, having thus attained a voice, now confronts us with a call to occupy an ethical position.

For Badiou, ethics has nothing to do with acknowledging the victimhood of the Other.[39] The ethical subject is immortal because the ethical subject can transcend the limitations imposed on what Badiou calls the "human animal," which is enslaved by its particularities of biological and social life within a given situation. This subject sees immortality of the Other. Mija's voice is the sound of the Real that ruptures the law of patriarchal society through a new signifier of the desire, her poem. Seeing the Other as immortal, her poem is a new signifier that creates a new time and space in which the dead girl, transcending the confines of the patriarchal signifier of femininity as the location of victimhood, comes to embody the immortal ethical subject. The film refrains from making any facile connection between Mija's personal history and the dead girl's trauma, and thus does not delimit Mija's action as personally motivated empathy. Mija answers the call to formulate an ethical position in relation to a stranger who, like Jacques Derrida's *arrivant*,[40] is out of our personal context yet demands our ethical response even while undoing our established mode of organic and psychical being. The river becomes a point that disrupts the preexisting cartography in which subjects' psychic and social positions are ordained. Mija's body, losing its linguistic meaning through her loss of words to dementia, which in turn signifies the loss of the linguistic body that guarantees the position of the subject in the Symbolic order, is the Real body. The dead girl returns through Mija's voice, and her poem is a manifesto affirming that ethics must always include the invisible and nameless Other. Thus, she embodies the Real, a point on a new ethical map of intersubjectivity. The river is the field of the Real that disrupts the sovereign cartography of the patriarchal system in which the girl was drowned.

Other films hint at what might lie beyond the horizon of the patriarchal nation-state and yet are unable to draw the field of the Real against the grid of that cartography. Consider Alice Rohrwacher's *Corpo celeste*[41] and *Happy as Lazzaro*.[42] In the former, the wind and the river mark points of disruption of the process that seeks to inscribe the Symbolic order upon an adolescent girl's body in the form of Catholic confirmation. In a moment of magical realism, a sudden gale rises around her. In another, she wades into the river, soiling her pristine white confirmation dress. These moments signify a momentary unmooring of the subject, who teeters between the boundaries of the Symbolic and the Real, which is signified by the magical wind and the water that alter her appearance. But rather than announcing the emergence of the subject of the Real, they serve only to give substance to her sense of entrapment and her desire to escape her properly assigned place in the map of religion, family, and community. The appearances of magical objects, the wind and the water, are visual devices that show momentary disturbances of the subject's movement in the sovereign map. The magical eruptions of natural objects appear briefly, only to be sutured back to the Symbolic order before they can usher in any destructive effect of the Real. We are left with a young woman who remains ambivalent in relation to the patriarchal monotheistic system. She is anchored in a reality that is only slightly disturbed by uncanny objects. The film is missing an image or a gesture that shows what it looks and sounds like to be the emerging Real subject. This absence signals the film's inability to suggest what lies beyond the cartographical horizon of the patriarchal monotheistic system: an ethical subject of the Real, the subject of feminine jouissance.

In *Happy as Lazzaro*, we also encounter a mysteriously rising wind that seems to convey the Real of subjects tethered to an exploitive social order, allegorized by the system of quasi-feudal serfdom under which they toil. The exploited tobacco farmers can neither speak nor rebel and have no agency to reconfigure their subjecthood: their lives are defined by the book of debt, impossible to repay to the big Other, who is represented by the landlord. What escapes the Symbolic order of the oppressive social regime finds its expression in the mythic winds that the farmers seem able to conjure. Furthermore, the landscape itself becomes a place of mythic rebirth into the divine subject of the main character, Lazzaro. After falling into a ravine, apparently to his death, he reemerges decades later in the same shape and form, shadowed by a mythic wolf. Neither he nor the farmers, however, are emancipated from their condition of serfdom. Their position is limited to that of a mythic Otherness that is tied to the Symbolic order, in which they remain unable to transgress the map that the system has defined. This limitation is made clear by the film; it does not push the oppressed peoples' filmic presence as the disruptive stain on the landscape that transforms the landscape into a point of eruption where an ethical formulation of subjectivity as subjects of the Real becomes possible. The film maintains the phantasmatic tone throughout, but it remains just a tonality, and as such it does not contain images or sounds of jouissance that drive characters to the brink of the Symbolic. When they move from the rural setting to contemporary urban confines, they fail to disrupt the rubric of either place, just like the mythic wind that appears and disappears without ever becoming a destructive force unleashed onto rural grids. Lazzaro, with all his mythic qualities that defy the laws of nature and society, drops dead as he tries to rescue his neighbor from a financial predicament. Both films lack the disruptive force of Lee Chang-dong's river and sawed-off tree. These films do not transform the disruptions of the elements of magical realism into formal disruptions through which the Real subject emerges. Hence, the apparent impossibility of the Real body, as those filmic bodies are simply the Othered body within the Symbolic order. In the following sections, I continue to explore the Real body in the South Korean horror film *Thirst* and the Chinese realist film *Still Life*, using the concept of the Real body, both in terms of form (across and beyond genres) and of transnationality.

The Abject Real Body and the Nation-State

In 2018, South Korea felt the first tremors of allegations of sexual assault and misconduct perpetrated by notable, powerful men. Among the most egregious offenders is Kim Ki-duk, one of the most globally recognized South Korean auteurs. Kim has won top awards at Cannes, Venice, and Berlin and remains the only Korean filmmaker to have done so. His victims report that he has sexually assaulted female actors and staff over a span of years, a campaign of terror that has caused some women to abandon their acting careers. His films, however, actually allow for a critique of his own actions and of the local context of sexual violence from which his actions derive.

Kim's films often dare to confront the obscene underside of modern South Korea's bourgeois society, that is, its violent patriarchal foundation. Kim creates female characters who confront the Law of the Father in pursuit of their own ethical principles and imperatives. Female characters in Kim's films, such as those in *The Isle*[43] and *Pietà*,[44] choose to occupy the "no-man's-land" outside the Symbolic order that binds the patriarchal nation. They do so despite understanding that this entails not only what Lacan calls the "second death," that is, the loss of the comforts and protections that the Symbolic order provides,[45] but also the likely destruction of their biological bodies. In the second death, however, biological death is not the focus. It primarily references the symbolic death that places the subject in the Real.

I have mentioned that while the Symbolic order constructs reality, the Real remains invisible. Like the fingerprint that confronted my student when he opened his new iPhone to rupture the fabricated "reality" of capitalism, female characters in Kim's films figure as subjects of the Real who disrupt the smooth surface of the Symbolic order of patriarchy. They superimpose their own ethical position onto it and define their relationship to the Other on ethical principles other than those that the law of the patriarchal nation prescribes. What may be construed as universal emerges from the feminine subject's being "part of no-part," being out of place in the social totality that the Symbolic order and the big Other dictate and impose. Films like *The Isle* and *Pietà* examine how those at the margins of bourgeois social totality might enter an ethical relationship with one another and how the subject of feminine jouissance strives to shape that relationship.

In *The Isle*, the central character, unnamed and mute (the film never explains whether her silence is due to a disability or by her choice), has no clear social identity. She ekes out a living by managing a collection of floating piers scattered around a lake where men come ostensibly to go fishing but mainly to hire prostitutes. The woman pilots a boat to bring provisions and prostitutes to these floating cabins. The floating pier community replicates a larger social relationship that serves as a space of obscene phallic jouissance that commodifies and humiliates the feminine body. The location is, just like all the characters, unnamable yet familiar enough to be nearly any specific locality of South Korea. Hence, we can see the film as a national allegory that reveals gender as central to intersubjective conflicts. When the woman confronts the phallic desire of a man she encounters, she expresses how its violence mutilates the feminine subject by inserting fishhooks into her vagina, thus mutilating the most prized phallic object of desire located in a woman's body. The film uses a sparse soundtrack. There is no dialogue in the bloody scene of mutilation. The scene is rendered through the economy of realism, in this case offering no escape to the viewer, who must face the gaze of the mutilated feminine body, revealing to us that there is nothing but the wounded flesh behind the veil of feminine mystique.

The film silently concludes how feminine jouissance has recreated the world. The final scene radically departs from the film's established realist aesthetics. A naked man slowly swims up to an island and disappears into a forest. The camera zooms out to a bird's-eye view to reveal that the forest into which the man disappears is a woman's pubic hair and the island, her body. This is the male subject of desire pursuing phallic jouissance and reckoning with feminine jouissance, which swallows its ground and transforms it into a territory where he must face its abyss. The floating pier and the lake serve as a metaphoric stand-in for the material space where that desire unfolds.

In *Pietà*, a mother, bereaved of her son, rewrites the law into a social space where his killer must enact universal ethics, which leads him to sacrifice himself, not just for the sake of fulfilling the mother's revenge but for all lives that have not been freed from desire within the Symbolic order where scenes of desire are staged. The universal nature of that sacrifice is not conveyed through narrative or plot but rather through the image of gruesome destruction of the male body as the vessel and reservoir of desire. The killer secretly ties himself to the underside of a truck driven by one of the women he brutalized. As the truck drives off, we see shots of the killer's face, calm with the conviction that this self-sacrifice is an ethical act, and of the trail of blood his disintegrating body leaves behind. The musical score in this long sequence of destruction—an imaginary detour from the horror of self-mutilation—casts it as something sacred, but the red trail of blood and flesh that follows the movement of the vehicle as it traverses the landscape works as a point from which the gaze emanates. Beholding the national space, striped with this stain, unsettles our sense of intimate belonging to that familiar space.

Kim's films represent the destruction of middle-class social mores through inserting the Real body that cannot be assimilated into the bourgeois purview of the Symbolic and Imaginary contour of human subjects, often through violent imagery. This has made Kim unpopular among the most avid guardians of those social norms: the bourgeois itself, including many feminists, many of whom are deeply invested in liberal values. However, it is possible to read his films as feminist texts that open up a critical space for analysis of the violence done to the feminine body by the patriarchal nation.[46] It is a brutal irony, then, that the filmmaker himself has staged his own theater of cruelty on the very film sets where he, in depicting the gendered, sexualized violence that the hypermasculine patriarchal nation imposes upon the feminine body, forces open the space of critical treatment of that violence. The film set, in this context, becomes a space where the feminine subject is thoroughly objectified and rendered abject. It is a scene of obscene enjoyment, in which Kim plays the role of progenitor and sovereign masculine subject, and his female staff and actors play the abject feminine.

Agamben's camp, as the space where the sovereign power of the nation-state inscribes itself in the body politic,[47] is again relevant here. It is a space, defined by the nation-state, within which the normal functioning of the law is suspended or altered to allow this violent, defining inscription to happen without disturbing those whom the law is intended to benefit. The sovereign, that is to say, the state or capitalist entity, holds the bio-power to strip life within the camp of rights and take away the political meaning of life, as an element that endows the subject with self-consciousness that the proper citizen of the nation-state enjoys. The abject subject embodies this bare life. Kim's sexual violence has a performative dimension, in that he impersonates the bio-power of the patriarchal nation. The bare life of the abject body appears along gender lines in response to the powerful looking of the sovereign figure, in this case ironically coinciding with that of the maker of films that interrogate, and even condemn, the abuse of such power.

Abjection, however, does not just refer to life that is the simple object of the sovereign's looking. An example of this simplicity is in the Foucauldian "medical gaze" that "sees death everywhere immanent in life."[48] For Foucault, death is a means to subject life to sovereign power, because "[to] the extent that life becomes defined by death, is permeated by death, it becomes permeated by power."[49] At this juncture, Joan Copjec draws our attention to Lacan's notion of second death, which goes beyond the Foucauldian power's death grip that permeates life. I have discussed the second death in chapter 1, and here I suggest that we recognize the connection between that concept and abjection. Lacan's reading of Antigone[50] allows us to see how the symbolic death that the subject of abjection undergoes reframes abjection as a possible means of subversion. Antigone's tomb does not merely enclose her corpse; it also becomes the locus where the subject of the Real breaks down the law of the state.

To see the emancipatory possibility inherent in the position of the abject, I return to my earlier suggestion of combining critical frameworks: that of the bare life that emphasizes physical injury, with Agamben's camp as the locus for that violence, and Julia Kristeva's notion of emancipation through abjection. Looking at them through Lacan's notion of symbolic death, we arrive at the abject body as the body that undergoes a symbolic death in order to open up the Real and subvert the sovereign power, whether it be the power of the nation-state or of a social organization, such as capitalism, that overdetermines subjectivity.

The feminine body on Kim Ki-duk's film set, like the female characters in his movies, is a metaphor for the abject body imprisoned in the camp. The abject, imprisoned, physical form is that of *homo sacer*, a being whose life may be taken by sovereign power with impunity. Because it is always in the grip of the power of the patriarchal system, the abject body of *homo sacer* is available to be punished and injured by the law, or those the law designates as proper social subjects, at will. The abject body is excluded from juridical thinking and practice, which exist to protect the civic body of the nation-state and its subjects. However, because the difference between *homo sacer* and the proper national subject marks the contour of the sovereign nation-state, the abject body also delineates the limit of the nation-state and, thus, is never outside its national, geographic, and ideological boundaries. The camp is a spatial organization within the nation-state of this paradoxical coexistence of juridical and extra-juridical spheres of being. Bare life, designating *homo sacer*, is banned from the juridical space because it lacks civic and political rights.[51] As such, it can be sequestered, imprisoned, even killed, but not with the goal of destroying it utterly. The juridical order needs bare life to delineate and clarify the limit of law. It defines itself against the body that carries bare life. What emerges is the contour of the civic and politically meaningful body. The women on Kim's film sets, though not exemplars of bare life that can be killed with impunity, demonstrate the limits of women's full recognition as civic subjects who are protected by the law. These limitations are, however, not themselves confined within the camp, as the body of *homo sacer* is more widely required by society to fulfill the purpose of providing definition, by way of contrast, of the proper subject. Recognizing this power relationship, we arrive at the conclusion that we are all, as national subjects, *homines sacri*.[52] The national subject's body is the surface upon which sovereign power writes itself.

Similarly, the prisoners who were held in Nazi concentration camps in World War II were, though confined within a space where the regular juridical order was suspended, never outside the physical and conceptual boundaries of the German nation-state. Their meaning spread beyond the camp that housed them. As Agamben makes clear, as long as there is a mapping of the extermination camps, denoting an exception to the national civic body, that national civic body itself remains part of the nation-state's construction of the camp. Power is permitted to intervene without any reservation inside the camp even as the biopolitical borders demarcate the line of the politically meaningful life of the citizens and their identitarian properties. Thus, the biopolitics inscribed on bodies in German prison camps in World War II also defined the German body. The blueprint of the biopolitics of the camp overlaps with the space of the nation-state. The underlying implication is that if sovereign power can destroy, for example, a Jewish body, the same technology can be carried out upon the German body. This is Agamben's general position: if the Jewish body is *homo sacer* as such, then the German body is also *homo sacer*, the body upon which sovereign power inscribes itself. It is, as Agamben states, the situation where "organisms belong to the public power: the body is nationalized."[53]

This boundary thinking regarding the civic body and that of *homo sacer* creates a cartography of the sovereign nation-state that maps out the locations of both the proper civic body and the abject body that houses bare life. We imagine our place within the nation-state through this cognitive mapping. We know where we are and how to behave in the spaces we inhabit. Lacan's position that the body *is* language rings true here. The space of the nation-state is conveniently organized around the ideals of, for example, modern capitalism and supported by the social, political, judicial, and linguistic apparatuses that sustain life within it. Proper gendered and sexual subjects, that is, linguistic subjects, also occupy this space as national subjects. In analyzing this mapping, we can also locate the space that Agamben describes as coinciding "neither with any of the homogeneous national territories nor with their topographical sum, but would rather act on them by articulating and perforating them *topologically* as in the Klein bottle or in the Möbius strip, where exterior and interior in-determine each other."[54] Here Agamben is conceptualizing an extraterritoriality that counters a strictly cartographical delimitation of the modern nation-state.

I posit that although the sovereign nation-state includes space that can be understood as the Agambenian camp, extraterritoriality is structurally inherent in the cartography of the nation-state and that the abject body that emerges within it holds the possibility of emancipation. *Thirst*, directed by Park Chan-wook, and *Still Life*, directed by Jia Zhangke, problematize the boundaries of the proper nation-state and its Symbolic order through the abject bodies that open up extraterritoriality within those boundaries. I compare these films to explore how comparable social subjects, particularly subjects of abjection, might find filmic expressions across different film forms and nationalities. The abject bodies of these subjects are the Real of the sovereign states that forcefully impose extraterritoriality, the sphere of the Real body, upon sovereign cartographies. Although it is beyond the scope of this book, we can further explore such comparisons as a way to articulate a new regional paradigm of cultural critique, in line with the transnational critique I have outlined. In light of this, Naoki Sakai and I both propose the establishment of trans-Pacific studies as a new discipline, one that can overcome the institutional limitations and biases of ethnic and area studies in US academia. We envision this new discipline as a source of new paradigms that address modernity, nation, and subjectivity in the historical and social contexts that comprise East Asia.[55] Such comparative thinking would keep the contradictions that emerge across the region central to academic and analytic focus, as the region participates in shared geopolitical and geocultural realities.

Abject physical forms of the Real body appear in both *Thirst* and *Still Life*, though in very different ways. In *Thirst*, as I will elaborate later, it is through the graphic disintegration of the bodies of vampires. In *Still Life*, abjection is expressed more obliquely, through an elliptical depiction of the uprooted lives of those displaced by the Three Gorges Dam project, China's paradigmatic modernization project. Although this film does not show abjection through the spectacle of violence meted out by the nation-state on the human subjects' bodies, as we observe in a close reading of the film, it uses images that unsettle its own sense of realism as the tenor of its cinematic aesthetics. While *Thirst*'s abjection pivots around the feminine body, in *Still Life*, the landscape in ruin itself represents the abject body that reveals the Real of the nation-state. In *Still Life*, the territorial nation-state rewrites the cognitive map of the displaced people at the margin of state capitalism on the ruins of the habitus, rendering the body politic abject by violently altering its temporal and spatial coordinates via the modern nation's time-space organization.

The experience of modernity literally and figuratively demolishes all signs and sites of the premodern, prior to the modernity that state-sponsored capitalism constructs. In one scene, the film depicts the traumatic impact of that destruction in muted images of people, weeping as they watch the destruction of their habitus right before their eyes, on a TV screen placed sideways in relation to the film viewers and appearing at the corner of the film frame. Migrant workers, who are mobilized to carry out that very destruction, are together silently watching this image within an image in their dilapidated rooming house. These images present an oblique look at abjection as if it's something that we, the film audience, do not have direct cognitive and emotional access to. Although *Still Life* got a national theatrical release, a number of Jia Zhangke's films are either banned in China or do not get shown to the wider national audience. As a global auteur whose films are celebrated in prestigious international film festivals, Jia through his work interpellates the global audience into facing local trauma. We can assume that the way Jia visualizes the local trauma in *Still Life* reveals the filmmaker's awareness that those who cannot face the image of abjection are indeed those who are safely away from the kind of destruction that the film depicts. We sense the effect of abjection obliquely again in, for example, the form of an unnamed young boy who has no distinct place in the narrative and no secure place in the nation's cartography but appears twice in the film. First, he slips into the common room of a migrant workers' dilapidated boardinghouse, his skeletal frame clad in only his underpants. And as the main character, a migrant worker named San-ming, sits watching silently, the boy takes a cigarette out of a pack that happens to be lying around, lights it, and exits smoking. Next we see him sitting on a boat full of migrants crossing the Yangtze River, belting out a popular love song with prepubescent eagerness. It is as if he breaks into the narrative only to draw our attention to the lacuna that the unrepresentable trauma of modernity leaves behind. Because there's no proper language to describe it, it will erupt in an unexpected place and form: the abjection we observe in the boy's crisscrossing of marginal social space. I will return to this film later in the chapter. Now, I turn to *Thirst* and its depiction of the visceral expression of traumatic abjection that the Real body signifies.

Monstrosity of the Real Abject Feminine

In *Thirst*, two vampires overwrite the grids of the modern sovereign nation-state with bodies in the thrall of jouissance that those grids cannot contain. Sang-hyun, a priest, becomes a vampire through the transfusion of tainted blood after contracting a painful, fatal disease. The priest acquired the disease while subjecting himself to a medical experiment, which he has done because he chooses a medically rendered corporeal salvation of mankind over the church's symbolic salvation. The gradual destruction of his body by the virus is almost a visual match for his prayer litany, written by the filmmaker himself, which expresses a longing for his utter physical mutilation and destruction, a wish to lose his body limb by limb and organ by organ. In this prayer, the body itself holds an "a," an elusive object of desire. It seems that the prayer conveys the desire to tear the body apart in order to get at what it is believed to be hiding, the kernel underlying carnality. At the same time, it is possible to see that this prayer ironically longs to install the body in the Symbolic order. For this Catholic priest, the body is an "a" itself, an object that holds the promise of the patriarchal monotheistic system. The wholesome body, which he idealizes when he submits himself to the medical experiment that will presumably cure the ills of humanity, is the premise for rendering the body as a vessel to be broken into pieces only to reveal its sublime essence as the ideological object of the patriarchal monotheistic system. As such, its symbolic meaning (the faithful) survives biological destruction like that of martyrdom. Therefore, we can see the body represented in his prayer as the linguistic body.

As the vampire blood from the transfusion resurrects him from the death caused by the viral infection, the priest's body becomes the Real body, the undead body that can no longer be torn apart limb by limb, because the limbs and body parts will regenerate. As such, the body cannot uphold the Symbolic meaning to be written on the body, limb by limb, which the patriarchal monotheism promises. The body is no longer a signifier of linguistic meaning that supports the system. And the priest occupies an ambivalent place of jouissance: his own Real body places him on the path toward feminine jouissance, yet his desire for self-destruction implies that he upholds phallic jouissance in the patriarchal monotheism that the church embodies. The repetition of the prayer throughout the film spans the priest's different incarnations (the healthy priest, the infected body, the vampire) and serves simultaneously as the assertion, and destruction, of the linguistic body. It requires a feminine subject to usher feminine jouissance into this film.

Tae-ju, his "chosen one," is an orphan. She grew up to become a good wife and daughter-in-law but stages a mock escape every night by running barefoot through the neighborhood. Once the priest turns her into a vampire, she flies across the cityscape with an exhilarating sense of freedom and agency. The same abjection that relegates her to a marginal space within the sovereign cartography also carries with it the means for subversion and thus the possibility of emancipation. In Kristeva's terms, the abject body crisscrosses the borders between the safety of the orderly system and its monstrous other side. Abjection "as a source of horror," according to Barbara Creed, "works within patriarchal societies, as a means of separating the human from the nonhuman and the fully constituted subject from the partially formed subject."[56] The abject destabilizes all the boundaries and borders that bind the system and thus disturbs, as noted by Creed, "identity, system, order,"[57] and ultimately reveals that these categories cannot be successfully contained.

The abject, thus, becomes identified with the monstrous origin of horror and vice versa. It represents the nonhuman, the partially formed, as opposed to the fully formed civic body of the rightful human. We can likewise connect the abject more directly to feminine jouissance. Feminine jouissance does not refer to the biological or sexual satisfaction of the feminine subject. As noted, feminine jouissance is the manner in which the subject positions itself in relation to the master-signifier in the patriarchal Symbolic order (i.e., the phallic signifier) and the mode of enjoyment that the patriarchal Symbolic order enforces (i.e., phallic jouissance).[58] In *Thirst*, Tae-ju embodies feminine jouissance, not simply because she is identifiably a woman but because of her relationship to the phallic signifier. Her abjection and monstrosity pave the way for the monstrous enjoyment of feminine jouissance. It is monstrous because it collides with the patriarchal principles that aim to imprison the feminine body within the norms that dictate gender identity. Therein lies the possibility of emancipation.

Copjec argues that Antigone's choice to walk into the tomb demonstrates the act of transformation. Through this transformation, the ethical subject prevails against the law of the state, which draws boundary lines dictated by the Law of the Father.[59] Antigone inaugurates her own law against the law of the state. Tae-ju, though longing for emancipation from the suffocating law of the patriarchal family, is able to run barefoot only in the middle of the night and must return in the morning, until she is emancipated through the monstrous transformation of abjection. Her ruthless pursuit of blood is an expression of that radical transformation. She desires freedom; she reaches the limit of that desire within the family law and must therefore transform from human to monster to transcend that limit. Her hardened feet, calloused by her nightly perambulations, testify to her bondage. After her transformation, the healthy sheen of the renewed skin on the soles of her feet is the embodied evidence of her liberation. The fact that her monstrosity is enigmatically combined with increased pulchritude, as opposed to a more conventional physical monstrosity, shows that her transformation extends beyond her newfound prowess. The priest's agony over her bloodlust (and his own) shows that he, never having been so thoroughly excluded from the Law of the Father, never achieves full abjection and, thus, is never fully emancipated.

However, for a more comprehensive reading of this film, it is worth noting that in the end all jouissance is paltry; there is no such thing as complete and full enjoyment.[60] Although it might seem that, freed from conventional notions of morality, her jouissance is without hindrance, Tae-ju continues to suffer. The sun is always just below the horizon, threatening to destroy her. The pleasure she takes in killing never satisfies her perpetual thirst for blood. The priest, by contrast, is always plagued by ethical misgivings. This leads his character to try to avoid actually killing people. In an unexpectedly comedic turn, the priest tries to concoct schemes to obtain blood that clash less harmfully with the Symbolic order that promotes healthy life encased in the intact body. As a priest, the character Sang-hyun understands that enjoyment is paltry and pleasure is inadequate. As a monster, Sang-hyun must succumb to the pressures placed upon him by his desire for a precious object, namely, blood. The film shows this character's ambivalence about his own enjoyment through occasional deadpan comic delivery. It is as if the pressure of abjection bursts the seams of the horror genre.

The recognition that all jouissance is paltry has an important political implication. It reinforces Agamben's advocacy for a politics that is emancipated from law created and preserved by violence. Emancipation from law-making and law-preserving violence is an ongoing process that cannot occur in a singular, messianic event. This critique of violence draws from Walter Benjamin's differentiation of mythic (law-making) violence and divine violence that breaks down the law.[61] Divine violence might have a messianic undertone, but it is important to envision divine violence as that which creates revolutionary processes as neither static nor crystalized into administrative forms of realpolitik. Divine violence unleashes paltry jouissance that must keep rebinding itself without dwelling in a static form or structure. This impulse to "keep going" that constitutes our life drive leads to what I call the *emancipatory drive* of the subject of the Real—a concept I first elaborate in the introductory chapter—one that never settles upon a singular law of desire that announces the messianic end of social, historical contradictions around lack. We can remain on the trajectory of the emancipatory drive as we continue to move from one trajectory of desiring to a new articulation of desire, to continue that transformation of desire to emancipate ourselves from the given situation that dictates a singular form of desire.

Thirst struggles with paltry jouissance's political possibilities and limitations. In the next section, I will return to these limitations. Now, I will explore the possibilities. In this film, social and domestic space undergo the formal rendition of the field of the Real. Tae-ju's family home exemplifies this space. As often happens in Park's films, interior and private space create a sense of claustrophobia. This house, owned by her mother-in-law, is covered with darkly garish wallpapers and fabrics, and clusters of household objects crowd the tight colonial-style quarters. The incessant sound of old-fashioned, Japanese-style popular songs, with their arduous and banal melodies, drowns the entire space. Tae-ju's sense of imprisonment is heightened by these mundane devices that are ubiquitous in her daily life. Once she commandeers the locale by orchestrating her husband's murder, slaughtering unsuspecting guests, and taking her incapacitated mother-in-law hostage, she paints the entire interior of the house white. It becomes the space of feminine jouissance that no living being can escape. The destruction of the body in this house equates to destruction of the Symbolic order by the feminine subject of jouissance. Yet feminine jouissance has no place in society. Hence, the manner in which the film describes her destruction in the end. I will return to this point shortly.

We have established that the origin of enjoyment is the wounding that we undergo in the process of becoming a speaking subject as the result of signification. Our relationship to and experience of the world is mediated by language—the system of signification—through which we also develop the sense that we have lost our direct relationship to the Thing-in-itself. Although it is an impossible object that is never obtainable, and thus is the cause of our desire, this sense of having lost the Thing-in-itself constitutes our wounding lack. Enjoyment diverges into either the pleasure one can obtain within the Symbolic order through the phallic signifier or jouissance in pursuit of the Real where the phallic signifier signifies nothing. When we become speaking subjects, we enter the prison cell of signifiers. Therein, the wounding propels us to locate a proper object that we fantasize exists to heal the wound. Thus, the wounding allows a speaking subject to nominate their own object of desire attached to the phallic signifier. In doing so, we sublimate an ordinary object into the object that we fantasize completes us, healing our originary wound. This sets the stage for our experience of perpetual loss but also of the sense of community, of spiritual belonging, or of national identity through modernization. Nationalism, even fanaticism, has elements of this psychic process, although their phenomenal manifestations are historically determined. So does the sexuation process, in which we are forced to abandon desires that are not appropriate in the patriarchal order. It is in this sense that we understand jouissance as the pursuit of a thing that we believe will heal that wound. This wound indicates the cut that separates us from what we believe we once had, namely, originary plentitude. Bruce Fink is one theorist who recognizes that we respond to the sense of loss that results from wounding—our realization of what we don't have—by choosing one of the two different forms of jouissance: phallic and feminine. And each includes our furtive, unspoken understanding that the Symbolic order will not be able to provide an authentic healing.[62] The big Other holds no object of desire, only the promise of its ability to deliver.

As established, phallic jouissance is derived from belief in a phallic signifier, an object that we believe can satisfy our most aching desires. The subject of phallic jouissance fantasizes that it can obtain the very singular object of desire and thus put an end to the perpetual longing left by the wound received upon entering the Symbolic order. The wizard of Oz can produce the one thing needed to make you complete. Mr. Wonka will hand you the candy that never gets any smaller no matter how long you suck on it. Within this fantasy, the subject of desire always gets what he wants; the hero arrives at his goal every time. Capitalist modernity promises this path, with cyber consumerism as a perfect manifestation of phallic enjoyment. It creates a new experience of time and space by shrinking the temporal and spatial barriers between the subject and its object of desire. El Dorado is perpetually here and now.

For an example of how this economy of desire plays out, I return to a scene from *Still Life*, specifically the one in which local thugs stage a show for migrant workers disembarking from a boat on the Yangtze River. They present a sleight of hand: A charlatan turns Chinese renminbi into a US dollar, instantly fulfilling a promise to "make" money in a parody of modern capitalism's promise to deliver. Next, the thugs search San-ming's (the main character's) bag to extract payment for having demonstrated the money-making trick. There is nothing in the bag except a few limp articles of clothing. In the next scene, we see him producing, from that very bag, a bottle of rice wine and other objects that he intends to use to obtain what he desires, namely, his long-lost wife, a quest in which he fails. This scene of clandestine desire introduces a crack in the film's realism and a point of fissure in physical space. Later, I examine how fissures like this throughout the film rewrite the sovereign cartography, the field of the construction of the modern capitalist nation. In this cartography, which maps national and capitalist desire, the two central characters, the miner San-ming and the nurse Shen Hong, always turn up empty. After an arduous pursuit of the objects of their desire—the restoration of their lost spouses and, by extension, a restoration of their presumed place within the Symbolic order—they go back to their hometowns without regaining what they have lost. Their desire is unfulfilled, and therefore, still felt. In the landscape of loss, the subject of lack embodies feminine jouissance, written over the desire of the nation, propelling the building of a new landscape.

Feminine jouissance recognizes that all objects of desire will fail to provide relief from wounding and loss. The subject of feminine jouissance accepts that all objects only affirm a fundamental lack that cannot be mended because objects are always a metonymic displacement of the thing itself, which doesn't exist in the first place. The originary object that causes our desire is itself a placeholder for the void at the center of the linguistic order. Behind the enlarged shadow of the object of desire that the regime of phallic jouissance casts, there is nothing. Feminine jouissance, therefore, organizes itself around this lack. The wounding loss is central to enjoyment.

The feminine is the historical truth of the masculine, as it supports the formation of masculine subjectivity in a specific historical context. The subject of feminine jouissance, however, can also disavow and resist the regime of phallic jouissance in which a desirable object, notably "woman," is continuously produced and nominated. Copjec implies that we must place the antagonism between the two kinds of jouissance in a historical context. Unpacking Lacan's statement that woman doesn't exist, Copjec posits: "Lacan is undoubtedly arguing that a concept of woman cannot be constructed because the task of fully unfolding her conditions is one that cannot, in actuality, be carried out. Since we are finite beings, bound by space and time, our knowledge is subject to historical conditions. Our conception of woman cannot 'run ahead' of these limits and thus cannot construct a concept of the whole of woman."[63]

In *Thirst*, Tae-ju's designated place in the home as "woman" is a placeholder for all the other social, sexual, and gender identities that the family and the state comprise. It is in this place that woman is at the center of the historiography of the modern nation-state. The film demonstrates Tae-ju's social location by showing her modeling her mother-in-law's creation, a traditional Korean wedding dress. It further illustrates the place she occupies by showing her occupying the dress shop in a mise-en-scène that emphasizes the separation between her and the outside world. Although one might argue that the nation-state is absent in a film in which the major catastrophe comes from Africa in the form of an incurable virus, the patriarchal nation-state always functions as an absent cause in any national cinema. Furthermore, the affect and artifacts that underpin social relationships in film draw from the political and cultural unconscious, thus enabling the cathectic relationship between the local audience occupying the position of the national subject, on the one hand, and the film text, on the other.

That woman doesn't exist implies that no woman can guarantee either sexual and gender difference, or the patriarchal social order that is predicated on that difference. Hence feminine monstrosity and its disruptive effect on the social order of the sovereign nation. When feminine desire turns monstrous, rendering the feminine subject abject, the Symbolic order that depends on her is destabilized. The feminine subject can eradicate what makes her a social subject: the historically contingent, rather than essential, features of identity. In refusing to accept the identitarian properties that impose a social identity, a new, unconfined subjectivity may emerge. This monstrous new subject, one that fails to conform to the phallic signifier that the nation proffers, defies the categorization that maps gender and sexual identities. It is the context in which the subject of the emancipatory drive appears in horror genre films. The emancipatory drive is a new trajectory of the drive where we transform our relationship to the traumatic lack, taking up the side of feminine jouissance that does not try to eradicate the lack through the phallic object, and our act of continuing on this trajectory constitutes our life drive. We enter that trajectory through our encounter with the Real. In horror films, the entire cinematic field can turn into the sphere of the Real. No one can escape it, and in the end, one could experience what it looks and feels like to exist in that sphere. But this aspect of the horror genre shouldn't lead us to a sanguine celebration of the genre's emancipatory potential, taking it for granted. I return to this point below.

Abjection and Emancipation across National Cinemas

The vampires, their abject, monstrous forms thus emancipated from the form of the body that the sovereign nation-state inscribes on the subject, pursue their perverse enjoyment and paint the Agambenian camp red. But the ultimate destruction of those abject bodies seems to suggest the defeat of the abject. They fail to claim victory over the Symbolic order of the modern nation-state into which they have momentarily injected their perverse enjoyment. The film shows the terrifying nature of abject desubjectivization—becoming inhuman. The gory destruction of their victims' bodies stands in stark contrast to their miraculous faculty to heal and recover the facade of beauty and completeness. This terrifying spectacle is the film's way of representing the destructiveness of feminine jouissance, as rooted in its Real body and its defiance of the narrative meaning-making. Recall here feminine jouissance in *Poetry* and *Oasis*, as points of comparison.

Feminine jouissance figures as a destructive force against the Law of the Father, escaping the camp that enwraps *homo sacer* in the sovereign state's social space. Subjects claim agency over their bodies by pursuing jouissance that destroys the patriarchal social order. Vampires fly unbound over the city with such exhilaration that they rewrite the cartography of bodily movement over the nationscape. They have also rewritten the meaning of blood. A foundation of the fantasy of the homogenous nation of South Korea and its patrilineal ideology, blood has been turned by vampires into a gushing flow of enjoyment that is not beholden to patriarchy. Even the priest's prayer for total abjection of the body can be read as an expression of desire to transgress bodily grounding and experience the kind of jouissance that is not permitted to a proper social body. In this light, the prayer's expression of longing for annihilation harkens not to spiritual transcendence but to the obtaining of an abject body, such as we see in horror genre films, where subjects turn monstrous in order to signify and embody the unspeakable pleasure of being beyond human ontology.

Abjection makes possible the emancipatory moments in which Tae-ju is able to escape the inscription of the family and the priest has a chance to escape the instrumental reason of religious institutions. Religion, no longer a medieval institution based upon the mythos of soul, has entered into an unholy union with medical institutions. By foregrounding the body and embodiedness of human subjects, religion now imposes a Foucauldian site of life wherein the sovereign power seeks to extend its power to death and to foster productivity within the boundary of the Symbolic order. Under this regime, life finds normative, acceptable form in gender and sexuality. Vampirism extends the body beyond this medical-sovereign logic. In this new locus, it becomes possible for the body to transform into the indestructible material manifestation of a jouissance-seeking machine that, unshackled, discards and replaces norms of gender and sexuality.

Tae-ju seems to straddle recognizable boundaries of gender. This character walks between legible gender lines, usurping typically masculine characteristics to force upon us the spectacle of the destruction of the feminine as prescribed by the Law of the Father. Tae-ju's visage turns radiant white, a sign of ideal feminine beauty in South Korea, but she also exhibits physical prowess and hunts, which are typically masculine traits. Jouissance, however, is feminine insofar as there is no ultimate object "a" that she hopes to obtain. For this subject of feminine jouissance, the hunt itself is the thing. However, the terrifying image of her hunting and taking humans in the cinematic space where there is seemingly no cinematically rendered space of contemplation on ethical relationship to the Other also reflects the inability of the film to thoroughly imagine feminine jouissance. Here, we see the film's struggle over the political limitations of jouissance. Horror genre films represent one of the few venues in which culture at large explores jouissance at all. In this sense, this film reflects the genre's limitations in imagining how the subject of feminine jouissance might forge an ethical relationship with the Other.

It is possible for us to construe the subject of feminine jouissance as a *whatever singularity*, a being capable of joining what Agamben calls the "non-state," an accidental community whose political project is to counter the sovereign state. That subject dwells "among beings . . . who would always already be this or that thing, this or that identity, and who would have entirely exhausted their power in these things and identities—among such beings there could not be any community but only coincidences and factual partitions. We can communicate with others only through what in us . . . has remained potential."[64] This "potential" being is in opposition to a united populace under the ideology and apparatus of the capitalist nation-state, where all subjects must serve a useful purpose. In fact, this "potential" exists only when there is always a certain remainder that cannot be utilized in the sovereign state. If the structure of the capitalist nation-state is defined by "land, order, birth," then *whatever singularities* rupture the boundaries of those three elements[65] through the force of the remainder that escapes their unity.

Genre films, as modern cultural texts, offer different ways in which the conceptualization of the body is related to ideas of land, order, and birth, all of which are mapped out in the spatial organization of the sovereign nation-state. Westerns depict the nation-state as built on the land and its order. In noir films, the urban landscape is an elaborately surveilled prison for the criminal body, a landscape of confinement in which order surrounds the individual. In Melville's neonoir *Le samouraï* (1967), during the sequence that depicts a citywide police manhunt, an image of the map of the city superimposes grids of order on the urban space that a criminal male body must traverse. In melodrama, we often see how the question of the birth/family and order/patriarchal law define and confine individuals within a set of identities. In Fassbinder's *Ali: Fear Eats the Soul* (1974), all three elements are the origin of individual and collective trauma. In this film, traumatic events evolve around a migrant black African man of Moroccan origin who marries a much older white German woman. This act simultaneously ruptures the order of the family and the state through racial Otherness that has no legitimate territorial belonging. The question of birth invoked here determines the source of national subjects' civic rights, as opposed to bare life, which lacks those rights, that is the foundation of the social order. In *Singin' in the Rain* (1952), Gene Kelly's character transgresses the boundary of the orderly social space. His enjoyment spills over the properly demarcated sidewalk into the street, until a policeman arrives to remind him of his spatial transgression and reestablish the proper order for movement.

In horror genre films, abject monsters rupture all three elements. They trespass the cartography of the nationscape because their bodily movements do not follow the proper lines that law, order, and the patriarchal lineage prescribe. While an accidental community is not in the film's purview, the vampires in *Thirst* also violently transgress those lines of demarcation. A "body genre" film, *Thirst* elicits a corporeal response to the spectacle of violence, allowing us to imagine what it feels like to be *whatever singularities* that rupture the elements that bind the nation-state and the body politic together. *Whatever singularities*, which we see as constituting an accidental community of the Real subjects of feminine jouissance, place themselves against all these elements and, in doing so, become abject. Their emancipation lies in the act of choosing what they withhold from society. What has remained "potential" approaches a state of nonbelonging. Feminine jouissance's nonbelonging is with reference to the phallic order or any static borders of gender, nation, and so on. It refers to something im-potential, to use Agamben's term,[66] which can be described as a remainder of the potential and contains an element that is not productive of the existing social order's ideologemes. It is that which a sovereign state cannot subjugate, a hard kernel of being that the nation-state cannot swallow and make part of itself. Again, I note that phallic jouissance and feminine jouissance do not form a binary along the lines of gender and sexuality. Phallic jouissance refers to enjoyment that is bound to fail. Feminine jouissance refers to the Real of the enjoyment that we fantasize, not a utopian alternative to the masculine.

By reasserting a Levinasian boundary between the self and the divine Other that the subject of feminine jouissance cannot cross, thus preserving the possibility of a social relationship within the given order, *Thirst*'s priest draws the line at which the ferocious flow of feminine jouissance must stop. The film visualizes that boundary as a mythic horizon in the final scene: as the two vampires die, the sea turns to blood and a leviathan leaps over the sanguinary waves. At this point, it becomes unimaginable for the flow of uncontrolled jouissance to continue to inundate the social space, as it is rerouted to the mythic space beyond the social.

The destruction of the abject in this film could be understood through a Jamesonian negative dialectic, where utopian solutions are fundamentally impossible. In what he calls the "extreme imagination of catastrophe prevalent in global cinema," Seung-Hoon Jeong sees "the end of imagination, the failure of imagining a new better community."[67] But Jeong also points out Fredric Jameson's position in which "negativity of our imprisonment in a non-utopian present teaches us 'negative politics.'" That is, "the negation of the negative status quo does not necessarily lead to a positive synthesis, but rather serves as a warning criticism for all different alternatives . . . debunking any imagined solution for all-encompassing systems as ideological illusion."[68] Jameson's notion of the utopian impulse in cultural texts is a means to reveal irresoluble contradictions, not identify solutions.[69] The ending of the film flows from the problems of the modern patriarchal nation-state, from which the vampiric desire to transgress emerges, to a Jamesonian impulse to mark the impossibility of easy solutions.

Crossing the Generic Terrain of Abjection

In *Thirst*, Park Chan-wook illustrates the jouissance that emerges from abjection with the film's visceral rendition of monstrosity. The film owes its effectiveness to the genre formula that capitalizes on the abjection of the gendered subject, particularly the feminine subject of jouissance. Horror is a genre that organizes itself around border crossings of the monstrous body that positions itself on the feminine side of jouissance. Other forms of film convey abjection through different methods of visualization and narrativization, representing the wounding of the modern subject, which renders the subject abject. Park Chan-wook's body of work contains several such examples.

Park sees his films as depicting problems that are fundamentally Korean.[70] His *Vengeance* trilogy undertakes the problematizing of the modern South Korean nation, in which the utter destruction of the body represents the destruction of modern subjectivity that sovereign power seeks to inscribe on the body politic. In his films, modern South Koreans are all *homines sacri*. On the surface, South Korea as a nation-state seems absent from this trilogy. The fact that the characters in these films do not appeal to the law but rather take vengeance outside the proper legal boundaries supports this notion of absence. The context of the trauma these characters suffer, however, is historically and locally specific, bounded by the modern sovereign nation. I have argued elsewhere that the visceral violence in these films, contained under the rubric of "Asia extreme" and infuriating to some film critics as simply gratuitous, is a symptom of a national trauma that does not provide cognitive mapping for a global audience.[71] In *Sympathy for Mr. Vengeance* (2002), we see the body politic, as defined by capitalism, in space where life itself becomes a spectacular commodity. Therein, the medical-industrial complex thrives by imposing the modern injunction that life must be healthy to be productive, and therefore it may commoditize human organs to achieve that aim. This is the aim of biopolitics that creates *homo sacer* through demarcation of the healthy civic body and its limit. The abject subject in this film confronts the nation-state's biopolitics.

Oldboy (2003), which I first analyze in chapter 1, dismantles the Law of the Father by breaking the incest taboo and undoing the Oedipal achievement that established the Law by upholding the big Other's prerogative to guarantee the gender and sexual identity of its subjects through an injunction to desire properly. Sexual objects signify the proper way of desiring, and the modern nation-state seeks to convince its subjects that the big Other guarantees the continuity of prosperous society by aligning gender and sexuality as the site for proliferating the modern body under patriarchal Law. *Oldboy* reveals an abject desire to transgress the big Other's injunction on the body. A historical and local contingency shapes the way the universal dimension of the patriarchal injunction finds its way into a particular situation. In this context, *Oldboy*'s big Other is a historical figure, the South Korean modern patriarchal nation. Its injunction reflects the nation's social need. In *Lady Vengeance* (2005), the hypermasculine patriarchal order is shown to be founded upon the big Other's obscene enjoyment, which hypersexual male violence represents. The abject, monstrous feminine subject strives to comprise her own ethical position against that order. In this trilogy, we see three monstrosities. In response, the modern nation-state scrambles to reproduce the proper social body's participation in an ever-increasing production of surplus value, which reasserts established gender norms. Park's trilogy thus shows the other side of modernity in a South Korean context through the monstrous subjectivity of abjection.

Like Park Chan-wook's work, Jia Zhangke's films deal with society's fraught relationship to modernity and the abjection of the social subject that results. In *Still Life*, the abject body belongs to the modern nation-state, if perilously. A woman is trafficked from one family to another, and her husband, San-ming, is a migrant laborer whose life remains precarious in the modern nation. The trafficked woman, whose visage we see mainly through long shots, meets with the husband who had purchased her decades earlier. She has been traded off, once again, to repay her brother's debt, and San-ming pledges to return her to his hometown after he has earned enough working on a building demolition site, specifically to buy her back. In the film, the structure that formed the foundation of communal life is torn down, bare-handed, by migrant laborers in a town about to be submerged under the new Three Gorges Dam. The mutilated landscape represents the unsettled social and political ground upon which these figures stand. Another woman, Shen Hong, comes to town searching for the husband who abandoned her in favor of a secure position in the booming developmental state. After dozing off in a friend's run-down apartment, she hangs a shirt on the laundry line in the early morning hours. Beyond this humble image, we see a monument lauding the Three Gorges Dam, all rendered through filmic realism. Then, suddenly rending the diegetic space of realism, the monument takes off like a rocket ship.

Žižek argues that "there is no a priori formal structural scheme exempted from historical contingencies—there are only contingent, fragile, inconsistent configurations."[72] This conclusion applies not only to art forms but also to the foundational theoretical schemes I invoke, including the big Other and feminine jouissance. Thus, to understand the application of theoretical schemes such as the big Other and feminine jouissance, we must look into the historical circumstances responsible for their particular shape. In comparing *Thirst* and *Still Life*, we recognize that these films capture historical contingencies that define the precise nature of abjection for those times and places. The universal principles of modernity and global capitalism find different paths and practices across the globe, and it is in these contexts that the local particularities of modern capitalism appear. Hence, contingencies are specific to local histories. The ways these films imagine abjection reflect different responses to the big Other, which is itself consolidated through historical contingencies. We can, therefore, examine the different phenomena of abjection and the presence and absence of feminine jouissance, for example, and their respective locality-specific social and historical contexts.

In this larger context, the space of the Real opens through abjection in the field of disciplining and punishing modern social subjects, even at the heart of family. *Thirst* translates that opening into a space of possibility for the imagining of an emancipatory figure of abjection who expresses her jouissance through subversion of familial and social boundaries. In *Still Life*, such a possibility is difficult to imagine. This might be the limit of its realist aesthetics, which refrain from excessive representations of monstrous jouissance. In this film, social subjects do not possess the means to impose a new set of ethics on the national cartography. They continually move on to the next location of exploitation of labor. If vampires are a spectacular metaphor for antihumanism as the new philosophical foundation of the modern subject, Jia's worldview is perhaps that his subjects are not antihuman enough for them to escape the nation-state's map of ontology. Victor Fan posits that Jia seeks to replicate the Western humanistic paradigm regarding modernization and its concomitant desubjectivization. In China's transition from socialism, for example, the humanist paradigm fails to show individuals the way to resubjectify as modern national subjects. Fan states: "What many of Jia's characters negotiate with themselves is the intricate relationship between individuation and deindividuation, subjectivization and desubjectivization. These individuals become aware of their subjectivities, yet they find themselves unable to make any personal decision (autonomy).... The transition from socialism to free market capitalism activated an awareness of one's subjectivity, as neither the state nor the party played the role of its symbolic substitute (for an individual's lack) any longer."[73] Jia's characters fail to abide by Cartesian humanism, and yet they are unable to find a new positionality outside of it.

Still Life, however, creates what constitutes "an aesthetic rupture" that counters the national cinema's hegemonic demand for "mimetic responsibility"[74] and the mandate that it must create a moral universe through the representation of humanity on the path of national teleology. The rupture that the film thrusts into the cinematic space is where we witness the Real of the sovereign nation-state, fracturing the map of developmental capitalism. San-ming and Shen Hong never find what they are looking for, nor do they ever meet or cross paths. What connects their disparate trajectories is their encounter with the disappearing physical and social landscape, signified by the ruins of thousand-year-old homes and the rusted skeletons of dismantled factories left over from an era before global capitalism. In this disappearing landscape, social subjects' spatial and temporal bearings are tenuous. As if to express this tenuous bearing of the social subject, the film's predominantly realistic style collapses with the appearance of a UFO. Although its flight crosses both characters' disparate spaces, their paths remain disjointed. The actions and events that drive these characters forward never intersect. This means that the characters' trajectories across the cinematic space do not follow a common teleological goal, because the formation of such goals relies on the subjective position, based on ideologies of state capitalism, that these characters at the margin of the development state have lost. But, poignantly, as subjects of trauma experiencing the violent destruction of their existential condition, as materialized by the landscape in ruins, they are unable to create a new subjectivity founded upon an ethical relation to the Other.

Although the camera captures the disappearing landscape, signifying the destruction of the social and historical space as the Three Gorges Dam's waterline encroaches, the trauma of that destruction is beyond the possibility of accurate representation. Hence, the film's abandoning of the implied responsibility for realism, as we see in the flying monument and the UFO. The ensuing disruption in the spatial cohesiveness, disappointing our formal expectation for realistic representation, makes apparent the ideological nature of realism. As such, the film reveals the Real of cinematic representation: the cinematic space enframes ideology. One of the ways in which the film disrupts the sense of cohesive reality is through inserting objects that break from narrative convention.

These objects—cigarettes, liquor, tea, and toffee—are exchanged by characters as gestures of connectivity among people at the margin of the developmental state. Such exchanges include a tender moment where San-ming hands a toffee to his wife before they bid farewell to each other, standing in a building under demolition in front of the open space where there used to be a wall. As we watch that exchange, we momentarily see the spectacular collapse of another building behind them; as the world collapses around them, they stand in silence without turning to watch the scene of the collapse. Ultimately, these gestures of exchange fail to build solidarity, as all scatter across the nationscape. These objects are floating signifiers, unmoored from a narrative that cannot make those objects and exchanges historically and politically meaningful.

In this manner, Jia destabilizes realism, where the primary function of objects lies in their usefulness in rendering coherent a narrative's action, as in Vittorio De Sica's *Bicycle Thieves* (1948). In the film, the protagonist and his wife bring their bedsheet to sell at a pawn shop, and we see, through the pawn broker's narrow window, shelves that line the walls, stacked with bed sheets. Unlike Jia's objects, this spectacle does not disturb the cinematic vision. It situates the viewing subject and characters within the logic of narrative and therefore maintains the narrative's mechanism rather than fissuring it. Objects in *Still Life*, in contrast, collapse the stylistic cohesion of realism that keeps the narrative's unity, and thus the humanistic cohesiveness of subjectivity, intact.

The closing sequence of *Still Life* is an extreme long shot of a tightrope walker balancing between two buildings that are being demolished, suspended in the midst of a wasteland of ruins, indifferent mountains, and rising water. Consider how this image fails to conform to the regime of realistic representation. The film eschews a national allegory by writing the sense of the crumbling time and space of the nation-state directly on the surface of the image. But it also subverts realism in space where capitalism assimilates local time to global capitalism's temporality, reorganizing local space into that of a pernicious state capitalism, achieving postmodern time-space compression.[75] As the ancient city is demolished and submerged, any sense of the continuum and comprehensibility of time and space is erased, leaving its unmoored inhabitants abject. Everywhere we look in this land of abjection, we see the Real of the capitalist sovereign state. Walking a tightrope depends on a sense of material confidence in the environment to which the tightrope walker's rope is secured. It is an ideological gesture that asserts a subject-object relation to sustain the sense of unified space. In tightrope walking between the two towers of the World Trade Center,[76] Philippe Petit asserts the certainty of its formidable materiality. The towers stood for that which is utterly guaranteed to continue in a reliable fashion. Through that act of certification, he emerges as a subject who is capable of controlling the material world. By certifying the materiality of things, the subject who thereby masters it is rendered that much more authentic. In *Still Life*, the tightrope walker's action, walking between the buildings soon to be destroyed and in the midst of the vast landscape of ruins, reveals that a concrete grasp of materiality, and therefore any guaranteed stability of temporal and spatial structure that the nation-state wants to assert in its territorial and ideological construction, is impossible. The image, thus, opens the visual field of the Real, and the tightrope walker appears as the Real body.

Michel de Certeau, emphasizing the centrality of physical space to cultural signification, states that there are "three distinct (but connected) functions of the relations between spatial and signifying practices [namely] the *believable*, the *memorable*, and the *primitive*. They designate what 'authorizes' (or makes possible or credible) spatial appropriations, what is repeated in them (or is recalled in them) from a silent and withdrawn memory, and what is structured in them and continues to be signed by an in-fantile (*in-fans*) origin."[77] Jia's tightrope walking, in making these functions untenable, opens up the field of the Real, unraveling the ideological assertion that produces the modern national subject's position. It is a "landscape of abject experience."[78]

In staging an encounter with the Real, film reveals the symbolic violence inherent in the regime of representation. Across a significant genre divide, both *Thirst* and *Still Life* take on this challenge: *Thirst*, by cleaving to genre as a fulcrum of the Real, and *Still Life* by creating a rupture in the generic, through which the Real emerges. Despite differences in the way they articulate the Real, they both reveal the subversive possibility of the Real body: The destruction of any material or symbolic guarantee for the national subject as advertised by the modern sovereign state. In *Thirst*, this destruction creates fissures in the sovereign camp's boundary. In *Still Life*, the abject landscape of ruin is the field of the Real, no longer the future site of the sovereign grip on subjectivity. A comparative study of these films opens a new framework of analyses for national cinemas, a framework that reckons with the social contradictions shared by various national and regional configurations as they participate in the global geopolitical and geocultural dynamics of modernity and global capitalism.

At this juncture, I summarize the critical intervention that this chapter makes in the theory of subjectivity and cinema: the locating of the Real's materiality in the Real body that is founded on feminine jouissance. The Real body embodies a position of the ethical subject that undertakes a rewriting of the sovereign cartography and never settles for a sovereign law of desire that sustains the Symbolic order. This subject turns the act of continuing with feminine jouissance into what Badiou calls a "nonliteral law,"[79] as opposed to the law that describes and legitimizes a particular form of society and subjectivity. I posit that this term describes the new law, which confronts the law that defines and dictates spatial and temporal configurations of the Symbolic order and the linguistic body of phallic jouissance that it supports. Taking up this ethical position gives meaning to the lives of the characters in the films that I have analyzed. Mija's life is worth living because she sacrifices it, as the Symbolic subject, to allow the Real body of the dead girl, Agnes, to appear and speak against the Law of the Father that supports patriarchal violence. In doing so, Mija captures Agnes's singular being, which emerges right in front of our eyes: Agnes's person appears, for the first time in the film, after the poetic subject's voice becomes hers. When, in a break from realism, she turns and looks directly into the camera, we encounter feminine jouissance in the body of the Real. Tae-ju rewrites the law of desire into the law of the drive: that one never gives up on feminine jouissance. The new path of the drive that opens up there is emancipatory; it keeps the subject confronting the law of the desire prescribed by the Symbolic order. The subject of the emancipatory drive never settles into a singular trajectory of the drive. Through Mija's sacrifice and Tae-ju's "keep going" with feminine jouissance, we see the Real body emerge. It is through the Real body that the cinema of the Real visualizes the new subject of the Real.

CHAPTER THREE

The Chronotope of the Drive in the Cinema of the Real

The Emancipatory Drive and Somatic Disjointure

In the previous chapters, I have explained how the emancipatory drive articulates the psychical structure in which we emerge as the political subject and the way we connect the transformation of the trajectory of our desire to the act of political emancipation. Now we turn to the subject of the bodily drive, a term that is predicated on the Lacanian concept that all drives are bodily. The subject of the bodily drive enters the emancipatory drive by encountering the drive of the Other. This encounter prompts the subject to transgress their temporal and spatial location within the Symbolic order. Through this transgression, the subject creates a new chronotope in which the subject embarks on the path of emancipation. Tracing this transformation, this chapter further develops the radical potential of being a viewer. The cinema of the Real dislocates the viewing subject's position of knowing and subsequently makes falter our desire to know through seeing as the foundation of subjectivity. In this chapter, we continue to expand the emancipatory possibility that the cinema holds for the body that traverses cinematic time and space, creating the emancipatory path for the bodily drive.

To look closely at how the cinema can visualize this process, we now turn to Michael Haneke's *Caché*.[1] The film opens with what seems to be an establishing shot of a house seen from across the street. A long, stationary shot with a soundtrack of chirping birds, it shows people going out of, into, and around a nondescript house on a quiet street. The image then begins to track in fast-forward, revealing that what we are viewing is actually video footage, over which we hear George and Anne, a bourgeois Parisian couple, expressing bewilderment about the meaning and the origin of the tape they have just received. Mysterious tapes continue to arrive. The taped images eventually lead to the Real of French history, imperialism, and the Paris Algerian massacre of 1961, which ultimately shatters George's and Anne's ways of being—a common theme in the cinema of the Real.

We, the audience, experience a shattering effect beyond that of witnessing the unraveling of bourgeois life. This shattering comes primarily from the experience of the disruption of our position of looking via the gaze that appears in the form of the disembodied perspective of the camera, displacing us from a comfortable cinematic point of view. The gaze, as Jacques Lacan theorizes, punctures our field of vision and confronts our looking. As a hole in the meaning in visual space that disrupts meaning-making, it marks the point in which the Symbolic order, which guarantees meaning given to objects, falters. Let us recall the sardine can in Lacan's story of Petit Jean: the tin was seeing Lacan. We can say that *the sardine can thinks Lacan* as he watches it floating on the surface of the waves. The object gazes at you from a place where you least expect to encounter an experience of being looked at.[2] This encounter with the gaze shatters the sense of your own subjectivity, founded upon the belief that you can determine the meaning of the object that you look at.

In *Caché*, we do not know whose subjective position of looking we have just occupied and then been evicted from, so we lose the ground from which we can safely survey the world and claim knowledge of it. The subjective position lands directly under what we perceive to be the menacing gaze of an unlocatable entity that has materialized through the cinematic apparatus. We believe that this situation generates an ontological threat, because the gaze that we encounter restricts our scopic drive, specifically, because we solidify our subject position through the scopic drive that nominates our *objet a* that elicits our desire. In *Caché*, the manner in which the taped images are introduced render the images in the field of our scopic drive as uncanny objects that the existing chain of signification cannot contain and threaten the way of knowing and being that the scopic drive affirms. Our desire to know through seeing as the founding element of subjectivity falters here as we encounter the gaze that appears in our field of vision as the limit of our knowledge, a black hole at the very heart of the object that we behold. The meaning of the image that endows an orderly worldview for us disappears in the black hole that the gaze opens up in the field of the image. Where we want to see a meaningful object, we see the gaze, an unknowable and unnamable Thing, the meaning of which escapes the Symbolic order as the guarantor of all meaning.

As such, the gaze marks the point of entrance to the Real. The Symbolic order is founded upon the Real (the way things really are), but the Real reveals the path to overturn the Symbolic order: If we were ever to see how many Oompa Loompas were maimed or killed on Wonka's factory floor, we would be less able to believe in the mythic quality of Everlasting Gobstoppers. We might even begin to see the structural destruction of the Other's life in the factory system as a point that can fissure the entire enterprise. At that point, our scopic enjoyment of candy, which propels the bodily drive toward it, would cease. Thus, Wonka's chocolate factory tries to make sure there are no holes in the visual field that gazes at us, with reasonable, temporary harm coming only to those whose moral shortcomings run afoul of the Symbolic order that Willie Wonka's factory seeks to establish. Pointing toward the Real, the gaze holds the emancipatory possibility: we emancipate ourselves from the trajectory of the scopic drive that consolidates our desire to phantasmatic possession of the object the meaning of which is ideologically supported. Thus, the scopic drive sustains our fantasy of a specific chronotope as a location where our desire unfolds—we stage our desire for objects in specific time-space coordinates—trying to rectify the lack through phantasmatic possession of *objet a*. The gaze, by opening up the other scene beyond the scene of the scopic drive, organized by the Symbolic order, places the subject outside the preexisting chronotope of desire, where the meeting between the desiring subject and its object of desire is impossible. In that sense, the gaze allows us to transform our drive, to liberate ourselves from what the primary signifier promises: elimination of the lack by clearly delineating the temporal and spatial location of the *objet a*. Cinema often enacts this premise and permits us to occupy the place of the subject who knows through the masterful position of looking. *Caché* makes such a position impossible as, in this film, we encounter the gaze, materialized by the camera eye, that emanates from the black hole where the *objet a* (in this film's case, knowledge of the nature of the image) is missing. The encounter with the gaze is the encounter with the Real of our scopic drive. This leads to the emancipatory drive in the act of looking.

Next, we need to locate decisive moments in which the emancipatory politics of subjectivity emerges in the visual field. We explore those moments by looking at the chronotope of the drive, a temporal and spatial point in which the emancipatory drive forces us to change the trajectory of our desire. We thereby reformulate the bodily drive with emancipatory political possibilities. In the following, we clarify at what point the bodily drive becomes the politically emancipatory drive while examining the existing discourse relating to the drive.

To sum it up, in the field of the emancipatory drive, the subject experiences disjointure in the form of subjectivity that materializes in the bodily dimension. In this sense, disjointure gives us a view into the way the Real body that I have conceptualized thus far emerges.

The bodily drive emerges from the chain of signification. To this extent, the bodily drive is chained to the signifier. This also marks the difference between humans' scopic drive and, say, a shrimp's visual capacities. A student in my undergraduate film theory class, distraught by the Lacanian concept of the subject—split, unconscious, its coherence only precariously hanging by the thread of a signifier—once blurted out in class one day that shrimps can see far more colors than humans. I replied that it's too bad that shrimps don't have language, though even if they did they wouldn't know how to grapple with all those colors they see, the meaning of which cannot be easily harnessed. For us, the expression of the language-driven drive is extremely corporeal, hence the linguistic subject reveals its desire in the bodily drive. I will observe the bodily drive through two examples. The first happened to an art teacher I once knew. He had always made his college-age students hand over their cell phones upon entering the art studio and kept the phones until the end of the class. One day, a student refused to follow this rule and, after the teacher made it clear that keeping the phone was not an option, clutched the phone to her chest and ran from the classroom in tears. As such, the student, as the linguistic subject, uses the body to manifest desire for an object, the cell phone, which is mistaken for *objet a*. Thus, desire becomes the bodily drive. Bodily jouissance within the bodily drive is, in this formulation, inherently phallic. The bodily drive in this context places the student in a parallel trajectory to *objet a*, a path that cleaves closely, but never intersects with, the actual object. Through the bodily drive, the desiring subject gets even farther away from *objet a*.

The other example is the bodily drive of the experience of psychotic breakdown. Psychosis places one outside the primary signifier, the name of the Father, but the drive still obtains a linguistic dimension. The drive plays itself out in a scenario that has proven to allow the subject to find its expressivity, a bodily expression that locks the psychotic subject in a singular trajectory. Physical symptoms like ringing ears, shaking, and shrieking that are involved in a psychotic breakdown are a form of language that stages a protest against the name of the Father. When one experiences these symptoms, one is on a warpath shaped by the narrative in which one places oneself and the Other in a specific spatial and temporal configuration, a chronotope of trauma. We see another example of the bodily drive in Jordan Peele's *Get Out* (2017). For the group of body-snatching white bourgeois in this film, the drive to harness material and epistemological power that undergirds racism (itself a linguistic enterprise with arms and physical violence) manifests its bodily dimension: to occupy the Black body.

All drives are bodily and entail bodily jouissance. This jouissance is written on the body, and the aforementioned psychosis exemplifies a form of the bodily jouissance that wages war against the name of the Father,[3] the master signifier that holds language together. In this manner, bodily jouissance could be emancipatory. The bodily drive could also be emancipatory in being indifferent to social goods, signified and represented by the master signifier (the name of the Father), and thus indifferent to the self-interest that propels the subject toward obtaining social goods. In this way, the bodily drive can enable the subject to leave the trajectory of desire organized around the pursuit of goods. One must, however, traverse the trajectory of the bodily drive to create a new trajectory of the emancipatory drive. Bruce Fink notes that one must go beyond the master signifier that initially castrated/cut the subject, to formulate a new subjectivity freed from "fate," the desire of the big Other, for example, that of our parents.[4] The subject can devise a new position in relation to the cause of its symptoms—the castration/cut by the big Other that imprisoned the subject in the master signifier. This liberation from fate—imprisonment in a particular context of the traumatic encounter with the master signifier—provides us with a template for how the subject of the drive may negotiate entering a new trajectory of the emancipatory drive. To pin down the point of that entrance, we must first pay attention to the failure of the desiring subject and its connection to the drive.[5]

We have established that, for Lacan, subjectivity emerges through the experience of a fundamental lack, the sense that the subject has lost an essential part of itself.[6] As I have explained in previous chapters, the sense of wounding or castration that comes with the feeling that we have lost an important part of ourselves derives not from an empirical occurrence of physical loss but rather from a phantasmatic castration. This sense of loss occurs subsequent to each of our becoming a speaking subject and our consequent entry into the Symbolic order. Language is a chain of signifiers, metonyms, and metaphors that continually displaces the Thing-in-itself, which we retroactively nominate after the emergence of language to constitute the material world to which we have access only through phenomenological experience. Enunciating our desire through language leaves something unsayable, a residue of what we want, a hard kernel that the Symbolic system cannot properly express. All this creates the nagging sensation that we have lost something.

The object that the subject believes it has lost and that, the subject believes, would eradicate the lack and the concomitant dissatisfaction that the subject suffers combines with the Real that there is, in fact, no object that could ever accomplish this to form the metaphorical rock and a hard place from which desire emerges. This unsatisfactory object that we aim to possess, the *objet petit a*,[7] is an inconsequential or incidental object, without inherent value, that functions as our object-cause of desire. But it seems to have the power to fill the hole that loss of the phantasmatic object has left behind. Slavoj Žižek notes an example of this *objet a* in Wagner's *Parsifal*. An arrow that has struck Amfortas will keep him alive as long as it remains impaled in his wound; it fills the hole of the lack he bears.[8] Nationalist ideology likewise nominates the sovereign nation as an obtainable object of desire. Through participation in the fantasy of obtaining its *objet a* through a national project that encompasses all facets of life, economic, political, military, and so forth, the national subject of desire emerges.

According to Žižek, desire sustains itself in a perpetual state of nonsatisfaction that, in turn, ties the subject's cathexis to a series of objects misrecognized as the cause of, and end to, its desire. The drive "stands for the paradoxical possibility that the subject, forever prevented from achieving his goal (and thus fully satisfying his desire), can nevertheless find satisfaction in the very circular movement of repeatedly missing its object, or circulating around it."[9] Žižek pushes the conceptual limits of the drive as articulated by Lacan and applies Lacan's injunction to "never give up on your desire" to the subject's drive. Here, the subject's drive fails to arrive at the goal that desire aims to achieve. It is through this failure that desire turns into drive. This drive to death that nullifies the seemingly life-giving desire to eradicate the lack via *objet a* paradoxically sustains life by eschewing a telos and allows us to envision the possibility of transcending pregiven ideologies that designate this very telos as our desire's goal. The drive involves an ontological state in which the subject derives its jouissance from the act of orbiting. In this formulation, it is the drive itself, not the objects it nominates, that generates jouissance, which cannot be described or represented in the Symbolic order. Jouissance's manifestation will always have a monstrous dimension, because it, by definition, doesn't belong to the proper order of things. Jouissance points toward an "elsewhere" of the Symbolic order. Its appearance can initiate a destructive assault on the senses, but it makes it possible to imagine an ethical subject that exists beyond all national and gender boundaries, a place where no patriarchal nation-state can claim it. This subject's drive does not aim at obtaining the fantastic satisfaction of desire through the *objet a* that the nation promises will deliver satisfaction. This principle expands cinema's conceptual and aesthetic boundary to include the ontological field beyond what is organized around desire as it is usually represented in cinema. In my conceptualization of the cinema of the Real, this ontological field includes the politically meaningful emancipatory drive. Cinematic subjects in the emancipatory drive can strike down the Symbolic order.

It is in this context that we can turn the drive into a political principle. Through the drive, it is possible for the subject to organize sustained resistance to the Symbolic order. This way, the drive keeps the subject anchored in feminine jouissance. This, then, is the emancipatory aspect of the drive.

Psychoanalysis reveals that desire, which ideological institutions such as the nation-state promise to fulfill, perpetuates the existing order. This revelation creates the possibility of a psychoanalytic resistance to ideology. Psychoanalysis helps us to recognize the existence of a universal drive that emancipates us from the economy of desire across historical and geopolitical space. Hence, I posit that the emancipatory drive propels us to continue to stay on the path of revolutionary changes across that space. This is the essence of the life drive: we keep going as a subject free from overdetermination. The universal emancipatory drive emerges from specific local contexts. For example, when we look at locality-specific trajectories of the drive emerging through overcoming particular local articulations of capitalism, we recognize the universal drive against capitalism. This is, by extension, how we recognize the universal dimension of historically specific situations and events.

It is in this context that I examine in this chapter the emancipatory drive in what I call the films of the chronotopic North: South Korean films that present the lands north of the border as a location of national trauma. This builds upon the transnational and transtextual analyses that I have engaged in previous chapters. I examine the heterogeneous perspectives on subjectivity that globally diverse national cinemas convey by reading film texts from different local contexts, without limiting analytical engagement to frameworks that are segregated along the boundaries of regions and nations.

Before I begin to articulate the chronotope of the emancipatory drive, I will further flesh out theoretical elements that open up the conceptual pathways that allow us to arrive at the emancipatory drive. This process expands on what I have already done in the introductory chapter. I begin with Alenka Zupančič's summary of the Lacanian drive: We enter the drive as we "pass through desire and insist on it until the very end."[10] That is, once we traverse our fundamental fantasy that supports desire, we arrive at the drive. Zupančič continues: "At the heart of desire a possible passage opens up toward the drive; one might therefore come to the drive if one follows the 'logic' of desire to its limit."[11] The object of the drive, which binds the relationship between the subject and the Other, is the satisfaction itself. This object "coincides with the itinerary of the drive, and is not something that this itinerary 'intends' to attain."[12]

I posit that the emancipatory drive extends beyond this point of subjects' arrival at the drive, to the path that includes universal emancipation. This trajectory should be a structural component of the drive. Guided by this position, now I continue to examine the traversal of the drive to the emancipatory drive by looking at the moment the bodily drive enters the trajectory beyond that of privatized bodily jouissance.

An example of such privatized bodily jouissance occurs in Billy Wilder's *Double Indemnity*.[13] Fred MacMurray and Barbara Stanwyck play murderous lovers who meet in a busy grocery store, mingling with housewives, browsing and touching commodities on shelves as they discuss their plan to kill Phyllis's (played by Stanwyck) husband. The act of plotting the murder is a point on the trajectory of their bodily drive. Their jouissance redefines the grocery aisles into a private space of bodily jouissance where the lovers are indifferent to the preordained goal of social relations, the successful exchange of goods for capital. Joan Copjec reads this scene as an example of private jouissance overflowing into the public sphere.[14] At the end of the film, the fulfillment of their aim, the murder, fails to deliver any good as an object of desire. The outcome is the destruction of the lovers' proper position in the Symbolic order.

For a discussion of the politically emancipatory drive, I return to *Caché*. In the film, the gaze opens our view into a strange time and space. It is the chronotope of the drive of the Other that forces our bodily drive to transform into the emancipatory drive, revealing the fissuring of the nation-state, in this case, France. The gaze that marks the place of the unknowable Other points to the Real of history, an open wound at the heart of the nation's historiography. The specific wounding in this case is the Paris massacre of 1961, in which the French National Police killed at least forty Algerians, and likely far more, during a demonstration. This time-space configuration, which the characters encounter through mysterious videotapes, will eventually lead the character of George to face the Real of history he has disavowed, which is outside George's and Anne's existential and epistemological limits. Overriding their temporal and spatial modes of being, the Other's drive forces them to enter its own chronotope of wounding and thus destabilizes the subject position from which their claim to see and know emanates. As we similarly observe in South Korean cinema of the North, to which we turn to later in this chapter, the chronotope of the emancipatory drive confronts the chronotope of the nation-state.

Confronting the Other's drive, we often feel a need to pin down the exact shape of the body of the Other. The force of the drive does not, however, originate from some cohesive embodied-ness of the subject of the drive. This informs my differentiation between the bodily drive and the emancipatory drive. I argue that the subject of the emancipatory drive appears through somatic disjointure. I draw this term from Eric L. Santner's notion that the modern subject of capitalism is rendered visible and made into the body of the state via a "jointure of the somatic and the normative."[15] In this formulation, the subject's body is always regulated along the line of the norm. This notion can be put to use beyond a reiteration of the perspective of Foucauldian biopolitics. It is because it holds conceptual space for delineating the psychic formation through the distribution of pleasure involving the use of the Other. A patriarchal capitalist nation-state regulates the desiring body as a location of productive agency, crucially through the law that regulates the way of desiring in which the use of the Other is inscribed, as in, for example, the use of women. While "woman" as a particular arrangement of partial objects is "not all," patriarchy gives us a picture of woman where the disjointure inherent in that arrangement is hidden. As I have noted in previous chapters, this aligns with the Lacanian idea that the subject represents a mode of arranging partial objects, such as limbs and organs, into the feminine and the masculine.[16]

Caché extends this line of thinking about the body. George suspects that the tapes were sent by Majid, an Algerian immigrant whose fate was entangled with George's family through the Algerian war and the Paris massacre of 1961, when they were both children. However, there is no agentic body, either visualized or implied, from which this looking emanates. As the plot of the film develops, this absence disappoints many viewers, some of them strenuously seeking to locate just that body. Through the look that belongs to an unlocatable entity, George (and the audience) watches a taped interaction between himself and Majid, during which Majid slits his own throat. This clandestine event occurs in Majid's slum apartment, where, as the cinematography and mise-en-scène imply, no presence of a diegetic witness is possible. The gaze indicates a location of subjectivity outside the purview of the cinematic frame that binds the field of looking and knowing. The unflinching gaze frames the final scene of the film, where we see an extended long-take long shot of George's and Majid's young sons conversing, standing in the middle of a crowd. The scene appears out of context in terms of the plot; there is no thread that plausibly allows us to make sense of this meeting. Furthermore, we do not know the content of their conversation, as we hear only the ambient street noise. This scene inspires the viewing audience's cinematic desire to put the disparate pieces of evidence together into a plot that can answer our questions: Who made the tapes? Has Majid's son had the agency to look all along? A resolution—that racial and class differences might be overcome though the meeting of the sons of a poor Algerian immigrant and a French bourgeois—is what we expect from narrative cinema. The film at least partially adopts this convention, even while its modernist formal elements partially deconstruct the form of narrative cinema.

Haneke's politics of the gaze—leading us to the emancipatory drive that disrupts the scopic drive that searches futilely for *objet a*—penetrates this narratively ambiguous film and requires us to accept that in this instance the gaze emanates from no visible anthropomorphic source. The gaze belongs to a subject position that cannot be traced and harnessed to the normative body. This is the subaltern's gaze that conveys a persistent vision emanating from an ontological and epistemological location outside the discursive and aesthetic regime of mainstream cinema.

I extend this notion of the subaltern to the body that appears only through disjointure, as partial objects that make no sense vis-à-vis "the jointure of the somatic and the normative." The subaltern should be understood as an assemblage of partial objects, from which we cannot assemble a body as the location of the legible and legitimate desire within the chronotope of the bourgeois nation-state. The subaltern thus appears through somatic disjointure; its disembodied gaze is upon us.

The body that signifies desire can break and dissolve into a state of somatic disjointure. In *Entre ses mains*,[17] Laurent Kessler is a serial killer who dispatches women with a scalpel. In the final scene of the film, Laurent immobilizes Claire, the woman with whom he believes he is in love, gripping her neck. Instead of immediately stabbing her as he has done with other victims, Laurent struggles to keep his knife hand away from Claire's neck. It is as if the hand belongs to a stranger, or as if he is fighting an uncontrollable stranger inside, embodying the bodily drive that ferociously seeks jouissance through impossible objects, in this case, woman. Laurent fatally drives the scalpel, his phallic prosthetic, into his own body. Thus, the force of the death drive aimed at failing to obtain *objet a* defeats the bodily drive toward the use of the feminine Other for its bodily jouissance. This defeat renders Laurent somatically disjointed. Had the feminine body been put to its commonly accepted use, which means the realization of phallic jouissance that depends on the unobstructed availability of the feminine Other, somatic jointure would have been maintained for both parties. Her killing would, in this manner, function as the way to extract enjoyment through the objectified Other in its extreme form. Because Laurent is unable to come in close physical contact with women he desires, the only means with which he can enter the feminine body is via a phallic proxy, the scalpel. By overcoming the force of his own somatic jointure, signified by the hand that seeks to penetrate the feminine body, Laurent arrives at somatic disjointure, which relieves Claire from the position of the usufruct object for his bodily drive. Laurent represents the subject that separates itself from the deterministic track of the bodily drive and relocates to the emancipatory drive, in which the feminine subject continues to exist. The ending scene shows Claire walking out of the building where Laurent's body lies, out of the alleyway, and toward the crowded cityscape over which a Ferris wheel looms, as if metaphorizing the movement of Laurent's death drive. Laurent's ethical choice has pushed Claire into a new trajectory, the life drive keeping her going on a path other than what she ever imagined.

In the cinema of the Real, we encounter the Real of subjectivity through the somatic disjointure of the subject of the drive. Somatic disjointure thus indicates that the transformation of subjectivity, the transformation from the bodily drive to the emancipatory, has occurred. In *Timbuktu*,[18] the setting for this disjuncture is an African village under siege by jihadists. The film opens with images of the jihadists shooting at local artifacts. It is as if they are aiming to reconfigure psychic and material topography by destroying objects that have underwritten the historiography of the location. The assertion of a new historiography involves a new organization of social space by creating and nominating "sublime objects of ideology," to use Žižek's term. This involves the inscription of new meaning on the existing objects that shape and define subjectivity. For the jihadists in *Timbuktu*, the meaning attributed to women lies in the veil and other coverings violently forced upon them as a way to redefine their subjectivity. In addition, everyday artifacts such as musical instruments and a soccer ball are coded under Sharia law as subversive to the regime. The jihadists' ideology is, however, confronted by local reinscriptions of the meaning of objects, time, and space, that is, the chronotope of resistance.

The first confrontational reinscription is in the form of a mad woman who asserts that she simultaneously exists in Haitian, European, and African time. The only uncovered woman in view, her apparent madness allows her to navigate the force field of ubiquitous physical discipline and punishment meted out to the body politic. Her body, which transgresses the imposed topography, marks where the lines of somatic disjointure lie within the brutal Islamic regime's somatic and ideological jointure. In a bird's-eye-view shot, she blocks a military vehicle in a narrow dirt alley. The long, flowing, colorful tail of her dress covers the earth, and her arms spread-eagled almost to the width of the alleyway: a brief but breathtakingly beautiful moment of the embodied defiance that announces the disjointure from the powerful somatic and ideological inscription of the law. Later, the village youths defiantly play soccer with a nonexistent ball, creating an object that mediates a disjointure of subjectivity within the law. Because Sharia law prohibits anything Western, including sports, the regime will mete out severe punishment to those who play soccer or own a ball. In a series of long shots that draw the viewer into the visceral emotionality of witnessing quiet subaltern resistance, the boys run, score, cheer, and pass the invisible ball as a jihadist militants' vehicle circles around them. In another scene, a woman is arrested and endures public beatings because she, an unmarried woman, has been caught uncovered and singing in a room with a group of men playing music. In the midst of her punishment—covered in a black hijab that obscures the contour of her body and, by extension, the singularity of her desire, forcing somatic jointure upon her unruly body—she bursts into song, a wailing pitch with the beauty of her voice still intact. Her voice is itself a point of somatic disjointure that expresses her drive to keep going in a space of public persecution and to overwhelm the torturous inscription of power on her body with the life drive. Thus, this subject of feminine jouissance enters into the path of the emancipatory drive that counters ideological and political violence. *Timbuktu* creates the chronotope of the emancipatory drive where the subjects rewrite delimitations imposed on their unique being, both temporal, by refusing to abide by the historiography that the law seeks to enforce toward the telos of jihadist utopia, and spatial, by erupting out of social spaces in which the identities and duties are to be performed.

In *Incendies*,[19] Nawal Marwan, a political prisoner, participates in the militant protest against the Christian regime's massacre of Muslims during the Lebanese civil war. Nawal becomes known as "the woman who sings" among prisoners and prison guards. Throughout her incarceration, filled with assaults and torture, Nawal's singing voice penetrates prison walls stained with blood and human waste. The voice emanates from the chronotope of the emancipatory drive, which the threat to her life cannot silence, and it signifies the life drive that sustains her in the face of fascist power. In this space of survival and resistance, the life drive overwhelms the will to annihilate and to enforce on the subject the temporal trajectory toward certain destruction. This is the chronotope of the emancipatory drive.

Steve McQueen's *Widows*[20] includes a sequence that demonstrates just how difficult it can be to imagine the chronotope of the emancipatory drive as a field of human existence where somatic disjointure occurs. In the beginning of a single take that lasts more than three minutes, a white Chicago politician, who is campaigning to be reelected, gets into his chauffeured car. Facing a Black opponent and having just addressed a Black community on a stage set up in the ghetto, the politician cynically rants at his aide, negating his own public speech about ideal community. As viewers, we see only streetscapes during the conversation. As the politician's car emerges from the ghetto and the scenery changes from tenements to mansions, the camera pans slightly right to include the chauffeur in the shot as if to reveal that the driver, who is Black, is confined to the obscene desire of the Other. The ride through the city captures the seamless continuation of space and time in which the Black face floats, confined within the flat surface of the image. The Black subject, whose drive remains muted and invisible, serves as a reminder that by confining Blackness, our society can fantasize blocking the emancipatory drive from emerging, and the bodily drive of the ruling bourgeoisie continues on its death-drive trajectory.

Repetitions that constitute the bodily drive, such as Laurent's serial killing, exist in a silent, self-absorbed world where subjects direct physical, psychic, and political force toward the Other, who exists as a partial object that fails to deliver the subject from the wounding cut at the heart of their desire. These repetitions, however, can be interrupted, and in the resulting gap or fissure, the ethical subject of the emancipatory drive can emerge to engage with the Other's own emancipatory drive. The ethical relation to the Other becomes possible when the subject engages with the Other's drive.

Here, let us pause to consider the way different thinkers theorize the ethical subject and its relationship to the Other. For Paul Eisenstein and Todd McGowan, the point of true solidarity between subjects lies in the recognition that the Real of our subjectivity is, in fact, the lack.[21] Alain Badiou states that love, a framing of one's relationship to the Other, entails lovers' experiences of the world from two points of view, not one.[22] The ethical subject likewise emerges from the ashes of the singular bodily drive through an experience of the world from the perspective of two points, two drives, rather than one. Applying Badiou's concept of immortality, the subject of the politically meaningful emancipatory drive is the immortal subject, a truly human subject capable of discovering a truth that can be universally applied across social, political, and cultural divisions.[23]

For Badiou, the subject's encounter with a fissure through which they can break down the boundaries of a given situation occurs in the fields of politics, science, art, and love.[24] This encounter constitutes an event through which the subject begins to engage with a universal truth. To put the emancipatory drive in Lacanian terms, reaching the point of the fissure in the trajectory of the bodily drive can be a life-altering event that breaks down confinement to a pregiven situation in order to arrive at the truth of that drive, which is the emancipatory drive. To put the emancipatory drive in Badiou's terms, the subject who maintains fidelity to such an event—as long as the subject keeps acting in devotion to the revealed universal truth—obtains immortal solidarity with all subjects of the emancipatory drive. Just as Saint Paul encountered the resurrection, an event that tears down the situational boundary of pregiven religious and philosophical discourses,[25] we can likewise envision the universal capacity for all human subjects to transcend the pregiven order and its boundaries upon encountering an event that defies explanation or incorporation. This is an ethical act through which the subject cleaves to a universal truth that can alter history across borders. This act defines the ethics of revolution and the politically meaningful emancipatory drive.

The Chronotope of the Emancipatory Drive

At this point, it is helpful to summarize my theorization of the chronotope of the emancipatory drive and its psychoanalytic relevance. Combining existing theories of the drive with my own, I begin this section by reasserting that the subject of the drive appears through some somatic disjointure that renders the desiring body resistant to inscription by the Symbolic order. The chronotope of the drive involves atemporality, a repetitious return to the pursuit of *objet a* without the possibility of obtaining it. As critics from Žižek to McGowan have noted, the act of returning is itself the aim of the drive, generating jouissance from continually "not having it." In Martin Scorsese's *The Age of Innocence* (1993), courtly love exemplifies this jouissance, in this case through not having "the lady." Aching pleasure comes from touching her glove, kissing the handle of a parasol she might have held, and walking away from a chance to finally have her, aged and spent, when all the rules of bourgeois society no longer prohibit a union with the lady. This act of keeping on going, without actually arriving, is not simply about prolonging desire by postponing the final obtaining of *objet a*. It is an outright refusal of the promise that the object makes. The trajectory is initiated by desirous longing and continues along the tortuous, pleasurable path of not having. Or, as Melville's Bartleby the scrivener would say, preferring not to have it. Each repetition is, as Žižek notes,[26] a return to the curved space of desire where one continually encounters impossible objects that are never *objet a* themselves and where one is denied a straight and narrow road toward fulfillment.

The alternative to this scenario is that the desiring subject performs what Paul Verhaeghe calls a "hop-step-jump"[27] to the other side of desire, and of the drive, to an atemporal, curved space where the desiring subject formulates a different chronotope of the drive. The transformational aspect of the drive is found in this jump from the solipsistic bodily drive. The subject continues on this way through the same curved space, even after discovering that the Other does, in fact, lack the puzzle piece that fills the gap within, which came from becoming a social subject by relating to the world through signifiers. A transformed subject lives with the lack, becomes someone in love who sees the lover's lack appearing as a sign of her own way of having become a subject through a traumatic cut. Importantly, in the trajectory of the drive, where all objects are partial objects that hold no promise of filling the lack in us, we hop-step-jump over the abyss of the Other's lack while not losing sight of the Real of the situation that this abyssal lack is the foundation of our subjectivity. This jump across, from one way of desiring to another, has an ethical dimension. In this process, it becomes impossible to follow the law of desire as written; the subject must formulate a new relationship to desire itself.

My position on the drive is a corrective response to Mari Ruti's ethics of desire. Here, I am expanding on points I have made in previous chapters regarding her notion of desire and drive. Ruti advocates reconceptualizing desire primarily as a defense against the antisocial tendency exhibited by Lee Edelman's subject of the death drive, in which meaningful social and political actions seem impossible because the subject's aim is the pursuit of jouissance to death, through which the subject arrives at social and Symbolic death. I cite Ruti's statement at length:

> Though I concur that desire is endlessly deferred, perpetuated by nonsatisfaction ... I stress the autonomy—and therefore the politico-ethical potential—that arises from the fact that desire does fixate on specific objects.... The fact that no object ever offers definitive satisfaction does not mean that no object compels us. Quite the contrary.... We are capable of resisting the hegemonic messages of our social environment, including the attempts of authority figures to convince us of the mistakenness of our desire, precisely because we find certain objects incomparably mesmerizing. In this sense, the ethical promise of desire derives from its stubborn loyalty to its objects, including ones that we are told are socially inappropriate.[28]

In this statement, desire coincides with the drive that is politically meaningful: it allows resistance to hegemony. However, when considering the ethics of the drive, the emphasis should be on the fact that all objects are partial and that their properties or attributes cannot themselves be the starting point of political resistance and emancipation. The recognition that all objects are partial, and our subsequent refusal to cede our drive toward emancipation from the condition of existence organized around phantasmatic objects, is the starting point of the ethics of the drive. This recognition and refusal in relation to partial objects keeps us in the territory of the emancipatory drive. Desire requires a different kind of space that allows for the temporality of desire, which is forever moving forward to unfold toward a series of objects that further cause desire. What Ruti calls "the kind of (jouissance-filled) pleasure that we derive from objects,"[29] as opposed to death-drive jouissance, for which Edelman advocates, is the defense we put up to avoid the ethical call to transform our relationship to objects. We avoid that call as long as the preexisting context of the production of mesmerizing objects does not confront, undermine, and even destroy jouissance-filled pleasure. Within this context is the perpetual need to produce objects that cause our desire. I have conceptualized the life drive on the path of emancipation that involves a hop-step-jump from the death drive's overdeterminations. We must reformulate the slogan "do not give up on your desire" and its jouissance-filled pleasure to "do not give up on your life-drive jouissance," which is the starting point of the new path to the emancipatory drive.

Life-drive jouissance that interrupts the production of objects of desire, especially in the prevalent capitalist mode that propels the production of consumer products, is represented in the much-understated comedic film *All Is Bright*.[30] In this film, a French-Quebecois pair, reformed thieves Rene and Dennis, peddle Christmas trees that they have hauled from Quebec to Brooklyn. Recently paroled, Dennis wants to keep a promise he has made "in his head" to buy a piano for his child, who has been told by her mother that Dennis is dead. Dennis sells enough trees to fulfill the promise but loses everything to an armed robber. Along the way, he has befriended Olga, the morally upright, no-nonsense maid of a wealthy dentist. She offers to leave a window open in the dentist's mansion, so that Dennis and Rene can recoup their losses by stealing from him. The house holds abundant precious objects, including a Steinway grand piano and a safe hidden behind a painting.[31]

We anticipate that these ex-thieves, already established as expert safe crackers, will loot the safe, and they do come prepared with what seem to be the tools of the trade. We are even prepared to celebrate the bond of class solidarity between Olga and Dennis when he and Rene make off with that sublime object par excellence: cash. Instead, the two men painstakingly disassemble the piano and drive off in their hobbled trailer with the piano parts disguised as indistinguishable refuse for their cross-border journey back home. The life drive strikes the structure of the production of objects and object-relations, and the jouissance involved therein derives from the sublimation of objects in a way that confronts the law of the capitalist production and the enjoyment of the objects and their value within it. The film details in a lengthy sequence the way the piano is broken down, part by part, into unrecognizable material, signifying its transformation from a commodity to partial objects that exceed the commodity value, in direct violation of the law of production and enjoyment of objects in capitalism. It is notable that the promise that drives Dennis to sublimate a partial object, the piano, exists only in his head, not as a contractual obligation to procure or create an object of value within the law of capitalist production. When we see it reassembled at the end of the film, it stands in the snow-covered front yard of a humble working-class home. A partial object even after its reintegration, it does not mediate a united family with Dennis at its center. It marks life-drive jouissance.

Jouissance, with all its destructive potential, normally remains hidden in plain sight. I happened upon one such instance in a subterranean space in Hochelaga-Maisonneuve, Montreal. Wandering in this working-class neighborhood, I spotted a banner announcing a pro wrestling match hanging from the facade of a Catholic church. In the packed basement, rowdy spectators chanted "French *le!*" to the male wrestlers, one of whom had fleur-de-lis sewn onto the back of his pants, rather conspicuously marking the anal region. This is a scene where we witness jouissance of the queer bodily drive, conveniently sequestered in a church basement. The film *Prisoners*[32] shows how the bodily drive's jouissance might escape such subterranean confinement. The film represents jouissance in its most menacing form: the obscene usufruct of the Other through abduction and torture. The scene that might be confined to a church basement in Hochelaga-Maisonneuve erupts into the public space where jouissance, experienced as a personal act, has public consequences. A murderous Catholic priest keeps the desiccated remains of his victim tied to a chair in his basement. The macabre trophy shares the hidden space with statues of martyrs and saints. The institutional, properly mediated version of jouissance—sainthood and martyrdom—and privatized jouissance coexist as part of a broader society in which objectification and use of the Other obtains public meaning. This uneasy coexistence reflects Lacan's caution regarding jouissance. When it comes to your jouissance, Lacan warns: Watch out! You are in trouble, because "once you have started, you never know where it will end. It begins with a tickle, and ends in a blaze of petrol."[33] Lacan further asserts that "by protecting itself, [jouissance] makes Being itself languish," however, "it is Jouissance whose absence would render the universe vain."[34] Alongside these risks and necessities, jouissance marks the eruption of the Real of our Being and also our history. It is this relationship to jouissance that prompts Lacan to see it as on the side of the slave.[35] Lacan is, thus, not warning us off jouissance, which would be futile, but he is reminding us of its terrors. The caution against the excessive jouissance of the bodily drive might lead some critics to defend desire as a theoretical antidote to its ravages.

Ruti accepts that the relationship between desire and drive is messier than the simple dichotomy articulated by scholars like Edelman: desire is a regressive force, and the drive is a politically disruptive one. The complexity that is not captured by this compelling juxtaposition exists, according to Ruti, "not the least because . . . our most stubborn desires converge with the jouissance of the drive."[36] While true, what is missing in this line of thinking, where desire might bleed into the drive, is the leap from the bodily drive to the politically emancipatory drive that often emerges in the public sphere. Ruti describes Lacan's conception of the death drive as a "will to make a fresh start" by challenging "everything that exists."[37] She sees the death drive as what causes the subject to "repeatedly recommence its circling around the traumatic kernel of the lost Thing,"[38] enjoying not attaining its goal. Although this repeated return to the failure of not having the Thing indicates an enclosed subject who might leave social space behind, Ruti describes an antidote to the death drive. It is inherent in the definition of the death drive itself, as "room for a degree of 'rebirth' in the sense that each new cycle of the repetition compulsion repeats slightly differently—draws new elements, new debris of life, into the groove of the compulsion—so that when even the repetition is largely predictable, it is always also somewhat unpredictable. To the extent that something new is added to the repetition compulsion with every new enactment, one can still speak of a 'fresh start' of sorts."[39] Though this is a lucid and accurate definition of the death drive, we need to incorporate the time and space in which the drive emerges (the chronotope of the drive) in order to locate its political and emancipatory possibility.

In what Žižek describes as curved space where the subject of the drive is situated, the coordinates of our temporal and spatial relationships with objects can never be definitely calculated because our encounters with partial objects occur along the asymptotic lines of our drive, which converge infinitely but never cross.[40] Though frustrating, even maddening, this situation allows our separation, even liberation, from objects as we move through this curved field. In mediating our relationship to the Other, this same movement, which involves two subjects (rather than a subject and an object), makes possible innumerable coordinates and, thus, infinite opportunities for mutual emancipation. Each repetitious encounter with the Other slightly differs in terms of its numeric possibility of even more varied encounters, spanning the entire field of asymptotes that allow for the separation from objects and the tyranny of unfulfilled desire.

In Žižek's "paradoxical, curved space,"[41] the unobtainable "lady" of the courtly love exemplifies an impossible object, or "a paradoxical object," as Žižek puts it, which is specifically not an already existing positive entity. In this curved space, we undergo "endless detours and ordeals" at the end of which we discover that the object is nothing, accidental and inconsequential.[42] The subject of the drive emerges in the course of these "endless detours and ordeals" in a state of somatic disjointure. At that point, the relation between subject and object changes to a state where objects of desire no longer maintain the cohesive structure of subjectivity's normative somatic bonding, which always occurs in relation to objects on the part of the desiring subject. To understand the emancipatory possibility of the drive, we must realize that making "endless detours and ordeals" toward nothing does not describe a passive state, forced upon us by the circumstance that all we have are partial objects and that no object will liberate us from the lack. Rather, these detours and ordeals open a new path for the emancipation of the subject.

Imagine a child. She discovers, amid the discarded debris and refuse strewn about in a vacant lot, the most precious object she has ever seen: a scratched, but shiny, silver metal ball. The metal ball immediately becomes a stand-in for *objet a*, an object so mysterious and lovely that space and time seem to curve in deference to its permanence and perfection. She picks it up, examines it, moved by its mystery and beauty. She takes it home and immediately invents a game that allows everyone she loves to enjoy it as much as she does: Her family all take turns improvising discovery of the very metal ball. One family member hides it in a random place around the house, taking pleasure in having secret knowledge of its location until another family member discovers and rehides the object somewhere else within the house. The child cherishes her *objet a*, but in order to enjoy it completely she must separate herself from it by placing it in an even more deliberately curved space where nobody ever quite owns it. Her desire for a perfect object, and the drive to locate it in the reality of time and space, is emancipated from the object itself, and she is thus no longer subject to its inevitable failure to deliver. The entire saga is a blueprint of the emancipatory drive.

Ideological norms sustain themselves by bonding subjects to the objects that society nominates as properly desirable within a given mode of production, notably capitalism. The drive is the foundation of ethics because it paradoxically implies individual freedom from this bonding, by transforming that freedom to the drive for universal emancipation. Eisenstein and McGowan define the social subject as one who emerges after being severed from the natural world, through the acquisition of language, to become the subject of the drive. This cutting via linguistic signification, the source of our bondage, simultaneously makes possible the freedom to act differently from the perceived necessity of "naturally, culturally conditioned inclinations."[43] There emerges the opportunity to act ethically, to move beyond the trappings of ideology that sustain the experience of culture as natural, necessary, inevitable, and, I must add, beyond the bodily drive itself that we accept as both cultural and natural.

The Priests,[44] an otherwise unremarkable South Korean horror film, is an excellent cultural text that demonstrates how the subject of the drive emerges through language and signifier. The exorcizing priests attempt to force an invasive demon to say its own unique name in order to cause it to take corporeal form. The scene elegantly demonstrates how signifiers function. The name gives substance to the Thing-in-itself within the linguistic order. The demon, once named, becomes a religious and social phenomenon that must transubstantiate. In the film, the specified, localized, identified demon recites a litany of the historical and geographical locations it has traversed, boasting of how it has mutilated and altered the social conditions of these times and places. The demon has history and exemplifies a subject of the drive whose jouissance continues through many returns. But the signifier (the name) also allows society and community to render the demon impotent because the name relegates the demon to a proper place and time within the Symbolic order. This is why in this film, rituals, which express the law's own desire, are centered around naming. The possessed young woman at the center of the exorcism, vulnerable to what lies beyond the boundary of the Symbolic order that the church represents, is made safe by the priests who turn what was previously unnamed, and untamed, into a named corporeal form, then into an animal that they can capture in a small sack to throw into the river. The curved space of the drive is, thus, made straight by a signifier.

The drive transforms from bodily to emancipatory through the faculty, or rather failure, of looking, an important constituting element of the bodily drive as exemplified in a Lacanian reading of Velazquez's painting *Las meninas*.[45] The painting depicts subjects from many positions of looking. The field of vision of the painting includes Velazquez himself facing us in the middle ground. His canvas is on the left corner of the foreground, turned against our view. The turned canvas elides its content, however, we see a mirror in the background that reflects the image of King Philip IV and his queen, which leads us to believe that they are at the end of the painter's line of sight. In the center of the foreground, we see the Infanta Margaret Theresa, who looks in our direction and is attended by two ladies in waiting, who look at the child. Foregrounded on the right-hand side of the frame are two dwarfs looking in different directions; behind them stand Margaret Theresa's chaperon dressed in mourning and a guardsman, both of whom look in different directions. To the far rear end of the field is the queen's chamberlain standing sideways.

As such, there is no space for the viewer's scopic drive to contemplate a singular beautiful object. In this crowded scene, there appears a gap between the viewing subject and its object in the field of vision. The gap creates infinite possibilities of exchange between our position of looking and the objects in the scene. The field of vision should convey a unified position of looking with which we can identify. Instead, it confronts the viewer with its own gaze. Here, the act of looking does not materialize a finite subject position, since a unified position of looking is impossible. The painting gazes at us, not the other way around. As a stumbling block in the certainty of our own looking as an act of mastery, the gaze reveals that, encountering the image, we are seduced by possibilities of obtaining a wholesome object of beauty exemplifying an *objet a* and reminds us that our own scopic drive's furious movement toward that object will exist in a permanent state of frustration. The gaze blocks us from any epistemologically stable subject position, as is typically exemplified by the position of looking. The implied emancipatory possibility is the potential to free ourselves from the scopic drive that compels us toward the desirable image that generates scopic jouissance, and thus our own bodily drive, as organized around the desire to cathect ourselves to an *objet a*. The gaze frees the subject from the ideology of subjectivity based on the power of looking, which is often coded masculine. The fact that looking is culturally coded masculine implies that masculine subjectivity depends on the act of looking for its cohesiveness. The subject of the drive can, however, find the space to transform the scopic drive tied to an *objet a* into something potentially political and emancipatory in the field of the vision, curved by the gaze, that confronts the subject. The gaze marks the place of the Other, whose heteronomy doesn't align with our scopic drive.

The scopic drive is often aligned with the nation's desire. Films can capture the moment the national subject faces the gaze of the Other, which destabilizes national subjectivity organized around a specific way of desiring through looking. In the Israeli film *Policeman*,[46] a police anti-terror unit storms the hideout of a group of young self-proclaimed revolutionaries who are holding three Israeli billionaires hostage. These policemen, established in the film as trained to control and subdue Palestinian terrorists, legitimize state violence. Yaron, one of the police, zooms in on a non-Palestinian face, that of Shira, a young Ashkenazi Jewish woman, dying of a bullet wound sustained in the raid. As he kneels down to take a closer look at her face, we follow Yaron's line of sight to a close-up of Shira's face, her eyes wide as the final spasm delicately shakes her body. The shot-reverse-shot then cuts back to Yaron's close-up, but from a lower camera angle. This disrupted position of viewing conveys disturbance and shock: the image of the properly Jewish body, destroyed by the Jewish nation-state, functions as the gaze that disrupts the broad picture of the national myth of a unified ethnic nation. Although he knew the targets were Jews, Yaron is still jolted by the visual confrontation out of his position as a national subject through the shocking recognition that the state violence aimed at the Palestinian body can also target the Jewish body. The encounter has rendered tangible the way that the national desire aligns the field of vision with that of the bodily drive for the destruction of deviant subjects, which is its scopic object, whether they are Palestinian or Jewish.

The gaze Yaron encounters changes his scopic drive from one that identifies with the nation-state's position of looking, expressed cinematically by the point of view of his rifle, to a new mode of the drive that enters the curved field of the unknowable Other's drive: that of a dying Jewish woman whose body escapes the state's ideological boundary. Thus, encountering the limit of an epistemological and ontological position that has been sanctioned by the nation-state, the national subject's subjectivity undergoes transformation. Here, freedom from state ideology is possible, and through that freedom we find it possible for him to become an ethical subject in relation to the Other whom he can no longer objectify as a target of his military weapon. This constitutes a vision of the hop-step-jump from the scopic drive of the nation to the emancipatory drive.

In the process of liberating ourselves from the track of our bodily drive, we become what Santner calls "the subject-matter,"[47] where the "matter" connotes whatever exceeds the ideological construction of corporeality and identity of the subject that the modern nation-state mandates and normalizes. The subject of the drive who is capable of political transformation has several discernable qualities. First, this subject lacks Symbolic identity, or, as described by Eisenstein and McGowan, is homeless, because it refuses to take up a proper place in the Symbolic order.[48] I add that it does not have a proper place where it can entrench itself in the rut of the unwavering trajectory of the bodily drive. Second, the subject who holds the possibility of political transformation remains in a curved space where the Other continues to introduce disruptions to bodily jouissance. It constantly expands the curvature of spatiality, proliferating the asymptotic points within it. For this subject, "rather than filling the needs of the subject, the drive sustains the subject's desires as desires," continuing the state of the lack of *objet a*. In this state, "the drive meticulously avoids attaining its object, and it uses this object as a pretext for animating its movement."[49] This drive to continue movement despite the recognition that the quest to obtain *objet a* is fated to fail constitutes the position "never give up on your drive." This path on which we never give up on our drive expands its sphere to include the Other's drive in its quest for emancipation. By allowing the emergence of what exceeds the signifiers supporting the Symbolic order, the Other's drive, we become the subject of the emancipatory drive, exceeding the normative jointure of the embodied subject.

The Other's drive enters our field of vision when we see the way the subaltern, the subject whose vision and speech are beyond the hegemonic mode of aesthetic and political representation, sees and speaks. In the Iranian film *The Circle*,[50] we follow several women at the margin of the country's theocratic, patriarchal society as they try to survive in the state's chronotope, which overdetermines their every move. One, Nargess, is in a group of four women who have just escaped from jail. We never learn any biographical details about these women, nor why they were incarcerated, though the bruises on Nargess's face reveal something of her recent past. She, like other women in the film, lacks a legitimate and legible place in society; their social location describes the fundamentally criminalized position of feminine subjects. The film is shot entirely on location, on the streets of Tehran and in public buildings, further emphasizing this criminalization. The places that normally signify mobility become prisons for these women, whose femininity seems to signify unredeemable guilt to the big Other. The film's framing of Nargess also visualizes this sense of imprisonment by using common architectural elements such as doors, walkways, and walls to delineate boundaries.

In one scene, however, we follow Nargess's active looking, rather than watching her reacting to the omniscient surveillance of authority, which is sometimes visibly manifested and sometimes implied. On the street, she spots, in a stack of cheap copies of European oil paintings, Van Gogh's *Wheat Field with Cypresses*. Nargess explains to Arezou, a fellow escapee, that the painting depicts the hometown to which she has been attempting to return throughout the single day that comprises the film. Nargess indicates a hill in the painting by name; she points to a spot where, she says, she and her brother played as children. Nargess calls her hometown a paradise, convinced that all hardship will end once she gets there. Then she points to a place within the painting where, she says, the painter has failed to include some flowers, omitting a detail from the utopian landscape. In this scene, we occupy her position of looking, turning indexical signs into material elements of utopia. This scene then cuts to a shot of Nargess in full view, squatting alone on the far-left side of the frame in front of a gray wall. Dominating the center of the frame are vertical steel bars that throw shadows on the ground. The image of vertical lines reappears in a long corridor at the bus depot where Nargess runs away from the police. The image of vertical bars continues to appear throughout the film as an element of the city's chronotope, which visualizes women's imprisonment within the society.

At the end of the film, we find all the women, whose movement we have followed through Tehran, in a jail cell where metal bars once again visualize criminality and alienation of women. The meaningfulness of Nargess's encounter with *Wheat Field with Cypresses* is, however, undiminished. Nargess redraws her European Other's chronotope by imposing her own chronotope, in which her drive to look confronts the European Other's drive. Though imprisoned in the chronotope of the nation-state, she redefines the temporal and spatial organization of the image, creating its new meaning. The scopic drive of the audience falters as it encounters the newly imposed chronotope of the subaltern. Here, the scopic drive is no longer just the bodily drive, confined in the subject position of an audience in the theater. It becomes the emancipatory drive as it opens its path to the Other's drive to look and create meaning out of the world. The subject's own entrance into the emancipatory drive becomes possible as it accepts the Other's drive.

The Spanish comedy *Toc toc*[51] demonstrates how the drive obtains an ethical dimension through taking the Other into its curved space, wherein the Other's jouissance alters the trajectory of the subject's bodily drive. The film is about six people, each with a different repetition compulsion, who gather at an analyst's office. They wait interminably for the analyst, who has mysteriously booked all six for the same time slot and is supposedly making his way back from a trip overseas. As the patients try to interact, revealing individual narratives of the bodily drive, they each stumble upon a fleeting, unique moment in which their individual compulsions briefly pause. They come to realize that each moment, though unique, is a moment in which they allow the Others' symptoms to enter their own curved space of the bodily drive, in the form of a brief reprioritization of another's condition over their own. This moment forever changes the curvature of the drive to include the drive of the Other and allows each subject to imagine a future free of a previously inescapable bodily drive.

In occupying the subject position of an audience member watching *The Circle*, we allow into the field of our scopic drive the Otherness of Nargess's "symptom." Derived from her existence as a woman in a violent theocratic patriarchy, this effect of her Otherness finds expression in her act of looking. Her drive carves, albeit virtually, a new path in a Van Gogh landscape. It opens a hole in the visual space, which she demands we fill with missing flowers, like a blemish in an authentic visual field of a European landscape. The emancipatory drive allows us to break from the ideological constraints that place us in a chronotope of the nation-state where the teleology of the desire of the nation-state and capitalism unfolds, according to which we are meant to sublimate our personal adventure to pursue the sublime object of ideology. By refusing, alongside Nargess, to abide in that chronotope, we allow the kernel of the Other's desire to curve our own. The Other's insistence on an impossible object curves the space where normal temporal progression is materialized and visualized into that of an impossible time, where there is no temporal progression of the quest for objects of desire—a time without telos. Witnessing this transformation, we may allow our scopic bodily drive to obtain a politically emancipatory aspect. In the missing flowers, we recognize the kernel of the Other's desire and its ability to overwhelm the chronotope of desire of the nation-state. Making space for missing flowers in an altered landscape of the subaltern chronotope, we ourselves enter this new chronotope of the subaltern. We separate ourselves from the preexisting context of discourse and identity. This is the experience of freedom within the new chronotope of the emancipatory drive.

The Emancipatory Drive and History

In contrast to the emancipatory side of the drive as I have theorized, David Denny invokes the perversity of the drive in his reading of *The Hurt Locker*.[52] In the film, James, the main character, is a soldier in Iraq. He collects bomb parts as surrogates for the more proper commodities that overwhelm him, such as the wall of cereal boxes on the shelf of a warehouse-style grocery store. According to Denny, this behavior demonstrates the perverse side of the drive. Denny argues that this shows how James's drive locks him in a rut of repetitive engagement with, and futile utilization of, objects. In a world where there is no possibility of satisfying desire, it is the drive itself that becomes commodified. For Denny, by locking the subject in the rut of futile repetition, drives can be "sutured to the social in such a way that they fail to disturb the social."[53] Consequently, Denny sees James's drive as stuck in the economy of pleasure within the law of capitalism and as having nothing to do with subversive jouissance. Denny thus concludes that the drive can function as a perversion, rather than subversion, of the law. He argues that the drive has a conservative nature, due to its ability to conform to the repetition of a social norm and in its fidelity to its own excess.[54] "The subject of the drive," he asserts, "complements the real of capitalism in the way it remains stuck to enjoyment, to the way it endlessly circles around and gains satisfaction by way of the impossible objects and simulacra of consumption."[55] This tendency to circle is what I conceptualize as the bodily drive that could be bound within the orbit of capitalist expansion. One must take active steps toward an emancipatory drive that subverts the law of capitalism through the recognition that all objects are partial, a path that I have described. It cannot be conflated with the satisfaction of a perverse subject who is tied to the big Other as the guarantor of the truth and obtains satisfaction within the law without the potential for subverting the law.

The South Korean film *The Front Line*, discussed in chapter 1, illustrates how the architecture of the drive shatters the efficacy of satisfaction derived from perversity. In this film, set during the Korean War, the North and the South engage in an endless struggle to capture and hold a hill that has no particular meaning or strategic value and is important only insofar as it marks a point of advance and retreat in the cartography of war. In the cycle of capture and retreat, some North Korean soldiers discover a hole in a cave where the Southerners have cached precious goods: cigarettes, liquor, and food. The Northerners consume everything in the cache and, upon retreating, fill the hole with their own excrement for the Southerners to discover. After retaking the hill, the Southerners discover the defilement of their cache. Rather than replying in kind, however, they refill the hole with edible and usable goods. Eventually, both sides come to consume and replace what they find in the hole, leaving behind a regular bounty for their enemies when they inevitably retake the hill. The hole becomes a locus where North and South Korean soldiers communally share: first, goods that they think the other would desire, later thank-you notes, and eventually, homebound letters that soldiers from each army ask to be sent to relatives on the other side of a border that neither country's postal system will cross. This hole represents the Real of the law of the nation-state, around which the subversive desire to sleep (or at least sup) with the enemy Other arises. The goods hidden in the hole, though desirable, always remain associated with the original defilement of the first cache, reminding us of a Lacanian truth that all objects of desire are indeed shit. They also initiate a cycle of repetition, as do all objects that are mistakenly thought to have the capacity to satisfy desire. In this case, however, both parties engage with the drive of the Other and subtly alter each subsequent repetition until they reach the point where they are no longer tied to national ideologies. At the conclusion of the film, the main characters from both North and South watch as bombs indiscriminately massacre fighters from both sides and say that they can no longer recall the reason for the war to which they have dedicated themselves.

With each return to the same, meaningless patch of disputed territory, engagement and entanglement with the Other deepen, qualitatively transforming the relationship between subjects and their Others. In the end, the lives involved in the trajectories of the drive become so intertwined that the distinction between friend and enemy collapses, which undermines the hostility of war and the opposed national ideologies that sustain it. Such is the destructive force that the drive can mete out to the Symbolic order. The force of that destruction escalates, because each repetition and return contains something that exceeds the previous cycle of return: from excrement, to cigarettes, to photos of communist and anti-communist families, scattered and dispossessed. Both parties must recognize all, not as satisfactory objects but as signs of the lack inherent in the Other. These objects are stand-ins, ultimately meaningless in fulfilling individual and national desires, and those small, subversive acts introduce Otherness that transforms the field of the drive, allowing an opening for the Other's lack as its constitutional element. It becomes a space of the ethics of the emancipatory drive.

This circling around the site of desire (like the hole in *The Front Line*) that defines the drive should not lead us to conclude that the drive's trajectory will remain confined to the same arc. As scholars have pointed out, the satisfaction that the drive yields has nothing to do with the objects themselves. Satisfaction lies in the possibility of returning not to the exact same arc of movement but to a somewhat altered orbit where a new engagement with the Other occurs. In this way, the drive's trajectory involves the traumatic reformation of the subject, leaving it perpetually without identity or home. The subject of this drive may then recognize this traumatic reformation as the universal condition in which it can identify with the Other. This is the emancipatory dimension of the drive that scholars have noted, using slightly different frames of reference, such as Eisenstein and McGowan, in their concept of freedom, and Zupančič, in her own tracing of the trajectory of desire toward the space she identifies as *outside* of fantasy.

Cathy Caruth posits that trauma historicizes subjects.[56] This helps us to visualize the drive through which the subject arrives at a different chronotopical arc: atemporal returns in curved space as opposed to the chronotope of desire as written on teleology. At this point, atemporal returns obtain a historical dimension. For Caruth, the subject enters history as the subject relates to the Other through trauma. Caruth bases this position on Freud's account of the father whose child admonishes him in a dream. The child's admonition is a demand that the father face the trauma of death, an Otherness utterly traumatic to the living, rather than take refuge from the traumatic shattering of his reality (the death of his child) by dreaming that the speaking child is alive. Trauma brings Otherness—in the form of the Other in whose traumatic version of the lack I see my own—into the subject's very condition of existence. Trauma involves the appearance of the Other, to whose Otherness the subject must find a way to relate. The subject, in doing so, must recognize its own place in history as a context that creates the relationship between the subject and the Other whom it meets in a traumatic condition.

In terms of my theorization of the drive, the Other's drive opens up the arc of the emancipatory drive, and universal emancipation defines the trajectory of history. In *The Front Line*, each return represents a different arc, as each arc brings the subjects closer to the Other's traumatic lack. At one point in the film, a Southern soldier realizes that a young woman he encounters in a mountain trail is a notorious Northern sniper and that she also appears in a family photo of a Southerner who joined the North Korean communist army, a photo that was left in the hole with a letter from the communist soldier asking the Southerners to deliver it to his family in the South. The family in the photo has likely experienced extraordinary persecutions, even executions, as family members defect to the enemy side. The soldier is moved by the pathos of this fate, the loss of the right to life that the geopolitical condition has created, constituting the lack in a history-specific context, which the woman's younger self, as seen in the photo, had yet to confront; he finds himself unable to shoot her. To reiterate, we can recognize the personal loss that the Other suffers as the symptom of the traumatic lack informed by historical conditions. In this way, the subject moves from nation-time to something transcendent. This subject no longer lives by North or South Korean time but by the atemporality of the traumatic Real, atemporal here in the sense that no ideological and material system can eradicate the lack through temporally bound action. The traumatic encounter with the nation's Other, in shattering the existing trajectory of the bodily drive for a missing object (e.g., a united, independent nation), makes possible the subject's relocation to a new chronotope of the traumatic Real. This encounter is history-specific, and in it the subject must make room for the Other's trauma, along with its drive, immersed in a local and historical context.

As I have established in previous chapters, to interrogate how the Symbolic order works, as well as how we might subvert that order in various political and social configurations (such as nation-states), it is necessary to see the relationship between global conditions of subjectivity and their various local contexts. Aesthetic cinematic forms reflect global conditions of subject production: consider how genre films construct subjects. Cinematic forms are intricately involved in local articulations of trauma, which structure the social subject and scaffold social formations, both of which draw from the global condition, notably that of capitalism. Expressions of local trauma, however, can exceed the global aesthetic form. It is in this context that I take a close look at the local chronotope of trauma which the North represents in a South Korean context in order to articulate the subject of the emancipatory drive in a specific location of historical trauma. This will allow us to see how local trauma influences the global cinematic form. Through historical trauma, the subject experiences the lack at the heart of subjectivity itself. The ideological objects that stand in as the *objet a* for nations, society, and communities fail to mend the lack. Through trauma, the subject alters the trajectory of its drive and enters a different chronotope, one that separates the subject from the ideological foundation that organizes time and space in which the ideological subject exists. This shift introduces the emancipatory possibility for the subject.

Trauma opens the realm of the Real of our existence. In the realm of the Real, the subject enters the new trajectory of the drive, beyond the bodily drive that trauma has initially oriented toward survival through cathexis to objects. Out of the abyss of trauma, the subject of the emancipatory drive emerges. Trauma shatters the linear time and unified space that anchor subjects to a cohesive perception of reality. Subjects who experience trauma repeatedly return to this shattering, but trauma's repetitions don't fate the subject to remain in the same rut. Extrapolating from Caruth, we can argue that each traumatic turn is an event through which we encounter the Other anew, because in a traumatic event the Other arrives to alert us, as subjects of trauma, to the lack that constitutes us anew in a new historical context. This encounter unsettles my relationship to the Other, an object of my desire, to the degree that I must devise a new way of being, including a new relationship to the *objet a* that the Other represents. The Other outside the subject's own chronotope enables the subject to reconfigure itself, to open up to a new chronotope in which a new traumatic Otherness, the other time and space of being, appears. This new subject, whose interiority is defined by Otherness—in the classical Lacanian notion of the hard kernel as something in me that is more than me—is the subject of the Real. This subject's trajectory of existence follows the emancipatory drive that continues to create a new experience of the traumatic Real. Thus, trauma is not debilitation or annihilation but affirmation and continuation of life that endlessly expands through the emancipatory drive.

We can narrate history only through returning to that meeting with the Other, although the traumatic dimension of encountering the Other imposes a gap, repressed speech, and a cognitive blockage that prevent us from returning and remembering that meeting. The emancipatory drive breaks through that gap and blockage. Even though trauma's repetitiousness and circularity undermine linear temporality, returning to trauma and thus pushing through the gap and blockage allows subjects to place themselves in relationships with other subjects in the unique chronotopical context of being. This formation of relationship describes the process of our becoming historical subjects. Here, the traumatic Real pushes the subject from the personal experience of wounding to an arc of the drive that includes other wounded subjects.

Through varied repetitions, we hop-step-jump into a chronotope yet unknown, and through that act, we change the course of history. Once we land in a new chronotope of the drive, however, it's not always easy to continue on that drive toward emancipation. In *The Front Line*, both parties make that hop-step-jump, but because it is so difficult to imagine an existence beyond the fraternal nation, the film's conclusion after the hop-step-jump is the spectacular annihilation of the male bodies; the wounding from the lack of the nation leads to the material and psychical destruction of the subject, creating a nostalgic pathos for the lack of the nation that the bodily drive circles around. The wounded and broken bodies in this film cannot open up the new chronotope of the emancipatory drive beyond the drive toward the fraternal nation. Hence, the landscape is covered with putrefied body parts.

Different modes and contexts of wounding set the scene of encounter between subjects in different locations of historical trauma as the origin of that wounding. The experience of encountering the wounded Other constitutes the Real that shatters the chronotopic coordinates of reality, notably that of the nation-state. As Kojin Karatani would posit, there appears to me, on the horizon of my vision, the Other who is yet to speak[57] of its wound. The space where we meet the Other, who has hitherto been hidden in the official discourse, is the space of the Real of history. This meeting occurs in *Dooman River* (2010). The film is directed by Zhang Lu, a South Korean filmmaker who immigrated from Yanbian, an ethnic Korean enclave in China. In this film, a traumatic encounter with North Korean refugees in Manchuria places Chang-Ho, a young Joseonjok (ethnic Koreans in China) boy, in the historical context of the North as the chronotope of trauma, shattering his previous existence and thus forcing him to devise a new ethical subjectivity. His eventual death is, in a way, a logical extension of this transformation. I will shortly return to this film in my discussion of the chronotope of the North in South Korean cinema. It is a return to the scene of South Korea as one of the prime locations for observing the subject formation both in historical and theoretical context.

For now, continuing my transtextual and transnational analyses, I look at such a transformation of the subject in Michael Haneke's *Time of the Wolf*.[58] The film is set in an apocalyptic chronotope, an unnamed European country without distinct historical markers. The film never makes clear what has caused the end of the world as we know it, but it seems as if no meaningful act is possible, beyond the bodily drive for mere life. However, an ethical subjectivity emerges through a boy, Ben. We see a situation unfolding in a train station where there seems to be no possibility of escaping the rut of existence, where people have established a rudimentary social structure to ensure survival with limited resources. They wait for a train, which they believe will deliver them from the ruins of civilization to a new chronotope of existence, although it is not certain if such a train exists. The cinematography emphasizes, through the color palette, the destitution of living in the lack, as opposed to the phantasmatic abundance that the desiring subject pursues. The daylight seems cold, rendered in low-saturation tones; the train station is a gray, drab space where humanity is represented by the bodies covering the floor, sleeping, waiting, and occasionally acting out the overwhelming bodily drive for sex and for annihilation of others. There are no spectacular shots of the catastrophic ending of the world, simply an interminable stretch of rural landscape in which all humans are confined in the bodily drive.

In this world, Ben has experienced the disintegration of his family: his father was murdered, and his mother is increasingly alienating herself from her children, no longer a reliable source of protection and comfort. He has been quietly attending to the emerging tale of a mythic salvation shared among people. How that might be possible is not a focal point in this film, which erases all signs of the narrative intervention that we are used to seeing in apocalyptic movies. The boy decides to self-immolate, in accordance with the lore he has learned of a sacrifice that can save all humankind. Lying in a room filled with layers of restlessly sleeping bodies that have taken shelter in the train station, his nose profusely bleeding, Ben watches his mother across the room copulating with a stranger. The boy walks silently out of the building, toward a bonfire, feeds the fire, watches it rise, and begins to strip off his clothes. A minor male character in the film who has been involved in altercations with other residents around disputes over scarce resources happens to be on the guard duty that night and sees the child. This man immediately understands the boy's intentions.

After pinning him on the ground, the man holds the boy, his nose still bleeding, revealing the wound of his being. The man tells the child that it is enough that he was ready to sacrifice himself. Maybe, the man says, tomorrow all will be fine again; maybe even the dead will come back to life. As his speech continues, the camera pulls back to frame the scene of the two figures against the night, silhouetted by the bonfire at the lower center of the frame, with the looming darkness occupying much of the screen. The shot comes to rest and cuts to an image of the unnamed open rural landscape rolling past in daytime as if seen from a moving train. This image persists for about two minutes, before it cuts to black and the ending credits. It is not only the boy's gesture but also the man's response that completes the ethics of the drive. The movement that the final image of the landscape expresses metaphorizes this. Together, they create the movement of the emancipatory drive by including the life drive of the Other in a situation where the world-making drive has become impossible.

Let us here return to jouissance, which is inherent in the drive and accompanies the emergence of the Real. The drive perpetually and repetitiously circles the zone of jouissance that subverts the ideological constitution of proper enjoyment. But the most unsettling effect of jouissance, the eruption of the Real, can also be incorporated into the capitalist politics of surplus jouissance. The cinematic screen itself thus becomes a space where jouissance functions as a capitalist commodity.

I have argued in previous chapters that the cinematic screen can function as a field that exhibits the traumatic and devastating effect of the Real. Through the screen, subjects can be thoroughly overcome by irreducible Otherness, experienced through the traumatic relationship to the Other, in which the Other is more than the screen that reflects the subject of desire. According to Lacan, "man's desire is the desire of the other."[59] One deduces from this (somewhat ambiguous) statement that the Other both reflects my own desire and affirms my unified status as a subject of desire. But on the screen, the Other can reflect the kind of desire that is unbearably and irreconcilably different from my desire. There, the Other who knows my desire is instead the Other who cannot give me, as a desiring subject, what I want: my unified subjecthood.

The emancipatory side of the drive exists in this encounter with the Other, rather than in the circling around an empty, impossible object. In *Time of the Wolf*, the boy represents the subject who, having experienced the failure of desire and the limit of the bodily drive that emerges from it, enters the drive that holds the jouissance of transcending the boundary of the bodily drive as a social condition of existence. At this juncture, it is important to reassert that the drive's repetitions are not mechanical. The drive indeed emerges in what Lacan calls "tuché,"[60] a subject's repetitious chance encounter, not a designed or willed one, with the Real through randomly appearing objects. Together, the subject and its objects constitute a patterned mechanism of the subject's repetitious encounter with the Real that breaks apart the boundaries of reality. However, this repetition should not lead us to assume that the drive's movement is inevitably confined in the determined sphere of the production of partial objects. Imagining the drive as something stuck in such a rut reveals the tendency to think of the drive in predominantly topological terms. To go beyond the spatial imagination that confines the drive's trajectory within calculable coordinates, we need to consider the repetitions of traumatic symptoms.

Each traumatic turn can be an event that forces the appearance of Otherness in the subject's experience: of the Real, of history, of one's own subjectivity, or even of love. Even when a subject has escaped the Otherness of death, that subject undergoes a new subjectivization and changes her mode of being. Trauma allows the subject to continue life with the Otherness that trauma has introduced into the subject's existence. Repetitions of traumatic symptoms keep Otherness appearing—not just the fact of death, wounds, or dying but what it is about them that exceeds the subject's capacity to mourn, to monumentalize, and thus to recuperate the Symbolic order of life. Trauma opens up fissures in the Symbolic order as it reveals the impossibility of subjectivity by showing us what exceeds it. Alain Badiou and Élisabeth Roudinesco point out that in a psychoanalytic cure, the subject moves from the experience of impotence, which is a symptom of pathology and refers to the inability to function within the Symbolic order, to that of the impossibility of sustaining subjectivity as one knows it.[61] It is at this point that the symptomatic subject must devise a new subjectivity, which, I add, exceeds the Symbolic order's prescription of pathology and norm. Trauma forces a reformulation of the temporal and spatial order, beyond the chronotope within which the symptomatic subject has originated in the first place. One can say the subject continues to traverse many chronotopes while continuing to devise a new impossible subjectivity.

Cinematic space, when visualizing the impossibility of fulfilling desire, works as a field that the subject traverses to reach the Real of desire, the drive. This traversal is the process in which occurs the faltering of what Jacques-Alain Miller describes as "suture," a covering over of the lack, and the subsequent establishment of subjectivity in a chain of signification.[62] This unsuturing creates the possibility of an ethical and political act, because through it the subject can resist ideologies that depend on suture for their meaning-making. Drawing from my conceptualization of the cinema of the Real in previous chapters, I posit that the cinematic spectacle can convey the trauma of the Real through the viewing position in such a process of unsuturing. Through that position, the spectator enters and exists in the time and space of the Real. It might look like we have stepped into the game of *fort-da* that Freud sees as an enactment of the death drive. Freud observes a game that his grandchild, experiencing his mother's regular departure from the family home, has invented. In this game, the child throws a cotton reel away (*fort*) and retrieves it (*da*). It is read as the child's response to the mother's absence. However, it is not the child's enactment of the phantasmatic mastery over his loss, which might mitigate his suffering. The cotton reel functions as a little object "a," a precious missing object that his mother represents. This game enshrines "a," but as a disappearing, impossible object one can never get hold of. The repeated appearance/disappearance that the game stages metaphorizes the subject's relationship to "a," which the subject forever circles around without ever getting.

As we have seen, the death drive is, in Lacanian thinking, formulated as a matrix of the drive's ethical subjectivity. I reiterate that the subject of the emancipatory drive emerges through the repetitious encounter with the traumatic Real. The cinematic spectacle of the traumatic Real, thus, can open up time and space in which the subject's sensory perception that enfolds the bodily drive becomes a pathway to the emancipatory drive.

The Chronotope of the Emancipatory Drive in South Korean Cinema

The subject of desire is stuck in an endless cycle of the acquisition of commodities as objects of desire. For this subject, there is no satisfaction.[63] The fact that there is no end point of desiring nevertheless sustains the subject's belief in finally acquiring the piece, clipped off the edge of the subject's imaginary perfect self, that would make the subject complete if finally located. The emancipatory drive evokes a different kind of satisfaction. Consider the idea of perpetual revolution. Should the revolution achieve a new party state, the subject of the emancipatory drive would immediately launch a campaign that reveals the Real of the law of this state, which has established a new matrix of desire. As a perpetual critique of the law that reveals the law's abyss, rather than its reason and rationality, the emancipatory drive makes radical politics possible. Satisfaction for the subject of the drive, Todd McGowan notes, comes from the act of revealing the Real of any regime.[64] This is the emancipatory dimension of the drive. The South Korean films that I examine below engage with this sort of revelation. They display fissure points within the cinematic narration of the nation through the visualization of space in which the nation-state fails to function as a principle for organizing and fulfilling desire. In these films, the landscape of the nation becomes a no-man's-land, casting doubt on the national teleology that promises to fulfill subjects' goals, be that obtaining social goods or becoming a national subject comfortably situated within the national ideologies.

The economy of desire necessitates the creation of objects, and the law of the nation-state enables, but also depends on, their production. Since objects ultimately only reveal the lack, and thus generate dissatisfaction, the subject of desire will continue to depend on the regime's next cycle of production for its objects of desire. One can see from this how nationalism generates the law of desire: through national identification, the subject participates in a defined way of desiring. National subjectivity conforms to a particular collective way of desiring. In contrast, the subject of the emancipatory drive obtains satisfaction from the failure of subjectivity organized around collective desire. The ethnic Koreans of the North reveal a crack in this law of desire. In what I call the films of the chronotopic North, we also see the subject that resists the law of desire of the nation.

The Yellow Sea,[65] with its gritty cinematography and mise-en-scène reminiscent of gangster genre B movies, unfolds around Gu-Nam, an ethnic Korean in China, and his entanglement in the contract killing of a South Korean man who belongs to the elite class. Gu-Nam has gone deep into debt to send his wife to Seoul for work, where she subsequently disappears. He reluctantly accepts an offer made by Myun—a dog-meat dealer and crime boss in a town in Yanbian, a major domicile for ethnic Koreans as part of the colonial diasporas in China—as his only means to get to South Korea and search for his wife, who might have abandoned him and their child to start a new life. After Gu-Nam is smuggled into South Korea by human traffickers, the target of the contract killing is murdered by another gang, hired by a different man, for a different reason. Gu-Nam, now a prime suspect, goes on the run and discovers that Myun had no intention of helping him return to China. Stranded, on the trail of his missing wife, and on the run from both the police and Myun's gang, Gu-Nam eventually suffers a mortal wound while attempting to return to China and dies on a hijacked fishing boat in the middle of the Yellow Sea. After bleeding to death, his body is dumped unceremoniously into the sea by the fisherman, along with the box that contains what he believes to be the cremated remains of his wife. This anonymous double burial at sea, signifying a liminal space between nations, visualizes Gu-Nam's status as a man without a country.

The film organizes the narrative around, and spectacularizes, the destruction of ethnic Korean male bodies that are not quite rightly Korean. The film's affect derives especially from the savage body of Myun, who resembles an immortal in his sublime monstrosity. His final destruction forms the affective climax of the film. In the savage violence he unleashes when massacring the rival South Korean gang, his own indestructible body tears the fabric of South Korean national space by introducing a hard kernel that autochthonous status cannot contain, whether it is of the law or its underside, that is, criminality. His appearance reveals unmodern savagery from the North. This represents the Real of the South Korean modern nation-state that imagines itself to be unified by "somatic-normative jointure" in Santner's term: partial objects joined together to form a normative national body.

Characters like Myun in South Korean cinema of the North displace the affective shock of modernity, which proper national subjects suffer, into the savage Other within from the North. The spectacle of unmodernity that disrupts the chronotope of the modern nation works as "the cinematic suturing" that masks the lack at the heart of the nation's modern chronotope, that of a little object "a" that the modern nation promises to deliver to those who reside in the time and space of desire that the modern nation prescribes. The lack is displaced onto the body of the savage Other vis-à-vis the body that signifies plentitude through the somatic-normative jointure. In that spectacle, the body is "a perceptual surface"[66] at the center of the embodied cinematic experience. The cinematic spectacle in which the impact of engaging with the Real is displayed on the cinematic body affects the viewer's sense of chronotope, as that impact is registered in that body's temporal and spatial existence. As conceptualized in chapter 1, poetic shock refers to the effect of an image that exceeds the expectation of action in narrative, as well as the anticipated effect of the image itself. This excess disrupts the progressive unfolding of action in space visualized through sequencing that advances teleological progress in narrative. This is in contrast to the way the screen functions in classical narrative cinema, where the shock that the trauma of the lack generates is contained through staged encounters between subjects and their Others. Genre elements, such as the melodramatic in war and action films, absorb this shock by setting a limit on desire's trajectory. Melodramatic films sometimes accomplish this by dramatizing the trials and tribulations of an attempt to recover a lost originary object, such as the cohesive family or nation that supports the jointure of subjectivity. Here, desire is delimited and tamed to follow this particular trajectory of search and recovery.

The South Korean film *Nambugun*[67] shows the disruption of the jointure of the national subject that the generic form cannot recuperate. The film's title refers to communist partisans in South Korea, active during the Korean War, who occupied an impossible chronotope between warring states. The central characters are two male intellectuals who come to lose all meaningful objects through the war. Both men get separated from partners, fellow partisans whom they love, and although they closely follow the path of their lost lovers, they can never overtake them. One of the men sends a letter through another who is to join the combat unit to which his lover belongs, but the letter carrier later returns the letter to the sender, having been unable to deliver it. One loses a tooth and a spoon that partisans carry with them as a form of identification, symbolic of their readiness to keep fighting and take meals when they can. Corpses that wear a spoon around their neck are determined to be those of the communist partisans. The other loses a book of poetry that he holds dear and has carried close to his chest. In the end, both lose the meaning of war, the promise of a somatic-normative jointure of the nation-state. Their path is neither linear nor forward; it circles in a curved space. Their movement forms a geographic circle around the same mountain pass as they take flight from the enemy's military campaign to decimate them while trying to hang on to the terrain. The loss of small objects for them is a metaphor for the failed promise of the Symbolic order of the nation to anchor their position as the subject of desire.

Their desire for the nation, expressed by the corporeal struggle, becomes the bodily drive that is visually captured in scenes depicting actual circular movement in the mountain trails. In the dead of the winter, in the merciless mountain terrain that once provided them a superior tactical position but now functions as a death trap, they are surrounded by the vastly larger South Korean army, equipped with superb firepower supplied by the United States. With the decimation of their entire army imminent, the partisans advance a few steps, only to immediately retreat and retrace the same ground yet again. They continue in this manner until the decisive air raid stops that repetitious movement. The partisans' bodies lying in the blood-soaked snowfield represent what exceeds the somatic-normative jointure of the modern nation-state, both South and North, haunting histories built on piles of bodies. The film, however, fails to create an ethical position in relation to the Other, as I have outlined in my reading of *Time of the Wolf*. The bodily drive of the partisans fails to make the hop-step-jump from bodily drive to emancipatory drive. After the spectacle of the ruination, no cinematic sight or sound would allow us to read it otherwise.

Here, let us return to *The Yellow Sea* to illustrate the subject's failure to hop-step-jump over to the emancipatory drive. Associated with poverty, criminality, savagery, and filth, the North often figures in popular imagination as a space of the unmodern Other whose Otherness threatens to transgress the somatic-normative jointure as the ideological and material boundaries of the modern nation of South Korea. In *The Yellow Sea*, that unmodern Other, represented in a savage masculine body, encroaches on and turns any space in the nation (including an affluent Gangnam neighborhood) into a space for its own jouissance, threatening all the boundaries and limits of the nation proper. The film follows the process in which unmodern, ethnic masculinity disrupts the nation-state. In the course of that process, ethnic Korean men from China are revealed to be without a country with which they can enter a viable social contract. The only form of contract available to them is a murder for hire, backed by bad faith. The state ultimately has no control over these men as, like a war machine, they carve out their own pattern of furrows through the nation-state's landscape. They give a different meaning to what the nation-state's landscape contains. The harbor, for instance, is where they stage human trafficking, as well as lethal battles, tarnishing the image of the prosperous modern state, with its trade vessels and cargo imprinted with global conglomerates' logos. They unleash the kind of death drive that is bent on annihilating the human body rather than turning it into a value-producing commodity. This is the bodily drive that the capitalist nation-state wants to fantasize it has contained through industrialization, modernization, and the social foundation of the patriarchal family.

Badiou argues that violence can provoke an event that enables a human animal to transcend the state of being below ethics and to become the human-subject of ethics.[68] Something akin to Walter Benjamin's divine violence, Badiou's "evental" violence enables the human subject to recognize and organize into a political program a "truth" of the situation that indicates the way society can overcome the pregiven order. In this formulation, a human animal obtains subjectivity through "evental" violence. The kind of male violence we see in *The Yellow Sea*, lacking an emancipatory aspect, does not lead to such revolutionary violence; it tends to annihilate the possibility of the human subject of ethics. These men's excessive enjoyment, which lacks the capacity for politically meaningful resistance, completely inundates and destroys public space, turning it into the space of private enjoyment of murder and mayhem. The violent and bloody fight scenes that break out in a bus company's basement, a hotel room, and the open space of the harbor show how their enjoyment operates independently of the state authority that determines the grids of social space, as well as the personal space of pleasure, but it also fuels the destructive bodily drive; again, this is what Lacan warns us against: watch out! When the gangs occupy an ordinary family home, it also turns into a site of massacre. Their violent acts annihilate the social body that the nation-state wants to utilize as a source of capital production. But it also lacks the clear possibility of a political program. This representation of Northern men lacks a politically emancipatory dimension. Stuck in the bodily drive, the possibility of the emancipatory drive disappears. This is why the path of "keep going" in South Korean cinema often ends up with a pile of dismembered body parts.

Women of the North are often fleeting images in South Korean cinema, but it is possible to locate, transtextually, the feminine subject at the center of the disruption of somatic jointure as inscribed by the norm. In *About Elly*,[69] by Iranian filmmaker Asghar Farhadi, a woman wreaks havoc on the somatic-normative social space. Sepideh is a young mother whose uncompromising desire to include Elly, a young teacher, in the family fold during a multifamily vacation to the seashore leads her to fabricate a situation in which all present must depend on Sepideh's narrative and mobilization of actions and events. This reveals the unspoken and invisible (at least initially in the film's diegesis) yet determinative foundation of social relationships ruled by gender-based oppressions at the core of family and social organization. For example, Elly has to fabricate stories to be able to travel, because a woman's movement is always curbed by the gender norm. Within such a social relation, women must surreptitiously and subversively orchestrate familial and social interactions to create clandestine interior space in the shadow of the suturing apparatus, namely, signifiers of gender: women can never publicly let their desires be known outside what has already been scripted using those signifiers. This is why Sepideh's desire has such a devastating impact and leads to Elly's disappearance.

Sepideh surreptitiously devises ways to block Elly from leaving the seashore vacation in her attempts to tie the teacher to her perceived community of friends. Sepideh's repetitious attempts to do so reveal her furious drive to write her own narrative, with everyone in her community serving as players within it. Elly cannot reconcile Sepideh's drive with her own mode of being, which is beset by constant negotiations of her own space in a society where her every move is policed. The frenetic search for Elly after her disappearance leads to the spectacular unraveling of the facade of functioning social relationships, including family relationships, as the basis of the community. The prolonged scene of men searching the roaring sea for Elly's presumably drowned body is staged in a way that conveys the chaos in which all are submerged: silent yet furiously kinetic male bodies, having lost their individual contours and distinctions, are engulfed in, and spat out by, the raging waves. Everyone in Sepideh's community has lost the grounding that holds together their subjective positions through clear delineations of their sense of identities.

Farhady continues, in his later films, to show how the drive unravels the somatic-normative jointure, tearing apart the already overtaxed quilting points of society. This is the emancipatory aspect of the drive. Depictions of the horrifying effects of the very drive that has been digging a surreptitious and unknowable trench through the social fabric, erupting through quilting points, continue in his body of work. What has become crystalized by the time Farhady gives us *Everybody Knows* (2018) is this: the drive involves an ethical dimension, and cinema can show the emancipatory drive through the protagonist's ethical choice at the expense of his own secure place in social relationships.

Before we move on to *Dooman River*, I would like to reiterate that through the repetitiousness and circularity of the traumatic Real that undermine linear temporality, historical subjects may emerge as the subject of the emancipatory drive. The traumatic encounter with the Real historicizes the subject, not because that encounter secures the subject in a temporality of progression but because it reveals the historical context in which the subject emerges through a particular wounding that engenders a subject. It is in this sense that *Dooman River* gives us a historical subject in the main character Chang-Ho.

In *Dooman River*,[70] the trauma of the Real exceeds and thus challenges the authority and cohesion of the narrative cinema, particularly in how it concludes with the inexplicable suicide of a child. Set in Yanbian, where the Dooman River marks the border between China and North Korea, the film is populated by North Korean refugees who have crossed the river in search of food and livelihood. They are fleeing hunger, the Chinese police, deportation, the gulag, and all variety of punishments in North Korea, barely eking out an existence in Yanbian, Manchuria. Chang-Ho, a Joseonjok boy, befriends a North Korean boy hiding in an abandoned building. This North Korean boy agrees to participate in the village boys' soccer match, only to be captured by Chinese police on the soccer field. In the midst of the soccer match that the police interrupt, Chang-Ho climbs onto the roof of the abandoned building and throws himself off. We have already witnessed, through Chang-Ho's point of view, the corpses of North Koreans and the rape of his sister by a North Korean refugee taken in by his benevolent grandfather. These incidents do not prepare us for his suicide, because the film does not provide space for narrative contemplation through shot compositions and camera movement that could enable the audience to claim mastery over, and knowledge of, the main character and his actions.

Dooman River avoids the spectacularization of trauma, but the traumatic Real peeks through ellipses in and the elision of spectacle. The film stages Chang-Ho's witnessing of his sister's rape through a long-take long shot of the child's back as he looks into the window that is made to conceal, rather than reveal, the scene of the rape. Death permeates the daily life of the border town that defecting North Koreans attempt to reach by crossing the river. Bodies of North Koreans wash ashore, and frozen corpses, having succumbed to exposure, hunger, and illness, are strewn on the ice and hillside, mostly captured in long shots. In the opening shot, Chang-Ho plays dead on the frozen river, mimicking a North Korean corpse that he has seen. The boy is enacting the traumatic engagement with the Other, here by assuming the ultimate form of Otherness: death. One can argue that this action foreshadows his physical destruction later in the film. Still, there is no arrangement of images and shots that walks the viewer through the logical process or progression that eventually arrives at his final choice. The gravity of the child's action is completely unexpected for the viewer, for whom the film's realism does not provide devices that allow the viewer to identify the child's psychological truth in order to make sense of the suicide. The film doesn't dwell on shots that would classically make such identification possible in cinematic realism, such as close-ups and long takes that follow the physical movement of a character through which viewers can contemplate the character's emotional and psychic state and see the character's actions as part of the logical trajectory of the narrative. *Dooman River* disallows a comprehensive reading of the despair the characters feel by refraining from the use of visual conventions that would enable the viewer to understand the child's suicide as the connection between individual and communal despair.

The spectator, whether an audience member in the theater or a character in the film, cannot easily find an explanation for this child's action; the film does not provide textual clues. This remains so even when we take into consideration that the boy is familiar with the death that surrounds him, his playing dead on the frozen Dooman River being one indication of this familiarity. The fabric of quiet realism that has sustained the film's style does not guide us to a plausible logic of an action that, when it occurs, does so abruptly. Here, we experience the traumatic Real that defies narrative containment.

This is quite different from the neorealist *Germany Year Zero*,[71] in which a child's suicide is well contextualized. In that film, the closing sequence consists of the child wandering through the city, having learned that his father, whom he has poisoned, has in fact died. As we follow the child aimlessly moving, picking up and playing with random objects in the city ruins, we don't have direct access to the "psychological truth" unfolding through meaningful actions in classical narrative cinema. However, we understand the mise-en-scène as the way in which neorealism visualizes interiority, and the spectator has been given ample time to observe the child's itinerary and to be affected by the emotionality arising from it. So when it occurs, the image of the child's suicide by falling, though shocking, does not have the disturbing effect that it does in *Dooman River*, where it shakes the spectator out of a position of knowing within the sphere of the narrative, located instead in the realm of the traumatic Real. Compared to classical European neorealist films, *Dooman River* involves a significant formal intervention to show the traumatic Real.

While *Dooman River* stages Manchuria as a confined space of the traumatic Real, *The Good, the Bad, the Weird*,[72] a hybrid of the Western, comedy, and action genres, uses Manchuria to express a desire to relocate the male body in a field where the imposition of bodily and national boundaries seems to be impossible and makes it difficult to securely place that body within the social relations of the modern nation. This film uses Manchuria as a chronotope of the unruly body that cannot be confined within the teleology of the modern nation-state. The film indulges in the spectacle of boundless space in which men's pursuit of the object of desire ends only with the anticipation of the repetition of that pursuit across the same boundless space. These men enjoy repetitious pursuit for pursuit's sake, indifferent to any utilitarian national project, desiring the pursuit of the goal itself, not the actual possession of the object of desire. Through most of the film, it is not even clear what the object is, as it is represented only as a marker on a treasure map, using a classical Western trope. The treasure hunt ensues across the vast, open land, involving the Japanese imperial army and Chinese and Korean bandits. In this way, the film's spectacle seems to visualize the drive, rendering Manchuria as the realm of the Real where actions organized around desire for a meaningful resolution of the lack cannot succeed.

However, the film textually eschews the traumatic effect of the Real, as it treats Manchuria as a field of the bodily drive of a solipsistic masculine subject, a sweeping landscape where that drive is unleashed only to return to the point of origin. At the end of the film, we anticipate that the same male contest will unfold again. Thus, the spectacle-driven film, with its highly stylized staging of masculine ruination, is unable to spectacularize trauma. There must be the traumatizing presence of the Other, as in *Dooman River*, in order for the film to convey the emancipatory drive. In *The Good, the Bad, the Weird*, the spectacular spatialization of Manchuria constitutes a pastiche presenting the space of male solipsism and excluding the traumatic appearance of the Other. This is why in *The Good, the Bad, the Weird*, although the force of the subject's circulating around the object of desire animates the spectacle, this force does not propel the arc of circulation into a new chronotope of the emancipatory drive where the Other's own emancipatory drive could enter.

It is useful at this point to clarify what I mean by the cinematic spectacle: It is a means to register the sensorial impact of the image on the subject's perception. It can involve the visualization of the event of traumatic wounding, which constitutes a relationship between the subject and its Other (object or neighbor). Subjectivity itself emerges through this wounding. The individuality of the subject is achieved through a wounding caused by the sense that one has lost a specific object, in a specific social context. When we experience such loss and the lack that comes from it, we grasp at different objects that stand in for the object cause of desire, that phantasmatic object that we believe we have lost. This sense of loss is the price that we pay when we enter the linguistic world and begin to enunciate and comprehend our desire through language. The particular mode of this payment is determined by the communality in which we exist. A different context of wounding in which we experience our own trauma thus becomes a different matrix for the subject of desire and for subjectivity, because we become social subjects by learning to enunciate our desire in our own language and what we desire is mediated by social relationships in which we exist. The cinematic spectacle can function as a field in which a subject emerges through a particular context of traumatic wounding. I have stated that trauma is an event through which the subject goes beyond the pregiven symbolic and ideological orders, and even the material boundary given to it, and loses everything that its previous subjectivity has held dear. In *Batman Begins* (Christopher Nolan, 2005), the Batman mask signifies a subject's becoming someone else through traumatic wounding. The traumatic ruination of self, anchored in the pregiven terms of subjectivity, can suggest a new configuration of subjectivity and the concomitant relationship between the subject and its Other and the objects that mediate it. The cinematic spectacle helps us, whether allegorically, realistically, or expressively, to visualize this process.

According to Lacan, anxiety occurs when the Other, "my neighbor," is too close.[73] This is because the Other presents an excess that the subject, as the unified being within the Symbolic order, cannot contain. Otherness is in excess of what constitutes the positive ground of identity for the subject. It marks the traumatic encounter with the lack that cannot be mended while underpinning our way of being: the Other's excess testifies to what cannot be had, swallowed, and digested by the subject, that is, the fundamental lack. And this encounter can lead to the end of subjectivity as we know it. Chang-Ho's suicide illustrates this: through his meeting with the North Korean Other, he encounters the loss and lack resulting from colonialism and imperial war that no nation-state can make whole. Chang-Ho's plunge is the film's way of imagining how we might respond to the anxiety-provoking presence of the Other making its plight known, as in the father's dream of his dead child admonishing him. This admonition should be read, "Wake up to my death, to its excessive Otherness, the trauma of which will shatter your subjectivity!" To respond, a subject must wake up to face Otherness, even if it shatters the subject's own hermeneutic boundaries.

The Good, the Bad, the Weird ultimately privileges solipsism over the unruly eruption of Otherness that would unravel its masculine subject. The film is unable to articulate the possibility of the emancipatory and politically meaningful drive. However, the spectacle of open landscape—in which subjects encircle objects that they are not actually interested in possessing but that have their meaning only as a metonym of the lost object—suggests ways in which the drive can be spectacularized. At the same time, we note Kaja Silverman's argument that films can disavow the "imaginary plentitude, unbounded by any gaze, and unmarked by difference"[74] that we often see in spectacle-driven films, which can generate the fantasy of ever-unfolding desire. It is noteworthy that *Dooman River* reveals the traumatic Real that stems from the encounter with the Other and forces the subject to devise an ethical position in relation to the Other, for which allowing that encounter to have a sensorial impact on your bodily drive is a starting point, through the lack of spectacle. That film, whose spatialization is reminiscent of Ozu's proscenium-framing of space that implies emotional distance between the spectator and the spectacle, refrains from spectacularizing the traumatic event and yet does offer the poetic shock of traumatic Otherness.

Some critics argue that the image positions us subjectively, that the phenomenological fact of viewing is coextensive with the subjective condition of modernity, and that the image thus makes possible "a filmic way of encountering the world."[75] These assertions imply that the cinematic way of encountering the world makes us believe that we can overcome the distance between subject and its Other, as it allows the subject to spill over into the world beyond the narrow boundary of "I," but the cinematic image can also convey the violent rending of the Symbolic fabric in which the subject is positioned. In that rending, pre-existing subjectivity is shown to be untenable, and the subject glimpses how to become something more. This view of the cinematic image complicates the logic of the sensorial for which traditional film studies have argued: the position that sensorial engagement helps formulate and found modern subjects and that the cinematic image offers a position that a subject can adhere to in order to face the disorienting and alienating world of modernity.

The aesthetic strategy of *Dooman River* that allows the traumatic Real, the untenability of subjectivity, to emerge counters the "phenomenological faith in viewing" that Jinhee Choi and Mattias Frey advocate, asserting that experiencing cinematic time and space allows the viewer to experience "ontological substance."[76] Films that I call the *cinema of the Real*, by contrast, focus on qualities antithetical to such a notion and emphasize that the phenomenology of cinematic viewing reveals the impossibility of a unified and cohesive modern subject. Rather than helping the modern subject to regain contact with the world through bridging the distance from it and restoring the world's knowability, as Choi and Frey argue, the spectacle of the traumatic Real reveals the phantasmatic dimension of knowledge. The cinema is not a protective barrier that screens the alienating world from the viewer and that the known-ness of the world is projected onto. Rather, it is a screen that projects a face one cannot recognize, the Otherness that exceeds one's ontological boundaries: not just the mirrored reflection of the masked face of Bruce Wayne but the kernel that points toward the extraneousness of the neighboring Other. The South Korean cinema of the chronotopic North responds to national anxiety about the nation's Other in the form of ethnic Koreans who exist outside the neoliberal cartography of modernity in which the South Korean nation-state seeks to claim its legitimate place. This is especially true of Manchuria, with its ethnic but unmodern Koreans. The screen reflects the face of the Other of the nation proper, the kernel of the Symbolic subject called "Korean." The spectacular destruction of the ethnic male body in the nation-state's territory reflects the nation's desire to cleanse that anxiety-provoking, uncomfortably near "neighbor."

Another aspect of the traumatic Real of the North is the harrowing history of Korean armed struggles against Japanese imperialism and on behalf of the Chinese and Korean communist revolutions. These conflicts occurred mainly north of the Korean peninsula and in Manchuria. This is the historical context, along with earlier Korean agricultural and industrial resettlement during Japan's colonial rule, that created a diasporic population, the unbearable face of the unmodern, which returns like a repressed memory to the South Korean modern nation. The films of the chronotopic North eliminate all traces of the communist aspects of the anti-imperial Manchurian struggles, because the South Korean nation-state's historiography and law cannot accommodate this pro-communist element in its imaginary Manchuria. This is why films like the recent *The Great Battle* (Kim Gwang-shik, 2018) voice a eulogy for Manchuria as a lost territory of an ancient kingdom that could have been a great unified Korean nation. The politically emancipatory drive that anti-colonial and communist struggle represented disappears in this picture. The films of the chronotopic North also evoke modernity as the geographical boundary that coincides with geopolitical demarcations. South Korea represents modernity as part of global capitalism vis-à-vis the unmodern North, where lurks menace that can be transported by easy airplane flights from China to disrupt the facade of the working social economy.

This kind of disruption is often curbed in South Korean films that feature Northerners whose bodily drive could unravel the somatic-normative jointure of the nation-state. They are safely relegated to space outside the proper body politic, and when they infiltrate it, they are properly punished or expelled. *The Outlaws* (Kang Yoon-seong, 2017) updates the well-worn trope of Joseonjok gangsters as the threat to communality, and *Coin Locker Girl* (Han Jun-hee, 2015) nominates a Chinese-Korean woman mob boss as the problematic social subject. Both films portray people that have no respect for humanity. In this type of film, we find the most anxious expression of this evaluation in the illegal organ harvesting and trading that the criminals engage in, for which the normative Korean body is an easy target. They objectify and commodify human bodies, revealing the foundational logic of capitalist social relationships. Thus, in these films, the Real of capitalism is relegated to the ethnic Other.

The North connotes the underside of exuberant accumulation and the movement of surplus value, shadowing it with its excessive inhumanity, as the Yanbian Koreans often represent. As ethnic Koreans who are de jure Chinese, they have no proper place in either the Korean or Chinese nation-states but exist in a liminal space. Gu-Nam's death in the Yellow Sea, a space of nonbelonging, symbolizes this liminality. In the last sequence of the film, Gu-Nam's allegedly dead wife appears in another in-between space, a train station. The film emphasizes its liminal status by providing no local marker to identify the station's location.

Cultural production can maneuver to cover up the Joseonjok's meaning as the hard kernel of Otherness within the notion of the unified ethnic South Korean nation. In *The Yellow Sea*, Joseonjok, represented as unmodern savages, use the large canine bones left over from the production of dog meat as skull-crushing lethal weapons. The excessiveness of this image actually provoked skits on a popular comedy show on network TV in South Korea. By rendering it farcical (these skits usually fail to be authentically comedic), these skits function as a way to tame and subsume the unbearable Otherness that such a grotesque spectacle signifies. In the end, many films that feature the chronotopic North tend to confirm, rather than confound or question, the South Korean national boundary as the boundary of modernity. Even in a gangster film like *New World* (Park Hoon-jung, 2013) that shows the obscene underside of hypermasculine capitalist enterprises where gangsters and legitimate businessmen easily switch roles to ensure the smooth operation of capital accumulation, the Joseonjok represent the brute force of a Deleuzian war machine—the illegitimate, underground organization that parallels, defies, and contradicts the legitimate body of governance, thus delineating and certifying, rather than destroying, the boundary of the modern nation.

At this juncture, recalling *Dooman River*'s aesthetic strategy of presenting the traumatic Real, I reiterate that the viewing subject can work as a formal element: eyes serve as a visual conduit that opens up the Real and the path of the emancipatory drive. The cinema of the Real can shock and push a spectator to the limit of cognitive grounding, which then leads to a new perspective: the vantage point of the subject position in the Real. The viewing subject whose eye sees the image but whose seeing leads to cognitive failure can be said to be a formal element of the film. Here, a set of eyes that see but fail to know is implicated in the organization of the spectatorship. Similarly, there is, in *Sympathy for Mr. Vengeance* (Park Chan-wook, 2002), the scene of an autopsy of a child. The child's father stands looking down upon the autopsy table. We hear the sound of the body cavity cracking open, but we see only a bright light, seemingly emanating from the cavity, which illuminates the lower half of the frame and the father's face as he stands watching the process. The viewing subject's position is that of not seeing, indicating that the viewer does not obtain the position of the subject who knows through looking.

Dooman River creates this subject position within the Real through different means. When *Dooman River* points toward the interiority of trauma for the viewer, it does not provide a comfortable position of knowing through looking. At an abortion clinic, as Chang-Ho's supposedly mute sister is about to undergo the procedure as the result of a rape, she calls out her brother's name before we see him fall. Earlier in the film, it has been established that she is not medically or morphologically unable to speak but rather that she stopped speaking after her father drowned in the Dooman River trying to save her from drowning. The death of her brother, the trauma to come, now allows her to speak. Here, speech, both in its blockage and its opening, marks traumatic loss. But even this representation of trauma does not offer any insight into a possible narrative resolution of both personal and communal trauma, as the presence of the disposable lives of North Koreans continues to open up the traumatic Real underlying perceived reality.

Theory of trauma considers temporality whether in terms of repetition or history. The theory of the chronotope of the drive calls for considering atemporality. Consider melancholic time as an example of atemporality. In South Korean cinema, we often see masculine subjects existing in melancholic time, especially in the melodramatic rendition of genre films that are built on the premise of the loss of a man's original family, especially in the melodramatic treatment of loss in war movies. When dealing with the traumatic encounter with the North, these films start with the melancholia of loss, then progress to melodramatic resolution. When the masculine subject's interactions with the North occur, resulting in the melancholic loss that threatens the somatic jointure of subjectivity, it is possible to reestablish the somatic jointure in melodramatic time, recuperating the nation-time that has been undone by the encounter with the traumatic Otherness that the North represents. Melodramatic time has a temporal arc of loss that extends to attempts at recovery. In melodramas, we often see recovery of a lost object tacked on at the end of the narrative arc as an ideological resolution, a reassurance that the subject does not suffer from loss of the object that, unless recovered, could unravel Symbolic subjectivity. But this recovery elides the fundamental impossibility of such recovery that the melodramatic pathos has visualized and dramatized up to that point. The recovery of the lost *objet a* is only phantasmatic. Among films that undertake the phantasmatic recovery of fraternal unity, as the foundation of somatic jointure, through the melodramatic form, we count *Tae Guk Gi: The Brotherhood of War* (Kang Je-kyu, 2004). This film represents the origin story of loss: the Korean War tears apart brothers and forces them to fight on opposite sides, necessitating fratricide. The melancholic loss that cannot be contained through the process of mourning sets off the drive around the lost object, and no monument will heal the originary loss. This accounts for the madness of the older brother in this film, who no longer recognizes his sibling. However, the melodramatic, relying heavily on the generic legibility of war films and action films, reframes the melancholic subject: the one stricken by madness miraculously comes to his senses during a bombardment of artillery and recognizes, that is to say, recovers, the lost object, his brother.

The goal is set to recover what is believed to be lost: the fraternal nation. Films like *The Suspect* (Won Shin-yeon, 2013) and *The Spy Gone North* (Yoon Jong-bin, 2018) imagine as the lost object the reunion of the Band of Brothers and, by extension, the unification of the nation-state. They present transcending the border between the North and the South as the emergence of a utopic chronotope that anticipates achieving the teleological goal of building a masculine nation. Men of North Korea thus signify the possibility of the somatic jointure, individually and also on the level of the body politic, while the other Northerners, especially ethnic Koreans in China, cross the border only to unravel the existing masculine network of law and capital in South Korea. If the films about such fraternity presume to recover, through the melodramatization of loss, the family of origin and by extension the phantasmatically unified nation, these characters, represented as unmodern savages from China, signify the impossibility of such melodramatic recovery. They belong to the other side of the melodramatic spectrum, which is what Linda Williams posits as the belated arrival at the impossible psychic place of pathetic loss: too late![77] They stand in a space of world-unmaking melancholia. Hence, their cinematic bodies are stand-ins for the locus of the affective shock of Otherness that exceeds the chronotopic boundary of the nation-state.

The melodramatic chronotope in South Korean war and action genre films, organized around objects that are lost and found, obscures the chronotope of the emancipatory drive and its threat to unravel the national narrative that coheres subjectivity through loss and recovery. The melodramatic arc in the narrative of loss and recovery prevents time from becoming unstable, undoing the articulation of nation-time. We see the melancholic time of loss and the melodramatic recovery of the lost object, such as the fraternal nation, in films featuring North Korean men who cross the border into South Korea to cement the chronotope of the nation. Action films about a North Korean operative and a South Korean lawman forming fraternal bonding are common examples. There are exceptions to this ideological maneuver of male genre films supported by excessive emotionality, notably *The Front Line* and *Nambugun*. Both films include scenes where Northern and Southern soldiers spontaneously sing an elegiac popular song together at the height of tense military action. This melodramatic eruption, fracturing the ideological boundary of proper national subjectivities, however, does not lead to reunification of fractured fraternity and the possibility of a unified nation. Melancholia remains unresolved, shown through the spectacular destruction and irrecoverable loss of male bodies that follows.

Another example of melancholic loss is in *Poongsan*.[78] In this film, the eponymous male character cannot determine which side of the divided peninsula he is on because he refuses to speak. He freely pole-vaults across the world's most lethal border, delivering goods and people across the North and the South without aligning himself with either side. His superhuman quality (his pole-vaultings are staged in mise-en-scène, tinged with surreal otherworldliness) is in line with his ability to not walk the ideological lines along the nations, a position that exceeds not only ideological but also topographical and somatic boundaries. When his tragic death occurs in midair, mid-vault, drops of his blood lightly rain down on tall reeds; we never see his corpse. It is as if his body has disappeared. This scene shows the impossibility of existing in excess of the nation-state, the impossibility of being of a somatic disjointure.

But somatic disjointure inaugurates the emancipatory drive. The subject of the emancipatory drive exists in atemporal curved space of the chronotope of the traumatic Real. Kim Ki-duk's *Time*[79] creates, through somatic disjointure, an atemporal curved space in which desire and its object do not align. In the film, the impossible relationship between the subject and its *objet a* is staged by a woman who completely alters her look through plastic surgery; her body is the surface on which the desire of the Other is registered. Appearing to her lover as a stranger, she erases a historiography of both herself and her lover, who does not realize that the new woman he has fallen in love with is in fact the lover he thought had left him. The only visible remainder of that historiography is their photos, now nonsensical because they hold images that do not belong to a timeline that constitutes a historiography of love. Thus, the photographed images signify a kernel that derails the subject's attempt to consolidate the meaning of the object of desire, in this case, the woman. In this way, she places herself on the path of the emancipatory drive in which the impossibility of aligning desire with its objects is perpetuated. When the man finally realizes her ruse, he also undergoes a plastic surgery to change his facade. The stable location of each subject disappears, and each is left with only incidental details, such as a hand that feels familiar to the touch, which vaguely indicates the kernel of the Other's being. Thus, the surgical transformation reveals that the subject of desire, who desperately wants to read the Other's desire, discovers itself and the Other to be a collection of partial objects. That the subject of desire and its objects are collations of body parts, that is, partial objects, is alluded to through shots of sculptures that describe various body parts entangled in intimate positions that the lovers visit to mark the time when they enter the relationship of desire.

The failure to connect desire with its objects in this film opens up a chronotope in which one no longer obtains recognizable traits, such as the shape of a face, that are meant to anchor the desiring subject's location in time and the proper place in which desire is to linearly unfold. The failure of desire to achieve a productive subject/object relationship that supports all ideological positions, and the danger of being stuck in the drive where no object can fulfill impossible desire, constitute the traumatic Real of our existence as desiring subjects in *Time*. Therein lies the possibility of emancipation from ideology based on desire and the objects that elicit it.

Time's final sequence begins in the same way the film opens: a woman, her face completely covered by a mask, walks out of a plastic surgery clinic clutching a framed photo of a woman whose face is streaked with tears and mascara. At this point in the film, we understand the face in the photo to be, paradoxically, the post-operative image of the woman who underwent plastic surgery earlier in the film. Another, whom we identify as the very same masked woman pre-surgery, collides with the woman in the mask, causing her to drop the frame, which shatters on the ground. She profusely apologizes, and the masked woman walks away without a word, leaving the frame and photo behind. The other woman salvages the photo from the broken frame and proceeds to meet her lover, wondering aloud about the identity of the woman in the photo. The collision between two different selves signifies the circular time of the emancipatory drive: the subject repeatedly returns to the point of the loss of a cohesive subjecthood.

We coexist with our past and future selves in the trajectory of the emancipatory drive. No matter how many times we change our facade, the surface of the self where our meaning as a desiring subject is inscribed, we return to the chronotope of the emancipatory drive where we must abandon our imaginary position as the desiring subject. Through that return, we are emancipated from the demand that we embody cohesive identity. We, then, continue to hop-step-jump to the new arc of the emancipatory drive, the new coordinates of the chronotope. There, the Other who speaks to us of its wound appears. This is the greatest threat to desire that the Symbolic order inscribes on our temporal and spatial existence. The emancipatory drive, in which we live with the jouissance of the wounded Other, necessitates a change in the cinematic form that narrates desire.

CHAPTER FOUR

The Feminine Cinema and Feminine Universality

Space in the Feminine Cinema

What I call the feminine cinema is a form in which the creative practice and psychical work that constitute cinema of the Real converge. It creates the cinematic space from which feminine universality emerges. The universal feminine is the subject position that reveals the Real of the Symbolic order, which no signifier can obscure. To clarify its meaning through the conceptual work we have engaged in thus far, the universal feminine subject is not a particular woman or even women in general. The universal feminine subject expresses the gap in the constitution of the body and of subjectivity itself by exposing missing links in the chain of signifiers. The chain of signifiers is founded on the master signifier, notably the phallus, which is at the center of the complete and unified body and of a proper subject position as envisioned in the Symbolic order. In this sense, the universal feminine subject is, in fact, the subject of the Real founded upon feminine jouissance on the path of the emancipatory drive.

The universal feminine does not refer to a position that is tethered to a particular identity, gender or otherwise. In support of this point, I describe how the universal feminine subject emerges in local and historical contexts. Continuing transnational and transtextual analyses, I will look at how the universal feminine subject appears in local historical situations where "the world's conflicts meet in a singular way."[1] Specifically, the case of the Korean "comfort women" will help us to see this process. The feminine cinema is the locus of these probings.

At this juncture, I need to clarify the connection between film, specifically feminine cinema, and the real lives of the universal feminine subjects that we see in a local context, notably the comfort women, as well as other historical subjects. In the introductory chapter, I posited that the cinematic space is the life space. Through experiencing the Real as an ontological condition in the cinema of the Real—the process in which the gaze of the Real pushes the spectator from the theater to the street—we explore how we might change our understanding of the world and our place in it. This is why we theorize the political potential of spectacle, as did Sergei Eisenstein throughout his film theory and practice.

As I demonstrate how the subject in cinema embodies the universal feminine subject, I ask: What is the shape of a cinematic space that provides a topography of the psychic life of the universal feminine subject? Let us take a close look at the film *Head-On* by Fatih Akin,[2] a Turkish-German filmmaker. In the beginning of the film, we follow Cahit, a forty-something man who was born in Turkey and is now living as an alcoholic in Hamburg, Germany. Cahit is estranged from both the Turkish and German communities. Other Turks notice that his Turkish is not quite proper, and he lives in a cramped, filthy apartment in a state of permanent melancholia due to the death of his wife, who was German. He earns money collecting bottles at a club called The Factory, gets into fistfights in dive bars, uses drugs, and attempts suicide. The urban space Cahit navigates is mostly enclosed in shots of low-saturation lighting that frame the dark streets and unwholesome interiors. The shots, rendered to convey the sense of flatness of the visual surface, create a feeling of claustrophobia in the viewer. These cinematic elements form the "geographical metaphors"[3] of Cahit's psychic life, a fragmented and fractured existence. The visual representation of Cahit's psychic life is devoid of the establishing shots that would provide perspectives on this human subject in an organic relationship to his environment and allow us to visualize his ideological location in society.

Cahit then meets Sibel, a twenty-something woman of Turkish descent in a psychiatric ward. She attempts suicide to escape her patriarchal family's male violence and then marries Cahit to achieve that goal. Sibel aspires to an independent life as a hairdresser. She moves through the urban space with the fluidity of one who successfully straddles two different languages and cultures, but in the end, she has to flee the city to avoid the gender violence imposed by her family of origin. When her family discovers that Sibel staged her marriage to escape the family, she must literally run for her life to escape her brother's physical threats. Her father burns her photos in a symbolic declaration of her death. Sibel's family effectively expunges her from both public and private space. In Istanbul, her place of ethnic origin, she is often identified by locals as the Other. As a woman who does not respect the social norms of her ethnic and national community, she occupies a space plagued by identitarian violence whose aim is to enforce those norms, whether in Germany or in Turkey.

This film dramatizes the precarious relationship that Cahit and Sibel have with their surroundings by inserting extradiegetic sight and sound. The film opens and ends with a stationary long shot of a band of Turkish musicians: a female singer and six men playing traditional Turkish instruments. They are situated in front of the geographical markers of Istanbul, playing an elegiac song about an unfulfilled love. The opening scene cuts to long, low-light shots of Cahit collecting empty bottles after a concert. As the film follows these characters' tragic collisions, first with the German and Turkish communities in Hamburg, then with Turkish society in Istanbul, this band reappears four times, always in the midst of regular filmic action. Each time, the sound of their playing bleeds into the scenes, set in both Hamburg and Istanbul. At the end of the film, having failed to recover his relationship with Sibel in Istanbul, Cahit leaves for the hometown he barely knows. In the ending scene, first, his face floats in the window of the bus he rides, then his reflection disappears as the bus pulls away from the camera and the surface of the window darkens. Finally, a long shot of the bus moving through the cityscape cuts back to the band for one final song.

The repeated appearance of the Turkish band heightens the sense of fragmentation and diremption connected to the main characters. When we encounter them in the middle of the Hamburg landscape, the appearance of the band functions as the point at which we encounter the gaze: the kernel of being of those who are in a diasporic trajectory gazes at us. The band represents the Other scene that haunts European metropolitan space, in which Cahit and Sibel occupy an impossible subject position. They are within German society but do not belong to it. Neither do they safely belong to their community of ethnic origin. The gender violence Sibel experiences and Cahit's inadequate Turkish signify their problematic positions. When heard and seen in Istanbul, the band signifies their precarious ethnic identities. Cahit and Sibel show us the universal feminine subject position, which has no home in identity-based communalities such as the nation, and thus demonstrate the gap in the constitution of the ethnic and national body. This gap in the body and identity indicates feminine universality.

The film also suggestively uses the British rock number "Life Is What You Make It." The song seems superimposed on the map of Cahit's trajectory toward Sibel, one lost object moving toward another lost object: his hometown. As he waits for Sibel in the otherwise deserted lobby of an Istanbul hotel, Cahit repeatedly plays the refrain of this same song on a piano. The notes are then superimposed on the montage of his movement through the city. In the end, Cahit leaves the city, and the film concludes with the Turkish band; the members address the spectator by standing and bowing at the end of their song, the soundtrack for his departure scene. But the film repurposes the thematic code of "Life Is What You Make It" to cover the entire ending credit sequence. The pop song functions as the coda for a diasporic subject whose sense of belonging to a community is fraught with ambiguity. For this subject, both the primal scene of Turkish space and the diasporic European metropolitan space work as geographical metaphors of psychic life. Both are psychic spaces of the diremption that the universal feminine subject occupies. Neither German nor Turkish, they find themselves to be impossible social subjects in communalities that aggressively define them. The film allegorizes their impossible position through the violent confrontations that both characters experience. Cahit is sent to prison for assault in Hamburg. Sibel is severely beaten by local thugs in Istanbul. Although Sibel stays in Istanbul with a new husband and a child, and Cahit leaves for the place of his birth, this is by no means a homecoming for either. Sibel's family has erased her, and she has come to Istanbul as a refugee, now banned from a Western metropolis. Cahit's face disappearing into the black surface of a bus window implies that the national space, which a place of birth represents, will not secure his subjectivity. Crucially, the viewer cannot dismiss the dimly lit rooms and dark streets of Hamburg where Cahit and Sibel literally and figuratively hit the wall of their existence (the meaning of the film's German title, *Gegen die wand*, is "against the wall"). They are connected to this European space through the trauma of self-diremption. Feminine universality emerges through such trauma, revealing the Real of subjectivity that the Symbolic order structures. Feminine cinema shows the process of this emergence.

In the cinematic space, the movement of history unfolds. Here, history is the story of trauma. We encounter the context that has created the kernel of our being, which renders impossible the consolidation of the Symbolic subject. History sets the stage for the eruption of the Real, the way it is materialized. In this film, it does so by tracing how a diasporic subject traverses both the European metropolis and the ethnic nation, and in doing so it dramatizes the traumatic impossibility of belonging. In this space, we witness the eruption of the nation's unconscious, which is atemporal in the sense that it forever circles around an impossible object such as the ideologically cohesive body politic and exists alongside historical time's progressive movement. The foreign bodies that move about in violent engagement with social space in a European metropolis are the unconscious Real of Europe. The same can be said about their existence as the Real of their shared nation of origin, Turkey. They defy the progressive temporality that supports the nation-state through their repetitious, circuitous movements around the void created by their lack of the master signifier "home."

This homelessness informs feminine universality in defiance of the chain of signifiers that constitute the Symbolic order of the nation.

That the unconscious is atemporal can be demonstrated by an examination of psychiatric symptoms. While symptoms may have a historical point of origin, their recurrences override any sense of temporal progression. Traumatic symptoms unfold in a seemingly eternal time of ever-expanding space, in which the related thoughts and behaviors are endlessly repeated. To be sure, traumatic events often involve mortal threats to life, but Freud made clear that trauma is not just about a reaction to horrible events. Trauma also enfolds the experience of survival, even though we may be unable to explain exactly how we manage to survive. Cathy Caruth explains that in this light, disturbing dreams actually bear witness to our survival, not to our self-destruction.[4] Our consciousness has no access to how we have managed to survive, because the means of survival is itself traumatic. Thus, only our unconscious knows, although the symptoms that subjects of trauma exhibit can reveal how they have survived.

An example from the annals of psychoanalysis: Consider a woman who has undergone treatment for debilitating somatic illness and resulting psychic problems. Psychiatrists declared her cured, but they could not relieve her of one final symptom: she hears bagpipe music in her head, all the time, as if tuned to a radio station she couldn't turn off. She hears rock and roll tunes on the bagpipes, hymns on the bagpipes, the constant, vexing presence of an auditory hallucination. Her symptom defies interpretation; the kernel of her being could not be decoded and fully assimilated into the linguistic order. The persistence of this symptom, though frustratingly immune to resolution, nonetheless reveals that she survived unspeakable trauma. It is, thus, a sign of the life drive, not of the demise of a subject. It reveals that she has moved from the death drive to the life drive by insisting on living with the symptom that defies neat explanation and the final resolution society demands and, thus, contesting her belonging to the Symbolic order.

As I discuss in chapter 2, the life drive describes how we move from one trajectory of desiring to a new trajectory and how we transform our desire to emancipate ourselves from a singular form of desire for *objet a* as prescribed for us in the pregiven order of things (e.g., capitalist desire). Through the life drive, we move to a trajectory beyond that of the death drive. In this sense, the life drive means emancipation has occurred: from the subject/object relationship held in the existing trajectory of the death drive. We continue on this new trajectory until we reach the point of another hop-step-jump from that trajectory to another emancipatory trajectory. In the life drive, we continue on the path set by the emancipatory drive, which, as I have theorized in previous chapters, constitutes a trajectory where we continue to transform our own terms of being and consequently our relationship to the Other. Through our encounter with the Real of our existence—both the universal condition of lack and history-locality specific context of our wounding through the lack—we come to a place of allowing the Other's drive into the path of our own drive for emancipation. It is because we cannot emancipate ourselves from the pregiven mode of being without the Other's drive altering our own course. Thus, the life and emancipatory drives always have universality as their driving force. The subject of the life drive who remains on the path of the emancipatory drive is the universal feminine subject.

Throughout this chapter, this transition, this hop-step-jump from the death drive to the emancipatory drive, will be crucial to construing the universal feminine subject and feminine cinema. The universal feminine subject reveals the lack in the constitution of the body itself, exposing gaps in the chain of signifiers founded on the master signifier. The woman with the bagpipe symptom exemplifies these aspects by revealing something that exceeds the Symbolic and Imaginary boundary of the body: an unfathomable organ that creates the sensorium, which gazes upon us, emanating from the crack in topography of the Symbolic order that asserts the existence of a seamlessly sutured body where all organs are counted and scientized.

Movies are dream factories. They show us how we have survived, how we are able to live beyond the initial traumatic cut into our being, as seen in the cinema of the Real. The symptoms that cinematic dreams convey are, thus, not the simple masochistic and destructive restaging of traumatic events. Repetitions, the repeated staging of traumatic events, could (and often do) lead us to self-destruction, as though the purpose of the struggle is to find death. They are surely an attempt to master all that we cannot truly grasp with our conscious minds. But through traumatic experience, we confront the horror of the death drive in the cut in our being. We also discover the possibility of transforming our trajectory to the life drive. I posit that the feminine cinema allows us to participate in this "hitting the wall" of our pregiven subject position, a repetitive impact entailed by the death drive, and to answer the universal feminine subject's exhortation to move toward the life drive that keeps us going on the paths of emancipation.

Cinema's spatial organization reveals how the law of desire works as an anchoring point for the psychic life of social subjects in local and regional contexts. David Harvey states that spatial ordering produces regional and local truths and laws rather than universals,[5] but he also adds that the ultimate question is about how we "relate such local truths and laws to the universal reason."[6] Harvey adds that "even if it is accepted, as Kant himself held, that the universality of ethics is immune to any challenge from empirical science, the problem of the application of such ethical principles to historical-geographical conditions remains. What happens when normative ideals get inserted as a principle of political action into a world in which some people are considered inferior and others are thought indolent, smelly, or just plain ugly?"[7] But universality can defy "rootedness in locality" or attachment in place and dwelling.[8] The cinematic space is most often constituted using elements in a locality, but locality necessarily carries the kernel of the universal. The universal is present in the disturbance that occurs in the locality. Harvey argues that different locations, from Rwanda to Kosovo, tell us what "evil" means on the ground.[9] This view from the ground makes it possible for us to understand the universality of evil. I add that universality smashes norms established in the context of place and dwelling and does so with a truth like universal feminine subjectivity as an emancipatory position. Harvey argues for conceiving cosmopolitanism as "a principle of intervention to try to make the world (and its geography) something other than what it is."[10] This refers to actions that allow critical, political, ethical, and economic intervention to change the world. Harvey continues: "It entails a political project that strives to transform living, being, and becoming in the world." Spatial orientation figures prominently in this project because "the production of space is as much a political and moral as a physical fact. . . . The way life gets lived in spaces, places, and environments is . . . the beginning and the end of political action."[11] We can extrapolate that the political character of cinema lies in its capacity for rendering space formally and politically.

To constitute universality, we must identify particular local circumstances and situations in which universality may emerge and intervene. Harvey argues that the Western brand of cosmopolitanism must pay attention to the factors that make universality impossible. He argues that Western cosmopolitanism has been "infected by religious power . . . [and] by bourgeois sensibilities, pieties, and 'feel-good' justifications for their hegemonic project of global domination of the world market."[12] But we must also consider the global proliferation of capitalist desire that pursues this "hegemonic project of global domination of the world market." It applies to the neo-imperial aspirations of countries like China and Russia. For example, as I mentioned in chapter 2, the recent formulaic Chinese film blockbusters organize cinematic space as imperial space, whether in Africa or at the outer limits of the galaxy. These films replicate imperial ambitions and the narratives and visual tropes that we have seen in the West since the invention of the modern cinema. Here, a universal cinematic language is used to solidify the Chinese nation-state's capitalist interests and construct the prison house of nationalist ideologies. In considering physical and cinematic space as the matrix of emancipation and transformation for the living being, and for the world, it is necessary to theorize a space in which the universal ethical subject can emerge. I see that possibility in the feminine cinema, which, in its confrontation with the nation and empire, seeks to transform their spatial organization.

What is historically defined as women's film is inadequate to describe the *feminine cinema*, in which subjectivity founded upon feminine jouissance is the starting point of the emancipatory drive as the universal human condition. In other words, this cinema allows the universal feminine subject to emerge. To show this process, the feminine cinema devises a new mode of visual language. It is our tendency to "extrapolate generalized rules about the world from the experience of a spectacle,"[13] and the cinematic spectacle can suggest ways to examine and rethink those rules. The feminine cinema is not limited to or defined by women auteurs' work about women. Bong Joon-ho's *Parasite*[14] can be read as feminine cinema for multiple reasons. The film is widely perceived as a critique of capitalism, a thematic backbone of the filmmaker's body of work, so it is tempting to read subjectivity in *Parasite* primarily in terms of class antagonism. In the film, a down-and-out proletarian family plots to secure employment in a bourgeois household. They eventually entrench themselves in the bourgeois family's life, providing academic tutoring, housekeeping, and chauffeur service. The bourgeois home is the space where the downtrodden get to legitimately participate in capitalist social relations and pursue capitalist desires. The film stages our encounter with the Real of our social and psychic lives in the space where we pursue our capitalist desires. This film materializes the unconscious as the spatial existence just under the stairs and in the midst of every line of mundane movement in bourgeois domestic space. Although many films reveal the Real of capitalist desire, this one renders as visceral a terrifying encounter with the jouissance of the oppressed. Torrential floods in the film metaphorize the unstoppable jouissance of the underclass that overwhelms and inundates the bourgeois home, the proper location of capitalist desire.

The film also illustrates that the persistent presence of jouissance, no matter how pervasive, remains invisible in the public sphere, where actual political acts must be organized and carried out to render its emancipatory possibility visible and practicable. Jouissance alone cannot emancipate, especially if it is privately claimed, as happens in *Parasite*. Private jouissance might inundate a particular social space, but it holds no emancipatory potential to change the social space itself. Jouissance obtains a public dimension in *Parasite* when the proletarian emerges from the basement where he has been carrying on an invisible life that has been subterranean, both literally and metaphorically, to carry out the murder and destruction of the bourgeoisie. The film visually juxtaposes the sunny and expansive aboveground living spaces with the narrow subterranean realm where jouissance visibly permeates and produces deadly struggle among the working class. Two proletarian families compete for this subterranean space in order to continue their parasitic existence. They remain an aberrant and criminal element that occasionally disrupts the grid delineating bourgeois space. Their spatial intrusions are made surreptitiously, wandering aboveground through the proper space of the dwelling when no one is watching. However, by structuring the space of desire around the eruption of jouissance, this film exemplifies how feminine cinema reveals a point of rupture in Symbolic space.

In previous chapters, I have described the traumatic Real of our desire that is revealed by feminine jouissance, which emerges from confronting the underlying, unspoken truth: the phallic signifier only temporarily releases us from the lack, and phallic objects are empty of any capacity to deliver on the promise of plentitude.

Feminine cinema's stylistic decisions transform space, and, in so doing, undercut the phallic signifier. In the opening scene of the film *Girlhood*,[15] the image of sensuous queer female bodies transforms a sports field, an especially hypermasculine public space in an ethnic ghetto, into the feminine space of jouissance. The sound of girls bantering at night after the all-female football game is edited so as to completely overwhelm masculine space. Its echo is amplified to completely fill the pathways of a French *banlieue*, normally ruled by hypermasculine gang members and religious brothers. The girls' voices convey feminine jouissance and change the way social space is organized by rendering the space as a location of the feminine gaze, realized through the voice, to remind us of how our own desire anchors us in gendered space. These spatial and aural components express visible and audible elements of the feminine position of the subject who escapes the traumatic rut to which the master-signifier relegates them, analogous to how sound functions in the aforementioned example of a psychiatric patient who hears bagpipe music all the time. In each case, sound, like the feminine gaze, signifies something that the Symbolic order is unable to assimilate and contain. This is an example of a cinematic element that the feminine cinema uses to construct space and the universal feminine subject within it. The feminine universality expresses itself through aesthetic means, in its antagonism to the Law of the Father, as a cinematic expression of the emancipatory subject that knows no gender or sexual difference.

Feminine cinema goes beyond women's films whose narratives are anchored in the body of women, films made by women in which women characters drive the narrative. The feminine cinema I delineate here creates space in which we follow the life drive of the subject of feminine jouissance as the anchoring point of the universal subject on the path to emancipation.

To highlight this difference, I summarize feminist critique in film studies, particularly that put forth by Sue Thronham. Thornham focuses on feminist critique of film built around the notion of space in comparison to time: "Time is defined by such things as change, movement, history, dynamism; while space . . . is simply the absence of these things. . . . With time are aligned History, Progress, Civilization, Science, Politics and Reason. . . . With space on the other hand are aligned the other poles of these concepts: stasis, ('simple') reproduction, nostalgia, emotions, aesthetics, the body."[16] In this framework, time is masculine and space is feminine. Equated with the feminine, space is "always and simply there—immanent, static and to be traveled over."[17] Feminist cultural theory can be characterized as a struggle to "articulate 'a different temporality' . . . which is also a groundedness in space, place, and the body, and to insist on 'multiplicity' of stories [notably, women's] rather than a singular [masculine] narrative."[18] Here *space* refers to the landscape, the place where the narrative proceeds. Feminist critique, in this sense, would focus on a narrative space that follows the process of women's subjectification and consolidates a consistent subject position for women.

Thornham emphasizes that feminist film theory critiques the dominant ideology that defines time as masculine because it denotes progress, whereas space is construed as feminine because it represents stasis.[19] Time in narrative cinema is indeed teleological; it follows the path of the desiring subject to obtain the phallic object that promises the fulfillment of desire. In the cinema of the Real, as described in the preceding chapters, Real time is the chronology of the drive, in which the subject never obtains the phallic object, an imaginary supplement to the Symbolic order. The subject of the Real faces the Real of existence: the phallus does not exist, and its objective referents are phantasmatic. In the time of the drive, the subject circles around the void created by the lack of an obtainable phallic object. The time of the drive, therefore, does not run on a Newtonian clock. It is the eternal time of a circular path on which we encounter the lack. Therein, the phallic object that anchors teleology does not really exist. The chronology of the drive is not temporal in the conventional sense; it involves only repetitious encounters with the lack or the gap where the phallic objects are meant to be but never will be.

Feminist film theory, based on the critique of time and space that Thornham summarizes, focuses on how women filmmakers oppose the gender binary, superimposed on time and space, by introducing a new way of constructing space wherein a feminine subject's experience is rendered in bold relief. In this line of thinking, critics might ask how women filmmakers reformulate the representation of wilderness, as established in Western genre films, in which we experience space as a field on which masculine temporality is written. The feminine intervention would be in reorganizing space, particularly in Westerns, which as a genre rely on the representation of masculine space for its ideological efficacy. For example, Kelly Reichardt's *Meek's Cutoff*[20] uses the square frame that alters our experience of the landscape. This novel framing of space shows how a woman filmmaker pursues a formal intervention into the Western genre such that it can no longer configure time and space according to masculine manifest destiny, which depends on boundless wild space to tame into a garden. The film's formal device unravels the gendered subjectivity that Western genre films established through the genre-specific spatial and temporal organization. Such a formal choice constitutes a notable feminist intervention that feminist film theory recognizes.

At this point, we can take note of the tenets of feminist film theory, as laid out by Thornham: first, the notion of women filmmakers' auteuristic signature as something that marks "the particularity . . . that the text will be read differently"; and second, the examination of how films show "ways in which the sexuality and corporeality of the subject leave their traces or marks on the texts produced."[21] Feminist film theory asks what "a specifically female space-time framework looks like."[22] This body of theory further posits that to "transform representations of female corporeality, and the narratives within which they are produced . . . 'the overarching context of space-time, within which bodies function and are conceived . . . need serious revision."[23] Women filmmakers' work is regularly measured by these criteria.

To escape the confinement of the time-space of their given situation, women undertake *depaysement*; that is, a woman undertakes "to change scenery in order to displace herself from her own territory" in order to eventually "transform the known territory."[24] Women's film could represent seeing "women through women's eyes, telling stories from women's point of view,"[25] in her process of *depaysement*. This seeing and telling constitutes film feminism. If we see film as a "time-space of fantasy," film feminism takes note of the "critical promise of fantasy"[26] and thus queries what manner of space the critical promise of fantasy involved in *depaysement* creates.

What, then, is the intervention that the feminine cinema I theorize makes into the preexisting notion of women's film and feminist film theory? To answer this question, it is necessary to unpack the relationship between space and the subject in feminine cinema, using the Lacanian framework. In a psychoanalytic conception of psychic space, the consistent subject is the one who arrives at the limit of subjectivity. Within the psychoanalytic conceptualization of human subjects in space, one cannot constitute a consistent and stable subject position through any mode of occupying space. Psychoanalytic thinking thus disrupts the notion of cohesive and unified psychic and social space that is meant to support subjectivities anchored in identities.

From this perspective, there is always a subject of enunciation behind any subject of the statement. Theorist Dany Nobus describes this structure: "The subject of enunciation implies that the subject of the statement (the personal pronoun or name with which the speaker identifies in his or her message) is continuously pervaded by another dimension of speech, another location of thought.... [The subject's] utterance is also coming from somewhere else than the place which the message has defined as the locus of emission."[27] In other words, while the speaking subject occupies a proper place of statement, this "somewhere else" haunts all speech, originating from a place other than the site the speaking subject consciously occupies.

The feminine cinema I envision materializes, visualizes, and superimposes this other place over the grids of space in the Symbolic order from which the subject speaks. In the feminine cinema, the place of enunciation, which undermines an intended statement, is where the subject of feminine jouissance exists. Feminine cinema reveals feminine jouissance that constitutes the subject of the Real through filmic enunciations, that is, through image and sound as filmic language. In *Morvern Callar*,[28] the sound that fills private and public space indicates this other place of enunciation that undermines the set of statements that seek to define femininity. A metallic, mechanical hum continuously penetrates and unravels the verisimilitude of the diegesis. The sound here actually functions as the gaze, something that addresses us in the form of language that emanates from an uncanny space where we see no place of our own belonging. This sound breaks down the boundaries of space, which, in order to be meaningful to the speaking subject, must be divided along the ideologically cohesive spaces of diegesis. In this film, sound renders the diegetic space disjointed. The heightened metallic pitch of the oceanic waves and Christmas lights overwhelm the cinematic space by creating a jarring chasm between the sound and the image with which it is paired. The sound does not contribute to the meaning of the image or of the narrative in which it is heard. It is the sound of "somewhere else," the other place, the place of enunciation.

In feminine cinema, the voice of the universal feminine subject comes from this "somewhere else." In *Oasis*,[29] which I analyze in chapter 2, the image of the body of a severely speech-impaired quadriplegic woman (played by an actor who does not have a physical disability) invades the proper social space with sound that only she can hear. Recall the scene where we find her, wheelchair-bound, in a crowded subway station, which I analyzed in chapter 2 as a location of feminine jouissance. As she stands alone, singing, the station now rendered surreal, devoid of people and noise, we listen to her enunciate her desire, and it drowns out the pervading sentiment that the pathological feminine cannot speak. The sound reveals how the other place of jouissance, which the definition of a properly feminine body as the location of statement elides, suddenly breaks into the scene of established normalcy.

The film *The Last Princess*[30] provides a counterexample of such eruptions. The film is based on the biography of an actual historical princess, the daughter of the last emperor of Korea's Yi dynasty, an oppressive feudal Confucian regime that was deposed as the Korean peninsula was annexed by Japan in 1910. Forced to marry a Japanese nobleman, the princess is blocked from returning to Korea. It is a biographical fact that, while in Japan, she developed the symptoms of schizophrenia, was committed to a psychiatric institution, and subsequently stopped talking altogether. The schizophrenic princess is an allegorical figure of the feminine subject who escapes the demand of the empire that forces her to speak properly as a colonized subject. The film rehabilitates the schizophrenic, withdrawn from the linguistic order, as a patriot by fabricating her delivery of a rousing speech to the Koreans brought to Japan for forced labor and by dramatizing a fictitious escape attempt to return to her suffering mother nation, where her own biological mother was ailing. This rehabilitation amounts to a translation of the subject of the enunciation into the subject of statement. The narrative maneuver shows the double imprisonment of Woman, phantasmatic and factual. She is imprisoned within the empire and also in the colonized nation-state that makes her speak the language of nationalism as her statement. This confinement creates the fantasy that there exists only one unique and valid place of statement for the subject, held in ideological space as the subject of the nation's and empire's statement, with no disruptive enunciation dispelling this fantasy.

We turn now to the feminine cinema's topology, that is, the expression of space using geometric figures and forms. Topology metaphorizes subjects' movements in both material and psychic space. For Lacan, topological surfaces like the Möbius strip, the Klein bottle, and the cross-cap are representations of the contour of the subject.[31] For Lacan, topology is "the structure of the world in which the linguistic subject exists," and topology's "non-spherical applications" trace the movement of the subject without center and show "the very absence of the nodal point in the unconscious."[32] I posit that what Lacan articulates as the space of the subject is feminine, insofar as that space problematizes the phallic subject's progressive movement. The subject position that doesn't follow this progressive, trackable movement toward acquisition of the phallic object is the subject position of the psychoanalytic feminine. Feminine cinema describes a Lacanian topology of the universal feminine subject and reveals the unconscious landscape where there is no nodal point of absolute reference. This lack leaves the trajectory of our desire open to the unconscious force of the drive. The drive itself, lacking the nodal point, circles around the lack of a finally obtainable phallic object of desire. Our desire is thus doomed to fail to arrive at the phantasmatic point of fulfillment. As we have established, the universal feminine subject circling around in the death drive hop-step-jumps to the emancipatory drive.

Lacan considered the possibility of "mathematical formalizations" as a means of obtaining and transmitting knowledge of the unconscious, a way to access the unconscious without reference to, and thus interference by, signifiers and their subjective meaning.[33] Might this, then, also be the cinema's ambition, transmitting knowledge of the unconscious through spatial expression that does not anchor itself in the chain of signifiers? Consider Todd McGowan's assertion that all movies are horror movies, in the sense that they stage the encounter with the unconscious.[34] The feminine cinema stages this encounter and subsequent transmission of revealed knowledge of the unconscious by untethering the signifier of gender, race, ethnicity, social inclusion, and so on from its meaning.

This focus on the subject of the unconscious—ephemeral because she moves between the statement and the enunciation—is also the defense against affect theory's tethering of meaning to the signifier of affect. In this framework, the image that describes affect serves as the signifier of the stable, comprehensible signified, such that an image that conveys emotional affects is able to support and sustain the signifier's meaning-making. Affect, especially that which is generated by "haptic visuality,"[35] presupposes that vision is a conduit to the body, as it stimulates the sensation of touch. Forming an optical/tactile dyad, vision certifies the cohesiveness of the sensuous body as the fulcrum of "tactile epistemology"[36] and of the subject who knows herself, because the self corporeally experiences. Affect is here seen as the material evidence of the feminine (that is to say, woman's) experience that ascertains a subject position: affect registered on the body authenticates the feminine, that is, woman's, subjectivity.

I agree that vision serves as a conduit to the body, though this is just the starting point of my theorization of the cinema of the Real, wherein the image of the body, and the spectator's visceral experience of it, creates the somatic disjointure that characterizes the Real body. As I theorize in chapter 3, this term, the Real body, draws from the Lacanian idea that the subject represents a mode of arranging partial objects, such as limbs and organs, to achieve "jointure of the somatic and the normative."[37] The Real body in the cinema of the Real unravels that jointure. Patriarchy, for example, presents a cohesive interpretation of the signifier "woman," which hides the disjointure inherent in that category as an ideological arrangement of partial objects organized to meet the needs of patriarchal society and occludes the Real of sexual difference, namely, that woman, as such, does not exist. In the cinema of the Real, the image of the body can reveal the lines of suture along which the ideological body has been assembled and thus dismantle the body as a method of dismantling the ideology that secures the Symbolic order.

The body is an assemblage of disarticulated limbs put together following the blueprint of the Symbolic order. The Real body reveals the contour of those fracture lines, and therefore it is the embodiment of universal feminine subjectivity. The Real body conveys feminine jouissance in opposition to the linguistic and Symbolic body of phallic jouissance, which, built on the belief and trust in the phallic signifier, implies belief and trust in language itself, in the Symbolic order, and in its various projects.

The Local and Global Location of Feminine Universality

A Lacanian intervention in our understanding of space helps further articulate the universal feminine subject. This intervention allows us to expand the feminine beyond current feminist film critique and its focus on the development of new stylistic modes of visually representing women's counter-subjectivity and experience in social space. The Lacanian framework draws our attention to the emergence of the feminine subject as a universal subject of the Real in cinematic space. Cinematic representations of image and sound in this framework conceptualize space beyond a unified place from which to reformulate or reflect upon women's agency. The visual field is the topography of the drive, where the universal subject of feminine jouissance appears. What critics may see as, for example, "images that don't have apparent narrative purpose"[38] in films like Claire Denis's *White Material*,[39] can be interpreted as the locus in which the other scene, not framed by the theater of imperial imaginary, appears. In *White Material*, the feminine subject is emancipated from the narrativization of gendered historical time and space. These images without apparent narrative purpose are, in fact, signs of the colonized Other slowly submerging the spaces of patriarchy and colonialism and finally transforming space into that of feminine jouissance, where the phallic signifier loses all meaning.

White Material takes place in a French colony in Africa during decolonization, a time of turmoil. Maria, a white French woman, identifying with the imperial desire of her coffee- plantation-owning ex-husband's family, struggles to protect her crop from internecine warfare. Around her, images and scenes quietly unfold that are mostly invisible to her: child soldiers bathing in her bathtub, sleeping in her easy chair, taking her necklace and dress, surreptitiously moving around her property; her son's loss of grounding in the imperial Symbolic order and going native, which leads to his being burned to death by a sector of the African militia as a "white material" object that belongs to neither France nor Africa. Maria encounters an injured rebel fugitive bleeding to death in her son's bedroom to whom she inexplicably offers a blanket before walking away. These details don't function as motivations for causal action within the broader narrative but rather signify the unraveling of imperial patriarchal space, crushed under the intrusion of the Other space of the enunciation of the colonized. In this newly created space of the colonized Other, Maria becomes able to kill the patriarch of the plantation, who has denied her legitimate ownership. Her emancipation from imperial patriarchy, thus gestured, is representative of the eruption of the feminine jouissance that anti-colonial warfare liberates, although whether that jouissance will create the life drive that continues the emancipatory trajectory of anti-colonial war is unclear, considering how the bloody internecine conflicts ravage all life. Although it is unclear whether Maria will abandon the imperial desire and stay on the path of the emancipatory drive, she remains at the threshold of the Other space of feminine jouissance at the end of the film.

Defined in relation to space, the Real is "a dimension of psychical life that constantly menaces and threatens to topologically erupt from within and without the Symbolic register's machination of the signifier."[40] The eruption of jouissance into the Real is topographic in nature,[41] and therein lies the threat of the Real to the Symbolic. We perceive and locate the desire of the Other/the neighbor in a space we claim as ours within the Symbolic order. The Other's enjoyment enters this space in various sensuous forms, such as sound and smell, but the Real of the Other's enjoyment is that it is not definitively locatable as either within or without. The Other's desire operates within our psychic space, within the psychic space that the Other interprets as theirs (although we see the Other as without), and within the Symbolic order itself, thus disrupting the topology in which our secure position in the Symbolic order is arranged by the spatial demarcation of "our space" and "their space," "within" and "without."

In *Parasite*, the proletarian Other's jouissance is likewise not sufficiently located within or without with respect to the social and psychic space of the bourgeois subject. The filmic space of *Parasite* is the field in which the Other's desire disrupts the psychic and material life of the bourgeois subject. The film's elaborate sets comprise physical spaces in which classed subjectivities find structural and visual manifestations. Plush, green, horizontally expansive space signifies the wealthy, but the architecture of the interior emphasizes a surreal spatial heterogeneity. Formal compositions exaggerate the distance between the properly bourgeois space and its Other space, which exists simultaneously outside and inside. To graphically render the space of the poor, the film visualizes bodies in endless downward movement toward the literal bottom of the cityscape where the boundary between sewage and the human domicile is erased by a furious downpour and flood during a summer tempest. But the proletarian Other lurks also within the very walls of the bourgeois edifice. The film visualizes extimacy, a Lacanian term for this interior/exterior ambiguity, among social classes through a space that is simultaneously within and without the bourgeoisie spatial domicile, which is secretly teeming with the proletarian Other's jouissance: the basement. Two families, both hired domestic help, are entrenched in the capitalist logic of desire, which dictates that they compete for recognition as the most useful human capital. They engage in a spectacular life-death struggle in the basement, suggesting that proletarian bodies will continue to live and die there without the bourgeois subject's knowledge. The film's spatial construction shows the Real of capitalism that the bourgeois subjects disavow: the proletarian Other is in fact intimate to their existence "like a foreign body, a parasite"[42] living in a larger organism. As we learn from the bourgeois-proletarian relationship in *Parasite*, the Other's jouissance is the Real of my jouissance, and it creates topological disruption in my material and psychic space.

Cinema visualizes the movement of desiring subjects through topological mapping. The desiring subject's body is the surface upon which messages from the unconscious are written, revealing how signifiers obscure the lack at the heart of our subject formation, and how we encounter the big Other through those signifiers. Subjectivity is, thus, spatial. Signifiers of gender, for example, appear topologically as "the spatial imperative of subjectivity"[43] within the Symbolic order. These spatial imperatives and their results are seen in cinematic representations of physical space, as when Hedy Lamarr appears in a domestic melodrama wearing a blouse that matches the curtains in her house. Lacan's topology maps "the structure of subjectivity."[44] We can summarize Lacan's topological subject via the following statement: "I am thinking where I am not, therefore, I am where I am not thinking."[45] Here, the subject exists through thinking where it is not, not where it is. A woman might stand in a kitchen wearing a blouse that ties her to the curtains, but the meaning of the feminine cannot be harnessed by her spatial location.

The historical dimension comes to the fore in this *where*. History unfolds in physical space, drawn in topological maps, and the way we relate to the world is contingent upon our concept of our historical and geographical location. Dipesh

Chakravarty discusses the topology of capital by distinguishing between "History 1" and "History 2."[46] As in a Möbius strip, these two histories are neither definitively opposing nor contiguous. History 1 describes the history of modern capitalism, while History 2 refers to various politico-economic trajectories that are coeval to History 1 but cannot be incorporated or assimilated seamlessly into the hegemonic sphere of History 1.

From this structure, we can extrapolate different sets of relationships, arranged as on a Möbius strip, beyond those of modern capitalism and its others, as arranged in any one history. The desiring subject and its Other are in this space. Imperial desire and the colonized Other's desire encounter each other in it. Korean "comfort women," the Japanese imperial army's sex slaves, provide an example of that encounter. At the outposts of the empire, outside the purview of Japanese imperial citizens, they dwelled in camp-like quarters, a metaphorical expression of the imprisonment of the feminine subject. As such, they reveal the Real of imperial and national signification, that which the Law of the Father simultaneously institutes and disavows. Their presence is simultaneously hidden and massive in the empire, exposing the obscene jouissance of a patriarchal nation institutionalized through imperialism. Put more generally: You think you are in the space of a particular history (History 1, or Japanese imperialism, for example), but you are never entirely where you believe you are, because the Real that the Other brings into your space changes its configuration. Thus, you are thinking where you are not and are where you are not thinking.

Lacanian space, when applied in the feminine cinema, complicates film feminism's focus on the means by which women filmmakers revise maps and models of space. In Lacanian space, the Real subject—thinking where she is not and, therefore, being where she is not thinking—cannot be summed up as "woman" in a way that renders the signifier as meaningful. Thus, the feminine cinema as I theorize it is not simply about the dissolution of "located-ness and spatial boundaries" within patriarchy that results in "the loss of place that propels the female subject forward, freeing her from [the] place"[47] designated to her by patriarchy. Here, terms like *place*, *home*, and *landscape* are used interchangeably with the notion of space, implying a reliable topological firmament. In Lacanian space, a consistent and wholesome spatial designation of human subjects that anchors the subject in specific expressions of gender and sexuality is impossible, even when those expressions are effectively counter-hegemonic. In this way, Lacanian space draws out the ontology of the subject of the lack. What Thornham describes as feminine space is an element of representation rather than an ontological field. While accepting the value of film feminism's focus on women's films' reformulations of filmic space to indicate the possibility of emancipation, the feminine cinema I theorize aims to capture the emancipatory possibility in the universal subject of the Real, which transgresses the line of sexual and gender difference and occupies the position of the feminine, that is, the universal feminine subject.

To imagine how the universal feminine subject might appear, let us consider the actual case of a woman who, in undergoing analysis, arrives at the original scene of trauma: the empty house where she started to be able to read as a small child. It is her childhood home as she remembers it, but there is no sign of life in the image of this house in her mind. This absence, perhaps, corresponds to her inability to recall the content of the trauma that must have happened in that house. In this image, the world of people has disappeared, another clue that this house holds the scene of trauma. But she also connects the expression "nobody guarantees" to the house, building a connection between the words and the space. In this space, she experienced the traumatic realization that there is no guarantee for her place in the Symbolic order, the result of encountering the cruel superego. The absence of guarantees describes her death drive. At the same time, however, the words also mean that there is no guarantee that she will continue to be tethered to the Symbolic order where the big Other rules with punishing violence. Because *nobody* guarantees, she is free to signify the language differently. She sees empty space in language, allegorized by the Father's empty house, inserts her own language into that empty space, and opens the emancipatory possibility of rewriting the topography of the space of original trauma. The feminine cinema defines universal subjectivity by discovering a subject who engages in such an emancipatory linguistic act.

At the center of our existence is an empty space, because our entrance to the linguistic order has cost us metaphorical arms and legs. It is here that the subject enters the death drive, which is set off by the experience of death, caused by the metaphoric bloodletting of being cut off from the materiality of nature via the acquisition of language through the encounter with the big Other who demands that we speak, that we relinquish our natural life in exchange for the benefits of language. Somehow, we find a way to keep going, to turn the death drive into the life drive. The language that cuts us also allows us to enter the life drive. We continue to desire, we traverse the fantasy space of the death drive to which desire has led us, and, upon cutting open ourselves and the Other in search of that little object "a" that we fantasize will fulfill our desire, we reach the limit of our fantasy and finally enter the life drive that keeps us going in the drive for emancipation.

Recognizing that the Father's language does not guarantee meaning, we might invent a new language through which we can creatively and authentically speak of our cut, relate to the world, and carve out our space within it. To think about this new language, let us consider the dreams of an immigrant woman, an intellectual from a country that is in a perpetual state of geopolitical conflict. She lives next door to a Hasidic Jewish rabbi who is her late father's age, a venerable scholar of Judaic learning with whom she shares mutual affection and respect. One afternoon while working at her desk, she hears him pass her window and say a prayer for her in Hebrew. That night, he appears in her dream. In it, she sees a dark, gaping hole on her bookshelf, signifying her troubled relationship with the language that has nonetheless allowed her to traverse the spheres of the Symbolic order across two continents. The rabbi speaks to her in Hebrew. Although she does not understand the details of his speech, in the dream it feels like a gift. Via this image, she makes a plea with the Other to fill the lack that the language has imposed on her. The demand of the Other to speak properly within the Symbolic order could place her on the trajectory of the death drive, but it also prompts her to search for a language that will allow her to enunciate, so as to escape becoming moribund in the Symbolic order.

In a later dream, the Hasidic man weeps and says to her, "I always wanted to teach you mathematics." In this case, mathematics metaphorizes the language that includes empty space, Lacan's "mathematics of the unconscious," and disrupts the master signifier's all-encompassing grammatical logic. The other language of the feminine subject, that is, mathematics, allows her (or him, or them, as the feminine subject may carry any gender signification) to move from the death drive, in which she was placed when she encountered the cruel demand of the Father that she speak the proper language. In the dream, the rabbi (a symbolic proxy for the Father) expresses regret that he was not able to teach the language, which paradoxically indicates that she has acquired the language that challenges the Father's master signifier, as with the dream child's emptying of the house to fill it with her own language. In surviving patriarchal oppression on two continents and finding the ability to speak as an intellectual, she has indeed learned the mathematics and devised new linguistic tools.

Consider also cultural objects as signifiers. They are the little materials around which jouissance is congealed. They indicate a particular way of responding to, and living with, the traumatic cut. Ethnicity refers to the position in which subjects feel they have membership to a particular place of jouissance by desiring particular objects. But because we can change the trajectory of our desire and eventually redirect the drive through a new language, which, in Lacan's formulation, is a "mathematics," we can transform our relationship to these objects. One can, in this sense, move beyond ethnically formulated jouissance through the formulation of a new language. The new language, manifested in the unconscious as dreams and cinematically as changes in film form, allows the feminine cinema to achieve this transformation. The point of critique for the feminine cinema is—beyond the prevalent film feminism's concern about how female characters drive narrative—a realignment of jouissance through a new language.

Objects may bind us to our jouissance. Consider a defense against the seduction of objects waged by a woman who believes that love will always fail. She might say to a lover: "I probably love you, and nothing's wrong with this relationship, but I am breaking up with you anyway." For her, sexual relationship and love will continue to restage the scene of seduction in the language of the Father that defines our desire for the Other's *objet a*, which physical objects, in this case her lover, represent. Objects make possible consistent and holistic reality; they are the points at which ideology sutures us to that illusion of reality.[48] The object appears as the material evidence of reality. In the feminine cinema, we witness how reality falls apart when space does not convey a consistent and complete reality through objects, including the body, and instead they are presented to us as fractured by the way in which the cinematic space is organized.

We turn now to examples of the way the feminine cinema organizes space. *The Swamp*[49] reveals the violent undercurrent of desire in a decaying Argentinian bourgeois family. The film opens with the bodies of middle-aged men and women framed to include only their midsections as they, visibly intoxicated, languidly drag chairs around the poolside, their screeching noise and distant thunder filling the soundscape. The shot defines the space by denying us a holistic apprehension of the body as an object that can successfully suture space to represent a consistent and wholesome reality. In *Mood Indigo*,[50] a film that pushes the boundaries of techniques of animation, fantasy, and magical realism, both private and public space are unstable. A bourgeois house—an object that secures bourgeois social space—changes shape to reflect the disorder of heterosexual romance. The feminine body is diseased, and when she takes up residence as a wife, the very presence of her body becomes a malaise that dismantles the house inch by inch, room by room, until it becomes an uninhabitable ruin. In the process of the bourgeois ruination, the kitchen is an especially magical space, because it is the locus of a phantasmatic Black body that supports the household with a plastic physique that carries out ever more versatile functions. He is a chef, a housekeeper, a lawyer, and a chauffeur for the bourgeois household.

This surrealist depiction of space is a formal pressure point that reveals the Real of a European society that stringently guards its boundary of the proper European body. The Real of Europe is Blackness, an *objet a* that promises the consistent reality of the European bourgeois. Ultimately, however, even the Black body's versatile labor cannot stop the house from metamorphosing into an uninhabitable, hellish space where humans can no longer keep pace with its disconcerting transformations, brought out by the diseased feminine body.

This body expresses jouissance that finds its metaphor in the literal presence of a blooming flower that grows in her lung. Here the feminine cinema stages the arrival of the feminine subject of jouissance in a new space, a topography of the universal feminine in the ruin of the bourgeois house. The feminine cinema's emancipatory politics depends on formal strategies of constructing space.

I have mentioned that critics notice in Claire Denis's *White Material* "images that don't have apparent narrative purpose" and read them as ways of rewriting imperial space, away from the hegemonic trope where space serves as the ideological space of European progress. They are, in my formulation, the location of the gaze that reveals the empty space in language; film is, after all, the linguistic field. So film feminism, and the feminine cinema I articulate, might share a point of departure: the need to create changes in the methods of making meaning through image at the heart of the narrative cinema. But the focus and aim of the two diverge here. In the case of *White Material*, I posit that *depaysement* is not just about changing the imperial narrative convention, wherein the masculine project to tame savage land into a garden plays itself out in cinematic space. In feminine cinema of my theorization, the emphasis is on this sense of dislocation that functions to open up the Real, through which the universal feminine subject emerges. Thornham's work mobilizes affect theory[51] as a support for women's films' *depaysement*, arguing that women's haptic experience creates an emotional affect that takes them out of their pregiven position in social space. I must note that the haptic and its affect are not a guarantee and promise for a new subjectivity. The haptic and its affect suture a subject along the lines of the linguistic/visual template called "woman." But "woman" does not exist, except as the linguistic effect and the effect of bodily fragments sewn together following the lines of signification. Haptic experience, were it to be the gut-wrenching undoing of the position that women hold in the Symbolic order, would be a chasm whose opening leads to the dissolution of the Symbolic subject, marked by particular properties of identity, not a thread that binds together a sensuous body that materializes and promises a subject position such as "woman."

What, then, are the specific contours of the feminine subject in the topology of the feminine cinema? What, in other words, are the location and spatial configuration of the universal feminine? The feminine in feminine cinema is a signifier without the signified. A signifier stands in for the *objet a*, whose absence leaves a void in the field of desire, which is the field of the Symbolic order. It attaches to objects as proxies for the absent *objet a*, the cause of our desire for various objects. It hides that we have only the metonymy of what constitutes our desire, not the realization of desire through *objet a*. Alenka Zupančič identifies that which is "created and extirpated by advent of the signifying order"; it is called "the Thing."⁵² I extrapolate that it is the *objet a* that is "created and extirpated" by the signifying order, and as such *objet a* is at the kernel of our being as the desiring subject. The signifier veils jouissance that comes from circling around the void that the absent object creates. In the feminine cinema, it is possible that the void, as "a stumbling block of reality,"⁵³ exists in every representation.

Even when the void itself is not directly represented in film, we often see visual and auditory markers that indicate the void in the Symbolic order and its representations. In the horror film *The Babadook*,⁵⁴ we encounter an incomprehensible presence that invades the home of a young, widowed mother and her child. A mysterious, handmade picture book that accompanies this sudden appearance calls it "Babadook," which, it says, is "in the word or looks," and warns that "you can't get rid of [it]." Babadook is a cinematic rendition of the uncanny object that makes "you wish you were dead once you see it." There is a long and rich history of cinematic renditions of the uncanny Thing, or *objet a*, the appearance of which could kill you, from various incarnations of Nosferatu to John Carpenter's *The Thing* (1982). It appears to be outside our corporeal boundary, yet it often turns out to be the kernel within us, toward which we feel simultaneous attraction and repulsion. The subject forever asks, "What does it want?" This Thing lacks even a signifier that conveys the history and meaning of its existence. But the Thing is the Real of the subject who believes he or she is a secure and whole entity, definable by signifiers. In this film, the Babadook is a monstrous incarnation of the jouissance we claim in the Real, that is, in the void in the Symbolic order. It is in the mother and in the house, both of which are believed to be substantiated by signifiers.

In *The Babadook*, the mother enters the space of the death drive's lethal jouissance as Babadook enters her, both corporeally and psychically. As the mother is about to murder her child on the path of her death drive to annihilate her subjectivity, the child pleads with her for his life. He is, in essence, imploring her to come back from her lethal jouissance, to expel the Thing as the vessel of that jouissance, and to let him live. The touch of the Other, the child, on her face conveys this request and enables the mother to enter the life drive in which both the subject and its Other keep going toward a new articulation of jouissance on the path of the emancipatory drive. At the conclusion of the film, we see that Babadook continues to reside in the basement, where Mother feeds it earthworms and grubs she digs out of her garden, partial objects that she knows are inherently empty. Each time she enters the basement to feed Babadook, she faces the peril of entering the space of jouissance of the death drive, represented by the invisible force of Babadook that nearly overwhelms her. This example of the feminine cinema demonstrates the gaps in subjectivity. In the chain of meaning signifying "mother," there is a gap in which murderous jouissance, in the form of Babadook, resides. But passing the path of that jouissance, Mother enters the life drive that allows the Other's and her own life to prevail; as the subject of the life drive on the path of emancipation from the death-drive jouissance, she is no longer defined as "woman" or "mother," an imaginary and also judiciary position to be occupied in the Law of the Father.

Society and subjectivity are assembled through desire, specifically through the exchange of objects of desire. But there is an inherent gap in relationships based on desire. Zupančič makes this point by stating that "the very fact that I address my demand to the Other introduces something in this demand that eludes satisfaction; for example, a child who demands food from her parents will not be satisfied simply by the food that she receives."[55] I add that the demand for the satisfaction of desire that I make to the Other invokes horror in the Other, as my demand contains the dimension of enunciation (invoking "somewhere else than the place which the message has defined as the locus of emission," as Nobus puts it[56]), the abyss of my being. The *statement* covers over the abyss of my being that *objet a* as the Real object creates, giving lie to the certainty of meaning of all objects. It is something that we cannot grasp through any signifier, and it renders our location in the Symbolic order insecure. The *objet a* is not an a priori presence; language creates it. Feminine cinema shows the process of this creation, including through the monstrous Otherness in our reality depicted in horror films. It is as if the Babadook is created as a material presence through the mother's recitation of the picture book's rhymes that describe it. Yet the feminine cinema also shows how we can overcome that horror for the sake of the drive that allows life to continue in the emancipatory trajectory of the life drive rather than annihilating it, as the Babadook, avatar of the mother's death-drive jouissance, wants the mother to do.

The signifier is meant to protect us from jouissance,[57] especially the kind that the feminine subject experiences in *The Babadook*. The feminine cinema's unbinding of the signifier reveals frightening jouissance, but it also offers a way for the subject to leapfrog over the abyss that failure of the signifier has left and to arrive at the emancipatory drive. We see an example in *Zama*.[58] The eponymous Zama is an imperial administrator in the far reaches of eighteenth-century Argentina. The film opens with a medium long shot of Zama in profile standing at the seashore. The shot of the landscape is cropped so that Zama specifically is not presented in the imperial position of looking out upon and surveying the savage land. In the following sequence, an indigenous woman, a slave whose feet were mutilated as a punishment for trying to run away, publicly calls Zama out for peeping at a group of local women bathing on the shore, then chases him away. Here, Zama is denied even the voyeuristic point of view that conveys masculine mastery. He already occupies a liminal position within the empire. Born in the colony, Zama lacks a European identity; he has been waiting for the king's permission to leave the outpost and return to a more central location in the colony. Finally, when Zama has finished traversing the territory that the empire's law hasn't quite reached in pursuit of an elusive bandit who threatens the imperial rule of law, we find him unconscious on a small boat piloted by local people. He floats with them along a river deep inland, farther and farther away from the ocean, both his hands having been cut off by the very bandit he was to apprehend. An indigenous boy, meeting his eyes, asks the seemingly moribund Zama, in the boy's native language: "Do you want to live?" Which is to say, "Do you want to live by a different language?" Here, we see an example of the unbinding of imperial signifiers. An imperial subject is carried through the jungle, which the imperial epistemology cannot penetrate. There he will have to lose the language of the empire in order to bind his life drive, connected to space that is not truly locatable within or without the topology of the empire, and give up the empire's pursuit of the death drive.

Feminine cinema can also show us that "we have been misled into believing that the access to our fantasy is bound up with an all powerful Other who punishes every form of transgression. . . . The subject will devise the most elaborate neurotic scenarios to lure this Other, to defend against it, or even to claim responsibility and guilt so that the fantasy can remain intact."[59] The subject, in this manner, fills the lack in the Other with the fantasy. But we can traverse our fantasy and hit the limit of the fantasy frame. The subject is initially tethered to fantasy within a framework with the big Other as its architect. To maintain this fantasy scene, subjects recruit lovers and neighbors to play the role of placeholder. Sexism and racism are examples of this intersubjective configuration. But these various recruits are, of course, more than objects, the functional pieces that hold our fantasy together; they each come from their own history of suffering. History must therefore be at the center in our thinking of others whose wound speaks, cries out, implores, and offends. Through the mobilization of others as set pieces for our fantasy, we claim agency and subject position. In this fantasy, we occupy the interstices. We can stay within this exchange, that is, we can maintain the fantasy scene that fills the screen that the big Other erects. But we can also break free of this fantasy frame, by refusing to speak properly as the big Other demands. This refusal can result in following the death drive, because by not speaking properly we refuse to become proper linguistic subjects, which is to say, to become proper subjects of desire. But we can also, through this confrontation, speak in "mathematics," the language of the emancipatory drive, a new ethical configuration with respect to the Other. Not speaking properly can push us outside the fantasy frame prepared for us.

The film *Nightingale*[60] shows a feminine subject who responds to the imperial Father's cruel demand by wreaking havoc in imperial space, in this case the British penal colony of Australia. Clare, an Irish convict, struggles to carve out a path through the imperial topography in order to carry out revenge against the empire, whose obscene underside is manifested in the gendered violence committed against the colonized feminine body. The colonial space she traverses is haunted: She encounters the ghost of her husband, killed by the imperial soldiers, and that of an imperial officer she herself bludgeoned to death in revenge for her murdered husband and child. Corpses scream at her in a fantasy sequence, lodged in the middle of an otherwise realist film, marking the unspeakable Real of the empire that the realist form cannot contain. Overwhelmed by the Real of imperial violence, Clare must enlist the Black body's labor to navigate the imperial space. The film allows space for the revenge narrative of an indigenous man, Billy, whose whole clan was massacred by the imperial army. Billy guides Clare through the wilderness. In the end, the trauma of colonization cannot be overcome through the actions of a white woman wanting to carve out the space of the feminine narrative. Even the Black body that carries intimate knowledge of the land cannot claim space. Mortally wounded, he can only shout at the empire's edge, facing the Pacific Ocean: "I am still here!" After all the traversing of imperial space, the feminine subject cannot rewrite the map, but the film cuts open a gap in imperial space where the mathematical speech of women and indigenes can be imagined.

In a world organized around the phallic signifier, there is no name for the universal feminine. A chain of signifiers holds together the concept "feminine," through which patriarchy assembles for us a picture of "woman." We fear the feminine because it can unravel the system of signifiers neatly arranged around cultural objects. If the gaps in the signifier "woman" are exposed, the Real of woman is revealed: that she doesn't exist except as a signifier. Consider the example of a girl of about twelve who has suffered severe emotional and physical abuse at the hands of her parents. Her art teacher gives her a pencil drawing of her face. This teacher has helped her to start drawing, loaned her art history books, and let her know that he recognizes that her intellect is beyond her age. Her mind leaps over the confines of her family home. She hangs the portrait in her room, but then the housekeeper, an elderly woman who has served the family for many years, destroys it while cleaning the girl's room, puncturing the face of the framed image. Could this supposed accident be an expression of the fear of the feminine as the abused child begins to find a new aesthetic and linguistic mode of existence? Perhaps the housekeeper took it upon herself to censure the new kind of language, which I have been calling mathematics, following Lacan, that the girl has begun to develop in opposition to what has been allowed her by the phallic signifier: the speech of the feminine that is forever guilty according to the Law of the Father.

Women experience this kind of antinomy, involved in the unfolding of femininity, in all sorts of settings. Once, I, an Asian woman, was walking on the sidewalk of a New England college town. I was, as usual, the only person of color in sight. Walking fast toward me, a middle-aged white woman yelled something in my direction that I couldn't immediately comprehend. As she approached, I realized that the white woman was shouting, "Get out of my way!" As she passed, the woman slammed her shoulder into mine, shoving me off the sidewalk and knocking me to the ground. Stunned, I asked, "What was that about?" Her answer? "You take up too much space!" (I am easily the smallest person around.) Race imbues femininity with an even more sinister Otherness that often invokes such hostility.

White femininity, fantasized as a unified subject to be violently defended, is, like any ideal, fractured. Let us consider *Cléo from 5 to 7*.[61] The title character habitually examines her visage in a hand mirror, as if to ensure that the imaginary self remains intact. In one scene she drops the mirror, and it shatters. The broken shards reflect Cléo's face as a web of fractured images, suggesting that the feminine body is in a fragmented state, that it is imprisoned in the fantasy space of "woman" assembled through fragmentary body parts along lines drawn in the Imaginary field. The feminine is put together piece by piece, following an Imaginary map, fitting her into the Symbolic space she inhabits. Broken reflections reveal the quilting points that hold the body together. These fragmented parts, assembled and made to occupy a cartographical point in a patriarchal society, trace the shape of the linguistic and the Symbolic subject. In this process of assemblage, the feminine subject, in facing the Father's impossible demand that she occupy a designated space in a properly defined form, experiences so much pain that she might encounter the experience of death. In this film, Cléo suffers from a life-threatening illness, a physical manifestation of the death drive just beneath the facade of the unified "woman," which she cannot transform into the life drive, confined as she is in the world of the master signifier. This confinement is visualized through the framing of her image in various mirrors throughout the film, with no addressee who might receive the sound of feminine suffering, despite her many mirrored images in public places. Cléo gains some respite from this silent suffering when she befriends a soldier on furlough from the Algerian war, with whom she shares the pain of death in different contexts:

feminine suffering and the colonial war. She spends two hours with him the evening before going in to see her doctor, whom she expects will confirm her illness. The feminine is, in this sense, psychotic. Insufficiently shielded from the unconscious, the locus of the death drive, the feminine subject lives with the pain of the unconscious at every moment. When the pain of becoming feminine under the Law of the Father is no longer repressed in the unconscious, the feminine subject wails audibly. Melodramas and horror films are, for this reason, populated by wailing women.

In describing psychotic pain and suffering as aspects of the feminine, I'd like to restate the shortfall of the critical framework of affect theory, which focuses on how the emotions that arise from such pain and suffering are enmeshed in notions of consolidated identities such as class, race, gender, and sexuality. The theoretical foundation of the feminine cinema that I articulate here involves a universal feminine subjectivity that such a framework, which presupposes the feminine as a marker of identity, cannot explain away. To clarify that difference, let us examine affect theory's conceptual foundation. According to Hegel, "sense-certainty" relies on immediacy: "The force of its truth now lies in the 'I,' in the immediacy of my seeing, hearing, and so on; the vanishing of the single Now and Here that we mean is prevented by the fact that *I* hold them fast."[62] Affect theory requires this unified position of the conscious "I" that grasps the sensuous. This sensuous "I" is the locus of affect, and because the immediacy of the sensuous experience of this "I" seems empirically undisputable, affect is the authentic expression of subjectivity.

This immediacy is the foundation of the apparent unity of subjecthood, but this picture ignores the linguistic mediation that shapes subjectivity. Because "I" experience the immediacy of the sensuous, the affect generated therein is deemed to be the essence of subjecthood. My sensuous experience of negative feelings as a woman of color, for example, many affect theorists would argue, authenticates my identity. Yet, this is a circular logic: these feelings I experience are particular, because my identity is particular; these feelings also certify my unified being based on my particular identity, which is an authentic locus of affects. There is no room within this paradigm to consider the existential lack that language creates. My immediate sensuous experience is construed to guarantee that there is no gap between my subjectivity and my identity. And if such a gap were to appear, closing it would only be a matter of claiming the immediacy of my sensuous experience. The affects generated by that experience complete me. For the subject of feminine jouissance, the immediacy of my senses (seeing, hearing, and so on) opens up the chasm in subjectivity. The immediate sensuous experiences are those of disjointure of the sensuous body, and this Real body of disjointure is the location of the Real subject. In the feminine cinema that shows this disjointure, sensuous experiences constitute the mathematics of the lack, not plentiful resources and evidences of a positive subjectivity.

The feminine cinema shows the subject who responds to the lack at the heart of our being by transforming the language supported by the phallic signifier and its insistence on a plentitude of meaningful objects into the "mathematics" we apply to trace the universal lack. Through the mathematics of the universal feminine language, which says "no" to the phallic signifier, we can crack open the Real of history, understand how hegemonic language covers over the lack in a particular historical context, and discover how confrontation with that language can lead us to politically emancipatory acts. In 1987, one million South Koreans spoke the universal feminine language during the street demonstrations to organize an anti-fascist political movement. Their mathematics, spelling out "we want to live in a world where there is no torture," is language that was unthinkable under the military dictatorship. To revisit Zama's final scene, in considering the question "do you want to live?" Zama must decide to speak a language different from his own in order to enter the life drive. South Korean political subjects in 1987 found themselves, like Zama, on the threshold of the life drive and chose the path to become the universal feminine subject through the mathematics of emancipation. The feminine cinema presents to us how the speaking of this language looks and sounds, even if the universal feminine subject who has learned the mathematics is forever haunted by the weeping Father's cruel wish that she had not.

In what follows, I use transnational and transtextual analyses to examine the universal feminine subject that emerges in local historical contexts. At various points of structural rupture in local situations, we arrive at the universal. The proposition for the universal principle of subjectivity lies in the political struggle over the human condition where we engage with the local situation.

Comfort Women and the Universal Feminine Subject

At this juncture, let us consider Alain Badiou's concept of *the event* as the rupture of the preexisting order of things, including law and our own subjectivity in a given situation. *The event* opens up space for a universality that transcends differences in local situations.[63] For Badiou, Saint Paul is a philosopher of *the event*. In Badiou's *Saint Paul: The Foundation of Universalism*, Paul's gospel reads like that of a militant revolutionary out to change the world. Paul asserted a changed way of being human, free from the law that prescribes identities, what Badiou calls "identitarian verification,"[64] and free from the community that imposes identitarian boundaries. In that way, Badiou argues, Paul exemplifies a universalism that strikes down the pregiven order of things in different local situations. We see in Paul's words a description of the universal subject who emerges in *the event* and upholds a universal truth: "There is neither Jew nor Greek, there is neither slave nor free, there is neither male nor female. . . . Glory, honor, and peace for everyone that does good, to the Jew first and also to the Greek. For God shows no partiality."[65]

Neither Jew nor Greek, we are the eventual subject who encounters points in our timeline that bring about ruptures, disrupting the situation that has sustained our identitarian way of being. Through this rupture, we then experience an earth-shaking, law-breaking event that leads us to a universal truth. It is a singular truth, rather than *the* truth. In Badiou's system, it is important to pay attention to singularity of truth as "a" truth, to leave open conceptual and political space in which we continue to discover truths (in plural). We universally participate not in the truth but in what Badiou calls the "truth procedure," the process through which we remain faithful to a truth we uphold with conviction.[66]

When we embark on what Badiou calls the "truth procedure," we remain faithful to a universal truth that we ourselves have identified. We declare that we are the subject that is defined by a universal truth, and we live by this truth as an existential principle and as our personal conviction. Paul asks us to change the world and our existence in it. Badiou articulates the trajectory of the subject who does so through rupture, event, universal truth, and truth-procedure, following Paul's trajectory.

Through Paul, Badiou asks us to imagine a subject without identity and a law without support from existing ideologies: a radical new subject and a radical new law. This new subject and law are founded upon a universal truth and the process through which we remain faithful to a universal truth. According to Badiou, particular cultural values that societies hold, as well as public opinions, are bound to try to cling to the notion of identity-based subjectivity and law that is invested in that subjectivity.

Being neither Jew nor Greek, we don't live by a culturalist ideology that imprisons us within a preexisting community, and we cease to live as human subjects who see themselves mainly as victims who defend themselves through identity-driven values. Rey Chow once coined the term the "protestant ethnic," playing on Weber's "Protestant ethic."[67] Chow argues that identity has become a capitalist market commodity and the means to remain viable in the market economy. As such, claiming an ethnic identity has itself become an act of protest. The protestant ethnic Asians become crazy rich Asians. Against this identitarian ideology, Badiou argues for a militant eventual subject who fights for a universal principle. Jews were historically declared non-French and non-German through the nation-state's law that protects what it deems to be a fitting identity. I extrapolate that as neither Jew nor Greek, we are the universal *feminine* subject who cannot be defined by what a Jew or a Greek is not.

In the following, I seek to locate universal feminine subjectivity in a group of women who once disappeared from history's stage: Korean comfort women. How might they rupture the local situation—or "a determinate place where the world's conflicts meet in a singular way," in Balibar's words[68]—to speak for and participate in universal history?

Recently, a South Korean broadcast news team unveiled never-before-seen newsreel footage of Korean comfort women, just as the Allies were releasing them from one of many comfort stations in China and other Japanese-occupied territories where they had been kept by the Japanese military in sexual slavery.[69] This six-minute newsreel turns out to be the source of a widely circulated image in public discussions on comfort women. In it, a very pregnant comfort woman leans wearily against a wall along with several others, moments after their liberation by the US and Chinese allies. Also in the frame is a broadly grinning Chinese soldier, performing the role of protector, sitting next to women who look disheveled and distressed. The silent comfort women frozen in this image are people whose names we do not know, with one exception: the very pregnant comfort woman's name was Park Young Shim. Kojin Karatani connects the proper name to the singularity of the human subject: "The singularity of an individual is manifested in a proper name because a singularity—as distinct from a particularity—cannot be reduced to a bundle of sets, to any generality." Citing this statement, Eisenstein and McGowan explain that, for Karatani, the proper name indicates the subject who is capable of radical doubt, who ruptures the pregiven paradigm of communality,[70] of a nation, empire, and so on. The nameless comfort women are shameful objects that signify victimhood, their violated bodies metaphorizing the pillaged, colonized nation. In that way, they are "absorbed and enclosed within the paradigm of community" as its intimate Other, against whom nationalism can be distilled.

Even though we see their lips move, in a scene that is staged to have them mouth a "hurrah" for freedom delivered to them by the allies, we cannot imagine their voices as emanating from singular subjects. During the war, these women disappeared into the nation's, and the empire's, unconscious, into makeshift comfort stations on imperial war fronts and in commandeered civilian dwellings across occupied territories. After the war, they were banished from national memory until the 1990s, when they began to reemerge from those rooms, corridors, and doorways, the spatial configuration of their existence, drawn by imperial and patriarchal violence, which demarcated the zone of their bare life.

In this context, the feminine is a signifier, solidified by the body, in the topography of the nation and empire, and the comfort woman is a signifier solidified by the body assembled from battered and misused parts. It's not surprising that we often see the victimhood of the comfort women depicted as mounds of corpses.

As former military sexual slaves, the comfort women's femininity has been defined through the shame that has silenced them. The shame that is attached to femininity makes women disappear from public space in other contexts, too; such is the case of women involved in social movements in modern South Korea. The Gwangju Uprising of 1980 was the first large-scale armed uprising against the military junta and US imperial interests colluding with the military dictatorship in modern South Korea.[71] While the Gwangju Uprising is represented through masculine narratives in contemporary South Korea, the many women who played an active role and fought on the streets of Gwangju have disappeared from public discourse.[72] It has been revealed that these women have been hiding themselves from public view, often strenuously asserting their identity as mother and wife because of the sense of shame forced upon them by patriarchal society for having transgressed the boundary that demarcates women's space. They dared to speak out and declare their political subjectivity and thus infiltrated public space that is coded masculine. A female fighter relates that she was an ordinary citizen who had no history of participating in organized political struggles before the uprising. She says that she heard on the street that democracy grows in the people's blood, an indigenous adaptation of Thomas Jefferson's alleged statement that "the tree of liberty must be refreshed from time to time with the blood of patriots and tyrants." She subsequently decided that it was her ethical responsibility to fight for democracy and that if blood was necessary, then her blood would also flow in the street. Women fighters of the Gwangju Uprising have said that they went into hiding after having been publicly shamed in court, by their families, and in their communities.

Gwangju is a space where the problem of global capitalist accumulation found a local manifestation. Indigenous capital was required to reconfigure its accumulation process in order to maintain a high growth rate by continuing authoritarian capitalism under a military dictatorship. This reconfiguration was an extension of the process of the global capitalist reconfiguration represented by the Thatcherian and the Reaganite regimes. The democratization movement in the 1980s and onward, in which the Gwangju Uprising played a pivotal role and which eventually toppled the military dictatorship, is an example of a local situation that has a universal historical resonance. It participates in a universal history wherein a people's movement resists the global capitalist structure that defines the local economic and political condition, impinging on freedom and equality. But the universal subjectivity of women was erased as the democratization movement anchored itself in an identitarian narrative that is masculinist and nationalist.

The comfort stations are situated in a global space where imperial and neo-imperial interests enclose women's bodies to draw a line between civic life, with its political rights, and bare life, which can, in Agamben's explication, be banned from the civic sphere and killed with impunity.[73] In this case, the bare life is localized in the woman's body, the colonized body par excellence. But it is within the colonized women, not citizens with rights, that we must see the possibility of the eventual eruption of universal subjectivity. The comfort women are a fracture point in the ideological structure of the empire, as well as of the nation. This is why, after the World War II, repatriated comfort women had to be banished again from both the Korean family and the state, in which the structure and practice of the Confucian family and the Confucian state reflect each other as patriarchal apparatuses. Their bodies had to disappear from nationalist discourses, filled with the masculine heroes of liberation struggles. No war criminal was put on trial for the crime, and Japan made no acknowledgment of the institutionalized military sexual slavery until 2015's Japan-Korea Comfort Women Agreement. Abe Shinjo apologized for the conditions of the comfort women and the Japanese military's involvement while making no admission to it as a state crime committed on behalf of imperial and national interests. Curiously, the agreement does not clarify the actual details of the crimes committed. The comfort women themselves are excluded as the subjects of rights; they are simply victims.

It is still the case that the degree of violence the imperial army committed cannot be openly discussed in the public sphere in Japan; open acknowledgment of the empire's obscene jouissance cannot be assimilated into the national masculine mythos that undergirds the Japanese nation-state. So, for both the former empire and the postcolonial states, these women's monstrous difference from the normative feminine threatens to fracture the nations from within. This is where we locate the emancipatory possibility of the universal feminine subject, a point I pursue in the rest of this chapter.

When comfort women finally appeared in image-making beginning in the 1990s, from documentaries to feature films, they were represented mostly as wounded and mutilated bodies and also as corpses. Interviews of surviving comfort women in North Korea by a Japanese journalist in the late 1990s and early 2000s[74] include women who calmly disrobe to show all the markings of torture and sexual violence written across their bodies, from a disfigured tongue tattooed with poisonous ink as punishment for attempting to escape to breasts, bellies, and genitals covered with knife cuts, wounds from swords, and crudely carved Japanese words and names. But we must question whether their wounded bodies turn the gaze to us. Do they force us to occupy the place of the addressee, to undergo our own self-diremption through the gaze?

Before we answer these questions, let us consider the case of a Chinese film, Zhang Yimou's *Ju Dou*.[75] In this film, we see Ju Dou, an abused and wounded woman in a feudal patriarchal household in the 1920s, allegorizing the Chinese nation-state and its gender violence. In one scene, Ju Dou is about to take a bath in a barn. She is severely battered from the physical and sexual assaults she has endured at the hand of the elderly patriarch who purchased her as a bride. On a wall in the barn is a peephole, and behind this wall, the old man's nephew is ready to indulge in the spectacle of the sexualized woman's body. In an intricately built scene, the voyeur fixes his eye in line with the peephole, through which a single shaft of the brilliant sunlight penetrates the room. The male character's looking, his line of vision, and the light that follows its trajectory metaphorize the power of looking.

Ju Dou, meanwhile, on the other side of the wall and fully aware of the male subject's looking, first tries to gather a bundle of hay to cover the hole, but then she turns toward the peephole and fully reveals her bruised, battered body to the voyeur. She turns the gaze back on the voyeur, both diegetic and extradiegetic, who occupies the position of the masculine subject with the authority to look.[76] Confronted by the spectacle of gendered violence written on Ju Dou's wounded body, the voyeur lowers his eyes as if moved by the sight. His line of looking no longer matches that of the light. Here, Ju Dou implores the diegetic male subject and the extradiegetic spectator to lose their identities, their Symbolic positions, and to relinquish the glorious peephole through which they fantasize possession of the feminine body.

In staging this scene, the filmmaker transforms the filmic spectacle into a visual field where the feminine subject dismantles the powerful regime of knowing, of which visual penetration is the foundation. What secures the masculine subject's power to look is seeing the image as a surface to penetrate through looking in order to obtain possession of the underlying truth about the feminine Other. In having a feminine subject turn her wounded body to the voyeur, returning his look and exposing his voyeuristic desire, the film undoes the relation of looking that the gender order has established.[77] She returns the look that traditionally belongs to the voyeur's masculine position, signifying authority based on the power to control the visual field and objects therein.

In the cinema of the Real, something like Ju Dou's body may appear as a stain in the visual field that destabilizes the subject position that holds authority to organize the visual field and meaningful objects therein. In these films, the rupture in the field of vision occurs in a local situation. Local cinema develops formal devices that visualize trauma as a metaphorical stain, which a transtextual engagement, drawing from critical and aesthetic frameworks across geopolitical borders, renders legible. It can show how a globally reified field of vision, where the phallic signifier defines the feminine, might be reformulated and transformed in national cinemas. Zhang's high-saturation colors, for example, dominated by red and yellow, render the youthful woman's skin as a shiny surface that reflects the gaze. The disjuncture between the aestheticized optical object and its destructive effect on the masculine subject adds to the force of this film's cinematography.

The comfort woman's body represents the failure of the feminine to function in a patriarchal nation as a reproductive organ that perpetuates a unified patrilineal lineage. It has been made invisible in the patriarchal family-state in both Koreas, because the failure of the feminine function directly implicates the failure of the patriarchal family and nation and their phallic function. The comfort women's wounded and decaying bodies confront us like a monstrous cut in our field of vision rather than evidencing victimhood. This image lacks the aesthetic trappings of the spectacular feminine body as seen in *Ju Dou*. Its rawness seems to defy any possibility of aestheticization. But the comfort women's revealed bodies seek to fix us as an addressee of their enunciation of pain. To be the addressee of that suffering means that we occupy space where their body gazes at us, destabilizing our own subject position as the gaze would in principle. Here, to be the addressee is to lose identity.

The current cultural work around comfort women emphasizes the loss of femininity that the master signifier inscribes. The wounded female body is the wounded heterosexual body. This is why the discourse of their bodies is coupled to the rhetoric of shame, both for them and the audience, in the eyes of the big Other. To mitigate the shame, public discourse infantilizes these women. A South Korean filmmaker who made a feature film about comfort women (*Spirits' Homecoming*, 2016) even goes so far as to describe the survivors as "child-like." He states that these women, who are of his grandmother's generation, stopped growing old when they were abducted and forced into sexual slavery as girls (the majority of them were teenagers, some as young as twelve).

One documentary film, *The Murmuring*,[78] made by a queer filmmaker, has a different take on comfort women. The film follows six women who share a house that a Buddhist charity has provided for them, documenting their daily routines. The film also documents their political activities, including demonstrations in front of the Japanese embassy. At the time of Abe Shinjo's acknowledgment of comfort women in 2015, they had mounted twelve hundred protests over twenty-four years. The camera lingers on their various modes of bodily engagement with each other, emotional conversions, and tender physical contact. The film takes the time to show their shared pleasure in mundane daily routines, cooking, drawing, singing, drinking, and dancing together, allowing us to observe their individual and sensuous embodiment, facial expressions, and bodily gestures. In this way, the film queers them, which is to say the film places them outside the prescription that they inhabit their bodies within the boundary of heterosexual femininity. Within that boundary, they can only be the damaged body that signifies the failed feminine function. Through queering, they return as desiring subjects. In one scene, the camera lingers on one woman's bare back, exposed by the low cut of her revealing flowery dress. The dress seems extraordinary in comparison to the muted, often drab clothing that these women, many of them in their seventies at the time of filming, normally wear. She works on a drawing, a scene from her years as a comfort woman. In her surrealist depiction, space is constituted as a comfort station within which the faces of a Japanese soldier and a young girl float. The sun is the face of a dead comfort woman in the sky, and a lone pine tree stands. Drawing here is rendered as a sensuous act, a corporealization of remembering trauma. By juxtaposing her bare back with her aesthetic drive, the film allows her a mode of embodiment that is usually unavailable to comfort women in their political and cultural discourse. This embodiment shows a woman as the subject of the life drive, no longer mere material evidence of the death drive of the empire.

The closing sequence of *The Murmuring* comprises long-take, close-up shots of the naked body of one of the six women. The camera frames, in a chiaroscuro style, her wrinkled face, sagging arms, breasts, and belly. While she is shrouded in shadow, the effect is of a sublime sheen enveloping her body parts. This technique also renders the body queer,[79] as it cannot be easily comprehended according to the signifier of "woman." This body cannot be harnessed as a meaningful object in the chain of signification, because it estranges the spectator from the regime of looking that has now failed to give the spectator an instruction on how to make meaning of this image as something other than an image that stares back at us. This is not the body that houses the shame of failed heteronormative femininity. It is the embodiment of the subject of queer desire erupting where it is least expected: the house of shame, meaning both the body and the domicile. This body gazes at us. It is the manifestation of singularity, which ruptures the chain of signifiers that has imprisoned comfort women in the nation-state's ideology of gender and sexuality. The manner in which this body, as a stain across the cinematic space, disrupts the chain of phallic signifiers secured by properly gendered objects, such as the body parts that constitute heteronormative women, and turns that cinematic space into the field of erupting singular subjectivity indicates what the feminine cinema can do in its formal arrangement of the body in space.

The Universal Feminine and Emancipation

The pain that the suffering subject lacks language to convey to an addressee is the Real of our subjectivity as the speaking subject. What escapes language is the *objet a*, a stand-in for our lack as the kernel of our being. Horror films show us what it looks and feels like to encounter the Real of our being in the shape of the *objet a*. There are two routes through that encounter: the universal feminine and the phallic, which is generally represented by the masculine. We see an example of the feminine route in *The Babadook* and the masculine route in *The Lighthouse*.[80] Both films deal with an *objet a*, that which escapes knowing and naming, and confronts viewers with an uncanny space beyond the limits of vision and knowledge. Another classic example of this uncanny space is Buñuel's *Un chien andalou* (1929), in which we see a character pulling, with great effort, on a rope that is attached to something yet to be revealed. The rope drags incongruent objects into our field of vision: a pair of Marist priests lying on the ground tied together, a grand piano, on top of which is tied a dead donkey. This is a vision of the incomprehensible *objet a* that reveals the shocking Real of objects given meaning in the Symbolic order. To visualize *objet a*, the best we can do is to build an image that reveals the void. This void is the location of the little object "a," the Real of the complete object we revere and desire, which signifiers cannot hide. In the following filmic analyses, I continue with the metaphoric Thing—recalling such an object in John Carpenter's *The Thing*—that stands in for an *objet a*. The characters in the film cannot harness the meaning of Carpenter's Thing, and as an *objet a* it destroys the human in its meaninglessness. To confront this Thing and to formulate a particular relationship to it is the starting point for the universal subject's emancipatory politics.

I return to *The Babadook* to compare the two routes of encounter with *objet a*, the Thing that exceeds my Symbolic existence. In *The Babadook*, the Thing is in the shape of the eponymous creature that lives in a family's basement. It comes out in the shape of a two-dimensional illustration to infiltrate the domestic space, turning it into the trackless space of the death drive's jouissance, where social subjects' Symbolic functions are untenable. That the mother is possessed by a jouissance that drives her to attempt to murder her son is one example of an untenable function. The mother sees phantasmatic holes and chasms in the walls, through which uncanny objects pour into her home—a representation of jouissance intruding upon a socially managed space, the family home—but she ultimately creates a liminal space where the Babadook may continue to exist, rather than exorcizing it. By feeding the Thing, an animated *objet a*, material from her conscious world (such as a bowl of earthworms from her garden), she keeps its death-drive jouissance from erupting into her life. Her encounter with the Thing no longer engulfs her with deathly jouissance. She lives with the destructive jouissance of the Thing by keeping it in the basement and provides it with only enough nourishment to keep it alive. Topographically separating her life drive from the death drive is the threshold between the basement and the rest of the house. She continues to feed the Thing, the Babadook, and keeps it alive in return for her life. Universal feminine subjectivity is based on living with the monstrous object charged with jouissance, the *objet a*, and containing it as the foundation of existence.

In *The Lighthouse*, in a turn-of-the-century lighthouse on an isolated island in Maine, we see glimpses of the *objet a* in the phantasmatic, mesmerizing objects that masculine subjects encounter, such as a mermaid and a monumental mechanical structure that emits mysterious blinding light as it rotates. The film offers no narrative exposition regarding the nature of these objects, although they are visual artifacts at the core of the visceral experience of the cinematic space. Two of the lighthouse keepers are seduced and held by these objects. One writhes orgasmically in the blinding light of the machine. The other man fantasizes about sexual congress with the mermaid, but within the fantasy the mermaid opens its mouth and lets out an inhuman wail, paralyzing him with terror. In the end, both men are destroyed by the Thing they cannot name or tame. They are swept away by the death drive that the Thing opens up. The last surviving man lies paralyzed, his eyes gouged out by seagulls that are eating him alive. The birds, like Hitchcock's, engulf the island like the furious force of the death drive.

The universal feminine subject, by creating liminal space, lives with the *objet a*, the Real of all objects, the encounter with which is lethal for the phallic, represented by the masculine, subject. In that space, she transmutes the Thing into a familiar object that she feeds. The phallic/masculine subject is seduced by the sublime monstrosity of the Thing that he encounters. He imposes the phallic desire on an *objet a*, which appears as a sublime object, and is then captured by the jouissance of the death drive. He cannot create liminal space where he can distance himself from the sublime object, and thus cannot, as the mother in *The Babadook* does, turn it into a familiar, banal object that does not satisfy his desire and also does not threaten him with annihilation. The jouissance of the death drive, which the sublime object inspires, kills him.

One can say that the life drive is, by definition, feminine, as represented by the mother in *The Babadook*. The masculine route, as we see in *The Lighthouse*, reveals the lethal nature of the Real in the sublime object, the unspeakable Thing that strikes down the chain of signifiers that sustains our Symbolic existence and with which the masculine subject is unable to live. The Real is the lack at the heart of our signifying structure and, therefore, the negation of life as we know it at the heart of the Symbolic order. The choice, then, is between life and death. In the world of sublime phallic objects of desire, the Real is simply too lethal for the phallic subject, who is ready to be lured by objects he hopes to possess and enjoy.

The Real of our existence is the lack at the heart of our signifying structure. This lack at the heart of our being is the universal condition. This lack turns the death drive into the life drive toward emancipation. But what happens when a subject lacks the lack? In *Ex Machina*,[81] we see an AI, Ava, created to emulate a speaking subject in the form of a woman. However, because her acquisition of speech does not cut her, Ava lacks the lack that constitutes the human. Ava, not having the lack, doesn't desire the phantasmatic little object "a" that the Other is supposed to (though never does) have. The Other for her simply figures as the means that she calculates will successfully allow her to achieve the goal of escaping the compound where she was created, a goal that, for her, is the calculable logical necessity. Unlike the subject of desire, who can never succeed at the goal of obtaining *objet a* and fulfilling desire, Ava actually succeeds. She abandons the programmer, whom she has seduced via her feminine facade and who helped her escape, and leaves him to die, locked in a cell in the abandoned compound. The programmer, as a desiring subject, humanizes her through his desire. His lack allows him to sublimate the Other, even though it is against his own interests. He helps her to destroy the AI technology and its creator, who also employed him. The programmer turns his back on what had defined him as a social subject. We can say our true connection to the Other can be made only if we can act against our own interest and are faithful only to our lack. When we do not compromise our own aching sense of lack and refuse to substitute accidental objects of desire for an unobtainable *objet a*, we become the subject of the life drive. This is the Lacanian side of the event, which is absent from Badiou's own conception of the event. Through our fidelity to the lack, we emancipate ourselves from the Law of the Father (that is, the law of desire). Only the lack can save us.

The comfort women encountered the death drive of the empire while they were, as bare life, denied the right to be the desiring subject, and thus the right to the death drive: Desire initiates the death drive of the imperial subject in the first place. In their encounter with the obscene jouissance of the imperial Other, comfort women experienced the death of the subject, that is, the death of the death drive that constitutes the human subject of desire. Murdered as desiring subjects, thoroughly rendered as objects, they were made to struggle along the path in the death drive of the empire and the nation. For universal feminine subjectivity to emerge in that situation, the subject must devise a movement through which she can turn the death drive into the life drive. Comfort women revealed their wounded bodies, and in place of the body that the signifier "woman" defines, we see the lack, a gaping hole, the imperial cuts opened in their bodies and in that signifier. The lack of "woman" gazes at us through the hole in gender and national ideologies. Their wounded bodies reflect our looking back at us and reveal our desire to belong to those ideological communities. Their gaze invites us to be part of their life drive, together formulating the path of emancipating ourselves from those communalities.

To emancipate ourselves from the position of the desiring subject on the path of the death drive, we must create space where we can imagine a different kind of subjectivity: that of those excluded from the proper national social space, not just comfort women but all universal feminine subjects, regardless of their gender coding. An example of a transformation into the universal feminine subject can be found in *Army of Shadows*.[82] The main characters in this film are French resistance fighters during World War II. They are inside French society but do not belong to it. This nonbelonging is translated into the precarity of their lives, which can always turn into bare life. The film shows this precariousness in a scene where a captured leader of the resistance is forced to run to the end of a target shooting range alongside other prisoners while a Nazi squad fires on them. Each one may or may not make it. Here, survival depends on chances calculated by the sovereign state that designates the zone of bare life. Whether you are shot or not, you are the bare life, just like Jewish life under Nazi rule. In the filmic space, we form solidarity with the excluded, the bare life of the oppressed. In the midst of this solidarity, we face the death drive of the fascistic nation-state and resolve to pursue our path to create the life drive and a mode of movement in which our fight against the fascistic nation-state keeps us going. Our movement becomes one of continuing to open up the space in the emancipatory drive for all.

Based on Freud's account, the Jewish nation was able to turn the traumatic death drive to a life drive when, after the killing of the Father (the Egyptian Moses), they installed Hebrew Moses as the origin of Judaism, a new trajectory of the Jewish life drive. Such a turn is possible through a mode of language that allows us to enunciate the existence of the subject of the lack. The Jewish subject's ontological lack is thus shown through the Jewish god, a deity who lacks a speakable name and as such signifies the lack.[83] In a terrifying encounter with the Real of our existence, that is, the lack, we turn the death drive into the life drive through the rupture of our assigned condition of being and our reliance on phantasmatic plentitude. Judaism achieved this through a new monotheistic god of the lack. The manner in which we configure our relationship to the lack, the manner in which we encounter and live with the lack, bears our singularity. The manner in which we obtain singularity is defined by our historical context, such as a South Korean context.

At this juncture, what Eisenstein and McGowan describe as singularity[84] can provide structural support for the universal feminine subject. Singularity refers to something in me that is more than me, something that emerges through the cut of language. Singularity is the unique scar and wounding we acquire as we become a linguistic subject, the result of a traumatic separation from nature. *Objet a* is another name for this unique, singular something, the shape of our wounding, that we cannot grasp through language, though in capitalist society, we often assign this singular object a name. Fill in any designer brand name of anything here.

We have noted through Karatani that names escape descriptions that rely on particular properties of race, ethnicity, class, sexuality, and so on.[85] Singularity appears through the proper names given to us, because these names fail to describe who we are, not because they pin down our identity. The name indicates the context of a subject that we cannot grasp. It shows an empty space in the chain of signification, the space that the unnamable occupies.

The singular subject's relation to communality also can take two routes: the phallic/masculine and the universal feminine. The singular subject positions itself vis-à-vis the nation-state as a subject who possesses the freedom to rupture the law. This is the universal feminine route. I juxtapose these routes using examples of two Koreans who lived under Japanese colonial rule.

As a nineteen-year-old student, Yoo Gwan Soon led an independence movement in 1919 that ultimately resulted in her death in the imperial prison from severe torture and starvation. My translation of her last known words are: "When the imperialists pulled all my fingernails, cut off my nose and ears, I could endure the suffering. The unbearable suffering for me comes from the loss of the nation. My only sorrow is that I have only one life to give to my nation."[86]

The other example comes from a poem titled "Terrifying Hours," by the poet Yoon Dong Ju. Yoon was a university student in 1941 when he wrote the poem, at the height of the Japanese imperial war. My translation:

> Who's calling me over there?
> In the shadow where dead leaves peek through the verdant, I am still breathing

I, who have never raised my hand, I, who have never left my mark in the sky with a raised hand
Who's calling me to lay this body in the sky
In the morning of my death, after all my work is done, dead leaves will fall without sorrow
Do not call my name.[87]

A few years after he wrote "Terrifying Hours," the poet was arrested in Japan for anti-Japanese activities. In prison, he was subjected to the Japanese military's biological experiments, among them having seawater injected into his veins. When he died in prison in 1945, at the age of twenty-seven, he left behind more than a hundred poems, some of which South Korean school children learn to recite.

Yoo Gwan Soon sees her body as an object to sacrifice for the nation, to fill the lack that the lost nation has left behind. She upholds the nation as the phallic signifier. Embodying the martyr at the altar of the lost nation, she accepts that she is to be sacrificed for the sake of the nation. The comfort woman, in contrast, cannot be sacrificed, as she is already marked to be killed with impunity. Here, the martyr's trajectory is phallic and is thus masculine. This martyr's body upholds the chain of signification by unifying the nation as a sublime object of desire that will render us perfect if only we can recover it. When the patriarchal nation is colonized and lost, its status as the phallic object is enforced by the martyr's body that signifies plentitude and promises to fill the gaping hole in the signifier, the nation. In turn, the lack in the martyr's body (signified in Yoo's last words by the lost appendages) implies a promise of being filled by the nation, the sublime object. Yoon Dong Ju, by contrast, exemplifies the universal feminine route. His response to the loss of the nation implies the subject that is not defined by attachment to the nation. This subject suggests nonbelonging in national communality, and the name he asks not to be called by is a signifier within that communality. The name simultaneously indicates an empty space, the space left by the unnamable in the chain of signification. By saying "do not call my name," Yoon is asking for a different way to respond to his wounding. He is not to be called "the unnamable" but rather is to be seen as the subject who is emancipated from the death drive around an empty space of the unnamable. He may properly be called the subject of the life drive. The colonized subject's nonbelonging, without a name particular to a communality and without the sky to stretch his hand toward to claim, expresses the universal lack that leads any particular subject to the position of the singular, universal subject.

The universal feminine subject says "no" to belonging to particular identities that the Law of the Father prescribes. Through this denial of the Law of the

Father, we claim universal feminine subjectivity. To see the universal feminine subject in transnational cinema in this light, let us look at a Hungarian film, László Nemes's *Son of Saul*,[88] set in the Nazi concentration camp Auschwitz. Saul is a *sonderkommando*, a prisoner assigned the task of removing corpses from gas chambers. In going about this grim business, he discovers a child still breathing. The child is revived, only to be murdered by doctors at the infirmary. Saul, determined to give the boy a proper Jewish burial, embarks on a search for a rabbi among the throng of newly arriving prisoners. This act is meaningful because it acknowledges that the child is not a "human animal" that Nazis can simply annihilate. As bare life, the child may be killed with impunity, but he may not be "sacrificed," which means that ethical and political meaning cannot be assembled around his death.[89] Through arranging a ritual burial, Saul declares the child's universal subjectivity. The singularity of his life, which calls for our ethical response to it, holds the possibility of transforming the human animal into the human subject, defined by the capacity to confront the death-drive jouissance (here, that of the totalitarian Nazi state). Saul changes the meaning of death from a simple annihilation, which is death by murder with impunity, to a sacrifice with ethical and political meaning. In doing so, Saul changes what is deemed human by Nazis. Saul's act also exemplifies freedom in the sense that the index of his freedom is the degree to which he can give himself law. In their explications of Kantian law and freedom, Eisenstein and McGowan state that when we give ourselves law, we do so completely against natural or culturally conditioned inclinations, against what we have accepted as necessary.[90] Through this universal freedom to give ourselves law, we disrupt natural and habitual causality, the chain of cause and effect. When we follow universal principles, our actions do not depend on the consequences that follow causality, tied to what society deems to be naturally or culturally necessary conditions. Freedom disrupts the causality that supports the existing law that determines the human.

Freedom originates from the break that language introduces into the natural world. As speaking subjects, we are no longer subjugated to the opaque rule of nature. Language cuts us from the law of nature, where there is only the instinctual drive for survival. Language involves signification, which is operable only through the law. We fix the law of language to pull ourselves from subjugation to the law of nature. Nature imposes necessity in the form of the quest for survival. Language gives us the means to make human life meaningful beyond our instincts for survival. Through language, and through the law that organizes language, we can act otherwise than as nature dictates; we can act based on morality and ethics.[91] Freedom thus entails breaking the law that ties us to a specific set of causality in order to formulate a new law of ethics.

We have seen that Badiou articulates how a new law might come about through *the event*: When *the event* happens, it ruptures the pregiven order of things constitutive of law. The rupture constitutes the subject of *the event*. According to Badiou, the evental subject exists "in the divided form of a 'not . . . but,'" and it is this form that bears the mark of the universal, that is, this division "guarantees universality."[92] "Not" is the potential dissolution of particularities, which the law names. "But" indicates the new task, the faithful labor for a new truth and a new law. Here, *the event* opens up the truth procedure, in which we remain faithful to a truth we have established through *the event*. Badiou calls this opening "grace,"[93] something that happens in defiance of all our calculations about possibilities and impossibilities and seems to come out of nowhere. Subjects of *the event* work together in this truth procedure. This is our universal possibility of becoming.

In the concentration camp under Nazi law, Saul claims freedom as he remains faithful to universality through a militant allegiance to a truth. Saul declares "not" as he insists that the child's life exceeds that of the human animal. This life is beyond the law of Nazism that sets the boundary between the politically meaningful life and the bare life. The act of burial Saul pursues corresponds to Badiou's "but," because it is more than a religious ritual. It is a passage through which the child becomes a human subject, exceeding the given boundary of the human/German and its animal Other/Jew. By extension, all Jews in the death camps become the human subject through this "not . . . but." Here, Jews are no longer particular subjects as determined by Nazis. Even though Saul fails to give a religious burial to the child, this passage has been made, and through that passage, not through a ritual, the Jews depicted in this film become universal feminine subjects of the life drive.

The film's square framing cuts off the field of vision for us in the audience, obscuring the spectacle of the gassed bodies and of those who march toward the gas chamber. This gesture denies us the pornographic spectacle that the Nazi death drive's obscene jouissance demands. This point of view also implies Saul's vision: initially, the limited frame makes it seem as if he is in a place where he cannot survey the world around him. However, the vision also allegorizes the kernel of all visions: the body that carries universal meaning cannot be captured through the frame that pornographizes it by rendering body parts as objects of obscene jouissance.

I return now to a scene of South Korean local history for a transtextual and transnational reference to the universal feminine subject who creates space out of the emancipatory drive for all through a political act. Yi Han Yeol, a college student, was killed by a tear gas canister during the massive anti-fascist demonstration in 1987. His death sparked the civilian revolution that toppled the military dictatorship. Yi's mother (Bae Eun Shim) became a prominent part of the democratization movement after the death of her son. In post-revolution interviews before her passing in January 2022, she was known to say that she lives to find her Yi Han Yeol, to see him somewhere, anywhere. She described placing herself in spaces that she believes Han Yeol occupies by going to political meetings and rallies. She asks herself, "Do my actions reflect how he would exist in this particular space in this particular moment?"[94] Asked if she ever found him, she would answer "no." Here, her search for her dead son is about keeping going, staying politically alive, and being faithful to a truth, although the lack persists in the form of her lost child. She will never find her lost object. For the universal feminine subject, the object that causes one to search forever cannot be found, but one's act of searching is not aimed at finally finding it but at circling the space where that object exists as something that is missing. The empty space where Yi does not exist is where his mother devises the life drive that allows her to keep going, weaving life out of deathly loss of the object, and to remain on the path of the emancipatory drive.

In our search for a universal feminine subjectivity that pursues the emancipatory drive in a local context, let us consider *In the Absence*,[95] a documentary about the sinking of the South Korean ferry *Sewol* in 2014. The disaster claimed the lives of 476 people, of whom 325 were high school students on a school trip. In the film, we hear from a handful of survivors and from volunteer body recovery divers recounting their traumatic encounter with capitalism's death drive and the concomitant criminal deregulation of industry that caused the capsizing. A diver describes how he touched, as he groped in the dark searching for corpses, a child's toes, curled by the cold in the deep sea. He held the child's body, as if in a hug, under its armpits. Locked in that embrace, he pulled the body up, face-to-face with the dead child. Another diver, who later committed suicide, describes dreams in which he plays hide-and-seek with a dead child. In his dreams, drowned children return to lead him back to the deep sea, where there is no light by which to catch them. The sinking was the result of the deregulation in all industrial sectors that the neoliberal regime had been relentlessly pursuing, undermining basic safety regulations. The trauma of experiencing the death drive of capitalism led South Koreans to organize nationwide candlelight protests, which continued from October 2016 to March 2017, to protest the corrupt, neoliberal regime. People of South Korea confronted the death drive with their own life drive. This act allowed them to envision the path in the emancipatory drive, claiming freedom for all to create the new law. This protest ended with the impeachment and imprisonment of the president, and allowed the ascendancy of a new centrist government, consisting of a number of people who were part of the democratization movement that had galvanized South Korea since the 1980s. The centrists lost the 2022 presidential election to the right-wing party, which is poised to oppress the labor movement that played a crucial role in South Korea's democratization but has been steadily weakening since the establishment of the civilian regime in 1993 during the expansion of neoliberal reform. This, and the fact that what South Koreans call the Candlelight Revolution of 2016–2017 failed to bring about the ascendancy of a revolutionary coalition of the labor party and the socialist party, implies that the capitalist nation-state's death drive continues. The revolution of feminine universality likewise continues, wherein the emancipatory drive emerges from the death drive through trauma, and the universal feminine subject replaces the national subject, which had been invented to claim the phallic jouissance of the nation.

Feminine jouissance, defying the signification of phallic desire, is the Real of our drive, and for it we incur a high price: the relinquishing of our belief in a master signifier. Here, our fascistic longing for a universal guarantor of meaning, lost in the Real, can take hold and turn us back toward the death drive. But it is possible to abandon the death drive that the traumatic lack in our existence has placed us in for the life drive that keeps us aiming to transform the world by emancipating ourselves from desire for a master signifier. We move beyond the awareness that we exist in the trajectory of the death drive, and we connect the transformation of our drive to a revolutionary act: to make way for a new law of feminine universality, to stand as the universal feminine subject in the plazas of the world, where many revolutionaries began.

Notes

Introduction

1. Tracy McNulty, "Demanding the Impossible: Desire and Social Change," *differences: A Journal of Feminist Cultural Studies* 20, no. 1 (2009): 34.
2. Slavoj Žižek, "With or Without Passion: What's Wrong with Fundamentalism? Part I," https://www.lacan.com/zizpassion.htm.
3. Eluned Summers-Bremner, "Reading, Walking, Mourning: W.G. Sebald's Peripatetic Fictions," *Journal of Narrative Theory* 34, no. 3 (Fall 2004): 304.
4. All drives are death drives because the drive is structured and propelled by the dead language of the Father. Jacques-Alain Miller states that the father's function is that of the dead language. Miller cites Lacan: "Don't believe that there's life of words because they change. Every tongue is a dead tongue, even the tongue you are speaking yourself." Jacques-Alain Miller, "To Interpret the Cause: From Freud to Lacan," *Newsletter of the Freudian Field* 3, nos. 1 and 2 (Spring/Fall 1989): 44.
5. Byung-Chul Han, *The Transparency Society*, trans. Erik Butler (Stanford, CA: Stanford University Press, 2015), 17.
6. Han, *The Transparency Society*, 17.
7. Han, *The Transparency Society*, 17.
8. Han, *The Transparency Society*, 17.
9. Cited in Hilary Neroni, "Following the Impossible Road to Female Passion: Psychoanalysis, the Mundane, and the Films of Jane Campion," *Discourse* 34, nos. 2 and 3 (Spring/Fall 2012): 305.
10. Mari Ruti, *The Call of Character: Living a Life Worth Living* (New York: Columbia University Press, 2014), 14.
11. Todd McGowan, *Capitalism and Desire: The Psychic Cost of Free Markets* (New York: Columbia University Press, 2016), 28. McGowan further suggests that capitalism's successful hold depends on this aspect of our desire, that it can be sustained only by the lack of the object that can end all dissatisfaction.
12. McGowan, *Capitalism and Desire*, 31.
13. *The X Files*, season 6 episode 2, "Drive," directed by Rob Bowman, written by Vince Gilligan, aired November 15, 1998, on Fox.
14. *Wild Tales (Relatos salvajes)*, directed by Damián Szifron (Burbank, CA: Warner Bros. Pictures, 2014).
15. Slavoj Žižek, "Neighbors and Other Monsters: A Plea for Ethical Violence," in *The Neighbor: Three Inquiries in Political Theology*, ed. Slavoj Žižek, Eric C. Santner, and Kenneth Reinhard (Chicago: University of Chicago Press, 2013), 142.
16. Žižek, "Neighbors and Other Monsters," 138.

17. Žižek, "Neighbors and Other Monsters," 138.

18. Jacques Lacan, *The Seminar of Jacques Lacan, Book XI: The Four Fundamental Concepts of Psychoanalysis*, trans. Alan Sheridan (New York: W. W. Norton, 1978), chapter 5.

19. Alenka Zupančič, *The Odd One In: On Comedy* (Cambridge: MIT Press, 2008), 164. This is how Dolar theorizes comedy. This helps us to see why comedy, where a piece of the Real emerges through repetition, is an essentially traumatic existential experience. Consider the entire body of Charlie Chaplin's and Buster Keaton's work, organized around repetitions of loss, confrontation with the Symbolic order, and so on.

20. Catherine E. Shoichet, "These Former Stanford Students Are Building an App to Change Your Accent," CNN, December 19, 2021, https://www.cnn.com/2021/12/19/us/sanas-accent-translation-cec/index.html. It is worth noting that this group of former students are of various ethnic and racial backgrounds. This shows how a midwestern accent is perceived as a positive marker of a universalizing element as an ideological object of desire.

21. Žižek, "Neighbors and Other Monsters," 144.

22. Cited in Tony Partridge, "Bong Joon Ho's *Parasite* Viewed in the Context of Pasolini's *Theorem* and Deleuze's Filmic Theories," in *Parasite: A Philosophical Exploration*, ed. Thorsten Botz-Bornstein and Giannis Stamatellos, (Leiden: Brill, 2022), 102.

23. Partridge, "*Parasite* Viewed in the Context of Pasolini's *Theorem* and Deleuze's Filmic Theories," 102.

24. Summers-Bremner, "Reading, Walking, Mourning," 304.

25. Summers-Bremner, "Reading, Walking, Mourning," 303.

26. Summers-Bremner, "Reading, Walking, Mourning," 305.

27. Summers-Bremner, "Reading, Walking, Mourning," 304.

28. Summers-Bremner, "Reading, Walking, Mourning," 304.

29. Žižek, "Neighbors and Other Monsters," 176.

30. Ruti, *The Call of Character*, 22.

31. Ruti, *The Call of Character*, 22.

32. I am grateful to Mark Stein for sharing Dov Eschel's story with me.

33. Of his years in his home country, Dov Eschel said, "I was Polish. I was Austrian. I was German. I was Lithuanian. I never moved."

34. Jennifer Friedlander, *Feminine Look: Sexuation, Spectatorship, Subversion* (Albany: State University of New York Press, 2008), 32.

35. Friedlander, *Feminine Look*, 38.

36. *Blow-Up*, directed by Michelangelo Antonioni (Beverly Hills: Premier Productions, 1966).

37. McNulty, "Demanding the Impossible," 34.

38. Dominick LaCapra, *Writing History, Writing Trauma* (Baltimore: Johns Hopkins University Press, 2001), 5.

39. LaCapra, *Writing History, Writing Trauma*, 8.

40. Žižek, "With or Without Passion."

41. Žižek, "With or Without Passion."

42. Žižek, "Neighbors and Other Monsters," 177.
43. National *Gugak* Center, Oral History Collections #12, https://www.gugak.go.kr/site/program/board/basicboard/view?currentpage=2&menuid=001003002006&pagesize=10&boardtypeid=26&boardid=1424&lang=ko.
44. *Even the Rain* (*También la lluvia*), directed by Icíar Bollaín (Palm Desert, CA: Vitagraph Films, 2010).
45. Neroni, "Following the Impossible Road to Female Passion," 303.
46. Neroni, "Following the Impossible Road to Female Passion," 304.
47. *Cuties* (*Mignonnes*), directed by Maïmouna Doucouré (Paris: BAC Films, 2020).
48. *Tomboy*, directed by Céline Sciamma (Paris: Pyramide Distribution, 2011).
49. *A Taxi Driver* (택시운전사), directed by Jang Hoon (Seoul: Showbox, 2017).
50. Richard Rushton, *Deleuze and Lola Montès* (New York: Bloomsbury, 2020), 92.
51. Rushton, *Deleuze and Lola Montès*, 10.
52. Rushton, *Deleuze and Lola Montès*, 45.
53. *That Uncertain Feeling*, directed by Ernst Lubitsch (Los Angeles: United Artists, 1941).
54. Hannah Arendt, *Eichmann in Jerusalem: A Report on the Banality of Evil* (New York: Penguin Books, 1963), 136.
55. Arendt, *Eichmann in Jerusalem*, 136.
56. Arendt, *Eichmann in Jerusalem*, 136.
57. Arendt, *Eichmann in Jerusalem*, 136.
58. Arendt, *Eichmann in Jerusalem*, 104.
59. Arendt, *Eichmann in Jerusalem*, 104.
60. *The Bitter Tears of Petra von Kant* (*Die bitteren tränen der Petra Von Kant*), directed by Rainer Werner Fassbinder (Berlin: Filmverlag der Autoren, 1972).
61. Robert O. Paxton, *The Anatomy of Fascism* (New York: Knopf, 2004), 219.
62. Bruce Fink, *The Lacanian Subject: Between Language and Jouissance* (Princeton, NJ: Princeton University Press, 1995), 68.
63. Fink, *The Lacanian Subject*, 68.
64. Jacques Lacan, "The Function and Field of Speech and Language in Psychanalysis," in Lacan, *Écrits: A Selection*, trans. Bruce Fink (New York: W. W. Norton, 2002), 103.
65. Alessandra Raengo, *Critical Race Theory and* Bamboozled (New York: Bloomsbury, 2016), 186.
66. Raengo, *Critical Race Theory and* Bamboozled, 9.

Chapter 1

1. *The Front Line* (고지전), directed by Jang Hoon (Seoul: Showbox, 2011).
2. Héctor Rodríguez, "Questions of Chinese Aesthetics: Film Form and Narrative Space in the Cinema of King Hu," *Cinema Journal* 38, no. 1 (Autumn 1998): 86.

3. Rodríguez, "Questions of Chinese Aesthetics," 87.
4. Rodríguez, "Questions of Chinese Aesthetics," 87.
5. Rodríguez, "Questions of Chinese Aesthetics," 86.
6. When we study transnational cinema, we are most likely to engage with transnational cinematic auteurs. Regarding film auteurs, Seung-hoon Jeong states: "Today's film auteurs are less independent artists struggling against the capitalist industry than managerial art planners looking for ways in which their vision and the audience reaction can intermingle in the market logic. What matters is to design a film that is ambiguous and contradictory enough to welcome various conflicting views in balance so that spectators do not stop at passive film consumption but can contribute to film promotion and even intermedial film culture through active critical engagement. Bong Joon-ho, who performs this task globally, is the most successful global Korean auteur." While acknowledging the pressure that capital places on auteur films, we recognize that transnational cinema's auteurs straddle the lines of visibility and opacity, originating from thick layers of local contexts and global transparency. I posit that the auteur films I analyze in this book are those films that achieve formal innovation that renders the Real visible and conceptually accessible to the global audience, thus allowing us to comprise a new way of categorizing transnational cinemas. Seung-hoon Jeong, "*Parasite* from Text to Context: An Ethical Stalemate and New Auteurism in Global Cinema," in *Parasite: A Philosophical Exploration*, ed. Thorsten Botz-Bornstein and Giannis Stamatellos, (Leiden, The Netherlands: Brill, 2022), 42-43.
7. Joan Copjec, *Imagine There's No Woman: Ethics and Sublimation* (Cambridge, MA: MIT Press, 2002), 178–96. I first introduced this reading of Joan Copjec in Hyon Joo Yoo, Introduction to *South Korean Film: Critical and Primary Sources*, vol. 3 (New York: Bloomsbury, 2021).
8. Paul Verhaeghe, *Beyond Gender: From Subject to Drive* (New York: Other Press, 2001), 15.
9. Verhaeghe, *Beyond Gender*, 95.
10. *Offside*, directed by Jafar Panahi (New York: Sony Pictures Classics, 2006).
11. Verhaeghe, *Beyond Gender*, 80.
12. It needs reemphasizing that the Thing-in-itself as the originary point of meaning of objects that appear to us through signifiers doesn't exist in reality. It is a point of designating that which exceeds the linguistic boundary revealing the inherent failure of language to enwrap the world with meaning.
13. Paul Verhaeghe, *Love in a Time of Loneliness: Three Essays on Drive and Desire*, trans. Plym Peters and Tony Langham (London: Karnac, 1999), 51.
14. For further elaboration on this, see Slavoj Žižek, *Looking Awry: An Introduction to Jacques Lacan through Popular Culture* (Cambridge, MA: MIT Press, 1992).
15. See Yoo, Introduction to *South Korean Film*.
16. For further elaboration on this, see Todd McGowan, *The Real Gaze: Film Theory after Lacan* (Albany: State University of New York Press, 2007).
17. Slavoj Žižek, *The Plague of Fantasies* (London: Verso, 2009), 292–93.
18. Verhaeghe, *Beyond Gender*, 73.
19. Samo Tomšič, *The Capitalist Unconscious* (London: Verso, 2015), 18–19.

20. Tomšič, *The Capitalist Unconscious*, 37.

21. *Breaking the Waves*, directed by Lars von Trier (October Films, 1996).

22. Jacques Lacan, *The Seminar of Jacques Lacan, Book VII: The Ethics of Psychoanalysis 1959–1960*, trans. Dennis Porter (New York: W. W. Norton, 1992), 248.

23. My position differs from Žižek's, as captured in the following exposition regarding the feminine jouissance that Bess demonstrates. Before we look at that exposition, it is useful to summarize Bess's actions. She submits her body to sexual violence that results in her death. This is a sacrificial act that she believes will bring back her husband from the state of paralysis, as if she resurrects the dead insofar as the state of complete paralysis signifies social death. Žižek states: "[Bess] undermines the phallic economy and enters the domain of feminine *jouissance* by way of her very unconditional surrender to it, by way of renouncing . . . some secret Beyond which allegedly eludes the male phallic grasp. . . . Bess' sacrifice is unconditional, there is nothing Beyond [a mysterious jouissance beyond the phallus], and this very absolute immanence undermines the phallic economy—deprived of its 'inherent transgression' (of the fantasizing about some mysterious Beyond avoiding its grasp), the phallic economy disintegrates. [*Breaking the Waves*] is subversive on account of its over-orthodox, excessive realization of the fantasy of the feminine sacrifice for the male *jouissance*. . . . The woman perturbs the phallic economy precisely by way of renouncing any Mystery and of totally and openly dedicating herself to her partner's satisfaction." Žižek, "Femininity between Goodness and Act," *Symptom* 14 (Summer 2013), https://www.lacan.com/symptom14/feminimity-between.html.

24. *Or*, directed by Keren Yedaya (New York: Kino International, 2004).

25. Raz Yosef, "Recycled Wounds: Trauma, Gender, and Ethnicity in Keren Yedaya's *Or, My Treasure*," *Camera Obscura* 72, vol. 24, no. 3 (December 2009): 47–48.

26. Anat Zanger, "Women, Border, and Cinema: Israeli Feminine Framing of War," *Feminist Media Studies* 5, no. 3 (2005): 351.

27. *Oldboy* (올드보이), directed by Park Chan-wook (Seoul, Show East, 2003)

28. According to Joseph Jonghyun Jeon, this loss of logos can be extended to the loss of history. My reading of Dae-su's act asserts the emancipatory potential in the loss of logos, as metaphorized by the cutting of the tongue. At the end of the film, Dea-su chooses the Real of the Law of the Father through that loss. In comparison, describing what I read as the loss of logos as "forgetting," Jeon focuses on what Dae-su's relationship to memory implies for the historical subject: "The most profound forgetting . . . at the end of *Oldboy* might be the forgetting not of the past but of the present. This occurs not due to any failure of apprehension or perception, but because, throughout the film, the formulations for understanding events and transcribing them into history have been so thoroughly damaged." Joseph Jonghyun Jeon, "Residual Selves: Trauma and Forgetting in Park Chan-wook's *Oldboy*," *positions: east asia cultures critique* 17, no. 3 (Winter 2009): 738.

29. See, for example, Max Horkheimer and Theodor W. Adorno, *Dialectic of Enlightenment: Philosophical Fragments*, trans. Edmund Jephcott, ed. Gunzelin Schmid Noerr (Stanford: Stanford University Press, 2002).

30. Homi K. Bhabha, *The Location of Culture* (New York: Routledge, 1994), 85–92.

31. Henry Krips, *Fetish: An Erotics of Culture* (Ithaca, NY: Cornell University Press, 1999), 178.

32. Krips, *Fetish*, 60.

33. Paul Eisenstein and Todd McGowan, *Rupture: On the Emergence of the Political* (Evanston, IL: Northwestern University Press, 2012), 45.

34. Joe Valente, "Lacan's Marxism, Marxism's Lacan (from Žižek to Althusser)," in *The Cambridge Companion to Lacan*, ed. Jean-Michel Rabaté (Cambridge: Cambridge University Press, 2003), 161.

35. Cited in Krips, *Fetish*, 159.

36. Yoo, Introduction to *South Korean Film*.

37. Jacques Lacan, *The Seminar of Jacques Lacan, Book XX: On Feminine Sexuality, the Limits of Love and Knowledge (Encore) 1972–1973*, trans. Bruce Fink (New York: W. W. Norton, 1998), 73–77.

38. Mary Ann Doane, "Film and the Masquerade: Theorizing the Female Spectator," *Screen* 23, nos. 3 and 4 (1982): 74–88.

39. For further elaboration on this, see Jennifer Friedlander, *Feminine Look: Sexuation, Spectatorship, Subversion* (Albany: State University of New York Press, 2008).

40. See McGowan, *The Real Gaze*.

41. See Teresa de Lauretis, *Alice Doesn't: Feminism, Semiotics, Cinema* (Bloomington: Indiana University Press, 1984).

42. Eric Cazdyn, *The Flash of Capital: Film and Geopolitics in Japan* (Durham, NC: Duke University Press, 2002), 175.

43. Cazdyn, *The Flash of Capital*, 175.

44. Cazdyn, *The Flash of Capital*, 179.

45. Thomas Elsaesser, "The Pathos of Failure: American Films in the 1970s: Notes on the Unmotivated Hero," in *The Last Great American Picture Show: New Hollywood Cinema in the 1970s*, ed. Thomas Elsaesser, Alexander Horwath, and Noel King (Amsterdam: Amsterdam University Press, 2004), 279–92.

46. For further elaboration on this, see Lacan, *The Seminar of Jacques Lacan, Book XX*.

47. Žižek, *The Plague of Fantasies*, 279.

48. These themes permeate Foucault's body of work, from *History of Sexuality* to *Society Must Be Defended*.

49. For further elaboration on this, see Lacan, *The Seminar of Jacques Lacan, Book XI: The Four Fundamental Concepts of Psychoanalysis, 1964*, trans. Alan Sheridan (New York: W. W. Norton, 1978).

50. See Žižek, *Looking Awry*.

51. Paul Virilio with Bertrand Richard, *The Administration of Fear*, trans. Ames Hodges (Los Angeles: Semiotext(e), 2012), 14–15.

52. *Hunger*, directed by Steve McQueen (Paris: Pathé Distribution, 2008).

53. Peter Bowen, "The Taste of Others," *Filmmaker* (Winter 2009), https://filmmakermagazine.com/archives/issues/winter2009/hunger.php.

54. See de Lauretis, *Alice Doesn't*.

55. Laura Mulvey, "Visual Pleasure and Narrative Cinema," *Screen* 16, no. 3 (1975): 6–18.

56. Alenka Zupančič, *Ethics of the Real: Kant, Lacan* (London: Verso, 2000), 16.

57. As noted, subject formation occurs through *the cut*, a wounding that institutes the lack. Through this lack we establish our relationship to the object, the thing itself that appears in the disguise of *objet a*, or the Other, my neighbor, who appears as such alongside that *objet a*. The Other is designated as the phantasmal location of that little *objet a*.

Chapter 2

1. For further elaboration on this, see Slavoj Žižek, *How to Read Lacan* (New York: W. W. Norton, 2006).

2. Regarding phallic jouissance, Bruce Fink states: "Phallic jouissance is the jouissance that fails us, that disappoints us. It is susceptible to failure, and it fundamentally misses our partner. Why? Because it reduces our partner, as Other, to what Lacan refers to as *objet a*, that partial object that serves as the cause of desire: our partner's voice or gaze that turns us on, or the body part we enjoy in our partner." Fink, "Knowledge and Jouissance," in *Reading Seminar XX: Lacan's Major Work on Love, Knowledge, and Feminine Sexuality*, ed. Susan Barnard and Bruce Fink (Albany: State University of New York Press, 2002), 37.

3. Regarding two different modes of jouissance, let us take into consideration Colette Soler's summary of Lacan's position: "Like the signifier, phallic jouissance is discrete and fragmented; it allows of greater and lesser amounts and can be appropriated by men or women, even though there is certainly a dissymmetry between the sexes when it comes to phallic jouissance. . . . There is what Lacan in Seminar XX calls other jouissance foreclosed from the symbolic. . . . Unlike phallic jouissance, it is not caused by an object correlated with castration [which is a little object "a"] and in this sense cannot be measured. This is why Lacan says . . . that it is beyond the subject. In contrast, phallic jouissance is not beyond the subject." Soler, "What Does the Unconscious Know about Women?" in *Reading Seminar XX*, 106–7.

4. Colette Soler, "The Body in the Teaching of Jacques Lacan," trans. Lindsay Watson. https://jcfar.org.uk/wp-content/uploads/2016/03/The-Body-in-the-Teaching-of-Jacques-Lacan-Colette-Soler.pdf (1984): 6.

5. Soler, "The Body in the Teaching of Jacques Lacan," 7.

6. Soler, "The Body in the Teaching of Jacques Lacan," 7.

7. Soler, "The Body in the Teaching of Jacques Lacan," 11.

8. Paul Verhaeghe, *Love in a Time of Loneliness: Three Essays on Drive and Desire*, trans. Plym Peters and Tony Langham (London: Karnac, 1999), 113.

9. Verhaeghe, *Love in a Time of Loneliness*, 82.

10. Soler, "The Body in the Teaching of Jacques Lacan," 14.

11. *Thirst* (박쥐), directed by Park Chan-wook (Universal City, CA: Focus Features, 2009).

12. *Poetry* (시), directed by Lee Chang-dong (Seoul: Next Entertainment World, 2010).

13. *Still Life* (三峡好人), directed by Jia Zhangke (Beijing: Xstream Pictures, 2006).

14. Verhaeghe says of the kernel that it "survives every confronting test with the pure signifier." Verhaeghe, *Beyond Gender: From Subject to Drive* (New York: Other Press, 2001), 73.

15. Hyon Joo Yoo, Introduction to *South Korean Film,* vols. 1–3 (New York: Bloomsbury, 2021).

16. Naoki Sakai, "Theory and Asian Humanity: On the Question of *Humanitas* and *Anthropos*," *Postcolonial Studies* 13, no. 4 (2010): 441–64.

17. We can observe a similar posturing as the West with material and militaristic power as opposed to its racial Other in China's blockbuster action genre film, *Wolf Warrior II* (2017), set in an unnamed African country. This film faithfully replicates genre conventions, ideologically and formally, of the Hollywood action-adventure genre film down to its colonial and imperial fantasy.

18. Susan Buck-Morss, *Hegel, Haiti, and Universal History* (Pittsburgh: University of Pittsburgh Press, 2009), 79.

19. Naoki Sakai and Hyon Joo Yoo, Preface of *The Trans-Pacific Imagination: Rethinking Boundary, Culture, and Society,* ed. Naoki Sakai and Hyon Joo Yoo (Hackensack, NJ: World Scientific, 2012), x.

20. Kwame Anthony Appiah, *Cosmopolitanism: Ethics in a World of Strangers* (New York: W. W. Norton, 2006), 173–74.

21. Appiah, *Cosmopolitanism*.

22. Jinsoo, An, "Introduction," *Journal of Japanese and Korean Cinema* 7, no. 1 (2015): 1–9.

23. Buck-Morss, *Hegel, Haiti, and Universal History,* 79.

24. Buck-Morss, *Hegel, Haiti, and Universal History,* 79.

25. Mark Seltzer, "The Serial Killer as a Type of Person," in *The Horror Reader,* ed. Ken Gelder (London: Routledge, 2000), 103.

26. Cathy Caruth and Catherine Malabou, for example, address the psychical and material dimension of trauma as the cause of the new subject, albeit with different points of emphasis. See, for example, Caruth's *Unclaimed Experience: Trauma, Narrative, and History* (Baltimore: Johns Hopkins University Press, 1996) and Malabou's *The Ontology of the Accident: An Essay on Destructive Plasticity,* trans. Carolyn Shread (Cambridge, UK: Polity, 2012).

27. See Giorgio Agamben, *Homo Sacer: Sovereign Power and Bare Life,* trans. Daniel Heller-Roazen (Stanford, CA: Stanford University Press, 1998), 119–88.

28. Anton Schütz, "The Fading Memory of *Homo non Sacer*," in *The Work of Giorgio Agamben: Law, Literature, Life,* ed. Justin Clemens, Nicholas Heron, and Alex Murray (Edinburgh: Edinburgh University Press, 2008), 123.

29. Schütz, "The Fading Memory of *Homo non Sacer*," 126.

30. Schütz, "The Fading Memory of *Homo non Sacer*," 126.

31. Agamben, *Homo Sacer,* 71–115.

32. Arne De Boever, "Politics and Poetics of Divine Violence: On a Figure in Giorgio Agamben and Walter Benjamin," in *The Work of Giorgio Agamben,* 83.

33. Justin Clemens, Nicholas Heron, and Alex Murray, "The Enigma of Giorgio Agamben," in *The Work of Giorgio Agamben*, 11.

34. *Oasis* (오아시스), directed by Lee Chang-dong (Seoul: CJ Entertainment, 2002).

35. See, for example, Immanuel Kant, *Groundwork of the Metaphysics of Morals*, trans. Mary Gregor and Jens Timmermann (Cambridge: Cambridge University Press, 2012).

36. Mari Ruti, *Distillations: Theory, Ethics, Affect* (New York: Bloomsbury, 2018), 36.

37. Ruti, *Distillations*, 36.

38. Ruti, *Distillations*, 37.

39. For further elaboration on this, Alain Badiou, *Ethics: An Essay on the Understanding of Evil*, trans. Peter Hallward (London: Verso, 2001).

40. See, e.g., Jacques Derrida, *Of Hospitality: Anne Dufourmantelle Invites Jacques Derrida to Respond*, trans. Rachel Bowlby (Stanford, CA: Stanford University Press, 2000).

41. *Corpo celeste*, directed by Alice Rohrwacher (Rome: Rai Cinema, 2011).

42. *Happy as Lazzaro* (*Lazzaro felice*), directed by Alice Rohrwacher (Rome: 01 Distribution, 2018).

43. *The Isle* (섬), directed by Kim Ki-duk (Seoul: CJ Entertainment, 2000).

44. *Pietà* (피에타), directed by Kim Ki-duk (Austin, TX: Drafthouse Films, 2012).

45. Jacques Lacan, *The Seminar of Jacques Lacan, Book VII: The Ethics of Psychoanalysis 1959–1960*, trans. Dennis Porter (New York: W. W. Norton, 1992), 270–83.

46. Hye Seung Chung takes this position in her book *Kim Ki-duk*, Contemporary Film Directors (Urbana: University of Illinois Press, 2012).

47. See Agamben, *Homo Sacer*, 119–88.

48. Joan Copjec, *Imagine There's No Woman: Ethics and Sublimation* (Cambridge, MA: MIT Press, 2002), 27.

49. Copjec, *Imagine There's No Woman*, 27.

50. Lacan, *The Ethics of Psychoanalysis*, 270–83.

51. See Agamben, *Homo Sacer*, 71–115.

52. Agamben, *Homo Sacer*, 71–115.

53. Agamben, *Homo Sacer*, 165.

54. Agamben, *Means without End: Notes on Politics*, trans. Vincenzo Binetti and Cesare Casarino (Minneapolis: University of Minnesota Press, 2000), 25.

55. Naoki Sakai and I articulate this new direction in *The Trans-Pacific Imagination*.

56. Barbara Creed, "Horror and the Monstrous Feminine: An Imaginary Abjection," in *Feminist Film Theory: A Reader*, ed. Sue Thornham (New York: New York University Press, 1999), 252.

57. Creed, "Horror and the Monstrous Feminine," 252.

58. Lacan, *The Seminar of Jacques Lacan, Book XX: On Feminine Sexuality, the Limits of Love and Knowledge (Encore), 1972–1973*, trans. Bruce Fink (New York: W. W. Norton, 1998), 71–77.

59. See Copjec, *Imagine There's No Woman*, 12–47.
60. Fink, "Knowledge and Jouissance," 34.
61. For further elaboration on this, see Walter Benjamin, "Critique of Violence" in *Walter Benjamin: Selected Writings: Volume I, 1913–1926*, ed. Marcus Bullock and Michael W. Jennings (Cambridge, MA: Harvard University Press, 1996).
62. Fink, "Knowledge and Jouissance," 34–38.
63. Copjec, *Read My Desire: Lacan Against Historicists* (Cambridge, MA: MIT Press, 1994), 222.
64. Agamben, *Means without End*, 10.
65. Agamben, *Homo Sacer*, 175.
66. Agamben, *Potentialities: Collected Essays in Philosophy*, ed. and trans. Daniel Heller-Roazen (Stanford, CA: Stanford University Press, 1999), 177–84.
67. Seung-hoon Jeong, "A Generational Spectrum of Global Korean Auteurs: Political Matrix and Ethical Potential," in *The Global Auteur: The Politics of Authorship in 21st Century Cinema*, ed. Seung-hoon Jeong and Jeremi Szaniawski (New York: Bloomsbury, 2016), 370.
68. Jeong, "A Generational Spectrum of Global Korean Auteurs," 370.
69. For this perspective, see Fredric Jameson, *Marxism and Form: Twentieth Century Dialectical Theories of Literature* (Princeton, NJ: Princeton University Press, 1971), and *The Political Unconscious: Narrative as a Socially Symbolic Act* (Ithaca, NY: Cornell University Press, 1981).
70. Kyu Hyun Kim, "Park Chan-wook's *Thirst*: Body, Guilt and Exsanguination," in *Korean Horror Cinema*, ed. Alison Peirse and Daniel Martin (Edinburgh: Edinburgh University Press, 2013), 201.
71. See Rebecca Garden and Hyon Joo Yoo, "Class and Ethnicity in the Global Market for Organs: The Case of Korean Cinema," *Journal of Medical Humanities* 28, no. 4 (2007): 213–29.
72. Slavoj Žižek, "The Real of Sexual Difference," in *Reading Seminar XX: Lacan's Major Work on Love, Knowledge, and Feminine Sexuality*, 72.
73. Victor Fan, "Revisiting Jia Zhangke: Individuality, Subjectivity, and Autonomy in Contemporary Chinese Independent Cinema" in Jeong and Szaniawski, *The Global Auteur*, 330, 332.
74. Rey Chow, "Toward an Ethics of Postvisuality: Some Thoughts on the Recent Work of Zhang Yimou," *Poetics Today* 25, no. 4 (2004): 678.
75. See David Harvey, *The Condition of Postmodernity: An Enquiry into the Origins of Cultural Change* (Cambridge, MA: Blackwell, 1991), 201–326. Universal capitalist time is superimposed on all locations, erasing historically overdetermined material specificities of life in different societies and changing the factory time of modernity into the postmodern virtual time of capital.
76. Jennifer Latson, "The High-Level Scheming behind Philippe Petit's Twin Tower Tightrope Walk," *Time*, August 7, 2015, http://time.com/3976999/philippe-petit-twin-towers/.
77. Michel de Certeau, *The Practice of Everyday Life*, trans. Steven F. Rendall (Berkeley: University of California Press, 1988), 105.

78. Helga Geyer-Ryan, "Effects of Abjection in the Texts of Walter Benjamin," *MLN* 107, no. 3 (1992): 511.

79. Alain Badiou, *Saint Paul: The Foundation of Universalism*, trans. Ray Brassier (Stanford, CA: Stanford University, 2003), 87.

Chapter 3

1. *Caché*, directed by Michael Haneke (Paris: Les films du losange, 2005).

2. Lacan gives us another example of the gaze in Holbein's painting *The Ambassadors*. The gaze emanates from the image of a morphologically complex three-dimensional skull in the foreground which, rendered in a style that is quite different from the rest of the painted surface, disrupts the visual unity consisting of two dignitaries surrounded by artifacts that signify the Enlightenment. Both examples of the gaze are from *The Seminar of Jacques Lacan, Book XI: The Four Fundamental Concepts of Psychoanalysis, 1964,* trans. Alan Sheridan (New York: Norton, 1978), chapters 7 and 8.

3. Bruce Fink's summation of the Lacanian understanding of psychosis allows us this position. See *The Lacanian Subject: Between Language and Jouissance* (Princeton, NJ: Princeton University Press, 1995), 44–48.

4. Fink, *The Lacanian Subject*, 68.

5. As mentioned in chapter 1, discussions of the Real's appearance have previously focused on locating "a quilting point" where "a perfectly 'natural' and 'familiar' situation is denatured, becomes 'uncanny.'" See Slavoj Žižek, *Looking Awry: An Introduction to Jacques Lacan through Popular Culture* (Cambridge, MA: MIT Press, 1992), 88. My approach emphasizes how moments of disruption create the possibility that the subject might begin to engage with an emancipatory act.

6. Lacan articulates this concept throughout *The Four Fundamental Concepts of Psychoanalysis*.

7. Lacan explains this term throughout *The Four Fundamental Concepts of Psychoanalysis*.

8. Slavoj Žižek, *Tarrying with the Negative: Kant, Hegel, and the Critique of Ideology* (Durham, NC: Duke University Press, 1993), 165–99.

9. Slavoj Žižek, *The Ticklish Subject: The Absent Center of Political Ontology* (London: Verso, 1999), 297.

10. Alenka Zupančič, *Ethics of the Real: Kant, Lacan* (London: Verso, 2000), 239.

11. Zupančič, *Ethics of the Real*, 243.

12. Zupančič, *Ethics of the Real*, 142.

13. *Double Indemnity*, directed by Billy Wilder (Los Angeles: Paramount, 1944).

14. Joan Copjec, "The Phenomenal Nonphenomenal: Private Space in Film Noir," in *Shades of Noir*, ed. Joan Copjec (London: Verso, 1993), 167–97.

15. Eric L. Santner, *The Weight of All Flesh: On the Subject-Matter of Political Economy* (Oxford: Oxford University Press, 2016), 89.

16. As I have noted in previous chapters, the feminine and the masculine are not gender identities, neither biologically grounded nor culturally constructed. They are subject positions that we take up in response to the impossibility of sexual difference. These positions depend on whether the subject organizes its desire around objects represented as phallic or not.

17. *Entre ses mains*, directed by Anne Fontaine (Paris: Pathé Distribution, 2005).

18. *Timbuktu*, directed by Abderrahmane Sissako (New York: Cohen Media Group, 2014).

19. *Incendies*, directed by Denis Villeneuve (Toronto: Entertainment One, 2010).

20. *Widows*, directed by Steve McQueen (Los Angeles: 20th Century Fox, 2018).

21. Paul Eisenstein and Todd McGowan, *Rupture: On the Emergence of the Political* (Evanston, IL: Northwestern University Press, 2012), 87–108.

22. Alain Badiou, *In Praise of Love*, trans. Peter Bush (New York: New Press, 2012), 22.

23. Alain Badiou, *Ethics: An Essay on the Understanding of Evil*, trans. Peter Hallward (London: Verso, 2001), 4–17.

24. Badiou, *Ethics*, 40–57.

25. Alain Badiou, *Saint Paul: The Foundation of Universalism*, trans. Ray Brassier (Stanford, CA: Stanford University Press, 2003), 65–85.

26. Žižek, *Looking Awry*, 56.

27. Paul Verhaeghe, *Love in a Time of Loneliness: Three Essays on Drive and Desire*, trans. Plym Peters and Tony Langham (London: Karnac, 1999), 199.

28. Mari Ruti, *The Ethics of Opting Out: Queer Theory's Defiant Subjects* (New York: Columbia University Press, 2017), 102.

29. Ruti, *The Ethics of Opting Out*, 102.

30. *All Is Bright*, directed by Phil Morrison (Los Angeles: Anchor Bay Films, 2013).

31. Throughout the film, the piano is established as the sublime object. Olga, a Russian expat, returns to the piano throughout the film, though her damaged fingers keep her from executing true virtuosity. She conveys longing through her touch and laments her inability to create the music she desires.

32. *Prisoners*, directed by Denis Villeneuve (Burbank: Warner Brothers, 2013).

33. Jacques Lacan, *The Seminar of Jacques Lacan, Book XVII: The Other Side of Psychanalysis, 1969–1970*, trans. Russell Grigg (New York: W. W. Norton, 2007), 72.

34. Jacques Lacan, "The Subversion of the Subject and the Dialectic of Desire," in Lacan, *Écrits: A Selection*, trans. Bruce Fink (New York: W. W. Norton, 2002), 305.

35. Lacan, "The Subversion of the Subject and the Dialectic of Desire," 296.

36. Ruti, *The Ethics of Opting Out*, 103.

37. Ruti, *The Ethics of Opting Out*, 111.

38. Ruti, *The Ethics of Opting Out*, 112.

39. Ruti, *The Ethics of Opting Out*, 112–13.

40. For further elaboration on this, see Žižek, *Looking Awry*.

41. Žižek, *Looking Awry*, 56.

42. Žižek, *Looking Awry*, 56.

43. Eisenstein and McGowan, *Rupture*, 144.

44. *The Priests* (검은 사제들), directed by Jang Jae-hyun (Seoul: CJ Entertainment, 2015).

45. Here I consider Aaron Schuster's reading in "The Lacan-Foucault Relation: *Las Meninas*, Sexuality, and the Unconscious." Lecture, Lacan contra Foucault Conference: December 4, 2015, https://www.academia.edu/26368827/The_Lacan_Foucault_Relation_Las_Meninas_Sexuality_and_the_Unconscious.

46. *Policeman*, directed by Nadav Lapid (Paris: Bodega Films, 2011).

47. Santner, *The Weight of All Flesh*, 85.

48. Eisenstein and McGowan, *Rupture*, 187–216.

49. Eisenstein and McGowan, *Rupture*, 195.

50. *The Circle*, directed by Jafar Panahi (Rome: Mikado Film, 2000).

51. *Toc toc*, directed by Vicente Villanueva (Burbank, CA: Warner Bros. Pictures, 2017).

52. *The Hurt Locker*, directed by Kathryn Bigelow (Santa Monica, CA: Summit, 2008).

53. David Denny, "On the Politics of Enjoyment: A Reading of *The Hurt Locker*," *Theory and Event* 14, no. 1 (2011): 23, https://www.researchgate.net/publication/265753061_On_The_Politics_of_Enjoyment_A_Reading_of_The_Hurt_Locker.

54. Denny, "On the Politics of Enjoyment," 24.

55. Denny, "On the Politics of Enjoyment," 26.

56. For further elaboration on this, see Cathy Caruth, *Unclaimed Experience: Trauma, Narrative, and History* (Baltimore, MD: Johns Hopkins University Press, 1996).

57. Kojin Karatani, *Transcritique: On Kant and Marx* (Cambridge, MA: MIT Press, 2003), 51.

58. *Time of the Wolf* (*Le temps du loup*), directed by Michael Haneke (Paris: Les Films du Losange, 2003).

59. Lacan, *The Four Fundamental Concepts of Psychoanalysis*, 38.

60. Lacan, *The Four Fundamental Concepts of Psychoanalysis*, 53–64.

61. Alain Badiou and Élisabeth Roudinesco, *Jacques Lacan, Past and Present: A Dialogue*, trans. Jason E. Smith (New York: Columbia University Press, 2014).

62. Jacques-Alain Miller, "Suture (Elements of the Logic of the Signifier)," *Screen* 18, no. 4 (Winter 1977): 24–34.

63. In McGowan's *Capitalism and Desire*, this is the starting point of theorizing the psychoanalytic subject. Todd McGowan, *Capitalism and Desire: The Psychic Cost of Free Markets* (New York: Columbia University Press, 2016).

64. Todd McGowan, *Enjoying What We Don't Have: The Political Project of Psychoanalysis* (Lincoln: University of Nebraska Press, 2013).

65. *The Yellow Sea* (황해), directed by Na Hong-jin (Los Angeles: 20th Century Fox, 2010).

66. Anne Eakin Moss, "The Permeable Screen: Soviet Cinema and the Fantasy of No Limits," *Screen* 59, no. 4 (Winter 2018): 425.

67. *Nambugun* (남부군), directed by Chung Ji-young (Seoul: Nam Production, 1990).

68. Badiou, *Ethics*, 40–57.

69. *About Elly* (درباره الی), directed by Asghar Farhadi (Le Cannet, France: Dreamlab, 2009).

70. *Dooman River* (두만강), directed by Zhang Lu (Seoul: Lu Films, 2010).

71. *Germany Year Zero* (*Germania anno zero*), directed by Roberto Rossellini (G.D.B. Film, 1948).

72. *The Good, The Bad, The Weird* (좋은 놈, 나쁜 놈, 이상한 놈), directed by Kim Jee-woon (Seoul: CJ Entertainment, 2008).

73. For further elaboration on this, see Jacques Lacan, *The Seminar of Jacques Lacan Book X: Anxiety, 1962–1963*, trans. A. R. Price (Cambridge, UK: Polity), 54.

74. Cited in Moss, "The Permeable Screen," 431.

75. Jinhee Choi and Mattias Frey, Introduction to *Cine-Ethics: Ethical Dimensions of Film Theory, Practice, and Spectatorship*, ed. Jinhee Choi and Mattias Frey (New York: Routledge, 2014), 3–4.

76. Choi and Frey, Introduction, 4.

77. Linda Williams, "Film Bodies: Gender, Genre, and Excess," *Film Quarterly* 44, no. 4 (Summer 1991): 9.

78. *Poongsan* (풍산개), directed by Juhn Jai-hong (Seoul: Next Entertainment World, 2011).

79. *Time* (시간), directed by Kim Ki-duk (Seoul: Sponge, 2006).

Chapter 4

1. Étienne Balibar, *Equaliberty: Political Essays*, trans. James Ingram (Durham, NC: Duke University Press, 2014), 32.

2. *Head-On* (*Gegen die wand*), directed by Fatih Akin (Potsdam, Germany: Timebandits Films, 2004).

3. David Harvey, "Cosmopolitanism and the Banality of Geographical Evil," in *Millennial Capitalism and the Culture of Neoliberalism*, ed. Jean Comaroff and John L. Comaroff (Durham, NC: Duke University Press, 2001), 299.

4. See Cathy Caruth, *Unclaimed Experience: Trauma, Narrative, and History (Gegen die wand)* (Baltimore: Johns Hopkins University Press, 1996), Chapter 3.

5. Harvey, "Cosmopolitanism and the Banality of Geographical Evil," 277.

6. Harvey, "Cosmopolitanism and the Banality of Geographical Evil," 277.

7. Harvey, "Cosmopolitanism and the Banality of Geographical Evil," 277.

8. Harvey, "Cosmopolitanism and the Banality of Geographical Evil," 287.

9. Harvey, "Cosmopolitanism and the Banality of Geographical Evil," 289.

10. Harvey, "Cosmopolitanism and the Banality of Geographical Evil," 305.

11. Harvey, "Cosmopolitanism and the Banality of Geographical Evil," 305.

12. Harvey, "Cosmopolitanism and the Banality of Geographical Evil," 304.

13. Caroline Levine, *Forms: Whole, Rhythm, Hierarchy, Network* (Princeton, NJ: Princeton University Press, 2015), 134.

14. *Parasite* (기생충), directed by Bong Joon-ho (Seoul: CJ Entertainment, 2019).

15. *Girlhood* (*Bande de filles*), directed by Céline Sciamma (Paris: Pyramide Distribution, 2014).

16. Sue Thornham, *Spaces of Women's Cinema: Space, Place and Genre in Contemporary Women's Filmmaking* (New York: Bloomsbury on behalf of The British Film Institute, 2019), 6–7.
17. Thornham, *Spaces of Women's Cinema*, 6.
18. Thornham, *Spaces of Women's Cinema*, 6.
19. Thornham, *Spaces of Women's Cinema*, 11.
20. *Meek's Cutoff*, directed by Kelly Reichardt (Brooklyn: Oscilloscope Laboratories, 2010).
21. Thornham, *Spaces of Women's Cinema*, 12.
22. Thornham, *Spaces of Women's Cinema*, 11.
23. Thornham, *Spaces of Women's Cinema*, 11.
24. Thornham, *Spaces of Women's Cinema*, 3.
25. Thornham, *Spaces of Women's Cinema*, 3.
26. Thornham, *Spaces of Women's Cinema*, 3.
27. Dany Nobus, "Lacan's Science of the Subject: Between Linguistics and Topology," in *The Cambridge Companion to Lacan*, ed. Jean-Michel Rabaté (Cambridge: Cambridge University Press, 2003), 62.
28. *Morvern Callar*, directed by Lynne Ramsay (Toronto: Alliance Atlantis, 2002).
29. *Oasis* (오아시스), directed by Lee Chang-dong (Seoul: CJ Entertainment, 2002).
30. *The Last Princess* (덕혜옹주), directed by Hur Jin-ho (Seoul: Lotte Entertainment, 2016).
31. Nobus, "Lacan's Science of the Subject," 63.
32. Nobus, "Lacan's Science of the Subject," 64.
33. Nobus, "Lacan's Science of the Subject," 65.
34. Todd McGowan, *Psychoanalytic Film Theory and the Rules of the Game* (New York: Bloomsbury, 2015), 19–23.
35. Laura Marks, *The Skin of the Film* (Durham, NC: Duke University, 2000), 178–81.
36. Marks, *The Skin of the Film*, 141.
37. Eric L. Santner, *The Weight of All Flesh: On the Subject-Matter of Political Economy* (Oxford: Oxford University Press, 2016), 89.
38. Thornham, *Spaces of Women's Cinema*, 137.
39. *White Material*, directed by Claire Denis (Berlin: Wild Bunch Distribution, 2009).
40. Paul Kingsbury, "The Extimacy of Space," *Social & Cultural Geography* 8, no. 2 (2007): 250.
41. Kingsbury, "The Extimacy of Space," 250.
42. Kingsbury, "The Extimacy of Space," 248.
43. Kingsbury, "The Extimacy of Space," 240.
44. Kingsbury, "The Extimacy of Space," 245.
45. From Lacan's *Ecrits*, cited in Kingsbury, "The Extimacy of Space," 253.
46. Dipesh Chakrabarty, "Universalism and Belonging in the Logic of Capital," in *Cosmopolitanism*, ed. Carol A. Breckenridge et al. (Durham, NC: Duke University Press, 2002), 82–110.

47. Thornham, *Spaces of Women's Cinema*, 4.
48. Slavoj Žižek, *The Fright of Real Tears: Krzysztof Kieślowski between Theory and Philosophy* (London: BFI Publishing, 2001), 55.
49. *The Swamp* (*La ciénaga*), directed by Lucrecia Martel (Lider Films, 2001).
50. *Mood Indigo* (*L'écume des jours*), directed by Michel Gondry (Paris: StudioCanal, 2013).
51. Thornham, *Spaces of Women's Cinema*, 73, 75.
52. Alenka Zupančič, "Ethics and Tragedy in Lacan," in Rabaté, *The Cambridge Companion to Lacan*, 174, 185.
53. Zupančič, "Ethics and Tragedy in Lacan," 188.
54. *The Babadook*, directed by Jennifer Kent (Kew, Australia: Umbrella Entertainment, 2014).
55. Zupančič, "Ethics and Tragedy in Lacan," 177.
56. Nobus, "Lacan's Science of the Subject," 62.
57. Judith Feher-Gurewich, "A Lacanian Approach to the Logic of Perversion," in Rabaté, *The Cambridge Companion to Lacan*, 196.
58. *Zama*, directed by Lucrecia Martel (Burbank: Buena Vista International, 2017).
59. Feher-Gurewich, "A Lacanian Approach to the Logic of Perversion," 200.
60. *Nightingale*, directed by Jennifer Kent (Sydney, Australia: Transmission Films, 2018).
61. *Cléo from 5 to 7* (*Cléo de 5 à 7*), directed by Agnès Varda (Paris: Athos Films, 1962). For comprehensive discussions of femininity in this film, see Hilary Neroni, *Feminist Film Theory and* Cléo 5 to 7 (New York: Bloomsbury, 2016).
62. G. W. F. Hegel, *Phenomenology of Spirit*, trans. A. V. Miller (Oxford: Oxford University Press, 1977), 61.
63. In this chapter, I refer to Alain Badiou's concept of *the event* as articulated throughout *Saint Paul: The Foundation of Universalism*, trans. Ray Brassier (Stanford, CA: Stanford University Press, 2003). References to Paul in this chapter are all from Badiou, *Saint Paul*.
64. Badiou, *Saint Paul*, 9.
65. Badiou, *Saint Paul*, 9, quoting Galatians 3:28 and Romans 2:10-11.
66. I draw the meaning of this concept from Badiou's *Saint Paul*, especially as theorized in chapters 1 and 3.
67. Rey Cow, *The Protestant Ethnic and the Spirit of Capitalism* (New York: Columbia University Press, 2002).
68. Balibar, *Equaliberty*, 32.
69. It is part of a Korean Broadcasting System 2020 report on the unearthing of this material in the National Archives and Records Administration, US: https://www.youtube.com/watch?v=wYb9tPs6ZRI. Many sources estimate that there were up to, and perhaps more than, 200,000 comfort women, the vast majority of them Koreans. See, for example, Amnesty International: https://www.amnesty.org/en/latest/press-release/2021/04/south-korea-disappointing-japan-ruling-fails-to-deliver-justice-to-comfort-women/.

70. Paul Eisenstein and Todd McGowan, *Rupture: On the Emergence of the Political* (Evanston, IL: Northwestern University Press, 2012), 170.

71. For more details about the Gwangju Uprising, see Georgy Katsiaficas and Na Kahn-chae, *South Korean Democracy: Legacy of Gwangju Uprising* (London: Routledge, 2006).

72. Among the materials engaged in locating these women's voices, I mainly refer, in this part of the chapter, to a South Korean documentary commemorating the fortieth anniversary of the Gwangju Uprising aired on SBS, a South Korean broadcasting network, in 2020. Its title includes the phrase "What is her name?": https://programs.sbs.co.kr/culture/sunmivideo/vod/65035/22000379498.

73. This concept of bare life is articulated throughout Giorgio Agamben's *Homo Sacer: Sovereign Power and Bare Life*, trans. Daniel Heller-Roazen (Stanford, CA: Stanford University Press, 1998), with part 2 fleshing it out in detail. References to the bare life in this chapter draw from this work.

74. *Newstapa*, "Sorrowful Homecoming," https://www.youtube.com/watch?v=GRmhsulHpLE (part 1) and https://www.youtube.com/watch?v=yaI3bdGh-8No (part 2).

75. *Ju Dou* (菊豆), directed by Zhang Yimou (Narita, Japan: Daiei, 1990).

76. I commented on this particular gaze of the subaltern in my book *Cinema at the Crossroads: Nation and the Subject in East Asia* (Lanham, MD: Lexington Books, 2012), 112.

77. For more on this point, see Rey Chow, *Primitive Passions: Visuality, Sexuality, Ethnography, and Contemporary Chinese Cinema* (New York: Columbia University Press, 1995).

78. *The Murmuring* (낮은 목소리), directed by Byun Young-joo (1995). This independent film was produced through grassroots funding; it credits four hundred ordinary citizens who participated in fundraising in the capacity of producers. Production company: 기록영화제작소 보임 (Girokyeongwha Jejakso Boim)

79. Jongwoo Jeremy Kim also sees the queering effect in this sequence: "Filming the Queerness of Comfort Women: Byun Young-Joo's *The Murmuring*, 1995," *positions: east asia cultures critique* 22, no. 1 (2014): 33–39.

80. *The Lighthouse*, directed by Robert Eggers (New York: A24 Films, 2019).

81. *Ex Machina*, directed by Alex Garland (New York: A24 Films, 2014).

82. *Army of Shadows* (*L'Armée des ombres*), directed by Jean-Pierre Melville (Paris: Valoria Films, 1969).

83. Eisenstein and McGowan, *Rupture*, 37–61.

84. Eisenstein and McGowan, *Rupture*, 163–86.

85. Eisenstein and McGowan, *Rupture*, 170.

86. You can read these words in Seoul's subway stations as you wait for your train to arrive: they are etched into the glass barrier that separates the track from the platform.

87. The original Korean poem is Yoon Dong Ju, 무서운 시간 , in the collection 하늘과 바람과 별과 시 (Haneulgwa Baramgwa, Byulgwa Si [Sky, Wind, and Stars]), published by 정음사 (Jeongum Sa, 1955).

88. *Son of Saul* (*Saul fia*), directed by László Nemes (Budapest: Mozinet, 2015).

89. Agamben, *Homo Sacer*.
90. Eisenstein and McGowan, *Rupture*. See the section on freedom, 137–61.
91. Eisenstein and McGowan, *Rupture*, 137–61.
92. Badiou, *Saint Paul*, 64.
93. Badiou develops this concept throughout *Saint Paul*. Notably, Badiou says, "The apostle, who declares an unheard-of possibility, one dependent on an evental grace, properly speaking knows nothing. To imagine that one knows, when it is a question of subjective possibilities, is fraudulent: 'He who thinks he knows something . . . does not yet know as he ought to know' (Cor. I.8.2)." One can say grace marks the point where preexisting knowledge disappears.
94. Even a conservative media outlet aired a eulogy that conveys the tenor of her interviews: https://woman.donga.com/3/all/12/3158158/1.
95. *In the Absence* (부재의기억), directed by Seung-jun Yi (NY: Field of Vision, 2018).

Bibliography

Agamben, Giorgio. *Homo Sacer: Sovereign Power and Bare Life*. Translated by Daniel Heller-Roazen. Stanford, CA: Stanford University Press, 1998.
———. *Means without End: Notes on Politics*. Translated by Vincenzo Binetti and Cesare Casarino. Minneapolis: University of Minnesota Press, 2000.
———. *Potentialities: Collected Essays in Philosophy*. Edited and translated by Daniel Heller-Roazen. Sandford, CA: Stanford University Press, 1999.
Akin, Fatih, dir. *Head-On (Gegen die wand)*. Potsdam, Germany: Timebandits Films, 2004.
Amnesty International. "South Korea: Disappointing Japan Ruling Fails to Deliver Justice to 'Comfort Women.'" April 21, 2021. https://www.amnesty.org/en/latest/press-release/2021/04/south-korea-disappointing-japan-ruling-fails-to-deliver-justice-to-comfort-women/.
An, Jinsoo. "Introduction." *Journal of Japanese and Korean Cinema* 7, no. 1 (2015): 1–9.
Antonioni, Michelangelo, dir. *Blow-Up*. Beverly Hills: Premier Productions, 1966.
Appiah, Kwame Anthony. *Cosmopolitanism: Ethics in a World of Strangers*. New York: W. W. Norton, 2006.
Arendt, Hannah. *Eichmann in Jerusalem: A Report on the Banality of Evil*. New York: Penguin Books, 1963.
Badiou, Alain. *Ethics: An Essay on the Understanding of Evil*. Translated by Peter Hallward. London: Verso, 2001.
———. *In Praise of Love*. Translated by Peter Bush. New York: New Press, 2012.
———. *Saint Paul: The Foundation of Universalism*. Translated by Ray Brassier. Stanford, CA: Stanford University, 2003.
Badiou, Alain, and Élisabeth Roudinesco. *Jacques Lacan, Past and Present: A Dialogue*. Translated by Jason E. Smith. New York: Columbia University Press, 2014.
Balibar, Étienne. *Equaliberty: Political Essays*. Translated by James Ingram. Durham, NC: Duke University Press, 2014.
Benjamin, Walter. "Critique of Violence." In *Walter Benjamin: Selected Writings*. Vol. 1, *1913–1926*, edited by Marcus Bullock and Michael W. Jennings. Cambridge, MA: Harvard University Press, 1996.
Bhabha, Homi K. *The Location of Culture*. New York: Routledge, 1994.
Bigelow, Kathryn, dir. *The Hurt Locker*. Santa Monica, CA: Summit, 2008.
Bollaín, Icíar, dir. *Even the Rain (También la lluvia)*. Palm Desert, CA: Vitagraph Films, 2010.
Bong, Joon-ho, dir. *Parasite* (기생충). Seoul: CJ Entertainment, 2019.
Bowen, Peter, "The Taste of Others," *Filmmaker*. Winter 2009. https://filmmakermagazine.com/archives/issues/winter2009/hunger.php.

Buck-Morss, Susan. *Hegel, Haiti, and Universal History*. Pittsburgh: University of Pittsburgh Press, 2009.
Byun, Young-joo, dir. *The Murmuring* (낮은 목소리). Docu-Factory Vista, 1995.
Caruth, Cathy. *Unclaimed Experience: Trauma, Narrative, and History*. Baltimore: Johns Hopkins University Press, 1996.
Cazdyn, Eric. *The Flash of Capital: Film and Geopolitics in Japan*. Durham, NC: Duke University Press, 2002.
Chakrabarty, Dipesh. "Universalism and Belonging in the Logic of Capital." In *Cosmopolitanism*, edited by Carol A. Breckenridge, Sheldon Pollock, Homi K. Bhabha, and Dipesh Chakrabarty. Durham, NC: Duke University Press, 2002.
Chow, Rey. *Primitive Passions: Visuality, Sexuality, Ethnography, and Contemporary Chinese Cinema*. New York: Columbia University Press, 1995.
———. *The Protestant Ethnic and the Spirit of Capitalism*. New York: Columbia University Press, 2002.
———. "Toward an Ethics of Postvisuality: Some Thoughts on the Recent Work of Zhang Yimou." *Poetics Today* 25, no. 4 (2004): 673–88.
Choi, Jinhee, and Mattias Frey. Introduction to *Cine-Ethics: Ethical Dimensions of Film Theory, Practice, and Spectatorship*. Edited by Jinhee Choi and Mattias Frey. New York: Routledge, 2014.
Chung, Hye Seung. *Kim Ki-duk*. Contemporary Film Directors. Urbana: University of Illinois Press, 2012.
Chung, Ji-young, dir. *Nambugun* (남부군). 1990.
Clemens, Justin, Nicholas Heron, and Alex Murray. "The Enigma of Giorgio Agamben." In *The Work of Giorgio Agamben: Law, Literature, Life*, edited by Justin Clemens, Nicholas Heron, and Alex Murray. Edinburgh: Edinburgh University Press, 2008.
Copjec, Joan. *Imagine There's No Woman: Ethics and Sublimation*. Cambridge, MA: MIT Press, 2002.
———. "The Phenomenal Nonphenomenal: Private Space in Film Noir." In *Shades of Noir*, edited by Joan Copjec. London: Verso, 1993.
———. *Read My Desire: Lacan Against Historicists*. Cambridge, MA: MIT Press, 1994.
Creed, Barbara. "Horror and the Monstrous Feminine: An Imaginary Abjection." In *Feminist Film Theory: A Reader*, edited by Sue Thornham. New York: New York University Press, 1999.
De Boever, Arne. "Politics and Poetics of Divine Violence: On a Figure in Giorgio Agamben and Walter Benjamin." In *The Work of Giorgio Agamben: Law, Literature, Life*, edited by Justin Clemens, Nicholas Heron, and Alex Murray. Edinburgh: Edinburgh University Press, 2008.
de Certeau, Michel. *The Practice of Everyday Life*. Translated by Steven F. Rendall. Berkeley: University of California Press, 1988.
de Lauretis, Teresa. *Alice Doesn't: Feminism, Semiotics, Cinema*. Bloomington: Indiana University Press, 1984.
Denis, Claire, dir. *White Material*. Berlin: Wild Bunch Distribution, 2009.
Denny, David. "On the Politics of Enjoyment: A Reading of *The Hurt Locker*." *Theory and Event* 14, no. 1: 2011. https://www.researchgate.net/publication/265753061_On_The_Politics_of_Enjoyment_A_Reading_of_The_Hurt_Locker.

Derrida, Jacques. *Of Hospitality: Anne Dufourmantelle Invites Jacques Derrida to Respond.* Translated by Rachel Bowlby. Stanford, CA: Stanford University Press, 2000.
Doane, Mary Ann. "Film and the Masquerade: Theorizing the Female Spectator." *Screen* 23, nos. 3 and 4 (1982): 74–88.
Doucouré, Maïmouna, dir. *Cuties* (*Mignonnes*). Paris: BAC Films, 2020.
Eggers, Robert, dir. *The Lighthouse.* New York: A24 Films, 2019.
Eisenstein, Paul, and Todd McGowan. *Rupture: On the Emergence of the Political.* Evanston, IL: Northwestern University Press, 2012.
Elsaesser, Thomas. "The Pathos of Failure: American Films in the 1970s: Notes on the Unmotivated Hero." In *The Last Great American Picture Show: New Hollywood Cinema in the 1970s*, edited by Thomas Elsaesser, Alexander Horwath, and Noel King. Amsterdam: Amsterdam University Press, 2004.
Fan, Victor. "Revisiting Jia Zhangke: Individuality, Subjectivity, and Autonomy in Contemporary Chinese Independent Cinema." In *The Global Auteur: The Politics of Authorship in 21st Century Cinema*, edited by Seung-hoon Jeong and Jeremi Szaniawski. New York: Bloomsbury, 2016.
Farhadi, Asghar, dir. *About Elly.* Le Cannet, France: Dreamlab, 2009.
Fassbinder, Rainer Werner, dir. *The Bitter Tears of Petra von Kant* (*Die bitteren tränen der Petra von Kant.* Berlin: Filmverlag der Autoren, 1972.
Feher-Gurewich, Judith. "A Lacanian Approach to the Logic of Perversion." In *The Cambridge Companion to Lacan*, edited by Jean-Michel Rabaté. Cambridge: Cambridge University Press, 2003.
Fink, Bruce. "Knowledge and Jouissance." In *Reading Seminar XX: Lacan's Major Work on Love, Knowledge, and Feminine Sexuality*, edited by Susan Barnard and Bruce Fink. Albany: State University of New York Press, 2002.
———. *The Lacanian Subject: Between Language and Jouissance.* Princeton, NJ: Princeton University Press, 1995.
Fontaine, Anne, dir. *Entre ses mains* (*In His Hands*). Paris: Pathé Disribution, 2005.
Friedlander, Jennifer. *Feminine Look: Sexuation, Spectatorship, Subversion.* Albany: State University of New York Press, 2008.
Garden, Rebecca, and Hyon Joo Yoo. "Class and Ethnicity in the Global Market for Organs: The Case of Korean Cinema." *Journal of Medical Humanities* 28, no. 4 (2007): 213–29.
Garland, Alex, dir. *Ex Machina.* New York: A24 Films, 2014.
Geyer-Ryan, Helga. "Effects of Abjection in the Texts of Walter Benjamin." *MLN* 107, no. 3 (1992): 499–520.
Gondry, Michel, dir. *Mood Indigo* (*L'écume des jours*). Paris: StudioCanal, 2013.
Han, Byung-Chul. *The Transparency Society.* Translated by Erik Butler. Stanford, CA: Stanford University Press, 2015.
Haneke, Michael, dir. *Caché.* Paris: Les films du losange, 2005.
———. *Time of the Wolf* (*Le temps du loup*). Paris: Les films du losange, 2003.
Harvey, David. *The Condition of Postmodernity: An Enquiry into the Origins of Cultural Change.* Cambridge, MA: Blackwell, 1991.

———. "Cosmopolitanism and the Banality of Geographical Evil." In *Millennial Capitalism and the Culture of Neoliberalism*, edited by Jean Comaroff and John L. Comaroff. Durham, NC: Duke University Press, 2001.
Hegel, G. W. F. *Phenomenology of Spirit*. Translated by A. V. Miller. Oxford: Oxford University Press, 1977.
Hur, Jin-ho, dir. *The Last Princess* (덕혜옹주). Seoul: Lotte Entertainment, 2016.
Jang, Hoon. dir. *A Taxi Driver* (택시운전사). Seoul: Showbox, 2017.
———. *The Front Line* (고지전). Seoul: Showbox, 2011.
Jang, Jae-hyun, dir. *The Priests* (검은 사제들). Seoul: CJ Entertainment, 2015.
Jameson, Fredric. *Marxism and Form: Twentieth Century Dialectical Theories of Literature*. Princeton, NJ: Princeton University Press, 1971.
———. *The Political Unconscious: Narrative as a Socially Symbolic Act*. Ithaca, NY: Cornell University Press, 1981.
Jeon, Joseph Jonghyun. "Residual Selves: Trauma and Forgetting in Park Chan-wook's *Oldboy*." *Positions: east asia cultures critique* 17, no. 3 (2009): 713–40.
Jeong, Seung-hoon. "A Generational Spectrum of Global Korean Auteurs: Political Matrix and Ethical Potential." In *The Global Auteur: The Politics of Authorship in 21st Century Cinema*, ed. Seung-hoon Jeong and Jeremi Szaniawski. New York: Bloomsbury, 2016.
———. "*Parasite* from Text to Context: An Ethical Stalemate and New Auteurism in Global Cinema." In *Parasite: A Philosophical Exploration*, edited by Thorsten Botz-Bornstein and Giannis Stamatellos. Leiden, The Netherlands: Brill (2022).
Jia, Zhangke, dir. *Still Life* (三峡好人). Beijing: Xstream Pictures, 2006.
Juhn, Jai-hong, dir. *Poongsan* (풍산개). Seoul: Next Entertainment World, 2011.
Kant, Immanuel. *Groundwork of the Metaphysics of Morals*. Translated by Mary Gregor and Jens Timmermann. Cambridge: Cambridge University Press, 2012.
Karatani, Kojin. *Transcritique: On Kant and Marx*. Translated by Sabu Kohso. Cambridge, MA: MIT Press, 2013.
Katsiaficas, Georgy, and Na Kahn-chae, eds. *South Korean Democracy: Legacy of Gwangju Uprising*. London: Routledge, 2006.
Kent, Jennifer, dir. *The Babadook*. Kew, Australia: Umbrella Entertainment, 2014.
———. *Nightingale*. Sydney, Australia: Transmission Films, 2018
Kim, Jee-woon, dir. *The Good, the Bad, the Weird* (좋은 놈, 나쁜 놈, 이상한 놈). Seoul: CJ Entertainment, 2008.
Kim, Jongwoo Jeremy. "Filming the Queerness of Comfort Women: Byun Young-Joo's *The Murmuring*, 1995." *Positions: east asia cultures critique* 22, no. 1 (2014): 7–39.
Kim, Ki-duk, dir. *The Isle* (섬). Seoul: CJ Entertainment, 2000.
———. *Pietà* (피에타). Austin, TX: Drafthouse Films, 2012.
———. *Time* (시간). Seoul: Sponge, 2006.
Kim, Kyu Hyun. "Park Chan-wook's *Thirst*: Body, Guilt and Exsanguination." In *Korean Horror Cinema*, edited by Alison Peirse and Daniel Martin. Edinburgh: Edinburgh University Press, 2013.
Kingsbury, Paul. "The Extimacy of Space." *Social & Cultural Geography* 8, no. 2 (2007): 235–58.

Korean Broadcasting System. Reporting on Korean Comfort Women. May 28, 2020. https://www.youtube.com/watch?v=wYb9tPs6ZRI.

Krips, Henry. *Fetish: An Erotics of Culture*. Ithaca, NY: Cornell University Press, 1999.

Lacan, Jacques. *The Seminar of Jacques Lacan, Book VII: The Ethics of Psychoanalysis, 1959–1960*. Translated by Dennis Porter. New York: W. W. Norton, 1992.

———. *The Seminar of Jacques Lacan, Book X: Anxiety, 1962–1963*. Translated by A. R. Price. Cambridge, UK: Polity, 2014.

———. *The Seminar of Jacques Lacan, Book XI: The Four Fundamental Concepts of Psychoanalysis, 1964*. Translated by Alan Sheridan. New York: W. W. Norton, 1978.

———. *The Seminar of Jacques Lacan, Book XVII: The Other Side of Psychoanalysis, 1969–1970*. Translated by Russell Grigg. New York: W. W. Norton, 2007.

———. *The Seminar of Jacques Lacan, Book XX: On Feminine Sexuality, the Limits of Love and Knowledge (Encore), 1972–1972*. Translated by Bruce Fink. New York: W. W. Norton, 1998.

———. *Écrits: A Selection*. Translated by Bruce Fink. New York: W. W. Norton, 2002.

LaCapra, Dominick. *Writing History, Writing Trauma*. Baltimore: Johns Hopkins University Press, 2001.

Lapid, Nadav, dir. *Policeman*. Paris: Bodega Films, 2011.

Latson, Jennifer. "The High-Level Scheming behind Philippe Petit's Twin Tower Tightrope Walk." *Time*, August 7, 2015. http://time.com/3976999/philippe-petit-twin-towers/.

Lee, Chang-dong, dir. *Oasis* (오아시스). Seoul: CJ Entertainment, 2002.

———. *Poetry* (시). Seoul: Next Entertainment World, 2010.

Levine, Caroline. *Forms: Whole, Rhythm, Hierarchy, Network*. Princeton, NJ: Princeton University Press, 2015.

Lu, Zhang, dir. *Dooman River* (두만강). Seoul: Lu Films, 2010.

Lubitsch, Ernst, dir. *That Uncertain Feeling*. Los Angeles: United Artists, 1941.

Malabou, Catherine. *Ontology of the Accident: An Essay on Destructive Plasticity*. Translated by Carolyn Shread. Cambridge: Polity, 2012.

Marks, Laura. *The Skin of the Film*. Durham, NC: Duke University Press, 2000.

Martel, Lucrecia, dir. *The Swamp (La ciénaga)*. Lider Films, 2001.

———. *Zama*. Burbank: Buena Vista International, 2017.

McGowan, Todd. *Capitalism and Desire: The Psychic Cost of Free Markets*. New York: Columbia University Press, 2016.

———. *Enjoying What We Don't Have*. Lincoln: University of Nebraska Press, 2013.

———. *Psychoanalytic Film Theory and the Rules of the Game*. New York: Bloomsbury, 2015.

———. *The Real Gaze: Film Theory after Lacan*. Albany: State University of New York Press, 2007.

McNulty, Tracy. "Demanding the Impossible: Desire and Social Change." *Differences: A Journal of Feminist Cultural Studies* 20, no. 1 (2009): 1–39.

McQueen, Steve, dir. *Hunger*. Paris: Pathé Distribution, 2008.

———. *Widows*. Los Angeles: 20th Century Fox, 2018.

Melville, Jean-Pierre, dir. *Army of Shadows (L'Armée des ombres)*. Paris: Valoria Films, 1969.

Miller, Jacques-Alain. "Suture (Elements of the Logic of the Signifier)." *Screen* 18, no. 4 (1977): 24–34.

———. "To Interpret the Cause: From Freud to Lacan." *Newsletter of the Freudian Field* 3, nos. 1 and 2 (1989): 30–50.

Morrison, Phil, dir. *All Is Bright*. Los Angeles: Anchor Bay Films, 2013.

Moss, Anne Eakin. "The Permeable Screen: Soviet Cinema and the Fantasy of No Limits." *Screen* 59, no. 4 (2018): 420–43.

Mulvey, Laura. "Visual Pleasure and Narrative Cinema." *Screen* 16, no. 3 (1975): 6–18.

Na, Hong-jin, dir. *The Yellow Sea* (황해). Los Angeles: 20th Century Fox, 2010.

National *Gugak* Center, South Korea. Oral History Collections #12. https://www.gugak.go.kr/site/program/board/basicboard/view?currentpage=2&menuid=001003002006&pagesize=10&boardtypeid=26&boardid=1424&lang=ko.

Nemes, László, dir. *Son of Saul* (*Saul fia*). Budapest: Mozinet, 2015.

Neroni, Hilary. "Following the Impossible Road to Female Passion: Psychoanalysis, the Mundane, and the Films of Jane Campion." *Discourse* 34, nos. 2 and 3 (2012): 290–310.

———. *Feminist Film Theory and Cléo 5 to 7*. New York: Bloomsbury, 2016.

Newstapa, "Sorrowful Homecoming." https://www.youtube.com/watch?v=GRmhsulHpLE (part 1), https://www.youtube.com/watch?v=yaI3bdGh8No (part 2).

Nobus, Dany. "Lacan's Science of the Subject: Between Linguistics and Topology." In *The Cambridge Companion to Lacan*, edited by Jean-Michel Rabaté. Cambridge: Cambridge University Press, 2003.

Panahi, Jafar, dir. *The Circle*. Rome: Mikado Film, 2000.

———. *Offside*. New York: Sony Pictures Classics, 2006.

Park, Chan-wook, dir. *Oldboy* (올드보이). Seoul: Show East, 2003.

———. *Thirst*. Universal City, CA: Focus Features, 2009.

Partridge, Tony. "Bong Joon-Ho's *Parasite* Viewed in the Context of Pasolini's *Theorem* and Deleuze's Filmic Theories." In *Parasite: A Philosophical Exploration*, edited by Thorsten Botz-Bornstein and Giannis Stamatellos. Leiden, The Netherlands: Brill (2022).

Paxton, Robert O. *The Anatomy of Fascism*. New York: Alfred A. Knopf, 2004.

Raengo, Alessandra. *Critical Race Theory and Bamboozled*. New York: Bloomsbury, 2016.

Ramsay, Lynne, dir. *Morvern Callar*. Toronto: Alliance Atlantis, 2002.

Reichardt, Kelly, dir. *Meek's Cutoff*. Brooklyn, NY: Oscilloscope Laboratories, 2010.

Rodríguez, Héctor. "Questions of Chinese Aesthetics: Film Form and Narrative Space in the Cinema of King Hu." *Cinema Journal* 38, no. 1 (1998): 73–97.

Rohrwacher, Alice, dir. *Corpo celeste*. Rome: Rai Cinema, 2011.

———. *Happy as Lazzaro* (*Lazzaro felice*). Rome: 01 Distribution, 2018.

Rossellini, Roberto, dir. *Germany Year Zero* (*Germania anno zero*). G.D.B. Film, 1948.

Rushton, Richard. *Deleuze and Lola Montès*. New York: Bloomsbury, 2020.

Ruti, Mari. *The Call of Character: Living a Life Worth Living*. New York: Columbia University Press, 2014.

———. *Distillations: Theory, Ethics, Affect*. New York: Bloomsbury, 2018.

———. *The Ethics of Opting Out: Queer Theory's Defiant Subjects.* New York: Columbia University Press, 2017.
Santner, Eric L. *The Weight of All Flesh: On the Subject-Matter of Political Economy.* Oxford: Oxford University Press, 2016.
Sakai, Naoki. "Theory and Asian Humanity: On the Question of *Humanitas* and *Anthropos*." *Postcolonial Studies* 13, no. 4 (2010): 441–64.
Sakai, Naoki, and Hyon Joo Yoo, eds. *The Trans-Pacific Imagination: Rethinking Boundary, Culture, and Society.* Hackensack, NJ: World Scientific, 2012.
SBS. "Commemorating the 40th Anniversary of the 5.18 Democratization Movement: What Is Her Name?" https://programs.sbs.co.kr/culture/sunmivideo/vod/65035/22000379498.
Schütz, Anton. "The Fading Memory of *Homo non Sacer*." In *The Work of Giorgio Agamben: Law, Literature, Life*, edited by Justin Clemens, Nicholas Heron, and Alex Murray. Edinburgh: Edinburgh University Press, 2008.
Schuster, Aaron. "The Lacan-Foucault Relation: Las Meninas, Sexuality, and the Unconscious." Lecture, Lacan contra Foucault Conference: December 4, 2015. https://www.academia.edu/26368827/The_Lacan_Foucault_Relation_Las_Meninas_Sexuality_and_the_Unconscious.
Sciamma, Céline, dir. *Girlhood (Bande de filles).* Paris: Pyramide Distribution, 2014.
———. *Tomboy.* Paris: Pyramide Distribution, 2011.
Seltzer, Mark. "The Serial Killer as a Type of Person." *The Horror Reader.* Edited by Ken Gelder. London: Routledge, 2000.
Sissako, Abderrahmane, dir. *Timbuktu.* New York: Cohen Media Group, 2014.
Soler, Colette. "The Body in the Teaching of Jacques Lacan." Translated by Lindsay Watson. https://jcfar.org.uk/wp-content/uploads/2016/03/The-Body-in-the-Teaching-of-Jacques-Lacan-Colette-Soler.pdf.
———. "What Does the Unconscious Know about Women?" *Reading Seminar XX: Lacan's Major Work on Love, Knowledge, and Feminine Sexuality.* Edited by Susan Barnard and Bruce Fink. Albany: State University of New York Press, 2002.
Summers-Bremner, Eluned. "Reading, Walking, Mourning: W. G. Sebald's Peripatetic Fictions." *Journal of Narrative Theory* 34, no. 3 (2004): 304–34.
Szifron, Damián, dir. *Wild Tales (Relatos salvajes).* Burbank, CA: Warner Bros. Pictures, 2014.
Thornham, Sue. *Spaces of Women's Cinema: Space, Place and Genre in Contemporary Women's Filmmaking.* New York: Bloomsbury on behalf of The British Film Institute, 2019.
Tomšič, Samo. *The Capitalist Unconscious.* London: Verso, 2015.
Valente, Joe. "Lacan's Marxism, Marxism's Lacan (from Žižek to Althusser)." In *The Cambridge Companion to Lacan*, edited by Jean-Michel Rabaté. Cambridge: Cambridge University Press, 2003.
Varda, Agnès, dir. *Cléo from 5 to 7 (Cléo de 5 à 7).* Paris: Athos Films, 1962.
Verhaeghe, Paul. *Beyond Gender: From Subject to Drive.* New York: Other Press, 2001.
———. *Love in a Time of Loneliness: Three Essays on Drive and Desire.* Translated by Plym Peters and Tony Langham. London: Karnac, 1999.
Villanueva, Vicente, dir. *Toc toc.* Burbank, CA: Warner Bros. Pictures, 2017.

Villeneuve, Denis, dir. *Incendies*. Toronto: Entertainment One, 2010.

———. *Prisoners*. Burbank: Warner Brothers, 2013.

Virilio, Paul, with Bertrand Richard. *The Administration of Fear*. Translated by Ames Hodges. Los Angeles: Semiotext(e), 2012.

von Trier, Lars, dir. *Breaking the Waves*. October Films, 1996.

Wilder, Billy, dir. *Double Indemnity*. Los Angeles: Paramount, 1944.

Williams, Linda. "Film Bodies: Gender, Genre, and Excess." *Film Quarterly* 44, no. 4 (1991): 2–13.

Woman Dong A, Obituary for Bae Eun Shim. January 1, 2022. https://woman.donga.com/3/all/12/3158158/1.

Yedaya, Keren, dir. *Or, My Treasure*. New York: Kino International, 2004.

Yi, Seung-jun, dir. *In the Absence* (부재의기억). New York: Field of Vision, 2018.

Yoo, Hyon Joo. *Cinema at the Crossroads: Nation and the Subject in East Asia*. Lanham, MD: Lexington Books, 2012.

———. Introduction to *South Korean Film*, vols. 1–3, and *South Korean Film*, vol. 3, edited by Hyon Joo Yoo. New York: Bloomsbury, 2021.

Yosef, Raz. "Recycled Wounds: Trauma, Gender, and Ethnicity in Keren Yedaya's *Or, My Treasure*." *Camera Obscura* 72, nos. 24 and 3 (2009): 41–71.

Zanger, Anat. "Women, Border, and Cinema: Israeli Feminine Framing of War." *Feminist Media Studies* 5, no. 3 (2005): 341–57.

Zhang, Yimou, dir. *Ju Dou* (菊豆). Japan, Narita: Daiei, 1990.

Žižek, Slavoj. *Enjoy Your Symptom! Jacques Lacan in Hollywood and Out*. New York: Routledge, 2007.

———. "Femininity between Goodness and Act." *The Symptom* 14 (Summer 2013). https://www.lacan.com/symptom14/feminimity-between.html.

———. *The Fright of Real Tears: Krzysztof Kieślowski between Theory and Philosophy*. London: BFI Publishing, 2001.

———. *How to Read Lacan*. New York: W. W. Norton, 2006.

———. *Looking Awry: An Introduction to Jacques Lacan through Popular Culture*. Cambridge, MA: MIT Press, 1992.

———. "Neighbors and Other Monsters: A Plea for Ethical Violence." In *The Neighbor: Three Inquiries in Political Theology*, edited by Slavoj Žižek, Eric C. Santner, and Kenneth Reinhard. Chicago: University of Chicago Press, 2013.

———. *The Plague of Fantasies*. London: Verso, 2009.

———. "The Real of Sexual Difference." *Reading Seminar XX: Lacan's Major Work on Love, Knowledge, and Feminine Sexuality*. Edited by Susan Barnard and Bruce Fink. Albany: State University of New York Press, 2002.

———. *Tarrying with the Negative: Kant, Hegel, and the Critique of Ideology*. Durham, NC: Duke University Press, 1993.

———. *The Ticklish Subject: The Absent Center of Political Ontology*. New York: Verso, 1999.

———. "With or Without Passion: What's Wrong with Fundamentalism? Part I." https://www.lacan.com/zizpassion.htm.

Zupančič, Alenka. "Ethics and Tragedy in Lacan." In *The Cambridge Companion to Lacan*, edited by Jean-Michel Rabaté. Cambridge: Cambridge University Press, 2003.
———. *Ethics of the Real: Kant, Lacan*. London: Verso, 2000.
———. *The Odd One In: On Comedy*. Cambridge, MA: MIT Press, 2008.

Index

abjection: abject body, 91–92, 93–94; emancipation through, 91; family and, 102; generic terrain of, 105–11; historical contingencies and, 107; horror and, 96; jouissance and, 105; the Real and, 107; in Jia Zhangke's work, 106; in *Still Life*, 93–94; in *Thirst*, 93, 96, 104

About Elly (Farhadi), 150–51

accents, 9, 210n20

aesthetics, 51

affect theory, 176, 190

Agamben, Giorgio: bare life, 195; the camp for, 79, 90–91; *homo sacer*, 79–80, 84–85; im-potential, 104; non-state, 103; on space, 4, 93; whatever singularity, 80. *See also* bare life

The Age of Innocence (Scorsese), 126

Aguirre: The Wrath of God (Herzog), 37–38

Akin, Fatih: *Head-On*, 164–66

Ali: Fear Eats the Soul (Fassbinder), 103

"all": "not-all," 14, 50; subjectivity and, 69

allegory, 89, 109, 166, 175

All Is Bright (Morrison), 128–29

An, Jinsoo, 77

Another Froggy Evening (Warner Brothers), 66

Antichrist (von Trier), 54, 69

Antigone, 91, 96

antihumanism, 107

Antonioni, Michelangelo: *Blow-Up*, 15–16

apocalyptic chronotopes, 142

Appiah, Kwame Anthony, 76

Arendt, Hannah: *Eichmann in Jerusalem*, 30–31

Army of Shadows (Melville), 202

arrivant (Derrida), 86

atemporality, 126, 139, 140, 159, 161, 167

audience's scopic drive, 136

auteurship, 173, 212n6

automation, 8

The Babadook (Kent), 185–86, 199, 200

Badiou, Alain: on cures in psychoanalysis, 145; ethics for, 86; on the event, 125, 191–92, 206; on love, 125; nonliteral law for, 111; on Paul, 191–92, 226n93; on the Symbolic order, 81; on truth, 192; on violence, 149–50

bare life, 79–80, 81, 91–92, 103, 193, 195, 201, 202, 205, 206

Batman Begins (Nolan), 154–55

Benjamin, Walter, 97, 149–50

Bhabha, Homi K., 47

Bicycle Thieves (De Sica), 109

Bigelow, Kathryn: *The Hurt Locker*, 137

biopolitics, 58, 92, 105–6

The Bitter Tears of Petra von Kant (Fassbinder), 31

Black bodies, 21, 183, 188

Blackness, 125, 183

blitzkrieg, 68

blood: democracy and, 194; in *Cuties*, 25; in *Pietà*, 90; in *Thirst*, 95, 97, 102, 104; in *Time of the Wolf*, 143

Blow-Up (Antonioni), 15–16

bodies: of ethnic Korean men, 147, 149; queer female bodies, 171

bodily drive: death drive and, 149; as destructive, 150; the drive and, 5; to emancipatory drive, 113, 132, 134, 149, 150; jouissance of, 129; nation-state and, 141–42, 149; queer bodily drive, 129; repetition and, 125; signification (chain of) and, 116; trauma going beyond, 140–41; in *Get Out*, 116–17

bodily jouissance, 117, 120

the body: abject body, 91–92, 96; as an "a," 95; body without organs (Deleuze), 58;

boundaries of, 39–40; cohesiveness of, 69; commodification of, 157; as commodity, 52; desiring body (Foucault), 57, 58; destruction of, 55, 95, 98; the drive and, 5; eyes, 57, 58–59; German body, 92; heteronormative body, 57; of *homo sacer* (Agamben), 79; impossibility of, 58; Jewish body, 92; jouissance and, 42, 184; as kernel, 43, 58; for Lacan, 56, 57, 73, 92, 113; as language, 92; masculine body, 63; organ without a body (Žižek), 58; otherness and, 43; as perceptual surface, 147; phantasmatic dimensions, 56–57; psychoanalytic body (Lacan), 56, 57–58; regulation of, 121; as sacrifice, 204; signifier and, 42, 73; social body, 102; subjectivity and, 42; Symbolic order and, 42, 95; topography and, 123; transformations of, 102; transgender body, 40, 57; vision and, 176; wholeness of, 95. *See also* bodily jouissance; Real body
body genre films, 104
Bollaín, Icíar: *Even the Rain*, 22–23
Bong Joon-ho: *Parasite*, 170–71, 178–79
Bosch, Hieonymus: *The Garden of Earthly Delights*, 59
bourgeois society, 53, 88, 114
Breaking the Waves (von Trier), 43, 54, 55, 213n23
Buck-Morss, Susan, 76, 77
Buñuel, Luis: *Un chien andalou*, 57, 199
Byun, Young-joo: *The Murmuring*, 197–99, 225n78

Caché (Haneke), 113–14, 115, 120, 121–22
camera, eye of, 58–59
the camp (Agamben), 79, 90–91, 92
Campion, Jane, 24
Candlelight Revolution, 208
capital, 180, 194
capitalism: body politic and, 105; death drive of, 207; desire and, 179, 209n11; emancipatory drive and, 137; global capitalism, 27, 45, 46, 76, 194–95; jouissance and, 143–44; modernity and, 99; the Real of, 71, 137, 157, 170; subject of, 121; temporality and, 109, 218n75; in *Parasite*, 170
Carpenter, John: *The Thing*, 185, 199
Caruth, Cathy, 139, 167, 216n26
Cazdyn, Eric, 51–52, 59, 64
Chakravarty, Dipesh, 179–80
Un chien andalou (Buñuel), 57, 199
China: Korean people in, 142; neo-imperialism, 75, 169–70; North/South Korea and, 35, 151–52; Three Gorges Dam project, 93; in *Dooman River*, 152
Choi, Jinhee, 156
Choi Dong-hoon: *Woochi*, 46
Chow, Rey, 192
chronotope(s): apocalyptic chronotopes, 142; creation of by subjects, 113; desire and, 115; of the drive, 115, 120, 159; of emancipatory drive, 119, 124, 126–37, 142, 146–62; entering a new, 141; of existence, 142; melodrama, 160–61; of nation-state, 120, 135–36, 147–48
chronotopic North, 119, 157
Chung Ji-young: *Nambugun*, 148–49, 160–61
cinema: life vs., 24; the past and, 28–29; politics of, 50–51, 169
cinema of the Real: generally, 3, 36, 40, 156; as cinema of failure, 69; depth of, 67; emancipatory drive and, 3, 17, 118–19; feminine cinema and, 163; feminine jouissance and, 10–16; form and, 33; life drive and, 24; organs in, 57; the Other's drive and, 16–24; poetic shock and, 24, 71; the Real and, 13, 28, 164; the Real body and, 72, 74, 176–77; the Real of subjectivity in, 123; shock and, 158; spectacle in, 52–53; subject in, 42, 57, 113; transnationally, 37; trauma and, 77; unconscious and, 66
cinematic form, 50, 51
cinematic space, 24, 108, 145, 156, 164, 168, 169
cinematic spectacle, 147–48, 154–55, 170
cinematic time, 156
The Circle (Panahi), 134–36
Cléo from 5 to 7 (Varda), 189–90
Coin Locker Girl (Han), 157

Cold War, 28, 46
collective trauma, 103
colonialism: colonial mimicry, 47; Japan and, 64, 195, 203–4; lost objects and, 78; modernity and, 45–46, 49, 78; trauma of, 188; in *White Material*, 177–78. *See also* postcolonialism
color: high-saturation color, 54, 65, 197; low-saturation color, 142; split (black-and-white, color), 62; in *Time of the Wolf,* 142
comedy, 30, 210n19
comfort women, 163–64, 180, 193–99, 201–2, 204
commodities, 2, 52, 143–44, 192
communal trauma, 83
communism, 157
concentration camps, 92
Confucianism, 175
constructivism, 18, 62
continuity editing, 55
Copjec, Joan, 5, 38, 91, 96, 100, 120
Corpo celeste (Rohrwacher), 86–87
cosmopolitanism, 169
Creed, Barbara, 96
cultural objects, 182
the cut: desire and, 18; Lacanian vs. Foucauldian, 79; language and, 77, 203; linguistic cut, 78; nature and, 10; of our being, 168; wounding and, 99, 215n57
Cuties (Doucouré), 24–26

Dancer in the Dark (von Trier), 54–55
Dardenne, Jean-Pierre: *Rosetta,* 53
Dardenne, Luc: *Rosetta,* 53
death and dying: biological death, 64, 86, 88; into life, 85, 91, 102; Otherness and, 144, 152; second death (Lacan), 43, 88, 91; space and, 207; of student activists, 206–7; in *Blow-Up,* 15; in *Breaking the Waves,* 43; in *Dooman River,* 152, 155, 158–59; in *Double Indemnity,* 120; in *Europa,* 62; in *Hunger,* 64; in *In the Absence,* 207; in *In the Realm of the Senses,* 65; in *Namburgan,* 148–49; in *Oasis,* 83; in *Oldboy,* 45; in *Poetry,* 85; in *Son of Saul,* 205; in *Sympathy for Mr. Vengeance,* 158; in *Thirst,* 104; in *Time of the Wolf,* 143; in *White Material,* 178; in *Wild Tales,* 7–8; in *The Yellow Sea,* 147, 149, 157–58. *See also* homo sacer (Agamben)
death drive: definitions, 1; absence and, 181; appearance of, 189; bodily drive and, 149; boundaries and, 11; of capitalism, 207; desire and, 201; to emancipatory drive, 168, 176; of imperial subject, 201; jouissance of, 128, 185, 200; for Lacan, 130, 145; life drive and, 4, 12, 28, 167, 181, 202–3; of nation-state, 202, 208; *objet a* and, 122; of the Other, 7; subject's entrance to, 181; trajectories, 7
de Certeau, Michel, 110
de Lauretis, Teresa, 50, 65
Deleuze, Gilles, 27, 28–29, 58
Denis, Claire: *White Material,* 177–78, 184
Denny, David, 137
depaysement, 173, 184
Derrida, Jacques, 86
De Sica, Vittorio: *Bicycle Thieves,* 109
desire: capitalism and, 179, 209n11; chronotopes and, 115; circling around site of, 139; for commodities, 2; the cut and, 18; death drive and, 201; vs. drive, 129–30; economy of, 146; ethics of, 127–28; feminine vs. masculine, 65; imperialism and, 180; the kernel of, 18; lack and, 50; law of, 19–20; narratives around, 41; for the nation, 148–9; nationalism and, 146; nation-state and, 119; *objet a* and, 114; objects and, 1–2, 4–5, 128, 146, 161–62, 186; the Other and, 1, 19, 125, 144; phallic jouissance and, 46, 65; the Real of, 53; satisfaction of, 55, 139; space and, 127; Symbolic order and, 13, 17; transgender desire, 57; verbalization of, 18; wounding and, 72–73, 125; Žižek on, 118
diegesis, 36–37, 40–41, 53, 65–66
disability, 81, 82–83, 85
disintegration of individuality, 56
disjointure, 116
divine violence, 97, 149

Doane, Mary Ann, 50
Dolar, Mladen, 8–9, 210n19
Doorman River (Zhang), 142, 151–52, 155–56, 158–59
Double Indemnity (Wilder), 120
Doucouré, Maïmouna: *Cuties,* 24–26
dreams, 181–82
the drive: the body and, 5; chronology of, 172; chronotope of, 115; as death drive, 209n4; vs. desire, 129–30; inauguration of, 67; for Lacan, 6, 119; of the Other, 6, 12, 19, 23, 134–35, 139; perverse side of, 137; Žižek on, 11–12

Edelman, Lee, 128, 129
Edison, Thomas, 52
Eggers, Robert: *The Lighthouse,* 199, 200, 201
Eichmann in Jerusalem (Arendt), 30–31
Eisenstein, Paul, 48, 125, 131, 134, 139, 193, 203, 205
Eisenstein, Sergei, 164
The Element of Crime (von Trier), 59–61, 62, 66–67
emancipation: feminine jouissance and, 14; the gaze and, 115; jouissance and, 170; language and, 26; politics and, 115, 184; politics of subjectivity and, 115; universal feminine and, 199–208
emancipatory drive: definitions, 2; bodily drive to, 113, 132, 134, 149, 150; capitalism and, 137; chronotope of, 119, 124, 126–37, 142, 146–62; cinema of the Real and, 3, 17, 118–19; death drive to, 168, 176; descriptions of, 3, 125–26; ethics of, 127, 139, 143, 151; feminine jouissance and, 119; feminine subjects and, 123; freedom and, 136, 139; history and, 137–46; in horror films, 101; life drive and, 167–68; in local context, 207; mathematics as language of, 187–88; moving to, 23, 132, 134, 149, 150, 168, 176; *objet a* and, 122; object of, 119–20; the Other and, 2; as political principle, 119; politics of, 120; repetition and, 144, 145; satisfaction of, 146; somantic disjointure and, 121–26, 161; subject and, 97–98, 107, 111, 116; survival, 167, 168; temporality and, 162; traumatic Real and, 141; universal feminine subject and, 16
emancipatory possibility, 91, 96
emergence of the Real, 143
empty space, 181
enjoyment, 17, 97, 98, 104, 115
Entre ses mains (Fontaine), 122–23
enunciation, 18, 19, 174, 178
ethics: of desire, 127–28; of emancipatory drive, 127, 139, 143, 151; of feminine jouissance, 81; human subject of, 149–50; the Other and, 37, 81, 86, 108, 125; subjectivity and, 31, 142; universality of, 81, 168–69
ethnic nationalism, 76
Europa (von Trier), 61, 68
Europe, 59–60, 61–62, 68, 135, 165–66
the event, 125, 191–92, 201, 206
Even the Rain (Bollaín), 22–23
Everybody Knows (Farhadi), 151
excrement, 63
existence, chronotope of, 142
existentialism, 37
Ex Machina (Garland), 201
extimacy, 179
extraterritoriality and territoriality, 93
eyes, 57, 58–59, 62

failure, 60, 69–70
family: abjection and, 102; disintegration of, 143; disruptions to order of, 103; fort-da, 145; roles in, 100; women in, 150
Fan, Victor, 107–8
fantasy, 3, 187
Farhadi, Asghar: *About Elly,* 150–51; *Everybody Knows,* 151
fascism, 31–32, 124. *See also* Nazism; South Korea
Fassbinder, Rainer Werner: *Ali: Fear Eats the Soul,* 103; *The Bitter Tears of Petra von Kant,* 31
father: child's admonishment of, 139; dreams of, 77–78; language of the, 183;

letter of, 11; name of, 116, 117. *See also* Law of the Father
fear of the Other, 56–57
the feminine: criminalization of, 135; emancipatory drive and, 123; embodiment of, 26; feminine desire, 101; feminine gaze, 171; feminine subjectivity, 13, 71; feminine universality, 165, 166, 171; gender identity (as not tied to), 13, 163, 220n16; life drive as, 201; materiality of, 176; as monstrous, 101, 106; point of view and, 53; resistance and, 50; as signifier, 194; speech of, 189; as truth (of masculine), 100. *See also* universal feminine subject
feminine body, 43–44, 78–79, 82, 89, 91, 122
feminine cinema: defined, 163, 170; emancipatory politics of, 184; jouissance and, 182–83; space and, 163–77, 180, 183; topology of, 175–76, 184; trauma and, 33; visual language, 171; voice in, 174–75
feminine jouissance: appearance of, 177; cinema of the Real and, 10–16; destructiveness of, 101–2; as disrupting time-space, 54; emancipation and, 14; emancipatory drive and, 119; ethics of, 81; gender binary and, 63, 96, 104; horror and, 64; ideological fantasy and, 49; lack and, 46–47, 64; language and, 14, 32; Law of the Father and, 25–26, 64, 102; nonbelonging of, 104; objects and, 72–73, 100; ontological status, 54; the Other and, 178; Otherness of, 74; patriarchy and, 54, 102; vs. phallic jouissance, 13, 17, 47, 89–90, 100; phallus and, 26; the Real and, 174; Real body and, 101, 110; as Real of our drive, 208; rejection of (by society), 98; spectacle and, 58; subjectivity and, 170, 190–91; the world according to, 63–66; wounding and, 100; in *Blow-Up*, 16; in *Breaking the Waves*, 55; in *Medea*, 54; in *Thirst*, 96
feminine pas-tout (Lacan), 50
femininity: normative expectations, 102; performativity of, 25; race and, 189; shame and, 194, 198; signification and, 197; white femininity, 189
feminist critiques of film, 172–73
fetishism, 47, 52
film theory, Lacanian, 40–41
Fink, Bruce, 32, 99, 111n2, 117, 215n2
Fontaine, Anne: *Entre ses mains*, 122–23
Foreign Correspondent (Hitchcock), 41
form: cinema of the Real and, 33; cinematic form, 50, 51; interiority and, 54–55; the Real and, 52–53; in South Korean cinema, 76–77; as transgressive drive, 55
fort-da (Freud), 145
Foucault, Michel, 57, 58, 91, 102
framing, 15, 173
freedom, 1, 8, 20, 139, 205
Freud, Sigmund, 5, 77, 139, 145, 167, 202
Frey, Mattias, 156
The Front Line (Jang), 35, 36, 137–40, 141–42, 160–61

gangster genre B movies, 146
gaps in subjectivity, 185–86
The Garden of Earthly Delights (Bosch), 59
Garland, Alex: *Ex Machina*, 201
the gaze: emancipation and, 115; as entrance to the Real, 115; feminine gaze, 171; field of vision and, 114; for Lacan, 77, 219n2; medical gaze, 91; the Other and, 20, 133; painting and, 132–33; politics of, 122; the real gaze, 62; shattering of subjectivity and, 114; sound as, 22, 53, 174; of subaltern, 122
gender: binary (and jouissance), 63, 104, 220n16; gender roles, 100; patriarchy and, 82, 106; subjectivity as gendered, 173
gender identity: as fantasy, 14; phallic signifier and, 39; Symbolic order and, 39–40
genre films, 28, 76–77, 103–4
geopolitics, 75
Germany, 56, 61–62, 164
Germany Year Zero (Rossellini), 153
Girlhood (Sciamma), 171
global capitalism, 27, 45, 46, 76, 194–95

god, 23, 48, 73
Godard, Jean-Luc, 10
Gondry, Michel: *Mood Indigo*, 183
The Good, the Bad, the Weird (Kim), 153–54, 155
The Great Battle (Kim), 157
Gwangju Uprising, 27, 194–95, 225n72

Haitian revolution, 76
Han, Byung-Chul, 4–5
The Handmaiden (Park), 46, 47
Haneke, Michael: *Caché*, 113–14, 115, 120, 121–22; *The Piano Teacher*, 3; *Time of the Wolf*, 142–43, 144, 149
Han Jun-hee: *Coin Locker Girl*, 157
Happy as Lazzaro (Rohrwacher), 86, 87–88
haptics, 176, 184
hard kernel, 141
Harvey, David, 168–69
haunting, 61
Head-On (Akin), 164–66
Hegel, Georg Wilhelm Friedrich, 190
hegemony, resistance to, 127
Herzog, Werner: *Aguirre: The Wrath of God*, 37–38
heteronormativity, 57
historical trauma, 28, 46, 49, 77–78, 82, 140, 142
historiography: contradictions of, 18; creation of new, 123; impossibility of, 60; methods, 76
history: displacement with pastiche, 49; emancipatory drive and, 137–46; historical contingencies, 107; memory of, 11; the Real of, 27, 31, 114; space and, 179–80; trauma and, 9, 46, 49, 68, 77–78, 82, 142, 166
Hitchcock, Alfred: blot, 40–41; *Foreign Correspondent*, 41; *North by Northwest*, 41; *Psycho*, 58
Holocaust. *See* Nazism
home, 167, 180, 181
homo sacer: bare life of, 79–80, 92; biopolitics and, 105–6; body of, 79, 91, 92; Jewish body as, 92; law and, 82, 84–85, 102

Hong Sang-soo: *Nobody's Daughter Haewon*, 53–54
Horkheimer, Max, 46
horror: abjection and, 96; feminine jouissance and, 64; the Other and, 186
horror films: all films as, 176; jouissance and, 64, 103, 105; monstrosity in, 101, 104, 106; the Thing in, 72; unconscious and, 176
Hu, King, 36–37
Humanitas/Anthropos binary, 75–76
Hunger (McQueen), 63–64, 68–69
Hur Jin-ho: *The Last Princess*, 175
The Hurt Locker (Bigelow), 137
hypermasculinity, 43

"I," 48, 72, 156, 190
ideation, 57
identification, 48, 66
identitarian violence, 165
identity: as commodity, 192; European identity, 68; names and, 203; vs. subjectivity, 190
ideology: feminine jouissance and, 49; fetishistic disavowal and, 48; freedom from, 134; ideological realm, 56; language and, 4; *méconnaissance* as sustaining, 48–49; of nationalism, 118; resistance to, 145; subject formation and, 192; of subjectivity, 133
image, fetishization of, 52
imaginary identification, 66
Imamura Shohei: *The Pornographers*, 59
immortality, 86, 125
imperialism: desire and, 180; jouissance and, 201–2; neo-imperialism, 45–46, 75, 169, 195; phantasmatic objects of, 56; the Real of, 38, 180; space and, 169
impossibility: of historiography, 60; of subjectivity, 145
Incendies (Villeneuve), 124
individuality, 56, 154
individual trauma, 103
industrialization, 61
inhuman, becoming, 101
inhuman kernel, 69
interiority, 54–55, 141, 153, 158–59

intersubjectivity, 10
intertextuality, 21
In the Absence (Yi), 207
In the Realm of the Senses (Oshima), 52, 64–66
invisibility of the Real, 89
Irreversible (Noé), 67
The Isle (Kim), 89–90

Jameson, Fredric, 104–5
Jang Hoon: *The Front Line*, 35, 36, 137–40, 141–42, 160–61; *A Taxi Driver*, 27–28
Jang Jae-hyun: *The Priests*, 131–32
Japan: cinema, 51, 59; colonialism and, 46, 47, 51, 64, 195, 203–4; Korean women in, 193, 195; pornography in, 51
Jeon, Joseph Jonghyun, 213n28
Jeong, Seung-Hoon, 104–5, 212n6
Jewish people: body of, 92, 133–34; *homo sacer* and, 92; Jewishness, 21; ontological lack, 202–3; *Eichmann in Jerusalem*, 30–31; in *Europa*, 61; in *Or*, 43; Ernst Lubitsch, 30
Jia Zhangke, 94; individuation and deindividuation in work of, 107–8; modernity and abjection in work of, 106; worldview in work of, 107; *Still Life*, 93–94, 99–100, 106–10
Joseonjok gangsters, 157, 158
jouissance: abjection and, 105; ambivalent paths to, 95; of bodily drive, 129; the body and, 42, 184; body as site for production of, 42; capitalism and, 143–44; of death drive, 128, 185, 200; emancipation and, 170; emotion and, 31–32; enjoyment and, 104; excessiveness of, 43; feminine cinema and, 182–83; feminine space of, 171; of feminine subjectivity, 13; feminine subject of, 105; gender and, 73; as hidden, 129; horror films and, 105; imperialism and, 201–2; as kernel, 42; kernel of, 43; of law, 31; life drive and, 9, 10, 128; manifestations of, 118; objects and, 11; obtaining, 11; of the Other, 57, 179; paltry (non) end for, 97–98; patriarchal social order and, 102; protection from, 186; public space and, 129; of the Real body, 82; representations of, 199–200; returning (act of) and, 126; signifier and, 42, 73, 185; social body and, 102; subversive jouissance, 137; surplus jouissance, 143–44; Symbolic order confronted by, 43, 81; traversing the fantasy, 3; visual depictions of, 41; in *Parasite*, 170–71; in *The Babadook*, 199. See also bodily jouissance; feminine jouissance; phallic jouissance
Ju Dou (Zhang), 196, 197
Juhn Jai-hong: *Poongsan*, 161

Kang Je-kyu: *Tae Guk Gi: The Brotherhood of War*, 159–60
Kang Yoon-seong: *The Outlaws*, 157
Kant, Immanuel, 30, 168–69
Karatani, Kojin, 193, 203
Kent, Jennifer: *The Babadook*, 185–86, 199, 200; *Nightingale*, 188
the kernel: generally, 41; of being, 74, 81, 165; the body as, 58; of desire, 18; as excess, 80; hard kernel, 141; haunting presence of, 42; inhuman kernel, 69; jouissance as, 42; lack of phallus and, 42; nation-state and, 104; of Otherness, 82, 158; as signifier, 216n4; subjectivity and, 44; Symbolic order and, 66; trauma and, 42
Kim Gwang-shik: *The Great Battle*, 157
Kim Jee-woon: *The Good, the Bad, the Weird*, 153–54, 155
Kim Ki-duk, 88, 90, 91; *Time*, 161–62; *The Isle*, 89–90; *Pietà*, 89, 90
Kim Seok-yoon: *My Liberation Notes*, 37
knowing: regime of, 196; through looking, 159
Korea: Japanese imperialism in, 157, 203–4; North vs. South, 35, 149, 160, 161; Yi dynasty, 175. See also South Korea
Korean people: anxiety around Otherness, 156; male bodies, 147
Korean War, 21, 78, 137, 148, 159
Krips, Henry, 47–48
Kristeva, Julia, 91, 96

244 | Index

labor: of Black body, 183; invisibility of, 71; migrant workers, 94
Lacan, Jacques: automation vs. tyche, 8; the body for, 56, 57, 73, 92, 113; the cut, 79; death drive, 130, 145; desire for, 144; drive for, 6, 119; extimacy, 179; father in work of, 11; *feminine pas-tout*, 50; film theory and, 3; on the gaze, 77, 219n2; on jouissance's terrors, 129; on language, 209n4; on location of subjects, 19; mathematics for, 176, 182; *méconnaissance*, 48–49; on objects, 59; on the Other, 155; on phallic jouissance, 215n3; quilting point, 45, 219n5; the Real for, 66; second death, 43, 88, 91; signifier as material cause, 42; on speech, 32; subject for, 116; subjectivity for, 117; Symbolic order for, 1; on topology, 175; visual drive, 20; women for, 55, 100
LaCapra, Dominick, 17–18
lack: desire and, 50; feminine jouissance and, 64, 73; objects and, 1, 146; the Real and, 201; subjecthood and, 13–14; subjectivity and, 117; wounding and, 117
Lady Vengeance (Park), 106
language: accents, 9, 210n20; acquisition of, 131; bodily drive and, 116; the body as, 92; the cut and, 77, 203; emancipation and, 26; of the Father, 183; feminine jouissance and, 14, 32; freedom and, 205; ideology and, 4; life drive and, 187; of nationalism, 175; *objet a* and, 186, 199; the Other and, 18–19, 32; the Real and, 72; seduction in, 183; signification and, 1, 18, 181–82; Symbolic order and, 182; trauma and, 77
Lapid, Nadav: *Policeman*, 133–34
The Last Princess (Hur), 175
law: of desire, 19–20, 111; *homo sacer* and, 79–80; jouissance of, 31; justification before, 30; Naziism and, 31; nonliteral law (Badiou), 111; of phallic jouissance, 82; vs. politics, 97; the Real of the, 138, 146; social space and, 90; somatic inscription of, 123; of the state, 91, 96; subjection to, 79; violence and, 97

Law of the Father, 102; feminine jouissance and, 25–26, 64, 102; feminine universality and, 171; inclusion in, 57; organization of, 58, 73, 96; Real of masculine desire and, 45; Symbolic order and, 29; universal feminine subject and, 204–5; in Kim Ki-duk's films, 88; *Oldboy* and, 106. *See also* father
Lee Chang-dong: *Oasis*, 81–85, 174–75; *Poetry*, 81, 85–86
Levinas, Emmanuel, 8, 104
life: affirmation of, 5; cinema vs., 24; productivity of, 105; trauma (continuing from), 144
life drive, 119, 128; generally, 11–12; cinema of the Real and, 24; death drive and, 4, 12, 28, 167, 181, 202–3; emancipatory drive and, 167–68; emergence, 9; entering into, 5, 186; as feminine, 201; jouissance and, 9, 10, 128; language and, 187; the Other and, 9, 10, 17; trajectories, 6, 8, 168; as transformational, 9; universal mode of being and, 10; women as subjects of, 198; in *Zama*, 191
life-drive jouissance, 128
The Lighthouse (Eggers), 199, 200, 201
linear perspective, 38
linear time, 141
linguistic order, 1, 28, 100, 132, 167, 175, 181
linguistic subject, 12, 72
the local and universality, 169
logos, 213n28
long-take shots, 43, 198
looking: diegetic space and, 65–66; feminine position, 53, 54; knowing through, 159; masculine position, 44; the Other and, 65; point of view and, 24, 114, 132–33; power of, 15; the Real and, 52, 67; refusals, 53
loss, 5, 159; wounding and, 99, 141–42
Lubitsch, Ernst: *That Uncertain Feeling*, 29–30

madness, 28
magical realism, 87
Malabou, Catherine, 216n26
Manchuria, 75, 142, 153–54, 156, 157

man vs. woman, 73
Martel, Lucrecia: *Zama*, 186–87, 191
martyrdom, 204
the masculine: gender identity, 13, 163, 220n16; hypermasculine entities, 43; masculine body, 63; masculine subjectivity, 45, 50, 100; masculine temporality, 173; position of looking, 44
materiality: of feminine, 176; nation-state and, 110; of penis, 64; of the Real, 110, 166; of space, 84
mathematics, 176, 182, 187–88, 189, 191
McGowan, Todd: on capitalism, 209n11; on desire, 41, 50; on the drive, 5, 6, 126; on fetishism, 48; on freedom, 139; on law, 205; movies as horror movies, 176; on singularity, 203; on subjects, 125, 131, 134, 146, 193
McNulty, Tracy, 1
McQueen, Steve, 63; *Hunger*, 63–64, 68–69; *Widows*, 124–25
méconnaissance (Lacan), 48–49
Medea (von Trier), 54
mediation, 9–10
medical gaze, 91
Meek's Cutoff (Reichardt), 173
melancholy, 159–60
melodrama, 103, 148, 159–60, 190
Melville, Jean-Pierre: *Army of Shadows*, 202; *Le samouraï*, 103
memory: of history, 11; national memory-making, 78
metaphor, 18
metonymy, 18, 19
migrant workers, 94, 106
Miller, Jacques-Alain, 145, 209n4
mimesis, 47
mirror stage, 48
modernity: capitalist modernity, 99; cartography of, 156; colonial modernity, 45–46, 49, 78; fear of, 61; as geographical boundary, 157; vs. premodernity, 94; remoteness and nonbelonging of, 54; shock of, 147; subjectivity and, 156; trauma of, 94; in Jia's work, 106

monstrosity, 95–101; in horror films, 104, 106; of jouissance's manifestation, 118; of Otherness, 8, 21; sublime monstrosity, 147; of the Thing, 200
montage, 165
Mood Indigo (Gondry), 183
Morrison, Phil: *All Is Bright*, 128–29
Morvern Callar (Ramsay), 174
Mulvey, Laura, 66
The Murmuring (Byun), 197–99, 225n78
My Liberation Notes (Kim), 37

Na Hong-jin: *The Wailing*, 64; *The Yellow Sea*, 146–47, 149
Nambugun (Chung), 148–49, 160–61
names, 20–21, 203, 204
narrative cinema, 40, 44, 55, 60, 65–66, 122, 148, 151–52, 153, 172, 184
the nation: bodily drive and, 141–42; desire for, 148–49; landscape of, 146, 149; national body, 51–52; national cinemas, 101–5; national subjectivity, 59, 146; national subjects, 148; national trauma, 105; as phallus, 204; the Real of, 35–36, 51–52; Symbolic order and, 78, 167; teleology of, 146; unconscious of, 166
nationalism: ethnic nationalism, 76; ideology of, 118; language of, 175; law of desire and, 146; psychic aspects, 98
national trauma, 49, 105
nation-state: abject Real body and, 88–94; bodily drive and, 148–50; body politic and, 104, 105; cartography of, 92–93, 94; chronotope of, 120, 135–36, 147; death drive of, 202, 208; desire and, 119; destruction by, 133; Holocaust and, 92; the kernel and, 104; in Korea, 78; materiality and, 110; oppression and, 81–82; the Other of, 140; patriarchy of, 73, 74; Real body and, 80–81; the Real of, 108, 138; as regulating the body, 121; social body and, 150; space of, 92–93, 95, 103; subjectivity and, 133–34; Symbolic order and, 93, 149; unification of, 160. *See also* China; South Korea
Nazism: destruction of symbols, 12; *homo sacer* and, 92; imaginary of, 78–79;

racial identity under, 56; resistance to, 61–62; *Eichmann in Jerusalem*, 30–31; in *Army of Shadows*, 202; in *Son of Saul*, 205–6
negative politics, 105
Nemes, Laszlo: *Son of Saul*, 205, 206
neo-imperialism, 45–46, 75, 169, 195
Neroni, Hilary, 24
New World (Park), 158
Nightingale (Kent), 188
Night of the Living Dead (Romero), 44
Nobody's Daughter Haewon (Hong), 53–54
Noé, Gaspar: *Irreversible*, 67
Nolan, Christopher: *Batman Begins*, 154–55
nonbelonging, 104, 157–58
North by Northwest (Hitchcock), 41
Northeast Project of the Chinese Academy of Social Sciences, 75
North Korea and China, 151–52
nostalgia, 141–42
"not-all": vs. "all," 14, 50

Oasis (Lee), 81–85, 174–75
object petit a: impossibility of obtaining, 15; as incidental object, 118
objects: colonization and, 78; connectivity and, 109; cultural objects, 182; desire and, 1–2, 4–5, 128, 146, 161–62, 186; of emancipatory drive, 119–20; feminine jouissance and, 100; fragmented objects, 63; jouissance and, 11; lack and, 1, 146; lost objects, 159, 160; as meaningful, 114–15; melodrama and, 148; misrecognition of, 47–48; *objet a* and, 131; partial objects, 122, 127, 128–29, 130, 131, 144; phantasmatic objects, 56, 118; the Real and, 40–41, 59; Real object, 73–74; space and, 130; stolen, 78; subject and, 130–31; sublimation of, 98; sublime objects, 220n31; uncanny objects, 114, 185; unsatisfactory objects, 118; war and, 148; wholeness and, 5; in *Still Life*, 99–100
objet a: cathexis to, 69; death drive and, 122; desire and, 114; emancipatory drive and, 122; encounters with, 199–200; *fort-da* and, 145; historical trauma and, 77–78; impossibility of possession, 65; language and, 186, 199; as lost, 159; objects and, 131; obtaining, 126, 133, 134; phallus as, 41; phantasmatic possession of, 115; the Real and, 72; Real body and, 73, 74; relationship to (forming anew), 141; as singularity, 203; subjectivity and, 78; temporality and, 126; visualization of, 199; Žižek on, 118
Ode to My Father (Yoon), 78
Offside (Panahi), 39
Oldboy (Park), 44–45, 106, 213n28
One Froggy Evening (Warner Brothers), 66
ontology, 24, 107, 118
oppression and nation-state, 81–82
Or, My Treasure (Yedaya), 43–44
Orientalism, 75
Oshima Nagisa: *In the Realm of the Senses*, 52, 64–66
the Other: anxiety about, 44; big Other (One Man), 6, 24–25, 28, 30, 32, 73, 74, 106, 179; chronotope of the drive of, 120; cinema of the Real and, 16–24; closeness of, 155; death drive of, 7; desire and, 1, 19, 125, 144; destruction of (enjoyment for), 79; drive of, 6, 12, 19, 23, 134–35, 139; emancipatory drive and, 2; ethics and, 37, 81, 86, 108, 125; ethnic identity as, 43, 56, 61, 157; fantasy and, 187; fear of, 56–57; feminine jouissance and, 178; freedom and, 8, 20; the gaze and, 20, 133; horror and, 186; immortality of, 86; jouissance of, 57, 179; language and, 18–19, 32; life drive and, 9, 10, 17; looking and, 65; love and, 125; as marginal, 81; Muslim Other, 56; of nation-state, 140; the Real and, 84–85; relationship with, 5, 130; the self and, 104; subjectivity of, 18, 19; touch of, 185; trauma and, 35–36, 141
Otherness: appearance of, 144; the body and, 43; death and, 144, 152; as excess, 155; of feminine jouissance, 74; interiority and, 141; the kernel of, 82, 158; monstrosity of, 8, 21; as overwhelming,

144; racial Otherness, 103; shock of, 160; trauma and, 139
The Outlaws (Kang), 157

pain, 69–70, 190
painting, 38, 132–33, 135–36, 219n2
Panahi, Jafar: *The Circle*, 134–36; *Offside*, 39
Parasite (Bong), 170–71, 178–79
Park Chan-wook: abjection in work, 105; *The Handmaiden*, 46, 47; *Oldboy*, 44–45, 106, 213n28; *Lady Vengeance*, 106; *Sympathy for Mr. Vengeance*, 105, 158; *Thirst*, 93, 94, 95–98, 100–101, 104, 105, 107, 110; *Vengeance* trilogy, 105
Park Hoon-jung: *New World*, 158
partial objects, 122, 127, 128–29, 130, 131, 144, 161–62
pastiche, 49
patriarchy: feminine jouissance and, 54, 102; gender and, 82, 106; of nation-state, 73, 74; phallus and, 39; sexuality and, 106; Symbolic order and, 57, 75; violence and, 86, 136; woman (as signifier) and, 177; in *Hunger*, 64
Paxton, Robert O., 31
Peele, Jordan: *Get Out*, 116–17
penis, 64, 65
performativity, 25, 91
perpetual revolution, 146
phallic jouissance: deprivation of, 45; desire and, 46, 65; disappointment of, 215n2; the end of, 59–60, 62; feminine body and, 89, 122; vs. feminine jouissance, 13, 17, 47, 89–90, 100; gender and sexuality order and, 104; jouissance of, 111n2; for Lacan, 215n3; law and, 61, 82; masculine body of, 63; objects and, 72–73; origins, 99; phallus and, 55; the Real and, 15; ruin of, 59–60
phallus: feminine jouissance and, 26; formation of subjecthood and, 50; as foundation of meaning, 40; having and not-having, 50; lack of, 42, 64; masculine subjectivity and, 50; nation as, 204; under patriarchy, 39; phallic jouissance and, 55; as signifier, 14, 15,

41–42, 98, 163, 171, 177; teleology and, 172; universal feminine and, 188, 191; in *Tomboy*, 26
phantasmatic objects, 56, 118
photography, 15, 140, 161
physical space, 110
The Piano Teacher (Haneke), 3
Pietà (Kim Ki-duk), 89, 90
place, as term, 180
pleasure, economy of, 137
poetic shock: definitions, 148; cinema of the Real and, 24, 71; the Real and, 26, 55, 56–62; Real body and, 74; as spectacle, 56; in *Cuties*, 25
Poetry (Lee), 81, 85–86
point of view, 10, 24, 36, 38, 114
Policeman (Lapid), 133–34
politics: of cinema, 50–51, 169; emancipation and, 115, 120, 184; of the gaze, 122; vs. law, 97; negative politics, 105; political emancipation, 113; pornography and, 64; of spectacle, 164; of subjectivity, 115. *See also* emancipatory drive
Poongsan (Juhn), 161
The Pornographers (Imamura), 59
pornography, 47, 51, 52–53, 63, 64
postcolonialism, 46. *See also* colonialism
potentiality, 103, 104
premodernity vs. modernity, 94
Prisoners (Villeneuve), 129
private space, 120
psychic space, 173–74
Psycho (Hitchcock), 58
psychosis, 56, 116
public space, 83, 129

queerness, 129, 198; queer female bodies, 171
quilting point (Lacan), 45, 55, 219n5

race and femininity, 189
racial Otherness, 103
racism, 116–17, 187
Raengo, Alessandra, 32
Ramsay, Lynne: *Morvern Callar*, 174
the Real: generally, 35; abjection and, 107; appearance of, 219n5; of being, 129;

boundaries of, 87; of capitalism, 71, 137, 157, 170; cinema of the Real and, 13, 164; cinematic form and, 51; contact with, 72, 77; of desire, 53; emancipatory drive and, 97–98; emergence of, 44, 59, 67, 143; of Europe (as Blackness), 183; eyes as opening onto, 59; feminine embodiment of, 64; feminine jouissance and, 174; form and, 52; the gaze as entrance to, 115; of history, 27, 31, 114; of imperialism, 38, 180; invisibility of, 71, 89; for Lacan, 66; lack and, 201; language and, 72; of the law, 138, 146; looking and, 67; of masculine subjectivity, 45; materiality of, 110, 166; of the nation, 35–36, 51–52, 108, 138; objects and, 40–41, 59, 72; the Other and, 84–85; pain of, 69–70; phallic jouissance and, 15; poetic shock and, 26, 56–62; political impact, 45; Real body and, 81; repetition and, 9; scholarship on, 50; space and, 10, 24, 40, 85, 107, 142, 145–46, 178; spectacle of, 59, 69; of subjectivity, 123, 125; subject position, 50; surface of, 67–68, 89; Symbolic order and, 3, 36, 38–39; of temporal being, 54; in transnational cinema, 43–49; trauma and, 40, 68, 140–41, 151; visual field of, 10, 55, 63, 110; visualization of, 45; wounding and, 72

the Real body: generally, 13, 71–80; abject forms of, 93–94; cinema of the Real and, 13, 72, 74, 176–77; feminine jouissance and, 101, 110; jouissance of, 82; linguistic systems and, 32–33; nation-state and, 80–81, 88–94; new subject appearing in, 71; *objet a* and, 73, 74; poetic shock and, 74; the Real and, 81; rewriting the sovereign cartography, 80–88, 110; subversive possibility of, 110; visual field and, 74; in *Oasis*, 83–84

realism: cohesion of, 109; formal techniques, 53; magical realism, 87; neorealism, 153; subversions of, 82; vs. surrealism, 65, 83; in *Dooman River*, 153; in *Germany Year Zero*, 153; in *Still Life*, 107

Real object, 73–74
Reichardt, Kelly: *Meek's Cutoff*, 173
religion, 102
repetition: automation vs., 8–9; bodily drive and, 125; cracks between, 9; emancipatory drive and, 144, 145; the Real and, 9; returning, 126, 138; trauma and, 141, 151, 168
representation: in Symbolic order, 83; of trauma, 159; of wilderness, 173
revolution: Candlelight Revolution, 208; perpetual revolution, 146
Rodríguez, Héctor, 36–37
Rohrwacher, Alice: *Corpo celeste*, 86–87; *Happy as Lazzaro*, 86, 87–88
Romero, George: *Night of the Living Dead*, 44
Rosetta (Dardenne brothers), 53
Rossellini, Roberto: *Germany Year Zero*, 153
Roudinesco, Élisabeth, 145
Ruti, Mari, 5, 81, 127–28, 129–30

sadomasochism, 31, 65
Sakai, Naoki, 75, 93
Le samouraï (Melville), 103
Santner, Eric L., 121, 134
satisfaction, 46–47, 55, 139, 146
schizophrenia, 175
Schütz, Anton, 80
Sciamma, Céline: *Girlhood*, 171; *Tomboy*, 26
scopic regime: enjoyment and, 17, 115; scopic drive, 20, 132, 133, 134, 136
Scorsese, Martin: *The Age of Innocence*, 126
second death, 43, 88, 91
seduction, 183
self-: destruction, 95; diremption, 166; immolation, 143
the self: the Other and, 104; seeing, 48; traumatic ruination of, 155
sensuous experience, 156, 190–91
sexism, 187
sexual difference: feminine and phallic as not, 50, 73; Symbolic order and, 39–40
sexuality: orgasms, 56–57; patriarchy and, 106; quilting point of, 55

Index | 249

sexual slavery, 193, 194
sexual violence, 85, 88, 90, 91, 159, 196
shame and femininity, 194, 198
Shinjo, Abe, 195, 197–98
shock, 147, 148, 158, 160. *See also* poetic shock
shot-reverse-shot, 44, 133
shots: close-ups, 27–28; establishing shots, 113; on location, 135; long shots, 109; long-take shots, 43, 198; money shot, 52; shot-reverse-shot, 133; wide-angle, 69
signification: bodily drive and, 116; femininity and, 197; language and, 1, 18; subjecthood and, 98; world (relationship to) and, 98
signifier: the body and, 42, 73; cultural objects as, 182; empty, 64; feminine as, 194; gap in chain of, 163; jouissance and, 42, 73, 185; the kernel as, 216n4; as material cause, 42; name of the Father as, 116, 117; phallus as, 15, 98, 171, 177; vs. signified, 42, 45, 184; Symbolic order and, 134; woman as, 177
Silverman, Kaja, 155
singularity, 80, 103, 104, 203
Sissako, Abderrahmane: *Timbuktu*, 123–24
social body, 102, 150
social class, 90, 128, 170
social space, 90, 150, 174, 177
Soler, Colette, 73
somantic disjointure, 121–26, 161
songs and singing: in *Oasis*, 83; in *Head-On*, 165; in *Incendies*, 124
Son of Saul (Nemes), 205, 206
sound as gaze, 22, 53, 174
South Korea: allegories of, 89; bodies of ethnic Korean men, 147, 149; body politic vs. nation-state, 105; China and, 35; colonial modernity and, 45–46, 49; Gwangju Uprising, 27, 194–95, 225n72; National Security Act, 2; patriarchy of nation, 106; protests, 191; resistance movements, 2, 203, 206–8; sexual violence and, 88, 90. *See also* Korea
South Korean cinema: chronotope of emancipatory drive in, 146–62; chronotopic North, 119, 156; colonial modernity and, 46, 78; form in, 76–77; globalization and, 77; reflections on teaching, 26–27; spectacle in, 52–53; women in, 150
space: of bourgeois home, 170; cinematic space, 24, 44, 108, 145, 156, 164, 168, 169; cultural signification and, 110; curved space, 130, 134, 136; death and dying and, 207; desire and, 127; diegetic space, 36–37; empty space, 181; feminine cinema and, 163–77, 183; feminine space, 171; framing, 173; history and, 179–80; human subjects in, 174; imperialism and, 169; materiality of, 84; of nation-state, 92–93, 95, 103; objects and, 130; ordering of, 168–69; private space, 120; psychic space, 173–74; public space, 83; the Real and, 10, 24, 40, 85, 107, 142, 145–46, 178; social space, 174, 177; time vs., 172, 173; uncanny space, 174, 199; universal feminine subject and, 200; urban space, 103, 164; visualization of, 146; in *Oldboy*, 44–45; in *Thirst*, 98. *See also* the camp (Agamben)
spectacle: of breakdown of subject and its body, 78; in cinema of the Real, 52–53, 145; cinematic spectacle, 147–48, 154–55, 170; feminine jouissance and, 58; of Korean male bodies, 147; poetic shock as, 56; politics of, 164; pornography and, 52–53, 63; of the Real, 59, 69; trauma and, 152, 156; of violence, 104
spectatorship, 54
speech, 32, 40, 159, 187, 189. *See also* enunciation
The Spy Gone North (Yoon), 160
the state: law of, 91, 96; non-state (Agamben), 103; violence of, 82, 133
Still Life (Jia), 93–94, 99–100, 106–10
subaltern, gaze of, 122
the subject: of capitalism, 121; destabilization of, 19; ideology and, 192; individuality of, 154; loss and, 5; melancholic subject, 160; object and, 130–31; speech and, 187; trauma and, 139

subjecthood: abjection and, 91; cohesion of, 162; desubjectivization, 101; formation of, 50, 100; "I," 48, 72; as impossible, 62; Lacan's theory of, 116; lack and, 13–14, 57; new subject (emergence of), 70, 192; phallus as forming sociality of, 50; political subjects, 113; reconfiguring, 87; signification and, 98; trauma of, 11

subjectivity: the body and, 42; boundaries of, 19; ethics and, 31, 142; existential subjectivity, 37; feminine jouissance and, 170, 190–91; feminine subjectivity, 71; gaps in, 185–86; as gendered, 173; global vs. local, 140; identity vs., 190; ideology of, 133; impossibility of, 59, 145; intersubjectivity, 10; the kernel and, 44; lack and, 117; limits of, 174; masculine subjectivity, 45; materialization of, 37; modernity and, 156; national subjectivity, 59, 146; nation-state and, 133–34; new (forming anew), 26, 145; *objet a* and, 78; of the Other, 18, 19; psychoanalysis and, 24; the Real of, 123, 125; rending of, 54; shattering of, 71, 114; as surplus, 57; transformations, 11; trauma and, 44, 108; traumatic Real and, 9; universal subjectivity, 205; whatever singularity (Agamben), 80; wounding and, 154

sublime objects, 220n31
subversive jouissance, 137
suffering, 1, 190
Summers-Bremner, Eluned, 11
surface, the Real as, 67–68, 89
surplus jouissance, 143–44
surrealism, 65, 83, 183, 198
The Suspect (Won), 160
Symbolic order: the body and, 42, 95; boundaries of, 87; desire and, 13, 17; disruptions to, 38, 39, 50, 51, 60, 68–69, 171; "elsewhere" of, 118; family and, 25; feminine desire and, 101; femininity and, 25; gender/sexual difference and, 39–40; jouissance as confronting, 43, 81; the kernel and, 66; for Lacan, 1; language and, 182; Law of the Father and, 29; nationhood and, 59, 78, 167; nation-state and, 93, 149; organization of, 17, 20, 72, 140, 163; the Other and, 9–10; patriarchy and, 57, 75; the Real and, 3, 36, 38–39, 60; representation in, 83; resistance to, 126; signifiers and, 134; smooth surface of, 89; sovereign law and, 110; trauma and, 33, 144–45; traumatic Real and, 39; the void in, 185; in *The Priests*, 132

symbolic violence, 110
Sympathy for Mr. Vengeance (Park), 105, 158
symptoms, 167, 168, 175
Szifron, Damián: *Wild Tales,* 7–8

tactile epistemology, 176
Tae Guk Gi: The Brotherhood of War (Kang), 159–60
A Taxi Driver (Jang), 27–28
teleology: failure and, 60; narrative and, 148; of nation, 146; phallus and, 172; of pornography, 52; postcolonial teleology, 46; temporality and, 16–17, 172; in *Still Life,* 108

temporality: atemporality, 126, 139, 140, 159, 161, 167; capitalism and, 109, 218n75; cinematic time, 156; circularity (in *Irreversible*), 67; different orders of, 16, 53–54, 123; emancipatory drive and, 162; linear time, 141; masculine temporality, 173; melancholic time, 159; *objet a* and, 126; the past, 28–29; past in present (haunting), 61; as repetitive and circular, 37; vs. space, 172, 173; teleology and, 16–17, 172; uncertain, 67; in *Dancer in the Dark,* 55

territoriality and extraterritoriality, 93
That Uncertain Feeling (Lubitsch), 29–30
theory, application of, 107
the Thing: definitions, 184–85; encounters with, 72, 199–200; Thing-in-itself, 18, 40, 98, 132, 212n12; thingness, 69
The Thing (Carpenter), 185, 199
Thirst (Park), 93, 94, 95–98, 100–101, 104, 105, 107, 110
Thornham, Sue, 172, 180, 184

Thorpe, Richard: *White Cargo*, 21
Three Gorges Dam, 93, 106–7, 108
Timbuktu (Sissako), 123–24
Time (Kim Ki-duk), 161–62
Time of the Wolf (Haneke), 142–43, 144, 149
Toc toc (Villanueva), 136
Tomboy (Sciamma), 26
Tomsic, Samo, 42
topography and topology, 123, 175–76, 179, 180, 184
transgender body, 40, 57
transnationality: global capitalism and, 76; as method, 76–77, 79; the Real and, 43–49
trans-Pacific studies, 93
trauma: cinema of the Real and, 77; collective trauma, 103; of colonization, 188; communal trauma, 83; of destruction, 108; expressions of, 140; feminine cinema and, 33; as historicizing subjects, 139; history and, 9, 46, 49, 68, 77–78, 82, 142, 166; home and, 181; individual trauma, 103; interiority of, 158–59; the kernel and, 42; language and, 77; life continuing from, 144; of linguistic subjecthood, 12; local trauma, 140; of modernity, 94; national trauma, 49, 105; origins, 103; Otherness and, 35–36, 139, 141; public aspects, 77; the Real and, 40, 68, 140–41, 151; repetition and, 141, 151, 168; representation of, 159; of self-diremption, 166; South Korea and, 45–46, 76–77; spectacularization of, 152; of subjecthood, 11, 108, 139; surviving, 167; Symbolic order and, 33, 144–45; symptoms, 167; transcendence of, 3; universality of, 10; visualization of, 154; wounding and, 28, 154, 155; in *Still Life*, 94. *See also* historical trauma; the kernel
traumatic Real: atemporality of, 140; chronotope of, 68, 140, 157, 161; desire and, 171; emancipatory drive and, 141; experience of, 162, 181; North Korea and, 157, 159; repetition of, 151; space of, 153; spectacle and, 24, 145, 152, 156; subjec-

tivity and, 9; Symbolic order and, 39; wound of, 78; in *Dooman River*, 153, 155, 156, 158; in *Poetry*, 86; in *Time*, 161

the uncanny, 40
uncanny objects, 114, 185
uncanny space, 174, 199
unconscious: cinema of the Real and, 66; horror films and, 176; of male European subjecthood, 68; of nation, 166; as not individual, 66; subject of, 175–76
the universal, 75–76
universal feminine subject: comfort women and, 193–99; from death drive to emancipatory drive, 168, 176; emancipation and, 199–208; emancipatory drive and, 16; emergence of, 170, 181, 202; ethics and, 31; Law of the Father and, 204–5; local and global location, 177–91; phallus and, 188, 191; space and, 200; voice of, 174–75. *See also* universality
universality: of being, 9; of ethics, 81, 168–69; feminine universality, 177–91; localities and, 169; Saint Paul and, 191–92; transnationality and, 75–76; of trauma, 10. *See also* universal feminine subject
unrepresentable, 52
urban space, 103, 164
utopia, 104–5

vampires, 74, 93, 95–96, 101, 102, 104, 105, 107
Varda, Agnès: *Cléo from 5 to 7*, 189–90
Velázquez, Diego: *Las meninas*, 132–33
Vengeance trilogy (Park), 105
Verhaeghe, Paul, 73, 126, 216n14
verisimilitude, 53
Villanueva, Vicente: *Toc toc*, 136
Villeneuve, Denis: *Incendies*, 124; *Prisoners*, 129
violence: Badiou on, 149–50; towards children, 188; divine violence, 97, 149; as forming subject, 149–50; identitarian violence, 165; law and, 97; patriarchy and, 86, 136; sexual violence, 85, 88,

90, 91, 159, 196; sovereignty preserved through, 80; spectacle of, 104; of state, 82; state violence, 133; symbolic violence, 110
Virilio, Paul, 61
vision and the body, 176
visual drive, 20
visual field: awry look of, 59; flaws in, 40; the Real and, 10, 55, 63, 110; the Real body and, 74; ruptures to, 197; as topography of the drive, 177; tortion in, 51
visualization: of *objet a*, 199; of the Real, 45; of space, 146; of trauma, 154
visual perspective, 38–39
voice, 174–75
the void, 185
von Trier, Lars, 40, 69; *Antichrist*, 54, 69; *Breaking the Waves*, 43, 54, 55, 213n23; *Dancer in the Dark*, 54–55; *The Element of Crime*, 59–61, 62, 66–67; *Europa*, 61, 68; *Medea*, 54
voyeurism, 21, 66, 187, 196

The Wailing (Na), 64
Weber, Max, 192
Western films, 17, 103, 173
the West vs. "the Rest" (Sakai), 75
whatever singularity (Agamben), 80, 103, 104
White Cargo (Thorpe), 21
white femininity, 189
White Material (Denis), 177–78, 184
wholeness and objects, 5
wide-angle lenses, 69
Widows (McQueen), 124–25
Wilder, Billy: *Double Indemnity*, 120
wilderness, 173
Wild Tales (Szifron), 7–8
Williams, Linda, 160
Wolf Warrior II (Wu), 216n17
women: in family, 150–51; gender roles, 100; in horror films, 190; in Lacan's thought, 55, 100; life drive and, 198; vs. man, 73; in melodrama films, 190; as not all, 50, 121; as not existing, 100–101,

184; as signifier, 177; in South Korean cinema, 150. *See also* comfort women
women's film, 170, 173
Won Shin-yeon: *The Suspect*, 160
Woochi (Choi), 46
World Trade Center, 109–10
World War II, 92, 195, 202
wounding: chronotope and, 120; the cut and, 215n57; desire and, 72–73, 125; enjoyment and, 98; feminine jouissance and, 100; lack and, 117; loss and, 99, 100, 117, 141–42; the Real and, 72; responding to, 204; singularity as, 203; subject and, 71, 105, 151; subjectivity and, 154; Symbolic order and, 71; trauma and, 28, 154, 155
Wu, Jing: *Wolf Warrior II*, 216n17

The X Files (TV show), 6–7
Yedaya, Keren: *Or, My Treasure*, 43–44
The Yellow Sea (Na), 146–47, 149, 157–58
Yi, Seung-jun: *In the Absence*, 207
Yi dynasty, 175
Yi Han Yeol, 206–7
Yoo Gwan Soon, 203
Yoon Dong Ju, 203–4
Yoon Je-kyoon: *Ode to My Father*, 78
Yoon Jong-bin: *The Spy Gone North*, 160

Zama (Martel), 186–87, 191
Zhang Lu: *Doorman River*, 142, 151–52, 155–56, 158–59
Zhang Yimou: *Ju Dou*, 196, 197
Žižek, Slavoj: on camera's eye, 58; on desire of the Other, 19; on drive, 11–12, 118, 130; on feminine jouissance, 213n23; on historical contingencies, 107; on ideology, 48–49, 123; on *objet a*, 118; on objects, 40, 130–31; organ without a body, 58; relationship with Other, 9–10; on repetition, 126; on spectacularity of the Real, 59; on subject's neighbor, 8; on Symbolic order, 81; on traversing fantasy, 3; on visual drive, 20
Zupančič, Alenka, 8–9, 119, 184–85, 186